FROM THE FINITE
TO THE INFINITE

From the Finite to the Infinite

SWAMI
MUKTANANDA

A SIDDHA YOGA® PUBLICATION
PUBLISHED BY SYDA FOUNDATION
SOUTH FALLSBURG, NEW YORK

Published by the SYDA Foundation
PO Box 600, 371 Brickman Road, South Fallsburg, NY 12779-0600, USA

ABOUT THE SYDA FOUNDATION

The SYDA Foundation is a not-for-profit organization that protects, preserves, and disseminates the Siddha Yoga teachings of Gurumayi Chidvilasananda, Swami Muktananda, and Bhagawan Nityananda. The SYDA Foundation also guides the philanthropic expressions of the Siddha Yoga path. These include The PRASAD Project, which provides health, education, and sustainable development programs for children, families, and communities in need; and the Muktabodha Indological Research Institute, which helps to preserve the spiritual heritage of India.

ACKNOWLEDGMENTS

Grateful appreciation goes to Shane Conroy for his cover illustration, to Cheryl Crawford for her design, to Bette Ziegler for her editorial help, to Cynthia Kline who reviewed the text, to Emily Poe and Eileen Considine for copyediting, to Anne Terry and Connie Upham for their help with the Index, to Les Bolton, Steve Batliner, Derek Beecham, and André Mireault for typesetting, to Madeleine Cranston, Robert Butler, Lissa Feldman, and Margarita Danielian for proofing, and to Pat Donworth, Gail Fairbank-Roch, Osnat Shurer, and Sushila Traverse who prepared the text for publication. — *Sarah Scott, Editor*

NOTE ON THE USE OF SANSKRIT

Sanskrit words are italicized the first time they appear in each chapter. The long vowels, "ā," "ī," and "ū," are marked with a diacritical above the character, and are held twice as long as the short vowels, "a," "i," and "u." The appearance of "ñ" signifies the *nya* sound, similar to the *ni* in the English word "o*ni*on." After the first usage in each chapter, Sanskrit words are set in roman type without diacritical marks. Sanskrit words not defined in context and other unfamiliar terms are defined in the Glossary.

Original language: Hindi

First published 1989. Second Edition 1994
Printed in the United States of America

16 15 14 13 12 11 10   10 9 8 7 6 5

ISBN: 0-911307-31-1   94-43555
                                   CIP

CONTENTS

FOREWORD

THESE LIVELY DIALOGUES OF SWAMI MUKTANANDA present a timely message for men and women of every nation who are searching for spiritual fulfillment. He teaches a profound self-acceptance that goes beyond our usual understanding of who we are, transcending the modern polarities of self-doubt and ego.

The man portrayed in these pages through a series of wide-ranging conversations is, one understands immediately, a robustly human and thoroughly authentic teacher, free of all pomposity. He reveals himself as tough-minded yet compassionate, humble yet commanding, subtle but unfailingly lucid, and loving but without attachment. The advice he offers is profound and at the same time eminently practical.

Arranged in the shape of a spiritual journey, the questions and answers in this volume chart an evolutionary voyage, from the earliest moments of awakening to the sublime attainments awaiting those who pursue the Siddha Yoga path to its goal. In his own words, "I'm not telling you fables. I'm speaking of the reality of the inner journey. I'm describing the greatness of man. I'm trying to bring home to you your own true worth." Swami Muktananda's words are charged with his intimate knowledge of every stage of inner growth, and they speak directly to anyone who has ever wondered: Who am I? Where have I come from? Where am I going? And how do I get there?

The people who appear in these dialogues bring to Swami Muktananda question after question on every aspect of contemporary life. To each questioner, he gives intense concentration, and in his answers, he minces no words and spares no egos. He draws parallels from classical scriptures and shares milestones of his own spiritual journey, which began in earnest after he found his Guru, Bhagawan Nityananda. A masterful raconteur, he moves easily through a gallery of sages, kings, pilgrims, and poets, telling their stories with sympathy and humor in order to drive home his teachings. He reminds his hearers again and again of the all-embracing quality of the love of God and the all-pervasive nature of the divine, closer to us than our own breath.

But Baba, as he came to be known by many thousands of people around the world, is more than an inspirational teacher. He possesses the remarkable ability — rare even among liberated beings — to give people the experience of what he speaks about, the experience of their own divinity. His purpose is always to release his disciples from bondage and to help them become spiritually independent by kindling the dormant *shakti* or energy within and guiding it to its complete expression. Any contact with such a Master — brief or long, in person or through his words — can be enough to untie the dynamic knot of energy that lies in each person.

Shakti, that transfiguring force which he likens to a supreme singer or dancer, is necessary not only to attain inner peace and liberation, but also to function effectively in daily life. The Shakti transmitted through Siddha Yoga, Baba emphasizes, is highly intelligent and dynamic. As a result, those who receive it experience more joy and participate more actively in the challenges of life because they begin to see the divine in everything.

He describes it in this way: "In the middle of the human body there lives a great Shakti, a divine energy, and it has tremendous power. Though it may be a tiny flame now, it is enough to burn up the whole world. Once that Shakti is awakened, once that fire is kindled, it will do its work for many, many people — not only for you. Either it is by the limitless grace of God that this dormant Shakti is awakened or if you move in the company of those who are near to God, who love God, then your Shakti too can be awakened. You should experience the Shakti. As long as you have not, this awakening has not taken place. As long as you do not know your Shakti, you do not know yourself."

Taking sure aim at every exclusionist notion of God, Baba points out that the great religious leaders taught not duality but unity among nations and within societies; that the notion of an immanent yet transcendent God is a basic concept in every major tradition; that alienation from one's own Self is tantamount to alienation from God and hence is abhorrent to Him; and that whenever religion becomes frozen into dogma or ritual, it fails to serve God's true design.

The path he offers is serene, balanced, and full of light. It constantly counsels turning within, yet it finds God in the world, in other people, within inanimate as well as animate objects. In his own words: "The God that I speak of is present everywhere, and He is particularly present within the heart. His nature is the highest bliss, supreme bliss. His body is pure light. Though He is without a material body, He can assume any number of bodies. Though He is without name and form, it is not difficult at all for Him to assume any number of names and forms. Another name of God is the conscious Self. It is God who inhabits the earth and makes it function; it is He who inhabits the body and makes it function. Just as I am seeing you distinctly, if you were to meditate, you could also see God."

From this collection of Baba's teachings, spontaneous and fresh as the day they were spoken, emerge the form and substance of a universal sanctity, and a clear road map for the journey.

Heyward Isham
New York City

Heyward Isham has had a long and distinguished career in the Foreign Service of the United States, serving in many places, including Berlin, Moscow, Paris, Hong Kong, and Haiti, where he was Ambassador. Trained as a Russian-language specialist, he now works as a consulting editor specializing in books from Russia and Eastern Europe. He met Swami Muktananda in 1981.

PREFACE
TO THE SECOND EDITION

During three successive tours of the west, Swami Muktananda ignited the fire of meditation in hundreds of thousands of people. In what he described as his "meditation revolution," even people with little apparent interest in spirituality would find themselves drawn by his love and attracted by the peace and power they felt in his presence. Admired by artists and statesmen, sought out by writers and thinkers and by other spiritual teachers, Baba was recognized as a figure of universal stature.

When someone first mentioned his name to me twenty years ago, an astonishing thing happened. I asked, "Who is Swami Muktananda?" but I never heard the answer. All I remember is that an exquisite blue light enveloped me. The room and everything in it disappeared. I basked in that brilliant light, feeling awe and a piercing joy. When the light faded and the room appeared again, I was left with my question—Who is he?—and the beginnings of an answer.

This experience, which happened in Berkeley, California, in the spring of 1974, was my first step on the Siddha Yoga path. A few weeks later, I met Baba in La Honda and took part in what I later found out was the ancient practice of sitting with the master to hear spiritual teachings.

Baba took questions from the floor, which were translated into Hindi. Before the translation was even finished, he would launch into his answer. I had never before heard anyone answer questions with such authority and certainty. He was intent that the person asking the question truly understand the answer, and seemed willing to go to any lengths to ensure that. Immersed in his inner joy, he sang verses from the poet-saints. He quoted in Sanskrit, drawing from his vast knowledge of India's scriptures. He would tell stories, again from the scriptures and from his own life as well. His answers were revealing in themselves, yet they also functioned at another level: the power of his state drew us inside, showing us how to look within ourselves to find answers.

Years later, I was given the opportunity of compiling a book of Baba's questions and answers, selecting passages from unpublished material that would best convey the immensely vibrant and poetic quality of Baba's speech. That turned out to be the easy part: whether he was writing or speaking, Baba's words brimmed over with poetic flavors — crisp, spicy, tender, sweet, and intensely devotional when he spoke of his own Master, Bhagawan Nityananda.

Not so easy was deciding which passages to include. To me they were all illuminating. But Baba was prolific, and a five-thousand-page book was impossible. So another question arose for me as I sat at my desk in upstate New York.

The snow was piled high outside. The transcripts were piled high inside. I examined each question and answer and asked, Does this one belong in the book? Usually the answer came quickly, but sometimes I would remain staring intently at the words on the page, seeking some clue. It was then that a brilliant point of blue light would sparkle at the top of the page just for an instant and dance away.

Baba speaks many times in these pages of a brilliant point of blue light that appeared to him in his meditations. He describes it as "the Blue Pearl." This light gave him great joy as it led him deeper and deeper in meditation, until finally he received a vision of his own inner being contained within that blue light. After this experience of enlightenment, Baba saw this same blue light pervading the entire universe.

So once again — as in my first experience of Baba — he answered my question in the form of this exquisite blue light. It was as if he were compiling the book himself. And Baba's energy reaches out from these pages. Those who have met him, either in person or through their subtle experiences, will recognize it and revel in it. The many who have not yet encountered him may recognize something deeply familiar here, some truths that they have glimpsed in their hearts but have not yet been able to bring into consciousness and make fully their own.

These questions and answers with Baba come almost entirely from his last two visits to the United States, Europe, and Australia, from 1974 to 1976 and from 1978 to 1981. Wherever he went, he opened hearts, awakened souls, and imparted the highest teachings. He gave hundreds of talks and answered thousands of questions. He spoke at small gatherings in people's homes and in town halls, later on at large public lectures, and eventually in his own ashrams, residential meditation centers that he established as he traveled.

The questions people asked covered a vast array of topics. Here they are presented in a sequence that traces the course of the spiritual journey, from its often surprising beginnings through the natural expansion of consciousness that comes with the awakening of the *kundalinī* energy. Baba describes in detail the struggles with the ego, the dwindling of ignorance as we learn how to open ourselves to the grace of the Guru, and the sublime experiences that herald the approach of the final attainment and the state of Self-realization. At the end of each chapter, Baba reminisces about what it was like when he was at each stage in his own journey.

Baba responds generously and precisely to the person asking the question, giving the particular answer best suited to that person. From whatever limited point the question begins, Baba always expands the topic, enlarges the angle of vision, and uplifts the questioner. Having arrived at the place where all his own questions have been answered, where even the seeds of doubt and fear within him have been burnt up, Baba takes us into greater awareness and deeper states of consciousness. For, while the questions are finite, the answers are infinite.

Sarah Scott
Monterey, California
September 1994

INVOCATION

Nityānandāya gurave
shishya-samsāra-hārine
Bhakta-kāryaika-dehāya
namaste chit-sad-ātmane

Om namah shivāya gurave
sat-chit-ānanda-mūrtaye
Nishprapañchāya shāntāya
nirālambāya tejase

Om saha nāvavatu
Saha nau bhunaktu
Saha vīryam karavavahai
Tejasvi nāvadhītam astu
Mā vidvishāvahai

Om shāntih shāntih shāntih
Sadgurunāth Mahārāj kī Jay!

Salutations to Nityananda, the Guru,
who rescues his disciples from the cycle of birth and death,
who has assumed a body to meet the needs of his devotees,
whose nature is Consciousness and Being.

Om. Salutations to the Guru, who is Shiva!
His form is Being, Consciousness, and Bliss.
He is transcendent, calm, free from all support,
and luminous.

Om. May we, Guru and disciple,
be protected together.
May we enjoy the fruits of our actions together.
May we achieve strength together.
May our knowledge be full of light.
May we never have enmity for one another.

Om. Peace. Peace. Peace.
I hail the Master who has revealed the Truth to me!

PROLOGUE

IN MY LIFE I HAVE SEEN THE GREATEST COUNTRIES, I have seen the most powerful kings, I have seen the wealthiest people, and no matter how many I saw and how great they were, I never saw them completely content, completely satisfied, completely filled with joy. I never saw them fearless; they were filled with fear. I never saw them smiling with great joy or laughing in bliss.

I have met great singers, and great actors and actresses, and they do their performing just for other people. As an audience we watch them and feel joy inside, but they don't feel it.

Once I visited a doctor's house. When I went there, they told me that the doctor had gone to see a doctor. I asked why, and they said he didn't feel well. I thought, Alas! He gives medicine to us, but he couldn't give medicine to himself!

This is what happens to every person: in the eyes of other people he may look complete and perfect, but he feels an inner lack and it troubles him.

No matter how many things you accumulate, no matter how much you earn, at the end of the day you put your elbows on your desk and rest your head on your hands. You are worried; you are filled with anxiety. You are not filled with joy. Who knows what you are worrying about? Who knows why you are so anxious? Only you know and God knows.

THE JOURNEY BEGINS

CHAPTER 1

Something Inside Seeks Truth

If a seeker is ready,
God will find a way to guide him.

Why are we living?

This is why we live: to experience supreme bliss, the highest enthusiasm, the highest ecstasy. A human life is mysterious and significant; it is sublime and ideal. In this human body, in this human life, we can see the Creator within, we can meet Him and talk to Him, and we can also become Him.

A human life is very beautiful. For this reason we should spread our own beauty in the world. We should spread this awareness of brotherhood. People should meet other people with great love and respect and honor. Divinity lies within everyone. To not respect other people is to not respect God.

I believe in humanity and I support humanity completely. I do not belong to any religion. I do not oppose any religion, nor am I in favor of any religion either. But I welcome humanity. It is my complete understanding, it is my firm conviction, that the human body is the temple of God. This is not a mere understanding — it has come from my own experience. In this temple the living God exists.

I welcome you all with all my heart and with great love.

I am in search of something, but I don't know what I am looking for. How can I attain what I'm searching for?

What you are searching for will bring you to itself. You are searching only because of That. Keep on searching; you will surely attain That. There is always the fruit of your labor. Some people get the fruit soon and some get it at a later time. Whoever you are, your effort will always be fruitful. Search with respect.

The only thing you have to know is where it is. You must have that understanding, because if it is in the east and you seek it in the west, it will prove painful. In fact, you are only looking for That because you don't know what it is. Once you know, then you will have attained it. In a way, you can't really find it because you already have it.

What do we need to realize our heart's desire?

Know God. There is nothing else that can satisfy the heart's desire, that can fulfill the heart. Whatever mundane satisfaction you give to it begins to bore it after a couple of days. Then you begin to pursue different things — not because they bring fulfillment, but because there is no alternative. A person can persuade himself that he is becoming fulfilled, but fulfillment is not anywhere near. Real fulfillment lies only in the inner Self, in God.

I have deep longing to realize the state of permanent inner peace, bliss, and freedom the yogis speak of. I think I need a Guru for that. Will you please be my Guru?

It is not that I accept you as a devotee — rather you accept me as your Guru. It is not the Lord who accepts people as devotees; it is the devotees who accept the Lord as their Lord.

If your longing is genuine, it is most valuable. In all philosophical schools it is this yearning, this intense longing, that is given the highest place. It is called *mumukshutva*, or longing for liberation, and it is the greatest quality of a seeker, greater than intellectual keenness or any artistic talent. One should be possessed so much by this intense longing for God that one shouldn't be able to sleep or to rest without wondering, "When will I see God? Who will show God to me?"

Such a person receives the Guru's grace quickly, and he also completes his journey and finds the Lord quickly.

Many obstacles confront me—I have no time to meditate, I am very tired from work, there are many demands upon me—yet something inside pushes me to keep searching.

That force inside you that keeps pushing you to search for something spiritual in your life is the real Truth.

Is it only for spiritual practices that you don't have time? Or don't you have time for anything else either? Everything else is ordinary, but this is most important. If you don't have time for the inner search that will take you to the highest levels of consciousness, what is the point of just eating, drinking, and living in the outer world? If you don't make time to work for your spiritual growth, what is the point of your human birth?

Just as you have divided up your time for the different things you do in your life, you should also find time for meditation, because this is far more important than anything else. If you can't find any time for it, at least meditate when you lie down to sleep. Start repeating the *mantra* and it will continue throughout your sleep. Even that will probably be enough for you.

The situation that I find people trapped in amazes me. They say they don't have time for realization, they don't have time for spiritual wealth, they don't have time for inner peace. They don't have even a hope of attaining any of these things if they continue as they are. What can you possibly get out of a life which is so intensely fast? At least do something for your spiritual growth when you lie down to sleep.

They say when you are ready, the Guru will appear. What should I do till the Guru comes? Should I make a conscious effort to search for him, or should I have patience and wait for him to search for me?

When the time comes, the Guru comes. But it's also very good to find the Guru. To find the Guru, you need great understanding; you need to know who the Guru is. And when it's time, the Guru will come. When you have a longing to attain God, when you have so much love for God, when you feel that you *have* to attain God, that there's no other way — then you will know that you are ready.

When a person has so much longing to attain God, then within himself he finds the Guru. There is a Guru within us, and afterward we meet the same Guru outside. The inner Guru also guides you, but you have to listen to him. What happens is that we don't listen to the inner Guru. We make him listen to us.

Therefore, it's fine if you try to find the Guru, but the Guru also comes in search of you. Before this happens, become ready for him, become worthy, and then the Guru will search for you.

What is the best way to search for your own true nature if you don't have a Guru?

By praying to God and by turning within through meditation. If you are really eager, you will certainly find a Guru sometime or other who will explain things to you. Furthermore, within everyone there is Shakti, spiritual power, which will have mercy on you and guide you from within. God has infinite power. If a seeker is ready, God will find a way to guide him.

Will one know without question his spiritual Master when he finds him?

Yes. If in the presence of a Master you experience profound change within, if you find yourself becoming transformed, that is a sure indication that you have found your Guru. If your state doesn't change at all, what's the point of being with such a teacher?

Why do we have to play the evolutionary game? Why not come into life already enlightened and without attachment and suffering? Why do we not begin already knowing our true nature? And if we did begin knowing, why did we forget our true nature?

You have to play this evolutionary game because for a long

time you have played the game of contraction. The truth of the matter is, there is enlightenment even in your attachment and your suffering, but you are not aware of it. If your contrary knowledge is straightened out, you become aware that you are enlightened. Now you see a snake in a rope, you see a thief in a pillar, you see money in a pearl shell, you feel like taking a bath in a mirage, thinking it is the Ganges. Because of this contrary knowledge, you are suffering. Once you get rid of it, you are all right. You already know your true nature. Just get rid of your wrong understanding. It is because of this wrong understanding that an individual soul suffers. Therefore, people take refuge in the wisdom of the Guru and in the knowledge of the Truth.

How does sādhanā relate to the rest of my life?

One's whole life should become sadhana, spiritual pursuit. The goal of sadhana is the inner Self, the spirit within. Through sadhana, what you attain in the end is all-pervasive Consciousness. If you could maintain Consciousness while acting in the world, that would be a very good sadhana. Be aware of this: whatever I am doing, I am doing for the sake of inner Consciousness. I am alive for inner Consciousness. Over and over again, make yourself aware of this: my eyes are seeing just for the sake of Consciousness. I am eating food regularly just to please Consciousness. My breath is moving in and out just for the sake of Consciousness.

This kind of understanding is called knowledge. Just as the bubbles that arise from the ocean and merge back into it *are* the ocean, in the same way, we are all bubbles arising from Consciousness. We exist in Consciousness, and we merge back into it. We are that Consciousness. This is called sadhana.

Is there anything that you can tell me to help me along the path?

The thing that will help you is to stay aware that the same Consciousness is within and also without, and that you are right in the midst of it.

In many of the accounts I have read, it seems that the journey is often long and difficult. Why is this so?

Once there was a Sufi named Malik-i-Dinar, who had a great desire to attain the Truth. So he set out in search of a great Guru who could tell him everything. On the way he met a dervish. Malik-i-Dinar asked him, "Where are you going?"

"I'm just walking," the dervish said.

The seeker said, "I'm in search of an inner Guru as well as an outer Guru who can teach me something. Do you know anything about Gurus?"

The dervish said, "I don't know anything about Gurus. I'm just walking. If you want to, you can walk with me."

So they walked along together, and they came to a big tree. The dervish went up to the tree and put his ear up against the trunk. He told Malik-i-Dinar, "This tree is saying that a thorn is hurting it, and it's asking us to please remove this thorn from its trunk."

"O Dervish," Malik-i-Dinar said, "forget it! I'm searching for a Guru! Why do you have to care about this tree? Come on, let's keep going!" So they walked for a couple of miles. By then it was evening, so they lay down to sleep.

In the meantime some other travelers arrived at that tree and saw a dervish sitting near it. He told them "Look! They say that wild bees hide in this tree, so remove this thorn and you will find honey." So the travelers removed the thorn, and they found so much honey that they filled twenty containers with it and they ate a lot as well. They planned to take it to the market and sell it for a nice profit.

In the morning when the dervish and the seeker woke up, the dervish said, "O Malik-i-Dinar, when we were walking by that big tree, I smelled honey. Let's go back there and get some so we can eat. I'm starving. I didn't eat all day yesterday." So they retraced their steps back to the tree.

By now there were lots of travelers there, all eating honey. Malik-i-Dinar asked, "Who told you there was so much honey in this tree?"

Pointing to the dervish they said, "There was a dervish sitting here who looked just like him. He was the one who told us about the honey."

Malik-i-Dinar and the dervish got a little honey to eat—although not enough to take with them—and then they moved on, because Malik-i-Dinar was still in search of the Guru.

Now people always want to find a Guru, but they never want to become a disciple. All day and all night they look for a great Guru, and they themselves don't become even a small disciple. How are they going to find a Guru?

As the seeker and the dervish traveled on, they came across an anthill. The dervish put his ear down on the ground to listen. There were millions and millions of ants inside the hill, and they told the dervish that a big rock was preventing them from building their house. They asked him to please move it.

"O Malik-i-Dinar," the dervish asked the seeker, "will you move this big rock? Will you help the ants? They want to build a house, but this rock is a big obstacle for them."

"What kind of a person are you?" Malik-i-Dinar asked him. "I'm in search of a great Guru, an inner as well as an outer Guru. And all you talk about is ants and rocks. I don't understand it! Come on, let's go."

While they were sitting there talking, the knife Malik-i-Dinar kept in his pocket slipped out and fell to the ground, but he didn't notice it. They traveled on, and when it was night, they went to sleep. The next morning when they woke up, Malik-i-Dinar put his hand inside his pocket for the knife, but it wasn't there. "I must have left my knife where we were sitting yesterday," he said.

"Well, let's go and get it," the dervish said. When they got to the anthill, to their amazement they saw that some people had moved the big rock and that underneath it were pots full of gold coins, which they were distributing among themselves. Malik-i-Dinar was outraged. "Who told you there was so much gold here?" he asked them.

They pointed at the dervish and said, "A dervish like this one—he showed us."

"Oh well," Malik-i-Dinar said. "Let's keep going." By evening he and the dervish had come to a river. A boatman saw the dervish from a distance and thought to himself, "It's a dervish. I should go and row him to the other bank."

Meanwhile the dervish showed Malik-i-Dinar a big fish that rose to the surface of the river and went back down, rose again and went back down several times. The dervish told Malik-i-Dinar, "This fish is coming up because it wants to eat the herb growing over there on the bank. If you give that herb to the fish, he will be free from his trouble. There is a big stone inside his gullet and he can't cough it up."

"Look," Malik-i-Dinar said, "it's nearly dark, and we should get across the river. The boatman is here. We should go. What kind of friend are you? You're always causing trouble!" So they got in the boat and reached the other bank and stayed at the hotel.

But the boatman went back across the river, thinking there might be other people to ferry across. And, as he had heard what the dervish said, he picked the herb and fed it to the fish.

The moment the fish ate the herb, it coughed up a ruby worth millions and millions of dollars. The boatman was so happy that he rowed back across to the hotel and offered his salutations to the dervish. "It was only because of your grace that I found this ruby," he said. "Now you may stay in this hotel for a whole year and you don't have to pay anything. I'll take care of the bills."

Malik-i-Dinar cried, "Just look at that ruby! Where did you find it?"

"It was inside the throat of that fish," the boatman said. "I fed the fish the herb, and right away it coughed up this precious stone."

Malik-i-Dinar began to slap himself on the head and moan. "I didn't get *anything*. All three treasures went to other people." Then he got very angry with the dervish. He said to him, "You knew everything, but you didn't tell me anything!"

The dervish patted him on the back. "O son," he said, "I knew everything, and I did tell you, but you didn't listen. I told you that the tree was creaking and telling us something, that the ants were telling us something, and that the fish was telling us something. I told you every time. But you didn't have the capacity to understand what I said. If you had been worthy, you would have found all those treasures.''

The dervish stroked Malik-i-Dinar on the back some more and then he left. Malik-i-Dinar sat there for a while and glided into a deep state. When he opened his eyes, he felt that he had received something after all. He felt his life changing. He thought about all the things that had happened, and he realized that the man who had been with him was the Guru he had been looking for.

So don't try to look for God, don't try to attain God, don't try to think about God. First attain worthiness within. God is not in a remote place. He is right within you, very close to you. But we don't try to understand what is within us. Our understanding is no better than Malik-i-Dinar's. He was looking for the inner Guru as well as the outer Guru, but he didn't listen to anyone.

The fact is that the supreme Guru is right within us. The inner Guru that he was looking for was also in that tree, in those ants, and in that fish. God has created this whole universe. This is God's playground and He takes different roles. It was God who played those different parts — only God and no one else.

When I Was Doing Sadhana

When I was young and full of energy, hardship did not feel like hardship. There was only one thing that filled my mind: How will I find God? Who will show God to me?

There was nothing else I was concerned about. I didn't care whether I lived or died or how I would get food or drink. I would keep walking throughout the day, and wherever I was when the sun set, I would lie down and sleep. If anybody invited me for tea or some food, I would accept and then resume my walking. Whichever saint I encountered, I would spend time with him for a while. If I lost interest in him, I would push on.

All the time, I kept chanting my mantra inside intensely. I did this "walking yoga" a great deal — walking and repeating my mantra. I was fond of long, long walks. The truck drivers used to feed me often. They would see me walking on the road and stop their trucks and ask me, "Have you eaten anything?" And then they would offer me food. In those days nobody minded giving away a couple of chapatis — food was very cheap.

This is how I moved from place to place, and I met many saints. At that time there were highly evolved beings in India — at least sixty of them — and I met them all.

Once I went to meet Anandamayi Ma in Bombay. At that time I was staying at a devotee's house near the ocean and she was staying nearby. In the morning I would take a walk on the beach. Somebody came up and told me that Anandamayi Ma was there. Immediately I went to her house. There were some people there and they said, "Hey, look here! You can't go in there!"

I said, "Oh, shut up!" And I went inside.

She had just washed her hair; it was wet, and she was drying it. She ran to get a cloth and spread it on a chair, and she said, "Babaji, please sit down!" Then she gave me a piece of fruit and we talked.

I have a lot of love for her. She is a great saint. I am telling you — even now there is a great woman saint. She is very, very old now. After we talked for a while, I left.

CHAPTER 2

Meeting the Master

*I welcome you all with all my heart.
This welcoming is my great mantra. The supreme
Truth is blazing within everyone. It doesn't matter
if you can't see it because I can.*

What is the inner Shakti?

Shakti is energy; it is the conscious energy of yoga. It is the same energy which creates a whole cosmos. It is a great energy.
I have not heard of this yoga before.
It is called *Siddha Yoga*, and this tradition is very ancient. It is not widely known because it has been kept a secret.
Why has it been kept a secret?
It has been confined to a small number of people. It is a great yoga, and there is really nothing secret about it. *Shaktipāt*, the inner awakening, is given openly. There are many, many trees, but sandalwood trees are very few. There are rocks and rocks, but every rock is not a diamond. That applies to Siddha Yoga: every *yogi* is not a Siddha yogi.
I don't understand why, after it was kept a secret for so long, you would now decide to spread it all over the world.
It is the Shakti itself which has taken that decision, which has decided that I should go out and spread it.

I have just met you, and this is all very new to me. How can

I develop trust in Siddha Yoga and come to love you?

Nothing is new. Everything existed in the beginning of creation, so it is very old. However, everything seems new to you because you are just learning about it. If you try to understand Siddha Yoga with your mind and intellect, your trust will grow by itself. You don't have to develop a new trust. You will have to develop love for yourself — not for me. Understand that if love arises within you, love arises throughout your whole world.

All of this is old; it is not new at all. However, what often happens is that a person changes an old thing into something new by just changing its name. Do you know why? Because people love new things. But in the entire world, only one Truth exists. Different people have given different names to the same Truth; they have given different forms to the same Truth and have made it appear as though it belonged only to them.

What truly exists is very ancient, and it is That that is called God or the Self. Today this is very new for you; tomorrow it will be somewhat new for you; however, by the third day, all this will be old.

You said that a Guru can make others like himself, but I have never seen anyone like you. Are there others like you? Perhaps your disciples back in Ganeshpuri?

Becoming like me doesn't mean that you will have a beard like mine or wear clothes like mine. It only means that you will be in the same place inside. Shakti is the very heart of a perfected Master, and when your Shakti is awakened, you enter his heart and you become just like him on the inside.

When I was listening to your lecture, I thought you were wearing a dark blue hat until I asked somebody next to me. I also saw a blue glow around your shoulder. But it wasn't a hat and it wasn't a blue glow. What is it?

You have the same light within you. It is a pity that we are not aware of our own Self. That divine light is the Truth, which is scintillating outside us and inside us all the time. This is true of every single one of us. Though that light lives within everyone, it manifests particularly through one who has practiced Siddha Yoga and perfected it.

I can assure you that what you saw was not a hallucination. I am happy that you have had that experience. It is only as long as that light is present within us that we appear attractive to others and that our form arouses love. But once that light departs from a person, his body is treated very differently. It is quickly buried or cremated.

That light is spread everywhere. I can see that same light around each one of you.

I've noticed that when you touch people, either with your hands or your feathers, there is a lot of energy flowing out. Do you have certain moments when you feel you are supreme Consciousness or is it a continuous level of energy? And if you have this, where did you get it?

Your question is correct. I do experience that I am the universal, all-pervasive energy. By giving shaktipat to people, I make them experience this energy; I make people come to know the Shakti. There is nothing surprising about it. Sometimes a person is afflicted with something contagious, and if that person comes close to you, you can also be afflicted with that disease. If one can receive the germs of a disease, what is so special about receiving the touch of Consciousness?

I received this energy through meditation and mantra, and through the grace of a great Guru. If there is a poor man and a wealthy person gives him a bundle of money, the poor man becomes wealthy immediately. In the same way, a Guru gives his bundle of conscious energy to a disciple, and he in turn becomes filled with energy. If a person's light is once kindled, with that same light he can kindle many unlit flames. If you have one lighted wick, you can light many other wicks. If you stay with me just as I stayed with my Guru, you too can receive energy and you can also give it to other people.

Why am I so skeptical about you? I am really trying not to be.

First of all, don't be skeptical about your own inner Self. Turn toward your inner Self, and just forget about me. Try to believe in your own inner Self. Whatever a person does, he experiences the fruits of his own action. So first of all, try to move toward the inner Self.

I want to know what impression you have of me and what advice you are willing to give me.

I never judge people individually. Just as one person dresses in a particular fashion and someone else dresses in another fashion, in the same way the soul takes different kinds of bodies. What is there to look at? What is there to judge? For me it is just the clothes that are different, the covering that is different: the inner Self is the same.

When I see you, I see another soul that is just like me. If you could think in the same way, it would be very good.

I have a friend whom I have known for many, many years, and it is my experience that since he has met you, he has changed enormously. It's hard to describe, but he just beams. I know it sounds silly, but it's very true. Would you describe what this quality is?

So now you can understand that he is one of the people who has changed. It's very good. Inside human beings there is divine effulgence and brilliance. When a person begins to open, this light comes out of him; it radiates from him. The world is made of light, and that light exists within you too.

Do you mind being the center of attention all the time? Do you mind not having friends?

There is nothing to like or dislike. When you receive that knowledge, you consider the whole universe as yourself. Nothing is different from you. There is no separate place, so there is nothing of which to become the center of attention. When you become perfect, you become aware that this whole universe is the flame of your own inner Self. When you receive this kind of knowledge, you don't need various feelings or thoughts. There is no necessity for me to invite people to be with me, because they are not different from my inner Self. If ten people come, there is no necessity for me to tell them to go away, because they are not different from my inner Self. When you become perfect, this whole universe becomes yours and everyone becomes your relative — the relatives of your own inner Self.

Yesterday I brought you flowers. Today I have brought myself.

No fruit or flowers could be dearer than you. Such is the greatness of a human being. Man has the power of compelling the Lord to come and stand before him. A man can see the kingdom of heaven within his heart. If he were to go a little further, he would become God Himself. All this is possible only for human beings. Techniques and money cannot achieve this divinity.

I feel unworthy of your blessings or of anyone's love. What shall I do about it?

By what meter have you detected your unworthiness? Something is wrong with the meter. It's not true; nobody is unworthy. You shouldn't listen to your meter. You are worthy of my blessing and of everyone's love. You must not use the meter of the mind to judge yourself ever again. The fact is that man is a most sublime being; he is not unworthy at all. You should think very highly of yourself. Don't put yourself down. There is no state that doesn't have God in it. If you can find something that is without God, I would like you to bring it to me.

Once you have received the touch of Shakti, there cannot be any trace of unworthiness left in you. When Shakti surrounds you, within and without, above and below, there can't be any room left inside you for impurities or unworthiness.

By the way, you should drink some milk and eat some butter and also some sugar. A meditator needs these things.

*I had an overwhelming experience recently. I was calling out
to the universe for someone to help me. Then I had a dream in
which I heard some chanting and I saw someone with a glow
of light radiating from him, but I could not see his features.
I was wondering if something was leading me to come here.*

It seems to me that you have been sent here through the dream.
Why did you get into a state in which you had to call out to the
universe for help? Don't let yourself get into a state like that.
Now you should have good days; you were born to see good
days. The Lord is sitting right here, and when we act in the outer
world, we should be aware of Him. None of our actions should
dishonor Him. Now you must take good care of yourself.

*I have come empty-handed, and I have nothing to offer
but myself.*

There is no gift greater than that. What else is there to give? But
don't take back what you have given!

I think you're just beautiful.

The camera in your heart must be very pure if it can reflect such
a beautiful photo.

*I have only one more question for you: do you ever get tired of
answering questions?*

I spend my entire life doing this.
I know. That's why I asked.
Questions and answers are the main subject of my life. News-
paper reporters come, and television interviewers, and if not
them, there are always the people at the programs.
And you don't mind?
No, it's very good. When I resolve people's doubts, I feel great.
For example, when you invite a friend home for a meal and you
see him eating the food, he is happy of course, but you also expe-
rience the same joy. So I experience a lot of joy in doing this.

THERE ARE SO MANY QUESTIONS TO ASK

Is it necessary for a meditator to have a Master? Can one reach the inner Self without a Master?

If a man could reach the inner Self without a Master, without a Guru, then Gurus wouldn't take birth.

Is there any significance to the name "Baba"?

In India people usually call an old man "Baba," and I am seventy years old, so it's very natural for people to call me that. "Baba" means father; it's a very pure word. And people who have attained the Truth and show it to others are also called "Baba." A child calls his father "Baba" because the father always wants good things for his child. In the same way, a disciple calls his Guru "Baba" because the disciple knows that his Guru wants everything good for him.

What is the purpose of your teaching?

The purpose of my teaching is to destroy all the negativities of the mind and to attain inner peace. Man is longing for happiness, and he does so many things for it. But still he doesn't obtain it. So I teach the way through which he can attain inner peace and happiness easily and naturally.

And this way is through meditation?

Yes, through meditation, and also through transmitting the inner energy. In the center of this body there is a divine, dormant energy. As long as this energy is dormant, one cannot become fully happy and great. For this reason I give Intensives in which I awaken the dormant Shakti.

Once that Shakti awakens, spontaneous yoga begins to take place. As that yoga continues, your health improves, and you attain inner peace and divinity. Through this yoga you can attain the power of clairvoyance, seeing faraway things, and clairaudience, hearing faraway things. Inside the heart there lies a flame that is full of peace and happiness, and once you perceive that flame, you experience those qualities.

This is my teaching. After you learn this, you become healthy and strong, and you can lead your life with great happiness and delight.

If God is omnipresent, who seeks whom in this human body?

This is a great question. To say it in a simple and direct way: God seeks God. Sundardas said in his poem, "You are looking for your own Self." So don't look for That, because you *are* That. Because of his contrary understanding, man looks for God. So God seeks God due to his own delusion. When his delusion is eliminated, he stops looking; he attains true contentment.

I read another poem by Sundardas on the same subject. Once the sun was walking down the road. It was feeling very cold, so it was asking everybody where it could find some heat to warm up. But is there anything in the world that is hotter than the sun?

The sun's younger brother — the moon — also started walking down the road. It was feeling very hot, so it wanted to find some coolness. But is there anything that is cooler than the moon?

There was a delirious man who was deluded and had been tied to his own bed in his own home. He began to say, "Release me! I want to go home!"

In this same way, God or the Self has forgotten its own true nature and says, "I want to attain the Self. I want to look for the Self." So the Self is looking for the Self, trying to attain the Self. It is a matter of great wonder.

Just as everybody else has done it, I did it too. You seek That within yourself, and you attain That within yourself. You attain your own Self, and then you say you found it.

What is the Self?

The Self is something that is very difficult to explain. Even the Upanishads say, *neti, neti,* "not this, not this." You cannot say anything about the Self; it is not a matter to speak about, not a matter of the mind.

All of us are instruments of the Self — you are, and I am too. Shaivism, a very high philosophy, says that the Self is Consciousness. It illumines all our psychic instruments — the mind, the ego, the subconscious, and the intellect. They are supposed to be inert, but the Self makes them conscious. The Self also illumines the senses. That Consciousness is called the Self. It is in the mind, but it is subtler than the mind. The mind can never know it, because the mind is the body of the Self.

By dwelling inside the mind, the Self makes it function. This indweller is the Self. It is of the form of nectar. To know it you have to meditate a bit. As you continue meditating, the mind stops thinking. The place where all the thoughts culminate — that is the Self. Think about this and understand this through meditation.

How can the Self forget the Self?

The Self hasn't forgotten the Self, but because of the outer senses and the mind, it appears that way. When a person is going somewhere, if he misses his road, he has to undergo a lot of trouble. In the same way, man sometimes forgets himself too; the Self appears to forget that it is the Self. This is called ignorance or *avidyā*. This is also called *māyā* or illusion.

What is the Siddha philosophy of the human soul?

In Siddha Yoga we understand completely that our soul is the soul of God. Just as space permeates everywhere, and you cannot break space into pieces, in the same way God, or Consciousness, pervades everywhere and everything. That is within us also. You cannot break Consciousness into pieces.
What happens to our human consciousness, as we know it, after we die?
Even after a human being dies, Consciousness remains the same because Consciousness is whole. Just as a person changes his clothes — when the clothes get old, he throws them away and puts on new clothes — in the same way, the soul discards this body and enters another body.

Another physical body?
Yes.
When does this process stop? When does a soul stop having to come to this planet?
After you become completely established in the soul, after you burn all your *karmas* — whether good or bad — in the fire of knowledge, the soul stops coming and going. That is called the state of liberation in this life. Once you become established in the Self, there is no more coming and going.

When you speak about God, to whom or what are you referring?

The God that I speak of is present everywhere, and He is particularly present within the heart. His nature is the highest bliss, supreme bliss. His body is pure light. Though He is without a material body, He can assume any number of bodies. Though He is without name and form, it is not difficult at all for Him to assume any number of names and forms. Another name of God is the conscious Self. It is God who inhabits the earth and makes it function; it is He who inhabits the body and makes it function.

Just as I am seeing you distinctly, if you were to meditate, you could also see God. As you go deeper in meditation and pass from one plane to another, you will see Him in four different forms. On the physical plane you will see Him as red light, on the subtle plane you will see Him as a white thumb-shaped light, on the causal plane you will see Him as black light, and on the supracausal plane you will see Him as blue light, sparkling and shimmering.

When you receive the Guru's grace and it begins to work inside you, in meditation you will be able to see the light that is God spread through every single blood corpuscle, every single molecule of flesh, every bit of bone. This is the God that I have experienced. Which other God do you want me to talk about?
Who can see God in this way?
Everyone can see Him. Everyone has the power of seeing Him, because He is within everyone.

How?

Meditation is essential. For that, one should turn within. Also one should associate with a Guru.

What is it from your point of view that the Western religions lack that creates the need for you to come to America?

Western religions don't really lack anything. The original doctrine of Jesus is very firm. It is not only in the West that religions have lost their appeal; religions in the East have also lost their appeal. After a while the so-called religious teachers change the teachings, and the religions move away from the original doctrines.

There are many religions which say that God is somewhere up there, but I revere the God within, and that is why people are immediately attracted to this. I not only tell them that God lives inside them, but I also awaken their Shakti, by means of which they can have a direct experience of the Lord within.

Besides, people today don't have much patience. They can't wait for divine grace to descend in the future — they want immediate results. Through the shaktipat that I give, they have some inner experiences immediately, so they are easily drawn to this path. That is all there is to it.

Do you believe that we will ever see a world where there is peace and love among all human beings?

Yes, that time will come. That is what I am spreading too. Every day during my lectures I say, "Respect everybody." First of all, respect yourself. If you can respect yourself, you can also respect others. You are not what you appear to be on the outside. You are something else on the inside, so discover that. Within a person there is the effulgence of God; you should see that radiance. Along with this light of God, there is so much joy. The purpose of human life is to attain that joy.

A person harms himself when he does not look within, when he looks only outside. If you have not attained the inner effulgence, the inner love, you are lost — you have not attained anything. There is an inner divine inspiration, and if a person has not drunk this inner inspiration, this inner nectar, he is not truly alive. Inside there is a beautiful radiance, a blue light that always shimmers, and if a person has not seen this scintillating blue light, although he is alive, he is not alive in a true sense.

I would like to know more about meditation.

When the Master's touch is received, meditation begins to happen spontaneously from inside, and different inner processes occur by themselves. As awareness turns within, more and more bliss begins to arise. The world within is great, it is vast, it is divine — and through meditation one gets to know that world. Within, there is the great kingdom of divine Consciousness, the kingdom of light, the kingdom of music. If one goes within, one is able to see that light and hear that music and experience that Consciousness. We keep looking for love outside ourselves, and in this constant search for love we become weary and tired. But when we go within and find love there, our weariness ends and our seeking is fulfilled.

Earlier this evening you stated that if one succeeds in finding inner peace, one will be able to see love in everybody and in all things. Does that mean that one might meditate for lifetimes on end and not attain this love, not succeed in finding it?

Unless something is wrong with the way one meditates, that cannot be possible. When there is an unpleasant stimulus applied to the mind, the mind feels some pain. There is no reason to believe that when the mind comes into contact with the source of bliss through meditation, it won't experience bliss. However, as long as the inner Shakti does not awaken, as long as it remains dormant, no matter how many years you meditated, it would be mere toil.

I have always associated meditation with withdrawal. Can you comment?

Meditation makes one very, very active. Siddha Yoga Meditation makes one intensely dynamic. Those people who try to get high on drugs may become lazy and withdrawn, but not the ones who do this kind of meditation. It makes you very dynamic, very adept. It brings you great skill in action.

On the way toward obtaining a state of happiness, does one have painful emotional experiences?

You may have a passing phase of painful feelings. But it is certain that if you go beyond that place, you will reach the place where there is pure elixir. If you happen to get into such a phase, you should try to befriend someone who is familiar with the inner Shakti. Spend time with such a person. You may have a period of painful feelings, but don't have any fear; beyond that lies bliss.

When you find a Guru, or the Truth, do the things you are attached to in daily life fall away and lose significance?

After finding your Guru, after finding the Truth, you don't have to renounce all these mundane things. They will not harm you. In fact, they are helpful. Even Lord Krishna, who was an incarnation of God, had a charioteer who drove His chariot and a treasurer who looked after His treasury. He had a palace and children and a family.

Worldly things do not get in the way. For instance, I am sitting in this chair. This chair has been placed here for me to sit in. What's the point of renouncing this chair? It can't harm me. Likewise, if a house is meant to be lived in, what's the point of renouncing it — particularly after you have attained enlightenment?

One might renounce it out of boredom during the period of *sādhanā*. But God has created this world for us to love; He has not created it for us to reject and hate.

How do you relate to the body?

It is because of this body that we are able to communicate with each other. If this body were not here, how could we communicate? It is because I am in a body that I am able to see you through my eyes, hear you through my ears, and speak to you with my tongue. The body is the vehicle of the soul. The soul lives in the chariot of the body, and it sees through the eyes, smells through the nose, speaks through the vocal cords, tastes through the tongue, grasps through the hands, and moves through the feet.

What are the practices that you recommend for our spiritual development?

For your spiritual development all you need to know is your Self. If you get to know your Self, you will get to know everything. The first and foremost question is: Who am I? Everything else comes later.

Self-discovery is the root of all actions, all duties, and all religious practices. First, know your inner Self. Everything is there because the Self is, and if the Self were not, what would exist? If *I* exist, *I* have a country, *I* have a family, friends, and relations, but if *I* am not, where will these things be? First, know your inner Self.

How can I get to know that?

There are many ways of getting to know that. If somebody were to ask me how to go to a certain country, I would say, "Go ask those who have been to that country." Get the help of someone who knows the territory and who can show you on the map. Or you can try to reach there by your own self-effort.

FINDING A GURU

Is it better to find a Guru, or to follow your own inner image?

It is difficult to receive guidance from within.

Then how do you go about it? It doesn't seem that there are many Gurus available.

Still, you will find a Guru. Once you are ready for a Guru, it is God's responsibility to make sure that your Guru comes to you in one form or another.

Then once I am aware, I will recognize him?

If you can, you certainly will!

I know that the teacher is within, but sometimes I need someone outside myself to objectify in a way that I can't. I try to see the teacher within, but I think I need someone outside.

When the inner Guru fails you, you should turn to the outer Guru.
I have no outer Guru.
If you could become a disciple, you would find many.
Can there be more than one outer Guru?
Until you have found your Guru, you can have any number of other teachers, but once you have found your Guru, he will be the only one. If you haven't found your Guru, you will keep flitting from one teacher to another, but once you have found him you will not feel the need to turn to anybody else.

Only that one is a Guru who can awaken your inner Shakti, who can make you aware of your inner reality, who can awaken your inner being. Until you have found such a Guru, you may have to go to many.

What do you do when you have not met a Guru of your own, when you are struggling by yourself?

If one has a sincere desire, he will certainly find his Guru. It is a law of God's creation that if you have a sincere desire for a Guru, he is bound to come in due course.

There is another plane that is the world of Siddhas, and there are many, many Gurus in that world. Anyone can descend from that world and initiate you. There is also a Guru within, and from this Guru too you can receive initiation. If a seeker is a true seeker, if a disciple is a true disciple, his Guru is bound to come to him.

What happens is that since there are so many problems in life, until you have found a Guru, your complaint is that you haven't found one; and when you have found a Guru, your complaint is that you don't have time for him.

How does one make contact with one's Guru initially?

That happens easily: by becoming aware of the need for a Guru, by reading something about it, by understanding its importance. You may hear something about the Guru or someone may introduce you to him — that is how you make contact with him. All of you have come here through somebody. In a very natural way you have become introduced to me and I have become introduced to you.

Now that we have been introduced to you, what's the next step?
Well, either you become my friend or I'll become your friend. A friend is one who has affinity with you in different things, in matters of eating and drinking and so on. My great addiction is meditation, so you should also become addicted to meditation.

If I am not able to see you again, will I be able to progress in Siddha Yoga?

Yes, you can certainly progress in Siddha Yoga; you don't have to meet me again. But remember that I have already merged in you. In the form of Shakti and the mantra, I have entered you. So even if you don't meet me in this physical body, it's all right.

Once Jalandarnath was traveling in search of his Guru. As he was walking, he saw his Guru, Gorakhnath, coming toward him. When they met, Jalandarnath bowed down to him.

Gorakhnath asked, "Who are you? Where are you going?"

"I am looking for Gorakhnath, my Guru, so I can do sadhana."

"I am he," Gorakhnath said.

So Jalandarnath said, "Will you please instruct me?"

"Sit here," the Guru said. "I will be back soon." Then he left and didn't return for twelve years.

Jalandarnath was cooked enough already, so he sat there. After twelve years had gone by, Gorakhnath started on the way back, but even before he returned, Jalandarnath had become perfect. He had attained full knowledge. Later he became a great Siddha being.

So even if you don't meet me physically, you can still progress and become perfect.

How am I going to keep in close contact with you after you go?

Even when I go away from here, I will not leave your heart, I will be there. I cannot leave your heart. Kundalini Shakti is all-pervading.

How will you know me? You only saw me three times!

When you remember me, I will remember you.

Can it be that you are a Buddha being in our midst and we don't recognize you?

Just by knowing me, nothing will happen; you have to know your own Self. Whether you consider me Buddha or Jesus or someone else only shows the greatness of your own heart. Nevertheless, you have to recognize your own inner Self; only that will mean anything. The supreme Truth that dwells within you also dwells within me, and I am only That. There is nothing else to say about me. In that Truth there is no change, no increase or decrease.

Shaivism says that whatever is here is also elsewhere; whatever is there is also here. When this is the case, why should a person put himself on a scale thinking that he is big or small? The great Self, Shiva, is within everybody, and there is no bondage or liberation in that Self. There is only purity, and that very Self exists within everybody. It is within you and also within me, and that is all we are.

By your grace, I received your touch on my forehead. I understand this to be shaktipat. Does this mean you are my Guru?

The touch was meant to give you shaktipat. I can be whatever you take me to be.

I Knew Even As a Child

I knew even as a child that God was the most valuable being and that there was nothing like being friends with Him. I knew that God was the greatest and most dependable friend and He would always stand by you. I wanted to make friends with Him, but I was told that it was very difficult. So I set out in search of someone who was a friend of God, with whom I could become friends. I finally encountered the supreme Friend's friend, and he enabled me to be friends with his Friend. And now instead of seeking friends in this world, the best thing for me to do is to make people His friends.

I met my Guru when I was very young. He came to my school. He used to love children, so whenever he came to our school, all of us would just leave our classes and follow him. The moment we followed him, he would start running and shouting. We would run after him, and then he would climb up a tree and sit on a branch. We would just stay there under the tree. He was a great runner, he had great speed. He was a great walker too, he walked very fast.

I don't know how to explain the kind of relationship I had with my Guru. When I first met him, I was still in school. I was almost sixteen. I was rather bored with my studies, but I was very active in play. I was very good at playing.

He would come to my school. He walked in a strange

way, in the state of an **avadhut.** *Wherever he went, the children would follow him. He was very happy with the children; he loved them. Even at the end of his life he distributed gifts to the children. So when he came to my school and I met him, I also began to follow him. I had this feeling that I wanted to become like him, that that would be much better than anything else.*

In those days he didn't stay in one place for very long. He kept walking and walking, day and night. He would walk forty miles a day, and then he would disappear. He wore just a loincloth, and he would walk and walk. Finally he went to Ganeshpuri where he settled permanently.

After I met him, I gave up school. I also started traveling. I traveled all over India. First I went to Karnataka where I began to study scriptures. I also met a great Siddha there, a great being called Siddharudha Swami. I traveled all over India. Finally I went back to Bhagawan Nityananda in Ganeshpuri.

I still had this feeling inside of wanting to become like him. So even after traveling so much, finally I went back to him. Then our relationship was fixed.

CHAPTER 3

The Inner Awakening

The Shakti transmitted to you will never leave you.

I find it hard to believe that by touching someone, you can change their experience of meditation, and yet I know people who say that this has happened. I would like to know exactly what happens.

It is natural that you have a difficult time accepting and believing that that can happen, because you have not had the experience yet. Hundreds of years ago nobody believed that iron could fly in the sky. People thought that was just a fantasy, but today it is true. You may not believe in it, but it is true; it does happen. Do you believe in contagious disease? If somebody has a bad cold, and if you're sitting next to that person, can't you also catch that cold? In the same way, if there is a person whose Shakti is awakened, a person who contains that divine power, who then gives that touch to you, why not trust that Shakti can enter into you also?

But this is not a matter for discussion. You have to experience it.

What is the meaning when I experience electricity coming up my spine? It feels as if something is opening up, but I find it hard to believe.

There are certain people who would not believe it even if celestial beings appeared to them, or even if God came and stood before them in His physical form. In the same way, in spite of these experiences of the Shakti, there are certain people who have no faith in the opening of the Shakti. It is a particular attitude that certain people have; such people even doubt the existence of God. When we actually experience the functioning of Shakti, why should we not believe that it has been awakened?

When you give shaktipāt, is this a total awakening or is this a temporary thing?

The process of shaktipat is like sowing a seed. When it sprouts, it grows into a tree, and then in the course of time it yields its fruits. It is a permanent process, not a temporary experience. Shaktipat is a process by which yoga happens spontaneously, so it is called self-propelled yoga.

So there is no procedure that is necessary in order to make that seed sprout? It happens automatically?

There is no special procedure. The only thing necessary is that a person have faith and love for this practice.

For the practice of shaktipāt, or for the Guru giving shaktipāt?

They are not separate — the Guru and shaktipat. The Guru is not the body. The Guru is the energy that flows through the body, so the Guru and shaktipat are the same. The Guru is not an individual being; the Guru is the grace-bestowing power of the supreme Lord, and therefore the power of the Lord that flows through a particular being is called the Guru. The power is the Guru; it is not the individual being.

Then the Guru is a symbol of devotion to a higher ideal?

He is not merely a symbol of the supreme Principle, but actually a storehouse of the supreme power. Only if the power is there can he be called a Guru. If that power is lacking, he cannot be called a Guru.

How do you decide who gets shaktipāt?

The Shakti is intelligent, conscious energy, so it knows whom to grab. The Shakti is aware of past and future; it knows who is fit. It is not good to distinguish between people, to see them as high and low, since the same inner Self lives within everyone.

To me all are equal. However, the Shakti catches some, while it does not catch others.

There is a story in the Bible about a farmer who cast the same seeds in three different fields. In one field the soil had been completely prepared, and there the seeds took root and grew. In the second field, the soil wasn't so well prepared, and there the seeds sprouted, but they soon died. The third field was full of rocks, and there the seeds didn't sprout at all.

The more receptive your heart is, the purer it is, the more you honor and revere the Shakti, the more quickly you are caught by it. In certain cases, it is just a matter of coming here. If your heart is pure and clean, if you have a longing for shaktipat, and if there is one who can give it to you, why should it take long? It doesn't take long to be affected by negative influences. Why should it take long to be influenced by good things?

What does the awakened Shakti actually do for us?

In the middle of the body is the source of great energy. In our present condition, that energy is dormant. If one receives the touch of a Siddha, a fully realized Master, that Kundalini is awakened. Then it is called Shakti; it is intelligent, conscious energy. It knows what is good for your constitution and temperament. After this awakening takes place, the Shakti causes the yoga best suited to you to happen inside of you.

There are so many different yogas: *rāja yoga, mantra yoga, laya yoga, hatha yoga,* and *dhyāna yoga.* But in all these yogas you need a teacher to teach and a student to learn. Since there are countless temperaments, it is difficult to find out which yoga is uniquely suited to a particular temperament. If you approach yoga in this way, it will take you a long time to reach the goal.

The term in Sanskrit that is used for all these yogas is *pantha. Pantha* means path, and the yoga we do here is the *pantharāja,* that is, the king of paths. As we follow Siddha Yoga, these various yogas happen to a person without his practicing them. Without his trying to learn them they just come to him. This is the result of Kundalini awakening. Just as nobody deliberately pushes the outgoing breath out or pulls the incoming breath in — it happens by itself — in the same way this yoga is self-generated and self-sustained. You don't have to do anything, you just sit back and watch it happen to you. This comes from shaktipat initiation.

Shaktipāt means transmission of energy from a Guru into a disciple. A Guru is one who can give shaktipat, who can transmit spiritual energy into you, and who can thus awaken your own energy, clear all the blockages from inside you, stabilize your mind in the *sahasrāra*, the highest spiritual center, and fill it with peace. The Guru has the power of awakening a seeker's energy by look, touch, sound, or by his thought. Just as among yogas there is Siddha Yoga, among Gurus there is a Siddha Guru, or a perfected Master, whose touch is sufficient to awaken us and to initiate all these processes.

This awakened Shakti cleans all the *nādīs* of the body and it destroys all the toxins, all the impurities, of the system. The Shakti is full of radiance. After this cleansing takes place, awareness rises automatically to the heart center. There are different places in the heart center. For instance, there is the center of higher Consciousness that we call *tandrāloka*, and if our awareness were to reach this center, we would be able to see many things, just as we see things on a movie screen. The awareness rises higher and higher and higher until it becomes stabilized in the crown *chakra*.

Here is the great effulgence, whose brilliance equals the light of a thousand suns. It is a blue light tinged with gold, and that is what one should be able to see. It is inside this light that we hear divine music arising and subsiding, and these celestial harmonies play there constantly. Right there in the middle of that light is a triangle. As that light vibrates, divine nectar begins to trickle, and as it flows onto the tongue of a *yogi*, he becomes rejuvenated from within. No matter how he looks from the outside, inside he becomes like a child. In the middle of the triangle there is a blue *bindu,* a blue dot, which is the goal of the yogis, and it is always shimmering and sparkling. It emerges from the eyes and hovers in front and then goes back to its place inside. It is so subtle that the eyes do not feel its movement at all. After seeing it, one becomes aware of who one really is. Although one's appearance stays the same, one's understanding of oneself totally changes.

In a dream a rich person may experience himself as a beggar going around begging for alms, but when he wakes up from the dream, he wonders, "How could I have experienced myself as a beggar when I am really so rich?" This is exactly what happens to a person through Siddha Yoga. After these experiences, one feels very happy that there are so many glorious treasures inside, and that one is so great. This Shakti is all-pervading. The incoming and outgoing *prāna* speaks a certain language, and a yogi understands that language. It is *So'ham, So'ham,* which means "I am That."

We should be aware of the nature of the Shakti because it is the energy that creates an entire cosmos. That Shakti emanates all the countless forms of the cosmos from Her own being. That same Shakti creates a new universe inside us. If that Shakti were to rise to the ocular centers and purify them, one could see distant things. That same Shakti, when it works in the auditory centers and purifies them, enables a yogi to hear distant voices. The same Shakti, when it comes to the tongue and purifies it, ensures that the words uttered by a yogi turn out to be true. The inner being is totally transformed, and the yogi becomes aware of the complete oneness of matter and Consciousness.

Then he can live his life in this world, considering the world to be a great friend. In the waking state our awareness is centered in the eyes, in the dream state it is centered in the throat, and in the deep-sleep state it is centered in the heart. In the fourth state, the transcendental state, it becomes centered in the Blue Bindu. Then, just as I am seeing you now sitting at some distance from me, one can see all pleasure and pain from a distance, and one is not overwhelmed by either of them.

All this happens by the mere touch of a Guru, by the grace of a Guru. The being whose picture you see here was my Guru. In this yoga the Guru ensures your spiritual growth.

Is there ever confusion or misunderstanding about what people expect to get and what is actually offered?

No, there is no confusion, because I give people what they already have. I don't give them anything new. I awaken *your* inner energy in you. I don't awaken *my* inner energy in you. Therefore, there is no uncertainty, no confusion. I kindle the love that you already have inside yourself, so it suits you very well.

Is it necessary to believe in the Indian religious tradition in order to accept or really profit from shaktipāt?

One does not have to be involved with the Indian religious tradition because all religious traditions in their essence are alike. What one needs is love; all traditions are about love.

Shaktipat is not exactly a religious phenomenon. If it is a religion, then it is a religion that transcends religions. It is not the monopoly of the Indian religious tradition. Shaktipat is something that in earlier times was also a part of the Christian tradition. You have heard how Jesus performed his ministry. If he communicated with anyone, immediately that person's mind was changed; that person would experience great love and happiness. That was the shaktipat of love.

Shaktipat is meant for every person. Our ashram attracts people from all different religions and faiths, and they all receive shaktipat. The energy that awakens is your own energy, which is right inside you. As a result of the awakening, it begins to blaze, and then it activates spontaneous yoga. All that we need is the Shakti.

Do you give shaktipāt to all those who desire it?

If people will take it, I can give it. You need to be a receptive vessel so that I can give it.

There was a saint named Swami Ram Tirth who visited France, America, and Japan many years ago. He used to sing, "O Lord, in this universe which is Your kingdom, there is everything that anyone could want. Your world doesn't lack anything. But my bag is very small. What can I do?"

Similarly, if people take it, I can give shaktipat to all. But make your bag big so that you can take this Shakti in. Open your pocket so that you can take it all in.

I'm thinking of taking the Intensive and I'm somewhat scared about two things: an explosion of physical ills that may be dormant, or the Shakti being more than I can handle. Would you comment?

After the Intensive your dormant ills may come up gradually and be expelled from the system, but they won't harm you at all. One day or another these physical ailments are going to spring forth anyway. How long are you going to subdue them by taking pill after pill? They will be expelled from your system, and when they're gone, they're gone.

It seems that you have great trust in the Intensive; you consider the Intensive very great, very sublime, very true. This is why you are scared, but there is no need to worry.

Do you take on people's karma, and do you feel pain in doing so?

When shaktipat is given, I don't have to take on the person's karma; it comes to me automatically, and it does cause pain. It lasts for an hour or two at night; at that time my whole body aches and the top of my head becomes hot and I get irritable. But then, as I become absorbed in meditation, it goes away. Just one moment of total absorption in meditation can burn up the sins of a thousand lifetimes.

In India saints would not usually give shaktipat the way I do. The traditional rule is that the seeker must fast and do *japa* and thus purify his body for several days, and then initiation may be given.

I met a lady who is one of the close disciples of the Dalai Lama. For the past five years she has been doing rigorous spiritual practices for the purification of various elements in her body. She will not be able to receive initiation until after the purification. I don't insist on that. The scriptures say that one should be made to fast for three days, and I don't demand even that. I follow the scriptural injunction about the three-day fast in my own way by asking people to eat a little less. Then we chant the divine Name over and over again because God's name has the power of purifying the body.

I want to attend the retreat, but I wonder about the cost.

There was once a great saint in Delhi who also used to give shaktipat. His name was Nizamuddin. He would spend his days living in ecstasy. One day a poor peasant came to him. This peasant had to marry off his daughter and he thought he could get some money from the saint. The saint said, "All right. You stay here for three days, and whatever money I get, I'll pass on to you." But during those three days he didn't receive a cent, and because of the bad karma of this peasant, even the saint had to go hungry.

The peasant complained to the saint, "I came with expectations and I stayed three days, but I didn't receive anything."

The saint said, "What can I do? Here, take my shoes to the market and sell them, and whatever money you make, take it home."

The peasant agreed and left with the shoes. He had hardly gone a mile when he saw a very rich merchant coming from the opposite direction with a caravan of camels laden with jewels, valuable silks, and plenty of food. Now the peasant was very thirsty and hungry, and when he saw a water bowl hanging from the rich man's camel, he asked for some water. As the man got off his camel to give the peasant water, he smelled a divine fragrance coming from the shoes in the man's hand.

"Where are you taking these?"

"To the market to sell them."

"Whose shoes are these?"

"Nizamuddin's."

"I'll buy them. You can take all the other camels in the caravan. Just leave the one I'm riding. Take the jewels and silk and everything the camels are carrying."

The merchant took the shoes and sat down under a tree, and he stayed there in meditation for two days. Then he went to Nizamuddin's ashram. He showed the shoes to him, and asked if he could become his disciple.

When Nizamuddin asked him how much he had paid for the shoes, he said, "I gave away my whole caravan—jewels and precious cloth and everything."

Nizamuddin laughed and said, "You got them dirt cheap!" This man turned out to be the greatest disciple of Nizamuddin; he became known as Amir Khusrau, and he composed great works.

Here they charge you a certain amount. You get lodging and food—and you also get Shakti. How much would Shakti alone cost? How much do people spend on nightclubs and movies? Think about it.

NOW YOU SHOULD LET IT GROW

I want to thank you very much for shaktipāt.

Now you should let it grow. I am particularly happy that a psychologist has received it because psychologists should be able to go beyond the mind, and that is possible only through shaktipat. Scientific researchers and psychologists must become familiar with shaktipat.

How can I help the Shakti grow, and how can I make my work more fulfilling?

If the Shakti unfolds fully within you, whatever work you do will become fulfilling by itself. If you meditate regularly every day with love and faith in the inner Shakti, it will grow by itself.

Aside from meditation, do I need to do anything else?

Meditation is a complete discipline. It has everything in it. You don't need to do anything else. As you get into meditation more and more, you will find your mind acquiring more and more strength. Have you read *Play of Consciousness*? Read it and then you will understand what is happening to you. The Shakti that has been working in you pervades the whole universe. It is not something trivial or insignificant. When the supreme energy of the universe is at work within you, do you need anything else? This will open up your heart and inner mind, and that is enough. This is what true religion is — it is not just ritual or dogma. Religion is this energy of the spirit.

I am one of the "wet logs" that takes a long time to ignite. This is my first Intensive, and nothing of apparent significance has happened yet. What are some possible explanations? What is the prognosis?

In the next Intensive I will dry that log. How long can it stay wet? Just for a little while. But when it dries up, don't get it wet again; keep it dry. Something will happen. When I come around during meditation, you can remind me by saying, "I am the wet log."

It doesn't matter; the Shakti will pursue you. You may not experience it for a month. It is all right if the log is wet, but your mind, your inner being, your faith, shouldn't be like a stone. That inner part should be soft. Then it's very easy to dry up that log. The reason nothing happens to you is not because the body is a wet log; it is only because your mind, your faith, is like a stone. The *Bhagavad Gītā* says that the more faith you have, the sooner your inner being can be ignited. Faith is the magnet that pulls God toward you. Faith is a chemical thing, a chemical that turns your grief into delight.

For the happiness of life, man should have faith. If you don't have faith, nothing works for you. If there is no faith between husband and wife, they don't get along with each other. If you have no faith in a doctor, his medicine won't work for you. If you have no faith in a lawyer, he can't help you. And if you have no faith in your neighbors, you don't get along with them. So in this Intensive the most important thing is faith; everything else is minor.

Does shaktipāt stop reincarnation?

Yes, shaktipat can stop the cycle of birth and death. And what it will do is keep you alive forever in true reality. Man has to undergo the cycle of birth and death; he takes birth and then he dies, and once again he takes birth and dies. What shaktipat does is make him free from both phenomena and keep him alive in true Consciousness.

Since I've had shaktipāt, I find that sometimes when I'm working, I meditate for just a few seconds and I feel a tremendous amount of peace and joy. I can work long hours, and I don't worry about the result of my work.

Shaktipat is a tremendous blessing. This Shakti does not render one poor. There are many people who have been helped immensely by the Shakti, even in their careers. There are lots of high-ranking Cabinet ministers and politicians among my devotees.

Shakti is the divine creative source which has created this universe. Though She dwells within us, we shouldn't think that She is as small as we are. One seer says that where there is pleasure-seeking, there cannot be liberation, and where there is liberation, there cannot be any pleasure-seeking. In other words, those who are pursuing liberation cannot seek pleasure. You must have seen holy men who look quite sad and indifferent and who hate pleasure. But it is different in the case of one who has been blessed by Kundalini, one whose inner Shakti has been awakened. In such a case, both liberation and worldly enjoyment take their seats right in the palm of your hand.

Is it possible that someone could have kriyās because of shaktipāt in a past life?

It is possible. When a person receives shaktipat and then dies before he reaches Self-realization, that Shakti will not go to waste. It continues to work in his next life and it may cause kriyas. Such a person is called a *yogabhrashta*. Then he takes birth in a highly developed family. He may become a Siddha from the time of birth. Then he is called *janmasiddha*, a born Siddha. My Guruji was a born Siddha. He had nothing to learn anywhere. All the *siddhis*, the supernatural powers, came to him when he was born. Shaktipat never goes to waste.

*In the past the teachings of the Siddhas were transmitted
more mysteriously and to fewer people. What is it about these
times that makes it appropriate for the teachings to be given in
such an open and widespread way?*

The past is past, and the new is new. The past hasn't stayed,
and now things have changed. In the past if an American
wanted to discover India, it took him perhaps thirty years. Now
it takes only thirty hours. So there is constant change. Just as
times change, in the same way religions also change.

There was a great Vaishnavite being called Ramanuja. For
many, many years his Guru did not give any *mantra* to him. He
only made him do *sevā,* or service. Then after all those years he
gave him the mantra. The moment Ramanuja received the
mantra, he started talking to everybody and said, "Repeat this
mantra. You will be very happy, and you will also attain God."

His Guru was amazed. He thought to himself, "I kept the
mantra a secret, and now this one is revealing it to everybody."

So he called in the disciple and said, "This is a secret
mantra, and you're revealing it to everybody. It's not good."

Ramanuja asked, "What will happen to those who have
received the mantra from me?"

"They will only benefit from it," said the Guru.

"If thousands of people benefit from this," said Ramanuja,
"and if only one person does not, and bad things happen to him,
so what? So many people will benefit from it."

So in the past everything was a secret, and now I reveal
everything. It's all right.

*You seem to be working very intensely giving shaktipāt to
multitudes, revealing secret knowledge. It is as if you are
working against a deadline. Is the human race in some kind
of trouble?*

What do you lose if you understand that something good is
happening in the human race? Why do you have to think the

other way? Understand it as a great day for humanity. All this time everything was secret, secret, secret, and I just revealed it. I didn't want to deceive humanity; I didn't want to deceive God. I encountered many difficulties in my *sādhanā*, and I realized that I should not conceal anything from people. I should reveal any knowledge that I have. Therefore, understand that a good day is coming for the human race.

What is the grace of the Guru?

The Guru's grace is the inner awakening. It is called Guru's grace when you attain the love of God. As man continuously revels in the external world, his inner path is blocked. When that path is prevented, he can neither understand himself nor others, nor can he experience any peace. Through the Guru's grace, the inner path is opened. Then man enters within and finds the abode of peace. When this happens, he understands himself and others, and his life is filled with bliss.

When the inner journey is opened again, when the inner energy is awakened again, that is called the Guru's grace. One attains supreme bliss because of that. To attain that you have to have an earnest desire within you. That is called *mumukshutva*. The scriptures call it a longing for liberation. You have to have this longing, this fire of love burning within yourself. You must wonder, "When will I meet Him? When will I attain Him?" When you have true longing to attain Him, at that very minute you do attain Him.

But Then I Received the Touch of a Great Being

For a long time India was under the control of England. However, on August 15, 1947, it became liberated. Just as India was a slave of another power, in the same way I was a slave of my own senses; I was under their control. On the very same day that Lord Mountbatten said, "India has become free," my Sadguru, my Gurudev, told me that I had also become free.

On this day sometime between eight and nine in the morning, my Gurudev offered me padukas, *his sandals. In those days I used to live in Vajreshwari. Where the ashram is now, there were three rooms, which were closed up; they weren't being used. I would visit my Gurudev at his ashram every day. Usually I stood far away from him, but today I went very close to him. He was wearing these padukas, walking back and forth; then he came and stood right before me. He came very, very close to me, and I began to sweat. I closed my eyes. He stood in front of me for a long time thinking that I would open my eyes. Then he said, "Hey!" and I opened my eyes.*

"Put these padukas on," he said.

I replied, "You have worn these padukas. How can I wear them?"

He laughed, and I said, "If you really want to give them to me, I will stretch my shawl out and you can place them in the shawl."

Then he lifted one foot at a time and placed the padukas in the shawl. I became extremely happy. I put them on my head, and as I did this, I almost lost consciousness. He was still standing right in front of me. I was facing south and he was facing north. He was muttering and he went inside to get something. I was standing there with the padukas on my head, and when he went inside, I left to go back to Vajreshwari.

I walked down the road, only half-conscious, until I reached the audambara *tree, which you see when you walk down there. After that I don't know what happened. I don't know how I walked to the little temple of the* Devi, *where the present ashram is, but I did, and I sat down in front of it for a long time, for hours on end. Maybe I sat there so long since it was the place where I was supposed to be. I'm still sitting here. I carried those padukas and sat down in this place. Until the end of time I am going to be sitting right here.*

My Baba's cook had made bhajias, *delicious fried plantains, and Baba had brought out a tray of them and asked, "Where is he? Where is he?" But I had left. So he saved the bhajias just like that on the tray. I went to him the next evening and he gave me those bhajias. I ate them until my stomach was really full. Then he said, "There are three rooms. Go and sit there." The three rooms were right here in what is now the ashram. So I came and sat down here.*

Jnaneshwar Maharaj said that everything comes to the person who obeys the Guru completely, who follows the word of the Guru completely. He doesn't have to go looking for anything. As I sat here, not only did I dwell just in India, but I began to dwell in the entire world.

I had pursued sadhana very well. I had attained a very good and healthy body. I had pursued hatha yoga and raja yoga; I had been to every holy place and every holy river. I hadn't spared a single saint of this country. But I attained nothing in the holy places and the holy rivers; I attained nothing in the temples. I felt that everything was as empty as I was. However, on the fifteenth of August, 1947, when I received my Guru's grace, I began to perceive God in every place; I began to feel the purity of the holy rivers. As long as you don't receive initiation from the Guru, you don't attain anything. Everything is nothing.

CHAPTER 4

The Guru

*The Guru is one who has understood the Truth
and who can make others understand it.*

What is a Guru?

There is really no one with whom the Guru can be compared;
a Guru is just a Guru. Still, one can say that the Guru is one who
awakens the inner Shakti of a seeker. The Guru is an embodiment of Shakti, of divine energy. The Guru is one who is able
to communicate spiritual experiences to others who are on the
spiritual path.

How does he do this?

The skill that he has in this field is unique and mysterious, and
no other person can see what he does. The energy that the Guru
uses, that he has realized within himself, is the energy of
Consciousness. It is very subtle. By means of this, he touches
the same energy in another person.

A Guru is not just an instructor who teaches you something; he is not just someone who can show you a few *hatha
yoga āsanas*. A Guru is one who can transmit the divine power
of grace; he is a dispenser of grace — that is what the scriptures
say. There are many teachers who can explain things and give
lectures on Vedanta. But that being is rare who just keeps silent,
who doesn't need to explain anything, but in whose presence
yoga happens in a seeker automatically. Only such a being is a
real Guru.

Ordinary teachers are never considered to be Gurus in our country. A Siddha Guru, a fully realized Guru, is one who has completely absorbed all the yogas — *hatha, laya, raja,* and *mantra* — and dissolved them into his own Consciousness and who teaches a seeker on a very subtle level. The moment he touches a seeker, yoga begins to happen within him. You can see the signs of this yoga on the physical level.

Is a particular Guru meant only for particular people?

Just as you understand what you are, in the same way you have to understand what I am. A Guru is there for all; there is no restriction that a particular Guru is meant for only a few people. Just as the sun and the moon are there for everybody, in the same way the Guru is there for everybody. There is no individuality in the Guru. There is no limitation of country or caste or creed.

The scriptures describe the Guru as burning fire. Whatever object comes into contact with fire is immediately burned, and the fire makes no distinction between one object and another. In the Guru the fire of knowledge, the fire of yoga, the fire of meditation, is always blazing.

Does the Guru choose the disciple, or does the disciple choose the Guru?

The Guru does not need to choose the disciple; the disciple needs to choose his Guru. In order to attain Self-realization, the disciple must choose his Guru well and with discrimination, because there are many kinds of Gurus floating around. You must choose a Guru who takes you to the goal directly, a Guru who belongs to the great tradition of Siddhas, one who has the Truth inside him, and one who teaches a straight and direct path, not one who teaches a little of this, a little of that, mixing it all and making a potpourri of all the paths. You must not choose a Guru who offers you a *sādhanā* according to your taste and ease, but one who offers you the true path to Self-realization.

The Guru is one who through *shaktipāt* can awaken the inner Shakti in you, one who activates your subtle body, and one who can still the restless mind. Therefore, it is the disciple who must choose his Guru after a great deal of thought and deliberation. There is no point in spending a lot of time with a particular Guru if he cannot satisfy your spiritual needs.

The word *Guru* is of great significance; just on hearing the word the disciple should start feeling the transformation within. If there is no change in the disciple after meeting the Guru, if he remains the same as before, it would have been better if he had stayed at home. Through association with a Guru, one must experience transformation within. Otherwise, what is the point of going to a Guru?

One must become a new being. It is not a bond of friendship that you establish with the Guru, and therefore you do not choose him as you choose your friends. The Guru must awaken you to the Self in you. He must destroy the undesirable aspects within you. He must untie the knot of divine energy that is within you.

In America, where there is so much searching right now, there is a great deal of confusion as to how you tell a true Guru from a false one.

You have to understand that in everything there will be truth and falsehood. From a false guru you come to know what a true one is. True Guruhood is a selfless service. It is not a business that helps you in your life. Mainly it is disciples who can test a Guru; casual observers cannot know who a true Guru is. But only a Guru can fully test another Guru.

A true Guru knows the Truth as it really is. A Guru is able to awaken the dormant energy in a disciple, which gives birth to a spontaneous yoga. Through this yoga a disciple becomes completely clean and free from addictions. A Guru should be able to transform the life of a disciple. He should be able to reveal the divine light of God, which exists within a disciple.

Even though divine effulgence is inside, it is very difficult for a person to know it. Only if a Guru makes the disciple enter into that divine light, only then can he be called a true Guru. For this the Guru should be free from expectations: he should not expect anything from a disciple.

If a Guru has such a nature, he can be called a true Guru. He remains absorbed in the bliss of the Self, in the intoxication of the Self. All his activities are God's. If a being leads his life in this way, he is called a Guru.

Guruhood is not a new discovery. A Guru is not somebody who invents new things. Even before creation, the source of the Guru was there. The lineage of Gurus comes down from before the beginning of creation. If new people separate themselves from this lineage and call themselves Gurus, it is not right. A Guru has to be from a lineage of Siddha Gurus.

In Sanskrit there is a saying: the path walked by the great beings will help you. Many new people have made up their own paths. Who has walked on their paths? What great beings have accepted these paths? The Guru puts his disciples on the path that the ancient beings have walked.

Most of all, a Guru is one who releases a disciple from bondage, from the noose in which he is trapped. In the heart there is a place filled with joy. This joy is independent, it doesn't depend on anything. He is a Guru who takes a disciple to that center of joy and makes him become established there. Only then can he be called a true Guru. Obtaining this joy, man becomes fearless. Then he is happy not only in happiness but in difficulties as well.

THE GURU AS DISCIPLE

Nearly always, Baba answered questions asked by other people, but occasionally he would become the questioner and ask devotees about their understanding of various aspects of Siddha Yoga. The following exchange took place with students at the final session of a Teacher Training Course held in Ganeshpuri in 1976.

Baba: Who can give strong shaktipat? Who can transmit the Shakti very powerfully?

One who remains completely one-pointed on the Guru and immersed in him.

One who sees only purity in other people.

One who follows exactly the teachings of the Guru. One who does japa and has devotion for the Guru.

One who has great love for the Guru and faith in the Guru.

One who has attained the ūrdhvareta state and is always absorbed in love for the Guru.

All of those are good answers. One who has attained perfection after doing sadhana, one who has assimilated the Shakti completely into himself, one who has made the Shakti pervade every pore of his body can give strong shaktipat. Even after doing all these things, one who doesn't give up his devotion to the Guru, one who always remains aware that everything happens due to the grace of the Guru can give the most powerful shaktipat.

Can you give me the reason why, when someone becomes a Guru, he is a Guru only for a while and then he brings about his own downfall? Why does he fall even after he has been a Guru for a while?

When he has ego inside himself.

When he forgets that he is a disciple of the Guru. One must never forget that he is a disciple of the Guru.

It's a very good answer.

A person is lost unless the Guru is served with love. A Guru would be lost if he forgot that all is attained through the grace of his Guru.

Perfect.

When one misuses his attainments for his worldly ends without surrendering to the Guru.

Very good.

When the Guru only teaches and stops following his own sadhana.

That's very good. When one does *tapasya* for a while, when one has devotion to the Guru for a while, he attains Shakti. At that time his old understanding goes away and he begins to think, "Well, I have Shakti in myself. Why do I need the Guru's Shakti? Can't I do everything with my Shakti?"

This kind of ego arises in him and then he begins to praise himself. He increases his pride and he tries to increase his *abhinivesha*, his identification with something that is not his own Self. He tries to spread propaganda about himself, and he forgets the sadhana that he had been doing. Then he falls in such a way that he never rises again.

THE STATE OF A SIDDHA

If Siddha Yoga was kept very secret for so long and shaktipāt was traditionally granted only to those who kept the company of a Siddha for three years of purification, what changed in order for so many to receive the Guru's grace?

This is God's law. Even though it was said that Siddha Yoga was kept very secret, still it always pervaded everywhere. Everybody did know it secretly.

In Siddha Yoga, shaktipat takes place. There are very few great beings who can grant divine shaktipat.

The lineage of Siddha Yoga has never been broken. Some Siddhas kept quiet and did not let anybody know, and some Siddhas came into the open and talked to others. But this lineage will remain indestructible. As long as the lineage of human beings continues, the lineage of Siddha Yoga will also continue.

Would you please talk about the state of natural samādhi that a Siddha lives in?

A Siddha's state is not something to just talk about, because it goes beyond words. A Siddha is one who has attained perfect freedom, who has become completely independent. One who has brought these inner senses and outer senses under his control is a Siddha. None of the senses can move him. His mind cannot be moved; it is always established in his own Self. He is completely absorbed in the bliss of the inner Self, and no one can separate him from that state. If someone has all these qualities, he is called a Siddha.

He lives in this body, but he is different from this body. He lives in this world, but he is different from this world. He lives among people, but even so he lives in a solitary way. Even though he performs actions, still he doesn't do anything. This is how a Siddha lives.

A poet named Shukadev says that a Siddha is one who has destroyed his notion of duality, who has become one. He is not conscious of bondage and liberation; he transcends even these states. He is alive, but it is as if he were dead. For him there is no friend, nor does he have an enemy. A person who has these qualities is called a Siddha.

These pictures that you see on the wall are of great Siddhas —Sai Baba of Shirdi, Zipruanna, and Hari Giri Baba. Even though they were all omniscient, they lived very simple lives. When you put a bundle down somewhere, it lies there very quietly. In the same way those Siddhas led their lives very quietly and with great serenity. Siddhas may not have anything with them except a loincloth, but even kings go to them to ask for things. They may not even know the notes of the musical scale, but still great singers go to them and ask, "O Maharaj, please bestow grace on me so that I can sing." These Siddhas are so important, they are so significant.

Generally speaking, it is better to become a Siddha rather than to ask questions about it. If you ask me how a mango tastes, I can't tell you. It is useless to describe the taste of a mango. I will tell you where you can buy a mango, and then you can eat that mango. Then you will really know the taste of a mango — that is what is important.

How does a Guru prepare himself for his role?

A Guru follows sadhana very intensely and also observes a very strict discipline. He keeps his mind under control and he is also very particular about his actions. He keeps his mind and his body pure; he keeps himself pure on all levels. After receiving his own Guru's grace, his Kundalini is awakened, and then this great yogic power begins to work inside, and his body becomes totally purified; it becomes like gold. Though a Guru may appear to be an individual human being, from head to foot he becomes Kundalini energy. His entire body consists of particles of Kundalini.

So this is how a Guru purifies his body. A Guru's main practice is that he doesn't allow any impure thoughts to stay in his mind.

Would you tell me exactly what a saint is?

If you really want to understand a saint, you have to have — at least to a certain degree — the qualities of a saint. In India someone once asked a great saint, "Tell me exactly the state of a saint, how a saint lives in that state of sainthood."

The great being replied, "If you asked me how a fish sleeps in the water, I would say you have to be born as a fish, and only then can you experience it. Just by staying on the surface you can't understand how a fish sleeps in water."

So if you want to understand the inner state of a saint, you have to turn inward and find that state. If you look from the outside, there are many different ways that saints live, and from that you can understand only a little. If you want to understand a saint completely, you have to turn inward.

But in spite of all this, I can say a little about saints. If you keep the company of a saint, your inner being changes. If you go to a saint, you don't remain as you were before; you are changed and you find a state of happiness within yourself.

Now, for instance, we pursue the mind, so we have become the secretary of the mind, of the senses, of the sense pleasures, and of the various things we depend on. But if you go to a saint, you become the boss of all these things — no longer their secretary. You become free of all these things. Such a change indicates that you have absorbed the qualities of that saint. If you are in the company of a saint, all your impurities and all your defects go away; they are transcended and you become faultless.

THE INNER GURU

Is my inner Self my own Guru?

The inner Self is your Guru if you have access to your inner Self. A Guru is one who can show you the way. If your inner Self can show you the way, very good. In meditation you should look for the inner Self and see if you can receive guidance from it.
I have tried to do that, but there are no results yet.
In that case you should now look for an outer Guru, and the inner Self can be your Guru later. You have the inner Self as a Guru at a later stage; you need another Guru at this stage, an outer Guru.

What is the difference between the outer form of the Guru and the inner Guru?

That is the true Guru who dwells inside. The true Guru has no form. The scriptures say that the Guru is the Self, so the inner Self is the true Guru.

As long as you do not receive the grace of the inner Self, outer wisdom is not going to work for you. The outer Guru dwells inside too. Remember that the Guru is not this body; the Guru is the grace-bestowing power of God. Lord Shiva said, "O Goddess, understand that I am the Guru who makes the mantra active and who makes the Shakti work inside." So the inner Shakti is the Guru.

I have been relating to the inner Guru as the Shakti. Now that you are here, is it important to establish a relationship with the outer Guru?

If you have the inner relationship, the outer relationship just develops naturally. It is only when you have a relationship with the inner Guru that you can perceive the Truth. If you have an outer Guru, you also have the same Guru inside. If you have a Guru on the inside but you don't have one on the outside, you don't have a Guru.

What if you don't have a living Guru, but you are following the teachings of a Master who is no longer on this earth?

If you are following the teachings of a particular Master, even if he is no longer in the physical form, by his grace you will be able to meet a living Master one day. If he is a realized Master, he will appear to you in a vision or he will give an indication in some other way, telling you to go to a particular living Master.

Many people have had such an experience. The Master is only concerned about the advancement of his disciple, so if he is not in the physical form, he will send you to a living Guru who can take care of you. Gurus are not interested in monopolizing disciples as their exclusive property. They are only interested in the progress of the disciple. Such Gurus, even if they have left their bodies, will always give messages from within.

Baba, when the lights are off and you are sitting on your chair, often I see your face become many different faces. I see a thick blue aura above your head, and very often your face disappears like a smoke cloud that vanishes. Your sweater and lungi just sit there without your body. Who are all these faces? What is this blue aura? What is this smoky disappearing of your body? Where do you go? When I see all this, I realize that you are certainly not an ordinary man. Is it good that I see all these things?

You have very good radar. The fact is this whole universe is pervaded with that blue light. It's not that the blue aura is only above my head — it's above everybody's head. Even though we chant for only a short while, during that time I become absorbed in the Self, and that is why you see the blue aura around me. Perhaps because you are looking at this blue aura, you don't notice my body. When we chant, I go deep within my Self; I go and sit in that place from which *Om Namah Shivāya* emanates. That's all. People who have a very good heart, who are very devotional, for them the Guru looks the way they want him to look.

Constantly I tell you that the Guru is not just this individual being; he is that light. Many times I have explained to you that the Guru is the one who is in the center of that triangle in the *sahasrāra*. After the divine realization of that Pearl within you, you see everything as one — whether it is inside or outside. So many times I have told you that everything is nothing but Consciousness.

What is the difference between Christ-Consciousness and the Consciousness of the Guru? What steps are necessary for one to enjoy Christ-Consciousness?

The only difference is that of language. The one you call Christ, we call the Guru. Christ revealed the kingdom of heaven to everyone, the inner kingdom of heaven. I too am talking about the kingdom of heaven within. I do not impose any creed on anyone. Meditation is not dogma, japa is not dogma, chanting is not dogma. The Bible has been translated into my mother tongue. Does it cease to be the Bible? We chant in Sanskrit while you chant in English. The only difference is that of language; the inner meaning is the same. To achieve Christ-Consciousness you need to go within. You need to go completely within and become steady in the heart.

What advice do you have for those of us who live where there are very few Gurus to choose from? How can we find the Guru who is right for us?

When seekership manifests itself in you, a Guru will come to you from somewhere or other. Even though a Guru may appear to be a limited human form, he is all-pervasive and he can give you messages from within, no matter where he is. Besides, there is the inner Guru, who is present in the midst of the sahasrara, the thousand-petaled center in the head. That inner Guru can show you the path to the outer Guru. It happens quite often in India that while meditating, an aspirant has a vision that tells him to go to a particular place and meet a particular Guru. Before attaining the vision of the final Truth, a meditator first has a vision of the Guru within. One can see that Guru, and that Guru is divine.

There was a great saint in Maharashtra named Tukaram; he received initiation in a dream from a being who had come from *Siddhaloka,* the world of perfected beings. In one of his poems Tukaram says that though the supreme Guru is Master of the universe, he makes a tiny house, as tiny as a sesame seed, and lives in that. That tiny house is like a dot, like a *bindu,* and a meditator is able to see the forms of many gods and goddesses, many deities, appearing and disappearing within that dot, within that house. Tukaram says that though the bindu appears to be so tiny, it holds in its belly all the three worlds of the macrocosm and the three worlds of the microcosm — the worlds of waking, dream, and deep sleep. These, too, are held in the belly of that tiny bindu. All this exists in every person and that is why I say that a human being is very, very great.

I am sitting here in this chair and my body is covered with clothes. If I were to look only at my clothes, I would not be able to know my body; I would know only my clothes. Likewise, if I were to look at my body, I would know only the body, not the bodiless One living within the body. It is only when I look at the bodiless One who dwells within the body that I come to know that I am That. If I become aware of who I really am, I become aware of my own worthiness, my own greatness, my own divinity.

How does one maintain the contact with the Guru so essential to spiritual development?

To maintain that contact you should sustain a pure inner love for the Guru, a pure inner affection, and follow his teachings. Then you will be continually in contact with him. If the Guru has planted the seed of yoga within you, and if by that means he has activated the inner yoga in you, he will always be working within you in the form of Shakti. The Guru always lives in your heart in the form of the mantra. See him right there — that is the best way of maintaining contact with him. A true Guru is one who can activate a mantra within the heart of his disciple and fill a disciple's heart with love and peace.

As long as I know the Guru is within me, is it all right for me to keep you at a distance, as I do everyone else?

Can you keep the inner Guru at a distance? If you could, then you could also keep the outer Guru at a distance. If you feel the inner Guru is close, then the outer Guru is also equally close, because it is the inner Guru that becomes the outer Guru.

INSIDE I NEED TO KNOW

I was looking at a picture of you above a doorway in my home, and it began to change. I saw you and many other saints and holy men pass by. Finally I saw the archway containing the statue of Bhagawan Nityananda. Then beneath the picture in the doorway I saw you appear and disappear several times in a body of white light. Tears were rolling down my cheeks. Was this real?

It is a real experience. This will happen many times — you will see me emerging from the Blue Pearl again and again. It is a very good experience.

Jesus said, "I am the Way, the Truth and the Light; no one comes to the Father but through me." Does this mean a Christian cannot accept a living Guru?

When Jesus was alive, he was a true being. He was a being who could give God's love to others. The Indian scriptures say that He is the Guru who gives God's love to others, who instructs others, who destroys all sins. This is what all the great beings have said. Mohammed also said that he was the way to God. Only through him could you come to God. Bistami and Mansur Mastana also said the same thing. Other saints such as Dho'l-Nun and Shankaracharya also said the same thing. Lord Buddha said, "I am the Void, I am the Emptiness." Whoever came said the same thing — that he was the only way. You should try to understand this with a sharp intellect. Everybody has said the same thing. Is everybody wrong?

I don't know how you manage it, but you are as beautiful as you were the last time I interviewed you. How do you keep your youth?

The secret of that is constant dwelling in the Self and a life of discipline. Living in inner Consciousness — that is the secret. I do not repeat the mantra of old age. I repeat the mantra of youth, and that is why I stay ever young. I love only the Self. I honor only the Self. I live my life in the Self. I find fulfillment in the Self. Since I function in the Self all the time, my youth keeps being enhanced. I don't repeat the mantras of old age, such as anxiety and craving for sense pleasures. There is no youth like freedom from anxiety, and there is no old age like anxiety.

The day before yesterday you said one should come to know what his relationship is with the Guru, and I would like to know what that relationship is.

Find it out. You can know it only through love. You can't know it by asking about it. You can know the relationship only through love.

Baba, did you ever have any doubts before and after meeting your Guru? You speak so strongly about doubts as the biggest blocks to enlightenment, yet you say we shouldn't have blind faith.

Yes, I had a lot of doubts. I had doubts about myself, always wondering, "Am I all right?" I would see a Guru in a certain way and wonder, "Now do I lack something or does he lack something?" I would always wonder in this way.

I had a lot of love for great beings and saints. I read their stories and poems. I always wanted to know what they had to say. I was in the company of many great beings and many poet-saints. I knew all of these beings whose photographs are on the wall. Those in the paintings existed before I came into this world; however, I know their poems by heart.

I traveled all over India and I stayed in the company of many, many saints. It is not that I doubted them, but I was always curious to watch their behavior and their way of living. I found that every saint was different. They looked different and it seemed they were in a different state, so I would always wonder what the reason was. As I kept traveling more and more, I understood more about them, and my doubts began to leave me.

Even now I always say, "Sit in a good boat." If someone has gone across the ocean of the world, you should really experience that from him. A Guru has to be very pure and clean. If a Guru speaks about the Self, you should try to find out whether he really experiences the joy of the Self or not. If he speaks about nectar, *rasa*, you should find out whether he really drinks the inner nectar or whether he depends on the outer nectar — from bottles.

What is your Consciousness like? What do you want?

All I want is that blind people should become conscious. My Consciousness is the same Consciousness which has given rise to this cosmos. God is Consciousness, and the Self is too. That is what I am, and that is what you are. What I want is that all of you become Consciousness.

What does it mean if one asks the Guru to be his Guru again in the next life? I'm enjoying this life so much, I would love to be reborn — only I cannot imagine living in the world without my Guru. Does this question impose any difficulty? Is it a nuisance to the Guru?

Is it your desire to make the Guru be reborn again with you? Why don't you finish your life with this lifetime! Eat, drink, enjoy yourself, and just finish it. However, if you are reborn again, the Guru will be with you one way or another — don't worry. As long as the sun and the moon exist, the Guru exists and you exist. After that, nobody will exist.

MILLIONS OF SIDDHAS
ARE BACKING US UP

Are there others with perfect Consciousness in other cultures? Would you name some, past and present?

There were many, there are many, there will be many — but we are not aware of them.

There is another plane of existence called *siddhaloka*, and many Siddhas live there. There is no sun or moon or star there, only the light of Consciousness that is the Blue Pearl, and that Blue Pearl illumines everything with a shimmering, scintillating light. Siddhas live in the midst of that light. This earth will never be without Siddhas — never. Some of them you know, and some of them you can't recognize. If one great being leaves this world, somebody else comes. God's storehouse is really huge. Siddhaloka, the world of great beings, is even greater than this world. Those great beings were so divine, so pure, and so sublime — and of course they went across the ocean of this world. We repeat their names, and now we too are going across.

There was a Siddha I knew named Zipruanna. Even now you would say he was crazy, because he slept on a heap of garbage. But he was a Siddha; he was a great, omniscient being. In spite of that, still his body never smelled; the garbage never affected his body because he was so pure.

Sometimes beings from that world come here to do some work— great beings like Jnaneshwar, Sai Baba of Shirdi, Zipruanna, and my Baba, Bhagawan Nityananda. They come because they get an order from that place to come here. They sow the seeds, and after sowing the seeds, they leave. When the seed is sprouted, it grows into a plant and becomes a tree with many branches. Then it bears a lot of fruit and it becomes a great thing.

Would you say something about Siddha Gurus and siddhaloka?

Even though it is so far away, the Siddhas who live in that plane can instantly come to the earth. That plane is made of pure Consciousness. There are beautiful gardens and forests everywhere. There is no moon, there is no sun; the whole plane is illumined by Consciousness. There is no thirst or hunger, there is no sleep. They exist just by the satisfaction of their experience of Consciousness. They are fully satisfied in their own Self, and they are constantly immersed in that bliss all the time. That is Siddhaloka.

The Siddhas who live there constantly watch the people who seek their help on the earth plane; they are constantly waiting to shower their grace on those who are in need of it. Sometimes they take birth on the earth plane, and their spiritual practices come to fruition automatically. Some Siddhas from that plane come and give initiation and then they go back. They possess so much freedom that they can do or undo anything. If they bestow their grace on someone, that grace never fails. It completes that person and perfects him. They simply awaken the inner Consciousness, and through this awakening they see that spiritual practices are culminated.

These beings reveal inner secrets that are hidden. If you once take refuge in the lineage of Siddhas, there are millions of Siddhas who are waiting to back you up.

Can you speak about visitors from other planes?

Siddhas from Siddhaloka can visit the earth plane immediately with the help of the Blue Pearl. They can come and move among us without our awareness.

Our contact with these saints is through the thousand-petaled lotus in the crown center. Within that lotus is a triangle, and this is the seat of all the Siddha Gurus. All our salutations, all our worship and prayers, are meant for these beings who are right within us. The supreme Guru exists in everyone's sahasrara. When you meditate, offer your salutations to all the thousands of Siddhas; then very naturally you will receive their grace to meditate.

I Have Seen Only One Nityananda

Before India attained freedom, there were many independent princely states. When I was young, I roamed from one place to another and met a number of these rulers, and I still know some of them. But everything changes; the wheels of destiny are constantly turning. Almost all those kings passed away and even their statues have been demolished. However, the statue of my Guru, of my Baba, will last forever. It will last as long as the sun and the moon rise in the sky. No one can touch it. It will remain as it is. I saw many presidents, I saw many ministers, but I have seen only one Nityananda. The famous men all change: their names change and they don't last. But people still bathe Nityananda and worship him; they drink the water of his feet. So remember this mantra — that the Guru protects you from time, from fear, and from death. I am extremely happy now because he told me to sit in Ganeshpuri and I sat there. I will sit there as long as this body lasts.

It is very difficult to talk about my Guru because he was a really great being. His behavior, his manner, and his discipline were beyond our understanding. He was a great and unique being.

He was free from company. His fingers were always completely outstretched; he never folded them. This indicates that when he gave up something, he gave it up completely.

He never got attached to it again. Generally, he spoke very little. Occasionally, he spoke a lot; however, it was hard to understand him. He was such an extraordinary being that although he knew the past, the present, and the future, he remained as though he did not know anything.

If anyone went to him becoming very small and humble, he would also be very humble, and he would talk to that person and give him instructions. If anyone went to him as a great scholar, or a rich person, or a person with power, he would close his eyes completely and turn inward and remain very quiet. In his vision he saw no differences. He did not consider anyone an inferior person, a low person, an ignorant person, or an illiterate person. Also he did not consider anyone to be pure, great, or very smart. He had equal vision. In his life he did not find anything that was good or bad. For him spirituality and worldly life were one and the same. Even if people asked him questions about their mundane life, he would answer those questions. He never felt that one should ask questions only from the scriptures, only about spiritual matters.

He was always in an intoxicated state. He got up every morning at three o'clock and went to take a bath in the hot springs. In the daytime he would remain lying down, absorbed in his own Self, and at night he would talk to his devotees. He had very simple food — just dal and vegetables, a little rice, and sometimes coffee. He used to sit on a very plain bench. He would lie on a very simple bed, and finally at the end he was sleeping on just a thin mattress.

People used to bring a lot of gifts for him. He never took any interest in them. However, the people around him made good use of those things. Even though lots and lots of people went to see him, they would all become very quiet in his presence. If anyone tried to command or discipline his devotees, he never liked it. As people kept watching him, they would feel him inside themselves; they would feel knowledge arising within them. They did not need to take courses. Even though his eyes were open, he never looked at other people. He liked to gaze inside, to gaze at his own inner Self, and to become absorbed in his own inner Self.

His eyes were always half open. He had a big belly because of the long inner retention of breath, or kumbhaka. *His body was completely dark. He wore only a loincloth. He was so handsome that not only did young people and adults watch him but even old people kept looking and looking at him. Without talking, he gave instructions. Without giving the touch, he awakened the inner Shakti. He did not have to hold question-and-answer sessions. Without speaking, he answered people's questions. It is very difficult to talk about such an extraordinary being.*

CHAPTER 5

The Shakti Unfolds

*When the Shakti is awakened, reality shows
itself to you of its own accord.*

*I am very new to all this, but I want to know how you look into
yourself.*

It is really nothing new to you. It is something that is old for
everyone. The Shakti has always been here and the inner heart
has always been here. In the middle of the human body there
lives a great Shakti, a divine energy, and it has tremendous
power. Though it may be a tiny flame now, it is enough to burn
up the whole world. Once that Shakti is awakened, once that fire
is kindled, it will do its work for many, many people — not only
for you. Either it is by the limitless grace of God that this dormant Shakti is awakened or if you move in the company of those
who are near to God, who love God, then your Shakti too can
be awakened.

   You should experience the Shakti. As long as you have not,
this awakening has not taken place. As long as you do not know
your Shakti, you do not know yourself. You cannot know yourself by just knowing your eyes or your nose or your ears or your
hands or by taking a certain name. It is a pity that most people
do not know themselves. One must get to know oneself through
the Self.

Can you explain what Shakti is and how it works?

Shakti is the creative power of God, which has created this diverse universe full of endless forms. Shakti is the divine energy, which manifests this variegated universe, which lives in it and also behind it in a concealed form. If we really want to understand what Shakti is, we have to reflect deeply on it. We should become acquainted with Shakti through meditation.

Shakti activates internal yoga. Shakti keeps our organism functioning properly. One could go on describing the work of Shakti endlessly. Shakti has become the outbreath and the inbreath. Shakti has become the four bodies and the four states of consciousness: waking, dream, deep sleep, and *turīya*. Shakti, in fact, has become everything. The Shakti has the power to create a new cosmos and to dissolve the old cosmos into Her being. Whatever you see around you is nothing but Shakti.

Does everyone have Shakti within them?

How can you stay alive without Shakti?

Is it the life-force?

Yes, it is the life-force, and much more than that. Shakti is the source of the life-force. One lives by Shakti. It is supremely divine and it lives in the body. It is a pity that we are not aware of it.

What is a chakra, and how does it differ from Kundalinī?

Kundalini is the all-pervasive Shakti, while a chakra is a point where Shakti is concentrated. The different chakras within the body control different nerves. These chakras have great importance. As long as they are not opened, we remain wandering in the outer world; once they are opened, we realize our inner perfection.

Do the chakras always open in ascending order?

Either it will start from the heart and go to the *sahasrāra*, or go from the heart to the base of the spine. Sometimes it opens first at the base of the spine, and sometimes in the heart. Wherever it starts from, it will go in order. One thing is certain — if one is open, all of them will also open.

Is there a God in your universe? Is there a supreme source that leads you?

Yes, the source is also called Shakti. You can describe it in different ways, but it is the universal source that has created this whole universe within itself. This Shakti pervades everything in this universe and it is one with all things; it makes everything work. In water there is coolness and in fire there is heat; that is the same Shakti that exists in all things. Different people give it different names, but there is one God.

If you would meditate with me, I could make you experience that Shakti. If I have to tell you verbally, all I can say is that it is a universal Shakti that pervades the entire universe. The yogis call it *Kundalinī*.

Where does it come from? What creates it?

It is self-existent. It does not have to be created by something else. It doesn't come from anywhere or go anywhere — it just is. It pervades the smallest and the greatest thing; it is everything and everywhere. The most important thing to know about it is that it lies within the center of a person's body.

And your teaching is to find it or harness it?

My teaching is that the Shakti lies within you in a dormant state and that one has to awaken it. Once the Shakti is unfolded, the inner yoga begins to take place spontaneously. That yoga happens by itself; you don't have to do it. Through that yoga one begins to understand that the great Shakti lies within, that it is ever present, that it is full of life. People who meditate find Shakti especially in the heart chakra and in the sahasrara. You too can find the Shakti if you meditate.

That is how you find the Shakti?

Yes, and also I cause people to experience the Shakti.

When you find that Shakti, how does it change your life?

It makes your life better, it gives you peace in your heart, and it also gives peace to your mind. You can do all your activities with greater joy, with greater ecstasy.

Into every spiritual man's life a little materialism must fall.
Can the Shakti make one a better bricklayer, a better doctor,
or a better baker?

Your question is beautiful! If the inner Shakti did not enable you to function better in your outer life, what would be the point of it? The Shakti that I speak of is not any ordinary energy. It is the energy of Consciousness, the divine creative energy, which creates an entire cosmos.

Once it is awakened inside us, it is perfectly capable of taking care of our outer life. In fact, it improves our outer life immeasurably. One who is a doctor can diagnose disease without too many instruments. A bricklayer can become a great expert in laying bricks. A soldier can fight with much greater vigor and courage. A baker will be able to bake the rays of Shakti into the bread he makes, and it will be extremely delectable. After shaktipat a musician can pursue music with much greater ease.

The Shakti affects not only humans but also animals and plants and trees. Some day come to our ashram in Ganeshpuri and see what giant mangoes grow on our trees. Shakti also moves animals very deeply. Quite often when I go to visit the cows in the cowshed, they start releasing their milk. The Shakti is the energy of enthusiasm, of greatness, of joy, and it stirs the heart of every creature.

Is there any particular tree or flower that has more Shakti
than another?

Certain trees are more effective in certain respects; different plants have different powers. Certain herbs have the power of curing diseases, while others can create new diseases. That too is a power. However, the basic Shakti is the same in all these plants, just as fire is one and the same but appears to be different when it manifests through different things. When fire manifests through a candle, it has one kind of look; when it manifests through wood, it has a different look.

There is only one Shakti pervading the whole cosmos.

It seems to become different when it manifests through different things. Suppose you have a piece of land, and you grow chilies and sugar cane on it. The soil is the same, the water is the same, and the manure with which you fertilize is the same; yet the Shakti manifests as sweetness in sugar and as pungency in chilies. The same water becomes sour in lemons and sweet in oranges. The air is the same, but when it blows through open spaces, it blows freely, and in the human body it works according to a certain rhythm in the form of the breath. The same air works differently in a soda bottle.

Though the basic substance is one, because of the different things it combines with, it appears to be different. It is the same Shakti that becomes poison in a serpent and nectar in the milk of a cow. The same Shakti seated in the human body activates spontaneous yoga.

Sometimes when I am around you, I feel the Shakti very strongly and sometimes I don't feel anything. Is it something that you do or that I do, or am I not open to experiencing the Shakti?

It is none of these. You have seen an automatic heater: once it has reached a certain temperature, automatically the heat is turned off. If it were to remain on, the room would get hotter and hotter and you would become giddy. The Shakti functions rather like an automatic heater. It is the divine energy, which creates a whole cosmos in one moment and dissolves it in another moment. It has the greatest power. It is confident and free. The sages describe the Shakti as a goddess: when She opens Her eyes, She writes out a universe, and when She closes them, She erases it in the twinkling of an eye. She has such power. However, the Shakti is also careful, and She adapts herself to the body; She knows how much it can take. You must have the capacity to bear the force of the Shakti. It is for this reason that we value celibacy, that we let the sexual fluid accumulate more and more in the body, and that we eat pure, nutritious food. The Shakti works automatically, and we must be able to bear Her impact.

*To what extent does Shakti control everyday life? Is everything
that happens, no matter how small, governed by Shakti?*

The fact is that whatever happens, happens for spiritual growth.
It is only that you are not aware of it. Everything, no matter how
small or big, is nothing but Shakti. This entire universe is Shakti.
It is Shakti who becomes the sun and illuminates the world. It
is Shakti who becomes the moon and cools the world. It is
Shakti who becomes the clouds and sends down showers. It is
Shakti who becomes the earth and produces the valleys and
plants and trees. Shakti has two aspects — masculine and fem-
inine — the aspect that looks after our outer life and the one that
looks after our spiritual life. So after you receive shaktipat,
whatever happens — whether it is big or small — consider it to
be a play of Shakti.

*What is it that keeps our minds tied to our contracted states
and unaware of our absolute or expanded state?*

It is we who have contracted our own understanding. It is our
own inner energy which has kept us in a contracted form.
Shaivism says that Shakti itself contracts and makes itself small.
That is called the world. If you unfold your energy, you attain
your own perfection.

THE FIRE OF YOGA

*I am new to meditation. At the retreat I experienced a flash of
red heat up and down my spine, but now when I sit cross-legged
to meditate, I feel a pinching sensation in the center of my spine.
Can you help me?*

You are already being helped. The flash of red heat that you
experienced up and down your spine was the heat of Kundalini,
but it won't burn you up — don't worry. The pinching sensation
that you feel in the middle of your spine is also the work of the

Kundalini, opening up the passage so it can rise to the higher centers. If you feel this heat or pinching again, welcome it, being fully aware that it is the touch of the highest Shakti of the supreme Lord.

When you touched my forehead, I felt fire in that spot.

My body is full of that fire, the fire of yoga. When I use the word *yoga*, I do not mean just a few postures; I mean real yoga. If you meditate, you will feel this fire being released inside you. This is the fire of yoga, the fire of love, the fire of true religion. This is the fire of peace and the fire of God.

The other night, while I was visiting a friend, she experienced a very bright white light surrounding my head. Around it was a yellow-gold light. Around both these lights was a shimmering blue light. She has never experienced this before or since with anyone else, and it happened for half an hour or more. That day for the first time I had put my forehead on the footrest in front of your chair. Is there any connection?

Yes, the footrest is full of rays of Shakti and you must have taken a few with you. Moreover, the Shakti is already awake within you, and that Shakti is light, which radiates all the time. What has happened is very good. If it happens again, let it happen. But now you'll have to meditate more!

I have had many wonderful meditation experiences of the Virgin Mother, of Jesus, and of a large white circle with eight spokes in it. I later learned that this was a Buddhist symbol.

Your visions are quite authentic and beautiful. What you need is to meditate more. You should get into the state called *samādhi*. Focus your awareness at the top of the head and let your inner visions be concentrated there. That is the real heart — not in the chest. Some people speak of the heart being in the chest, but in fact the subtle-body heart extends from the chest to the top of the head. In the chest is the seat of all psychic powers.

79

Do you hear inner music?

Yes, often.

Focus your attention on that music. Or you can focus on the light, because the light is enclosed by this music. Actually, the two are one.

During darshan I experienced a column of golden light up and down my spine. What is this light? Also, if I begin to laugh during meditation, should I leave the hall?

What you saw as a golden light is really the *sushumnā,* the central channel in the body, which extends from the base of the spine to the cerebrum. That nerve is very brilliant. Meditators often focus their minds on that. To have a vision of the sushumna has tremendous importance.

If you go outside and meditate and laugh in the streets, people will wonder. If you keep laughing here, you will disturb others. So what shall we do? You should go into the office and laugh there.

It's true — sometimes one does feel like laughing hilariously during meditation. There are people who begin to dance because of this rush of laughter within. It's a happy experience.

In my meditation I saw a burning white light. It was so bright that it blinded me and it scared me. What should I do?

When the inner divine light arises, you experience yourself burning, literally burning. You get so scared that you come out of meditation and run away. Although this light appears to be very ordinary, still it is great. Electricity is absolutely nothing compared to this. This light cannot be compared to anything, even the power of an atom bomb or nuclear energy. An atom bomb will destroy something, but after a while a new building or a new city will come into existence once again. However, the fire of an atom bomb can destroy only a person's life, a person's body. It cannot burn the *karmas* of the person.

The *Bhagavad Gītā* says that as the fire of knowledge arises in meditation, it is so powerful that it destroys the karmas of your countless lifetimes.

With great certainty you can understand that it is an auspicious day for you, because you perceived the burning white light. It will burn all the bad things inside you. Thank you. This is a beautiful question that you have asked.

Sometimes when I meditate, a tremendous amount of energy goes up my body to the top of my head, and it feels as if the top will blow off. What do I do with this energy? Where do I send it? How can I use it constructively in my daily life?

This is your imagination that your top is going to blow off. With respect and with courage, continue to meditate. Let the Shakti do whatever She wants to do, and if She goes to the top of the head, let Her go; She will also come down. Keep the Shakti free. Shiva, the Lord of Shakti, is in the sahasrara, and She is yearning to meet Her beloved. That is why the Shakti goes there. So it is a matter of great fortune for you.

Last night, my head was on fire and it was difficult to sleep. How can I pursue my sadhana, yet have peaceful sleep?

It happens in certain cases that when the inner Shakti awakes and begins to work, you will lose your sleep; however, that is no cause for fear. What you experienced as fire in the head is really the heat of Kundalini, and this will subside on its own. Even though you have this burning sensation in the head, the brain will not get heated up. Much more will be accomplished inside. Keep repeating *Guru Om, Guru Om* and focus your mind on the place where you feel the burning sensation, because that is the seat of the Guru. It is quite likely that sometime the Guru will emerge from within and stand before your eyes and you will be able to see him. The Guru lives in the crown center, but his seat is situated between the eyebrows. If you wish to reach the house of the Guru, you have to get clearance from the customs there. It is there that you have to obtain the Guru's permission to move upward. That seat is also called a *chakra*. It has two petals, and the two syllables *ham* and *sa* also exist there.

I have been doing sadhana by myself for a year. Sometimes I experience bright light and a roaring in my ears after meditation and while doing hatha yoga. Is this the Kundalinī? It has not been pleasant.

These experiences will become very pleasant later. You should stop worrying. Such experiences come when Kundalini is only partly awakened. When it awakes fully, you will experience the bliss of the light and the roaring. You will be able to see the inner light time and time again. Even if you were to start feeling a little restless, it would not matter. Just watch it and don't worry.

I have heard that the Kundalinī can be dangerous and that some people have been driven insane by it.

What you have been told is what the owls told the swan. Owls can't see in the daytime, and they tried to persuade the swan that the sun does not exist.

All the people here have awakened Kundalinis. How do they look to you? Do they look insane? Look at their faces, look at their glow. Those who have absolutely no knowledge of Kundalini cannot bear that you should have anything to do with it. They would like to drag you to where they are. Kundalini is not at all dangerous. However, there are some people who practice rigorous hatha yoga without a Guru, and it is the rigors of their sadhana that may cause insanity — not Kundalini. This awakened Kundalini will always guide you from within and it will give you messages from inside.

Now you should reduce your *āsanas* and increase your meditation. It is necessary for a meditator to drink a little milk and eat a little butter and also to eat a little sugar. It's quite likely that you may come up against more difficulties in the future, but don't have any fear. When you are meditating, if something happens that you don't understand, look upon it as the work of a living deity. Look at it with love and reverence, and then the Shakti will help you. The Shakti is the highest Goddess. She is all-knowing and all-powerful. We should remain aware of Her glory.

Sometimes my legs and back shake when I meditate. Also sometimes my spine hurts. What is happening? Is this okay?

It's not just slightly okay—it's very okay. I consider you to be very lucky. You haven't been here long and you have already received Shakti. If your limbs feel like shaking, let them shake. The pain that you feel in the spine is a creative pain, and the more the pain increases, the greater is your chance of enjoying bliss later.

Once Shakti has been received, one changes completely and all that was done before is completely destroyed; not the good things that you have done, but the bad things. It is not your merit, but your wickedness that is consumed. It is not your wealth that is taken away after the inner awakening; it is the misfortunes that are taken away. So now you should sit in meditation having the right perspective on yourself—that you are a most noble being.

The Shakti that has become awake within you is not ordinary human shakti; it is the Shakti of God, a living force. This Shakti is something that all the spiritual philosophers talk about. One who has received Shakti and becomes immersed in the limitless bliss of Consciousness, not only does he become liberated, but his entire family as well, including his ancestors. I am very happy that this has happened to you and I feel great respect for you. According to the scriptures, the mother of such a one is blessed. The earth also feels very happy that at least one more person has reduced the burden of sin that she has to carry all the time. Now you should develop through pure thoughts and a pure lifestyle. After this living force has become active within you, it is that which should absorb you, not idle chatter or gossip.

The reason you feel pain in the spine is that the central nerve, which is the hub of thousands of nerves, lies there. All these nerves begin to vibrate at this point when you receive Shakti and when you meditate with faith and love.

One who has unshakeable faith in the inner Shakti attains infinite knowledge by Her grace. One who has the same faith in the inner Shakti that he has in the reality of God is one to whom the inner Shakti reveals all Her treasures, all Her divinity, saying, "I am the Shakti, I am God." One should be able to recognize this great force that travels at the speed of lightning. We should store the Shakti up inside ourselves with reverence. Don't think that it only enables you to meditate; it can give you whatever you want. But you must store up the Shakti within you; otherwise you will lose it. If we do not observe any restraint and discipline in our life, if we do not observe any self-control in eating and talking, and if we do not meditate regularly, we will lose the Shakti. We should remember the inner Shakti time and time again.

Since receiving shaktipāt, is it possible that it is more difficult to meditate?

It's quite possible. The Shakti knows everything, including the needs of your constitution. Shakti is conscious, intelligent energy. It will make us meditate only as much as our body and our nerves can bear. So you should be happy in the will of the Shakti. If you were getting too much intense meditation, your body might become quite weak and even emaciated.

The other day a *yogi* came to me who was a very good yogi, but his body had become quite emaciated, and I told him not to meditate for a while and to eat more. Leave it to the will of the Shakti and don't worry about it. Sit regularly for meditation and let the Shakti run your ship. The ways of Shakti are quite mysterious. When you try to sit for meditation, you may not get it, but when you are driving to your office, you may be grabbed by the Shakti, because it is supremely free.

In the natural state will the Kundalinī become too powerful for the practitioner to handle? If so, how may we quiet the Shakti?

Kundalini is not like an automobile engine with gears— first, second, third, and fourth. Kundalini is the highest Shakti, She is the divine Goddess, She is the supreme Guru. God and Kundalini and Guru are one, so Kundalini knows how much She should work within you.

Is Kundalinī felt only in the spine or are there variations that can be felt only in the head, for example, rather than at the base of the spine?
You can feel it in any part of the body.
So if you don't feel it in the base of the spine first, it can be felt in other parts of the body?
Yes, you can feel it anywhere. It depends on where it pleases Her to be felt. There is no law that the Kundalini follows.

Could you talk about samskāras? What are they and how are they made?

According to the scriptures, *samskāras* are the impressions that become embedded in your psyche as a result of the various deeds you have performed. These impressions are embedded in the central nerve of the subtle body, the sushumna. They are like tapes that play from time to time. Sometimes they rise to the conscious surface. Sometimes they merge into their place in the sushumna and you lose awareness of them. It is not so easy to detect these impressions; it is only when your Kundalini is awakened that you can perceive them rising from within very clearly. They are the leftovers of the deeds you have done.

Samskaras are related to habits. All the thoughts we think and all the meditating and the chanting we do leave their impressions in our psyche. For this reason it is essential to stay conscious and alert. Whatever you think, whatever you feel, has its effect on your entire body, on its subtle constituents. Therefore, be extremely careful.

Either strive to keep your mind empty of all thoughts, or if you can't do that, let only good thoughts move in the mind. You may think you are thinking bad thoughts about others, but the fact is that all these thoughts are harming *you,* not others; and when you think good thoughts, those thoughts benefit you. The thoughts you think and the actions you do cast seeds within your mind, the fruits of which you yourself will consume later on. That is why I stress chanting so much. Chanting destroys all the old samskaras in the mind, and it purifies the heart completely. Not a single word that you utter ever goes to waste.

Whatever you chant stays forever in the inner atmosphere.

My first experiences of Kundalinī were very blissful, but now when I experience Kundalinī or have a very deep meditation, the next day there is a tremendous exhaustion and sometimes a very deep depression. Why this change?

It is due to the Kundalini that you sometimes feel that way. Kundalini itself contains all of this — depression and bliss and happiness and hopes. We live only because of this central channel in the subtle body; it is a storehouse of all our past karma. When your Kundalini awakens, all your qualities, one by one, come out, because Kundalini is expelling them from your system.

Sometimes you feel depressed and have negative thoughts and sometimes you feel hopeless. But don't worry; have full courage. When you are completely purified, when that Kundalini has thrown away all your bad qualities, then you experience supreme bliss. You meditate and realize that your bliss hasn't gone anywhere — it is right there inside you. It will never come and go; it will never decrease. That bliss will never become impure. It is always in one steady state, and it is always inspiring.

It is worth remembering that for some people when the Kundalini awakens, the mind may become completely restless and fickle, and there may be great depression. But the mind is depressed only to destroy that depression. So you don't have to be afraid. You should be supremely happy, thinking that your Kundalini, your inner Shakti, is awakened and is active inside you.

KRIYAS ARE MEDICINE

If you don't have kriyās, does it mean you are not allowing them to happen? Do they happen to everyone?

Kriyas do not happen to everybody. Understand that kriyas are medicine. If you don't have any disease, why should you take medicine? Kriyas occur if your body needs them. If there are blocks and impurities in the body, kriyas take place to remove them. In meditation more subtle kriyas will take place. You may have visions of lights or flames. No matter what experiences you have now, whether they are physical kriyas or visions of flames and lights, finally they will all merge in the final state, which is nothing but supreme happiness.

When you finish eating, or when you meet a friend whom you have not seen for a long time, there is a point at which you experience happiness. The experience is like a lightning flash; it remains for only a fraction of a moment. When that happiness is increased through *japa* and meditation, you will experience the supreme bliss, which is everlasting.

Since I have received your grace, things are happening in my body and in my head, but my heart seems to be slow to open. Please tell me something about that.

If your crown chakra becomes open, the heart will become open by itself. Keep meditating calmly. All these things are happening in order to open your heart. If you were to feel at one with these processes happening inside of you, the heart would open quickly. By considering yourself to be apart from the kriyas, it slows things down. Become one with the kriyas and the heart will open by itself.

I feel my energy is centered in my throat chakra. I think it might be blocked. How can I open my throat chakra so the energy can flow freely?

You shouldn't try to open it. The energy will open the door on its own, and it will flow freely upward. When you are doing sadhana, when you are meditating, the energy stops wherever it is supposed to work. Sometimes it stops in the navel, sometimes in the heart, and sometimes in the throat. Wherever the chakra is, it stops there. It also stops between the eyebrows and then it moves upward, becoming completely free. There are no more specific locations for it after that. So if your energy stops at the throat chakra, meditate on that space. There is a particular deity of this chakra. Understand what Shakti is; then everything will be all right.

When I am in meditation, I sometimes feel an intense pressure between my brows. Then I stop whatever I'm doing and wait until the pressure goes away. Can you explain this?

It's good to experience that pressure. It's not good to stop it. That is the path that leads you to the sahasrara, and it is the inner Shakti clearing the path by means of the pressure. Indian people apply either sandalwood paste or *kumkum* to their forehead at this place out of respect for that inner Guru. It is the Guru's seat. There is a chakra here called the *ājñā chakra. Ājñā* means command. Here you receive the Guru's command to go higher. So don't try to stop the pressure. Just let the Shakti move up. If you try to stop it, it is as if God comes to meet you and immediately you close the door. Don't do that. Let the Shakti go higher at its own pleasure.

I always have very peaceful meditations. How do I know when my sadhana is progressing if I don't see the different centers unfold before me?

Forget about the centers, forget about the chakras. You don't need to know about them. Keep meditating peacefully. What *chakra* means in our language is wheel. A wheel can turn this way or that way, but the important attainment of meditation is peace. The result of meditation is not the unfolding of centers or the perception of images or the vision of flames. The result of meditation is to increase inner peace. Peace increases inside on its own, spontaneously. Peace keeps growing and growing.

Lately as soon as I say my mantra, I feel great pressure in my neck. My head is pulled to one side or the other. Often it shakes violently. Can you tell me what is happening? Do I have a block in that area?

There is a knot at the nape of the neck and there is also a knot between the eyebrows. There are very strict customs officials sitting at these points and regulating your entry into the higher realms. Ordinary customs officials are quite casual, because they let drugs pass through and various other things. But the customs authorities here are very stubborn and they won't let any such thing pass. It is to open that knot in the neck that the inner Shakti causes these neck movements. This is a very good kriya. Sometimes I touch people on the nape of their necks in order to release that block. Sometimes I tap a person between the eyebrows, and that is to open up the knot there. So what is happening is very good and you shouldn't worry about it.

Is the experience of seeing a flame between the eyebrows a once-in-a-lifetime experience, or do enlightened beings see it constantly? Is it just another experience before realization?

Between the eyebrows there is a constantly blazing flame the size of your little finger tip. People who meditate by focusing their attention between the eyebrows do see a flame the size of a candle flame. Realized beings constantly see that flame between the eyebrows when they meditate; they also see many other things. In the sahasrara, realized beings see different kinds of flames; they see the whole universe inside the head. There are so many marvelous things existing there. A good meditator, even before he is realized, sees the flame between his eyebrows. This is also called the *guru jyoti*, the flame of the Guru, because this is the seat of the Guru.

Sometimes in meditation my tongue rolls up and goes back inside. Is it khecharī mudrā? If so, what is the importance of it?

This is khechari mudra. It happens automatically after shaktipat. It is very valuable because it is clearing a straight path to the sahasrara. There is nectar in the sahasrara, which falls on the tongue. When you taste it, your whole body is transformed from inside. You remain the same on the outside, but your inner parts completely change and you become younger. That is how much value khechari mudra has. After that, God's form appears like a sky of knowledge, and you continually soar in that sky. This is good. I thank you. You are hard working and energetic. You are not far from the Truth, you are very close.

When I try to get beyond ecstasy and bliss, I experience pain in the ear. How do I get rid of it?

The ears aren't going to disturb your bliss. Maybe you have some defect in your ear. Even if it hurts, let it hurt; try to go beyond that pain. There are some nerves in the ear, and if there are blocks, when the *prāna* moves through the nerves, they hurt for a while. You should learn how to bear that pain. Don't get scared and don't worry.

In meditation you come to a state where the ears are pierced; it's called *karnabheda*. There are many, many different kinds of states — sometimes the ears are pierced and sometimes the tongue is pierced. When the tongue is pierced, it moves upward and that is called *khecharī avasthā*. When you are going to hear the divine music, which is always being played in the inner space, at that time the piercing of the ears takes place. Once the inner ears are pierced, you begin to hear this divine music. You also acquire the power to hear people talking from a great distance. So don't worry, just meditate.

When I sit for meditation, my entire spinal column and head move back and forth from left to right like a snake. Brilliant white light bursts into my head, and I see colored lights. This began two years ago, after I received your blessings, and it was followed by an illness. Is everything going well with me?

Does an illness stay forever? It goes away after a while. With great peace, keep meditating and the illness will go away. If your head moves like a snake, let it move; don't stop it. The Self is of infinite colors; all the colors that exist in the world are the color of the Self. What you see is the Self.

It is a matter of great fortune that you see the brilliance of the Self. The scriptures say that light is the form of the Self. Have the awareness that this is the true Self. Keep pursuing sadhana. It will make your illness go away.

THE SHAKTI IS THE GURU

How many disciples can you guide?

Many. In the ocean, many people can bathe.
Is it direct guidance only for meditation or also for other things in life?
When you receive that guidance, it is not just for meditation. You receive the inspiration in meditation that guides everything in your life.
If a person whom you guide makes a wrong move in life, will you correct it?
Even if I don't correct him, the inner energy will certainly correct him. Also I can correct him. The Shakti will make you improve; it brings circumstances that make you improve.

How does one find guidance for shaktipāt yoga after initiation?

The Shakti that is awakened through shaktipat is the perfect Guru, and the more devotion you feel for the Guru, the more you revere and respect him, the more the Shakti will be pleased. In fact, to honor the Guru is to honor the Shakti. Shakti is intelligent and all-knowing. As you feel more devotion for the Guru, the Shakti will keep guiding you from inside and will do whatever needs to be done.

If I do not get any outer sign from you to indicate that my sadhana is going well, how can I know that I am doing the right thing?

You do not need any outer sign from me. Continue to do your sadhana, and your sadhana will guide you; it will tell you where you are. You will feel it. I am here and I am also there. When you go to a restaurant to eat food, does the waiter have to stand there and tell you, "Now your stomach is this full. Now you should drink this much water. Now you should eat more food"? Do you need outer signs for this?

So if you follow sadhana, it will tell you your own worthiness; it is the sign that will guide you. The Shakti that has entered you is me; it guides you and lets you know how far you have come in your sadhana.

Now that I can feel the Shakti slowly unfolding, will it continue to develop even though I may not be able to spend time with you in person?

Yes, your unfoldment will continue — provided that you see the Shakti as Baba. The Shakti of a Guru is the Guru himself. This process will continue. You should look at the Shakti as Baba.

If I am not a pure instrument for receiving inner guidance, what can I rely on for guidance after you leave America?

You should rely on God, on God's love, and on the mantra. You should have the understanding that your Self is completely pure. Rely on that. This body contains all holy places and is the abode of all deities. When this is the case, what do you have to be afraid of? The ocean of divine love exists within you, and in your sahasrara the inner Guru exists. When this is so, you don't have to be afraid of anything.

When I leave America, still you can rely on the Guru in the sahasrara. Even when I leave my body completely, still I will take only my outer covering; my Self will remain here with you in the form of Shakti. There is no place where I am not, there is no heart where I am not, because that Consciousness pervades everywhere. It pervades the sentient and the insentient, and it grows in subtle things. When this is so, why do you have to be afraid? I am with you all the time. But you should have understanding.

Are you rearranging the structure of my atoms?

Yes, it's true. What is happening is that the fire of Kundalini is burning away what you don't need and strengthening what is good for you.

Last night I felt that my heart was completely open and today I feel that I am more closed and tight. Why?

It happens. That too is a phase of the same process. Just stay calm. It is the doing of the inner Shakti. This alternation will continue for some time: sometimes you will find your heart opening up, and at other times you will find it closing and shutting tight. There are two phases of Shakti: one is expansion and the other is contraction. When She withdraws or limits Herself, you feel your heart is closing off, but it is the same process.

Why would the Shakti limit itself?

It is just a part of Her game.

Does shaktipāt, once received, ever stop of its own accord?

Not in most cases. However, if you were to slight the Shakti, Her work might stop. So treat the Shakti with respect and love over and over again, until all your work has been done.

Do all realized beings see the same lights and the Blue Pearl? Or does it vary for different people?

It's not like that. The inner kingdom of the Self is the same for everybody. Inside there are various brilliant lights, and they are the same for everybody. If you meditate systematically, certainly you will see them. No matter who is passing by this building, he will see it. The building will be true for him. In the same way, if you go deeper and deeper inside, you will come across these inner lights. The inner Self contains infinite lights. It is only because these lights exist that there is radiance in people and you feel interested in them.

So the experiences are the same for all the realized beings. However, every great being describes his experience in his own way. Jagadguru Shankaracharya said, "The Shaivites call Him Shiva. The Vedantins call Him Brahman, the Absolute. People who have devotion call Him the embodiment of devotion.

People who follow rituals believe that He is the giver of the fruits of their rituals. The Jains believe that He is void, empty."

Everybody describes the same One in different ways. Nonetheless, He is only One. Every person should enter inside and understand his own Self through meditation. For every person it is the same experience, the same God, and the same state.

God is not aware of different directions. For Him there is no difference between east and west, south and north. Do you know why? Because He is all-pervasive. If He were restricted to one place, different directions would exist for Him. However, it is not like that. He just pervades everything. Not only that, He has no sense of color differentiation either. A great being said, "O God, You are of every color. You contain red, black, yellow, and infinite other colors." Understand that all countries, all languages, all forms, all names, all colors, all actions, all religions belong to Him. So everybody has the same experience.

Can there be anything negative about Shakti?

Shakti can never have anything negative about it. It can never be spoiled. If there is something that is going to die, still the Shakti will be alive. Even if there is someone who is completely filled with disease, still this Shakti will be free from disease. Shakti pervades everywhere, and no matter how many years pass by, it doesn't change, it remains the same. There is no time limit imposed on this Shakti. It's not that Shakti is going to work for twenty years and that's it. It's not like that. Shakti will work forever—even at the end of time. No matter how much time passes by, still the Shakti will remain one and the same, one and the same.

Do heaven and hell exist, or are these imaginary worlds?
Do they exist during this life or after death?

The sages did not write the Puranas like novels. They wrote the truth. The worlds are true. A person who meditates very well is able to see heaven and hell through the power of his meditation. We have knowledge only of this world, but there are infinite worlds. One of them is heaven, another is hell, and there is also the world of the moon, and the world of Indra. Individual souls go to those planes.

I once saw a huge hell in meditation. It must have been my karma. I was brought right to the middle of a sewer and the sewage came up to my waist. After coming out of meditation, for a week I could still smell the stench of hell. After that, I began to believe that the Puranas were true and that the sages did not write novels. Later, I visited heaven in meditation. It was very beautiful there and so were the people.

So there are worlds such as heaven, hell, and *satyaloka*. The *Yoga Vāsishtha* has mentioned infinite planes. There are so many that you cannot even count them. They are the imagination of God, but for us they are true.

I would like to ask about the relationship of Shakti to the Blue Pearl. In meditation yesterday I started experiencing blue lights that were steady.

The Shakti is not other than the Blue Pearl. It is the vibration of the Blue Pearl that appears as the Shakti.

I Wondered If It Were a New Obstacle

When Kundalini travels to the auditory region, one is able
to hear celestial music that is intensely melodious; listening
to this music, one is filled with ecstasy. When She rises to the
ajna chakra — the lotus between the eyebrows — She releases
a divine perfume, like nothing ever manufactured by any
human skill. As one inhales these divine fragrances, one's
mind becomes absolutely tranquil, and one enters into the
samadhi state for a while.

Then there are the most wonderful, boundless places
within the sahasrara — the thousand-petaled lotus — and in
these places there exists a divine light whose brilliance equals
the light of a thousand suns of our solar system. In the midst
of the brilliant light there exists a supremely beautiful Blue
Pearl, as tiny as a sesame seed; and it is in this Pearl that
man's true worth lies. One should try to experience this
Pearl. When Kabir says that each one of us is carrying a
jewel, a most precious jewel in his head, he is referring to
this most glorious Blue Pearl.

After the Kundalini is awakened, we are able to go
deeper and deeper during meditation; we hear divine sounds,
we inhale these marvelous divine fragrances, and we taste
the sweetest nectars. Finally, we see this Blue Pearl, which
sparkles and shimmers and which is exceedingly beautiful.
This Blue Pearl is the wonder of wonders. It is extremely
subtle; it can pass easily through stone, and when it is active,
it travels faster than light. It is the vehicle by means of

which one can travel to different worlds in no time.

Even though one has had all these experiences, one cannot be called fully realized because there is still a great deal more. But when a yogi is able to see this Blue Pearl, his heart is filled with tremendous rapture, so much so that he does not experience himself as a limited, chained, individual being any longer. He discovers his own true worth; he realizes that he is divine, that he is God.

During meditation, sometimes the Blue Pearl emerges, shimmering and sparkling before your eyes, and then it goes in again to its dwelling place within the thousand-petaled lotus. It is a great mystery how this tiny Pearl can move in and out with such supreme freedom. It keeps on moving for a long time and becomes still only through the grace of the Guru.

After it has stood still for some time, it begins to expand, growing bigger and bigger and bigger, its radiance becoming more and more intense. And though in the beginning it appeared to be very tiny, as it goes on expanding it comes to embrace the entire universe. Such is the glory of the Blue Pearl.

Then within the Blue Pearl there appears a Blue Person, who is effulgent and beautiful. One should be able to see this Blue Person during meditation. I'm not narrating a fairy tale; I'm talking about the inner Truth, which you can discover during meditation. I want to make you aware of the purpose of Kundalini awakening.

When this Blue Person appeared within the Blue Pearl during my meditation, I was supremely amazed, and for a moment I wondered whether a new obstacle had come up on the path. I closed my eyes with fear. When I opened them again, I found the same Blue Person still standing there. His shape resembled that of a human being. Again I wondered whether it were a new obstacle that had come up, so again I closed my eyes with fear. When I opened my eyes, I found the same Blue Person still there. He was made of pure blue light. He went around me once and stood still before me. I was extremely careful. I was trying to find out whether it was a hallucination or a true vision. The Blue Person stayed, asking me to speak. I was deeply absorbed in meditation and my eyes were closed, but the Blue Person sparkled with such radiance that even though my eyes were closed, I kept seeing the blue light. He began to speak to me and I listened to his words most carefully. Then he started shrinking in size and once again he became the Blue Pearl, and the Blue Pearl returned to its home in the sahasrara.

This is one of the very last experiences of sadhana. It is only at this stage that any form of yoga — the yoga of devotion or the yoga of meditation or the yoga of knowledge — is truly fulfilled. There are further mysterious experiences, which yogis usually keep secret, and it is after those that one can be said to be completely realized.

Such is the nature of the divine Blue Pearl that lies within each one of us. It is for a direct, personal experience of this glorious Blue Pearl that one should try to have one's Kundalini awakened and activated.

THE PRACTICES

CHAPTER 6

Discovering Our Real Being

Steal reality from the grip of the senses, and then experience it and enjoy it. The name for this process of stealing is deep meditation.

What is meditation?

Meditation means total stillness of mind — a silent, empty mind. In this stillness you go into the inner Self. All of you know that when you sleep, you pass from the concerns of the waking state to oblivion, but that is not meditation. To be free of all external concerns and at the same time to enter into the heart and stay there for a while — that is meditation.

You tell us to meditate on our own Self. I don't understand how to.

Don't you remember to meditate on your body, on your children, and on your family? In the same way, it should not be so difficult to meditate on the Self. Keep meditating, and your meditation will reach the place of the Self. When you are meditating, look within. So many thoughts arise and subside, arise and subside. Try to understand the place from which they arise and into which they subside.

There is a gap between one thought and another. Have you ever thought about the stillness and stability that exist in the space between two thoughts? Of course, we don't take time in our lives to think about it. That is the Self. That is God. That is the Truth. That is Self-realization.

If you cannot contemplate that place, start repeating the name of God, focusing your attention there. As you repeat the Name, the mind will stop, and you will attain the state of stability. Then you will understand the Self. Meditation on the Self is very easy.

There is another technique, and that is to contemplate the space from which the breath arises and into which it subsides. When the breath comes in, there is a space where it merges before going out again. When the *prāna* comes in, let it merge there. Try to understand where the prana merges. Before the prana goes out, try to understand that state where the prana has merged within. This state — this stability in between the breaths — is Consciousness, is the Truth.

Could you give me a basic understanding of meditation?

Once there was a man who was very afraid of his own shadow and disgusted with his footprints. He was really sick of them, so he tried many things to erase them. He took many different courses from many different teachers; he even took the twenty-one courses of Nasruddin. Still the footprints and the shadow were not erased. Every day his fear and anger toward the shadow and footprints grew and grew. He was getting desperate. He thought if he walked very fast to another town, he would leave them behind. So he walked very fast, but the footprints were following him. He looked back over his shoulder and he began to walk faster. He gave another furtive glance over his shoulder, and still the footprints were following him. He thought if he ran very fast, he would leave them behind. He ran faster and faster. But as he was running he looked back and saw the footprints and shadow still chasing him. Finally, after running and running and running, he collapsed and died. He died, but still his footprints didn't leave him; they were right behind him. His sufferings were still there.

Instead of running, if that man had found a large shady tree, he could have sat under that tree in great peace, in great calmness. If he were sitting under the tree, there wouldn't have been any shadow and there wouldn't have been any footprints. He could have sat there very peacefully, at least for a while. We are also in the same predicament. We try to get rid of these sufferings, but we look back, and still the sufferings are chasing us. Instead of turning inward and finding a place inside the heart and experiencing supreme peace and bliss, we chase our suffering. We have different things that are our shadow and footprints — our fear and anger, our lust and greed, our desire and infatuation. But we never try to go inside and sit under that large tree right within us and experience that supreme bliss.

How do you meditate on the Self?

Meditation is not so difficult, but you have to turn within with great interest. You have to go deeper and deeper and deeper within yourself. The mind continually wanders in this world, in this infinite creation; it continually roams around watching different colors and different styles, and it gets so exhausted. It is so troubled by all these things. So what you do is turn that mind within; you make the mind perceive your own divinity. That is called meditation on the Self. You have to have some interest. If you have the interest, meditation is very easy. If you have no interest, meditation is very difficult. Therefore, have great interest and love for it. Meditation is beyond the sleep state, and it is filled with bliss. Turn within all the time. Learn how to free the mind. Become totally still. Then meditation will happen spontaneously.

In the Guru Gita, *one verse says to meditate on the inner Self, the tiny person within the heart. Does this mean that we meditate on our own inner form or on your form?*

The tiny person is thumb-sized and lives right in your heart in the form of light. That is your inner Self. You should meditate on that inner Self and not on me. If you meditate on your own Self, that meditation will be for you. That tiny light in the heart signifies your inner Self, but the Self also pervades the whole universe. If you once see that Being inside your heart, you can see Him everywhere outside too.

While I'm using the mantra, a light or color will appear sometimes. Where would it be best for me to concentrate?

Wherever your mind focuses itself spontaneously, let it stay there. If it focuses on the heart, let it stay there. If it focuses elsewhere, let it do that. It's good to focus the mind on the heart. The goal of the mantra lives particularly in the heart.

Why do you focus on the heart?

There is a divine place there, and the life in you really lives there. That's why we focus on the heart.

How can I open my heart?

To open the heart, you have to turn within, you have to go to the heart. Truly speaking, the heart is already open. When you receive *shaktipāt*, when you receive the Guru's grace, yoga begins to occur within, and then the heart *chakra* opens up completely. However, you keep yourself separate from your heart. Don't ever think that the heart is closed — the heart is always open. But you have to enter the heart, you have to turn within. You can do that through self-inquiry and meditation. For this reason we meditate.

I've experienced a great fear of opening my heart for many years. I've had moments of humility and love only through your influence, but mostly my heart remains guarded. I've tried to blast it open, shout it open, drug it open, get therapy to open it, and for years I've meditated on it. I've reached an impasse, and I'm afraid of the dryness inside. What can be done?

You cannot open it through drugs or anything external. The more you try to open it through these things, the more closed it will become. Only if you meditate on the Self, if you have love for the Self, will it be flung open.

Would you say that prayer is a form of meditation?

The final state of prayer turns into meditation. As a person continues to pray and pray, finally he loses himself in prayer. He merges himself into the prayer. That is when meditation truly begins. When a person forgets himself in prayer, meditation starts.

Is meditation totally passive? If not, how is it active?

You go completely within, deeper and deeper. Once you go within, your meditation makes a movie of your inner world. To see this inner movie is a great delight. It is a divine movie that cannot be duplicated on the outside. It is worth seeing. There are beautiful places inside and you must discover them. There is a divine light at the top of the head and there are divine melodies inside. You must hear them. An elixir flows inside. You should try to taste that elixir. All these other drinks — Coca-Cola, beer, whiskey — anybody can drink them. But this elixir is the true one. With just a little bit you will really get intoxicated, and you don't come down from that.

(From a five year old) What makes meditation so special?

Meditation is very special. Our life is based on it. When people work a little bit or when they have a fight and their mind gets very agitated, at that time they like to go to a room where there is no one and sit there by themselves quietly. Some people go to the ocean and go sailing. Some people go to the mountains and stay there for a while so that they can have some peace. Some people drink a lot; they sit in their rooms drinking, and it's a kind of meditation because their minds are released from that agitation a little bit. If you forget something, you close your eyes and you begin to do something similar to meditation; this is not real meditation, but you begin to ponder, and you become still because you want to remember what you forgot.

In ancient times people would give up a meal, but they wouldn't give up a meditation session. Food and sense pleasures can do something for your body, but they cannot go beyond your body. Dancing and eating and drinking and all your actions cannot reach the inner Self. You can reach your inner Self only through meditation; it destroys your sins and you begin to feel that you are pure. Through meditation all your senses become sharp and very subtle. Meditation gives you the power of understanding things that you normally cannot. Without meditation one cannot lead a happy life. Meditation keeps you ever young. Look at me—I'm old, but I still speak like a young man.

That is why you can skip a meal, you can give up some sleep, but you should never give up your meditation. Meditate regularly. Meditation is a great science. It transforms your inner being completely; it creates a new body inside you. Meditation gives you the power to be happy even when you are sad.

What is important in this world besides meditation?

Once meditation happens, importance comes to an end. Just as all the rivers merge into the ocean and lose their individuality, in the same way importance does not exist any longer. Meditation is the supreme happiness. There is no greater attainment than meditation. Therefore the *Bhagavad Gītā* says that in meditation a person attains his own Self; without meditation a person loses his own Self. People who have lost their own Self live in negativities and hatred. People who have attained their own Self live in positive feelings. They live with great joy and with great laughter.

When I sit for meditation, I wait for something to happen,
but nothing ever does. I feel good, but my expectations are not
fulfilled. Is this meditation?

You feel good, and that means something is happening. It does not matter if anything else is happening. Do not give up meditation. Keep meditating. To feel good, to experience peace and love and satisfaction are signs that something is happening in meditation. Whatever else might happen is only temporary.

I remain quite conscious of my surroundings during meditation. How can I lose myself in the Self?

Even if you remain conscious of your surroundings during meditation, it's fine — just meditate. As you meditate more and more, you will reach a center within where you won't hear outer noises. All that you have to remain aware of is "I am the supreme Truth, I am the supreme Truth."

Meditation is not the state of a dead person. It does not mean that you have to become like a rock or a log. The constant vibration of the Self, experienced within, is meditation. In simple words, when the mind does not think anything, that is meditation. If the mind is serene and free from changes, even if you hear outer sounds, it doesn't matter. Patanjali says that complete stillness of mental tendencies is meditation. He also says that to see oneness everywhere is meditation. So don't torture yourself thinking that you have to sit with your eyes closed, not hearing anything. True meditation is equal vision, and if you have that, even with your eyes open, you are still meditating.

May one seriously meditate without abandoning one's religious denomination and religious principles?

Absolutely! There is no relationship between meditation and religion. Just as sleep has nothing to do with religion, in the same way meditation has nothing to do with religion. You must meditate on your own Self. If you are a Christian, you are not meditating on Hinduism, you are meditating on your own inner Self. So meditation has nothing to do with religion.

Someone said to me that once when he was meditating, he got so far away from his body that he was afraid he wouldn't get back into it again. Can this be true?

If you were to get far away from the body and mind, you wouldn't be allowed to stay there longer than necessary. Don't worry, you would be sent back. Wherever you go in meditation, go without resistance. If you were to go to a place that is divine, far away from the body, why would you want to come back?

Why would you have the desire to return to this world after being in the world of God?

Recently while meditating, I become very sleepy and tired, so much so that my head often sinks to the floor. Sometimes I dream and sometimes I don't remember anything. Is this the working of the Shakti? Should I try to keep awake as much as possible?

You are truly meditating. The greatest sign of meditation is for the head to touch the floor. Just let it happen. Understand that you are getting good meditation. When you become free of thoughts in meditation, your mind becomes one-pointed. That is why you feel sleepy. It is a very good state. In meditation, one is drawn inward. Inside a human being there are four bodies, one within another. When you leave the gross body, which you experience in the waking state, and enter into the second body, called the subtle body, you experience the sleeping state. There you have dreams. When you leave the second body and enter into the third body, the causal body, you get into a much deeper sleeping state in which there are usually no visions. If you do have visions, they will come true.

One feels a little bit sleepy after coming out of meditation, just as one often does after emerging from a deep sleep. All the senses turn inward during the sleeping state and are resting. When you wake up, they all have to turn outward. At that time you feel that you are tired, but it doesn't last long. You may feel sleepy for a short time after meditating, but after a few minutes you feel very strong, don't you? In deep meditation you will find great strength.

Would it be considered a selfish desire to want to enter into true meditation?

To want to eat food — do you consider that a selfish desire? When you make an earnest effort for spiritual goals, that is not selfishness. If you have other desires that you want to be fulfilled through meditation — the desire to see other worlds or to acquire psychic powers — that would be selfishness.

How would one begin to meditate if he has not been in the presence of a Guru?

Start meditating anyhow, by hook or by crook. You can use God's name for meditation, and God will certainly send you some Guru or another because He has no shortage of them. Many people have told me that several months before they met me, they saw me in their dreams and received the mantra from me.

WHAT IS THE GOAL?

What is the relationship between meditation and love? Doesn't love arise from meditation?

Through meditation, love does arise. You do not meditate for the sake of meditation; you meditate for the sake of love. Meditate with great respect, and love will arise from within on its own.

Inside you, there is a divine center of love, just as there is a center of sleep. If you are always awake, and if you always think of sleep, you cannot derive the joy of sleep. You have to actually go to sleep. Only when you go to sleep do you reach the center of sleep. Just as there is a center of sleep inside the body, in the same way there is a center of love. There only love exists. Love exists there in happiness, of course, but it also exists even in unhappiness. There is love when you are living, and there is love even when you are dying. Only love exists there. One meditates to reach that state, and then meditation becomes quiet. So through meditation you derive love.

Sometimes I laugh uncontrollably in meditation. This happens when the Shakti rushes to my heart. I feel wonderful during these periods of laughter, but I fear I am disturbing other meditators or neighbors. Is this laughter good? What should I do so that I don't disturb others when it happens?

109

We meditate to be able to laugh! Laughter is the purpose of meditation. If you want to laugh but you stop yourself, wouldn't it be better if you didn't meditate? Laughter is the main expression of Siddha Yoga. When Siddha Yoga manifests in the heart, one person dances, another laughs, another sobs and cries. This laughter, if it is true laughter, will also get your neighbors to laugh. It shouldn't disturb them. Don't worry about it. If you want to cry, cry. If you want to laugh, laugh.

I worry about what I will really be able to gain from meditation.

The gain beyond which there is nothing more to be gained is the unfoldment of the inner Shakti. And the bliss that rushes as a result of this inner awakening is the kind of bliss, after tasting which, nothing more remains to be tasted. When the Kundalini awakes, you meditate more and more, and pure knowledge arises from within. As a result of this knowledge, you see the world as beautiful and holy; you see yourself as divine. You no longer see people as wicked, as depraved, as inferior. Once this knowledge has arisen, that is the end of all your searching. There is nothing more to know after that. So it is necessary to meditate with a calm mind and to go within. There is tremendous Shakti in that.

My Kundalinī often rises during meditation and goes up to the sahasrāra, but it does not remain there; it comes down immediately. Why? How can I keep it in the sahasrāra all the time?

Keep meditating. It will remain there on its own. When your meditation culminates, the Kundalini Shakti will be able to remain in the sahasrara because Shiva is there. Shakti lies at the base of your spine, and when it is awakened, it moves upward and becomes one with Shiva. There the union between Shiva and Shakti takes place. So it is enough for you to keep meditating. Once meditation starts, it will stop only after it culminates. It doesn't matter if it takes a bit longer. Keep meditating peacefully. It is a long journey, but it is accomplished within a short time.

Do you find that you can solve personal problems through meditation?

Yes, meditation will help you in every field; it is a friend to every pursuit. Meditation is like a great lawyer who can give you advice on anything. If you are sick, meditation will remove your sickness. If you are interested in business, meditation will help you in business. If you are interested in medicine, meditation will make you a better doctor. If you are interested in yoga, meditation will make you a better *yogi*. All talents and skills are unfolded through meditation. That is why we call it *Kundalinī Mahā Yoga*, the great yoga: it embraces everything.

How can I increase my creativity?

Meditate a lot. Meditation is the royal road to communication with your inner Self and to success in every field. Everything arises from the *ātman*, the inner Self. Knowledge comes from the Self, beauty comes from the Self, energy and intelligence too. All these qualities are expansions of the inner Self. If you were to move toward the inner Self, everything would come toward you.

I have been ill for several years. Will regular meditation help me become well?

Yes, certainly. Meditation has a great power of eliminating illnesses. Meditation and *japa* — silent repetition of mantra — will dispel your ailments slowly and gradually. Many kinds of sicknesses are destroyed in meditation.

Is enlightenment possible without meditation?

Enlightenment is possible without meditation if you practice knowledge, but even knowledge will show you meditation. If you only talk and talk, you are not going to attain God. It is very true that God is within everybody. However, you have to enter that inner place. If there is anything great in your life, if there is anything worthy of attainment, it is the Self.

Many astonishing things take place in this world. There are people who can perform miracles that make you feel wonderstruck. However, this skill, this art of astonishing others, lies only in the inner Self. Whatever in this world creates astonishment is because of the inner Self. Become completely still; have no thoughts in the mind. Become immersed in the inner Self; meditate only on the inner Self. Make your mind very pure. Worship the eternal Self.

Without meditation there is no enlightenment. The *Bhagavad Gītā* says that only through meditation can you perceive your inner Self. If enlightenment were possible without meditation, everybody would be enlightened by now. Only a meditator can be enlightened.

Is meditation essential for a meaningful life?

Meditation is a tremendous help in living a meaningful life. However, one should understand what meditation really is. Meditation is not just sitting with closed eyes. During meditation the inner Shakti awakens and, though outwardly you may seem to be doing nothing, inwardly much is happening. Whatever field we are in, we need that Shakti very badly because Shakti is the supreme singer, the supreme dancer. She balances the whole universe. She helps us to learn, to plan, and to function better. Shakti is necessary not only to attain inner peace and liberation, but even to function effectively in daily life. You need it to become young again when you have become old. Having become old, I became young once again. The Shakti transmitted through Siddha Yoga is not inert; it is not unconscious or unintelligent Shakti. The Shakti is dynamic, full of joy, and very active, and as a result you experience more joy, you participate more. You do not become withdrawn and sad.

Sometimes in meditation I achieve a state of great bliss, but I do not remain in this state very long. It seems as if there is nothing for my consciousness to hold on to, so my concentration wavers. What can I do to stay there longer?

Indescribable bliss is the very goal of meditation, of shaktipat. When you are experiencing this bliss, let your mind merge into it completely. There is a place inside where supreme bliss constantly vibrates; when your mind reaches that place, it experiences this indescribable bliss. When it returns from there, it leaves the bliss behind. As your mind returns, hold on to the Guru and repeat *Guru Om, Guru Om, Guru Om,* and then that bliss will come back. It is that state of bliss which people like me live in. We are continually drunk on that bliss.

For the last seven months I have been having indescribably pleasurable rushes of energy in the left side of my head. Would you please explain to me what is happening? What will the results be and how long will the results last?

This pleasure is not the kind that will stay for a while and then leave you. This pleasure springs forth from your heart chakra or your crown chakra, and once you experience this joy, it will never leave you. It will always increase, never decrease. This is the immortal bliss; it has no time and you cannot limit it. This is called the experience of the inner Self. There are so many things that you can experience, but this is the ultimate experience — the bliss of the inner Self. After experiencing this delight within you, you will have the same experience when you look at other people too.

There was a great Siddha called Krishnasuta who said, "The root of all happiness is *brahmānanda,* the bliss of Brahman, the bliss of the Absolute. After experiencing that bliss within me, now I can experience that bliss within everyone. The same bliss exists everywhere. It is all-pervasive, and it is of the form of *sat chit ānanda* — Existence, Consciousness, and Bliss." Truly speaking, this bliss is everywhere, but because of our dual understanding, we cannot perceive it. This is a very good question.

What is the ultimate goal of meditation? Is it an end in itself?

The ultimate goal of meditation is to know your own Self, to know God. Therefore, a person should meditate every day.

Within a person there is a great power which is dormant, so you should awaken and activate that power. This Shakti works in the entire world. It helps you attain God, it helps you to do your work, it helps you to throw away defects. Within a person there is great divinity. The knowledge of all the world's technology also exists in the heart. When the dormant inner Shakti awakens, automatically you get to know your own Self and you become one with God. Then this world appears as full of joy, then this world becomes heaven; then there is a balance in your society, in your country, in your neighbors, and you experience peace no matter where you are.

Is this always the result of meditation? Will I get there no matter what?

It is every person's right; every person has this. If you are alive, if you have a heart, you contain all of this; you have every right to attain it.

Is it possible to meditate and not get it? To do it wrong?

If you meditate wrongly, you will not see God correctly.

What is the wrong way to meditate?

If you do not learn how to meditate in a very disciplined manner; if you learn meditation from a teacher who has never learned how to meditate, who has never seen Him; if you try to go swimming with one who has never learned to swim; if you hold the hand of a blind person who has never seen the path — these are wrong ways to meditate.

WHAT TO DO WITH THE THOUGHTS

Sometimes when I meditate, a thought will come in. I don't want it there and I'm not sure what to do with it.

During meditation one should be very, very alert and vigilant. There are thieves, thought-thieves prowling around, who are very keen on stealing your meditation away. Don't let any thoughts arise. Meditate by emptying your mind of all thought. After meditation we can think to our heart's content.

Please tell me what to do with my thoughts during meditation.

If thoughts come during meditation, don't think about what you should do with them. Try to perceive where the thoughts arise and where they subside. This is also a great *sādhanā* of meditation — to watch your thoughts. It is said they arise from *chidākāsha*, from the inner space. Just as space exists outside, in the same way space exists inside. The Self exists in the space of the heart. Thoughts arise from that *ākāsha*, that inner ether. Watch them. They arise from this place; they subside in the same place too.

These thoughts are called bondage. There is no other bondage. Your own thought is bondage. Because of thoughts man is unhappy. Man is not unhappy because he doesn't have enough possessions. He is unhappy because of his thoughts.

You can stop those thoughts while repeating the mantra *Om Namah Shivāya*. Even the mantra is a thought. However, it is a pure thought and the others are not. They are impure. Therefore, stop all your thoughts with this one thought.

If you cannot stop them with this one thought, start watching them. Watch where they arise and where they subside. You can also watch how many countless thoughts arise. Among sadhanas, this is one of the best. Focus your attention on the heart, and see how thoughts arise and subside. As you keep watching them more and more, you get the knack of controlling them completely.

How can I get rid of thoughts about family or work during meditation?

Keep your thoughts gently aside for an hour or so. Tell those thoughts of family and work to be at peace for a while. Tell them, "After meditation I will think about you." If they don't listen to you, then don't listen to them. Be like a witness and watch what kind of thoughts are coming. Just watch them. One who watches the thoughts from a distance is different from the thoughts. He has no relationship with them. He is not from the same country. Don't be a thought yourself; be that witness. Then your thoughts won't cause you unhappiness.

During meditation what should I do about all the various jumbles of thoughts that keep streaming into my mind? Should I try to eliminate them and meditate about only one thing?

If you try to sweep the thoughts out of your mind, more and more they will rush in, and that is how your entire day will be spent. Instead of trying to sweep your thoughts away, switch your attention to the one who is the seer of those thoughts, the witness of those thoughts. It is not thought-waves that are the object of meditation. The object of meditation is the knower of those thoughts, the witness of those thought-waves. So keep focused on the witness of your thoughts. Thoughts are not objects of meditation.

Would you please talk about witnessing during meditation?

If you are repeating the mantra, you witness the mantra. If you are meditating on the Self, you witness the Self. Otherwise, you might remember your wife and children, your sense pleasures, or your friends. When you watch all these things from a distance, that is called being a witness. The witness is the one who really understands your inner being, inside and out. During meditation, whatever happens, whatever actions take place, the one who watches all those actions, being apart from them — he is the witness. He is Consciousness and he does everything.

To achieve the state of the witness is a great attainment. In Siddha Yoga I don't send you out to sit under a bridge and meditate there in solitude. I don't send you into a cave. I don't tell you to observe silence and go into solitude for twenty-one days or fifty days. Siddha Yoga teaches you to look at everything equally, to experience peace, and to be calm. The witness understands this body as body; it understands this world as world. This is the kind of understanding you have inside, and it is great. It is called the witness. It is Consciousness and it is without attributes. When the mind begins to play, the one who understands that play is called the witness. It can also be called the Self. And people who believe in God call that witness God. There is no one greater than that.

How can one achieve a state of nothingness during meditation, or even when not meditating? That in itself becomes an expectation.

It is not an expectation. To be in this state is called being a witness. This is the greatest state. Meditate a little bit more and you will attain this witness state. It will arise of its own accord. Now, for instance, there are so many people sitting there, and I am sitting here. So many people have their different questions, and I give them different answers. Even though I am doing this, still I am witnessing it, because I do not feel anything good or bad about it. This is called the state of being a witness. The senses do their own actions, they move in their own objects. But you are different from the senses; you are apart from the senses; you are the witness of the senses. To become aware of this, to live in the body but also beyond the body, is called being in the witness state.

You can attain this state through meditation. You should meditate very calmly. The fact is that you are already in the witness state, but you are not aware of it. To become aware of this state, you have to meditate. For example, at night you go to sleep and you have many dreams. Who reports them to you when you wake up? Does that being go to sleep when you go to sleep? If it goes to sleep when you go to sleep, who watches your dreams? That being does not go to sleep. It witnesses whatever happens in your sleep. For instance, a person is sleeping, and suddenly he begins to shout, "A tiger is coming! A tiger is coming! Run! Run! Run!" His wife wakes him up and says, "Hey, what's happening?"

He replies, "While I was sleeping, I saw a big tiger."

Who saw the tiger? Isn't that the witness? The witness always remains awake. The one who understands the waking state, the sleeping state, and the deep-sleep state, the one who understands all the actions of this body, the one who, even though he is living in this body, is still not attached to this body, that one is the supreme Principle, and that one is the inner Self, the supreme bliss. We are meditating on that Being, and we are trying to attain that Being who is already attained, who is already within us.

During meditation, after thoughts have ceased and I am sitting in stillness, I turn my awareness to the witness of that stillness. I seem to be at the edge of infinity, but I have trouble letting go. Why can't I slide easily into That?

To slide into That is meditation. You have obtained very good understanding. Now lose yourself; let yourself go. You will not reach infinity until you open the egg of ego. Only then will you emerge from the egg. Then you will enter infinity. Because of ego, we are still human beings. When ego goes, we are not human beings — we are God.

My mind runs away and my body is restless. Will you please help me to focus my mind on you?

During meditation just watch your mind and tell it, "O mind, this is God, that is God. O mind, you can go anywhere you want, but you are just going to come across God."

Then you won't have any trouble.

MEDITATION ON THE GURU'S FORM

Is it helpful to meditate on the Guru's form?

Yes, it is very helpful because the Shakti begins to work much more strongly. If there is a mind that is meditating continually on a woman's form, it becomes like a woman. Likewise, a mind that continually meditates on the Guru's form will become like the Guru.

Is meditating on the Guru the same as being with him?

It is very good to meditate on the form. The *Yoga Sūtras* of Patanjali say that if you cannot meditate on the Self, if you cannot meditate on the mantra, if you cannot meditate on the formlessness of God, meditate on the Guru. Meditate on a being who has gone beyond attachment and aversion, beyond the state of anger, on one who has become established in his own Self. If you do so, the inner Shakti awakens very quickly.

It is also true that you become that which you meditate upon. Everything depends on how you feel. If you meditate on somebody who has lust, that is what you get; if you meditate on somebody who has anger, you become angry; if you meditate on somebody who has greed, you also become greedy. Whatever we see, whomever we are with, that is what we become. This is how all sects, all groups, all religions, and all organizations arise. Somebody creates them, and you try to become like them, you try to fit in.

In reality, the Truth is so pure, so valid, so authentic. Even if you try to become something on the outside, you always do remain That on the inside. So it is good to meditate on the great beings.

In Play of Consciousness, *you talk about meditation on the Guru's form as the highest kind of meditation. Do you recommend this as a practice?*

Although I meditated on the form of my Guru, I did not only meditate on his body; I meditated on him with the awareness that he was the embodiment of the Self, and that Self also existed within me. Therefore, I always say, "Meditate on your own Self." However, the mind has an affliction. It always wants an object to contemplate. A girl thinks of a boy and a boy thinks of a girl. Something is always in your mind — your husband or wife, your child, your pet, your car, or some other object. We have become accustomed to having it this way. For this reason, I placed the form of my Guru in my mind instead of these objects. As I continued to meditate on him, I began to meditate on my own Self.

If you meditate sincerely on any form, without expectation and without deception, your meditation will bear fruit. Tukaram Maharaj used to meditate on a deity called Pandarinath. He would say, "As I meditated on Pandarinath, I was completely transformed. My whole body was rejuvenated. My sense of 'I' vanished. God revealed Himself to me. Now I am blessed. Vitthal, the Lord, has revealed Himself to me from within."

This is how I meditated on my Guru. I meditated on his form, but I attained my own Self from within. Every day you read about *gurubhāva* in the *Guru Gītā*. Identification with the Guru is sacred; it is a holy place. The Guru is constantly in the awareness of "I am That." You too should attain that awareness. The Guru is absorbed in the power of the Self, in the Shakti of the Self. As you meditate on the Guru, the Self will reveal itself to you. If you meditate in this way, it is called *gurubhāva*, and it is true meditation on the Guru.

How should one meditate on the form of the Guru? Sometimes I try to see your picture or your physical form. Sometimes I just see light.

What makes you think that the light you see is not the Guru's form? Should you be able to see the beard and the hat? That light is also the inner body of the Guru. Be content with that. As you see more and more of this light, you will understand that it can show you any form you want to see.

Which meditation is the highest meditation: So'ham or meditation on the Guru?

So'ham is the highest meditation. However, not everybody can do that. You may remain uncooked forever like that. For this reason, it is much better for you to meditate on the Guru. The mind has become accustomed to having something all the time — either a husband, or a wife, or children, or a dog, or a cat. If people don't have these things, they use a magazine. The mind always needs some object. Whatever the mind likes, it is much easier to hold on to that. The Guru is always in front of your eyes. As you watch the Guru all the time, it is easy for that object to fit in your mind.

Tukaram Maharaj used to say that he worshiped the form of God, and as he worshiped the form, he attained the formlessness of God. He went beyond name and form.

Therefore, the highest meditation is *nirvikalpa*, the still mind where there is no thought. If you don't get this kind of meditation, you can meditate on a Guru who has risen above attachment and aversion. In meditation, you incorporate the Guru into your being completely.

Is your presence as real in a photo as it is in this place?

The more real your heart is, to that same degree my presence is real everywhere. If your heart is real, my presence is real in a photo. Even in a stone it is real. I am real even in your sleep. It is real even in a name — and in everything. Once I read a poem of a great saint who said the Guru is true, the mantra is true, the statue is true — when you become true. If you are untrue, everything is untrue.

Would you speak on the use of your photographs in meditation and as a channel for shaktipāt?

No matter what photograph you meditate on with love, you are bound to draw that person's Shakti to you. However, that photo should be like a living being to you. You can see the photograph of my Guru here on my right. Even though I have completed my sadhana, I still worship his form and I become more and more complete, more and more perfect. There is a verse in the Vedas which says that by worshiping Shiva, you become Shiva.

When I study your picture, your face disappears. It also happened once when I watched you while we were chanting. Why is this?

That is a very good sign. This is a practice of meditation. In Patanjali's *Yoga Darshana* he says that it is very good to meditate on a being who has transcended attachment and aversion. If you want to meditate on a form, you have to keep watching it and watching it. When it disappears, understand that meditation is happening. People have this wrong understanding that if they have visions, they are getting meditation. But actually if you are watching something, it should eventually disappear from your vision. That shows that your mind has become completely still, that it has stabilized, and that's a very good sign of true meditation. Patanjali also says that meditation is to become free from mentation — then there are no thoughts in the mind; the mind just doesn't absorb anything from outside. It has become completely still. That is high meditation. So what is happening to you is very good; it seems that your mind has become very quiet and still. Because it has become still, it doesn't reach for anything from the outside.

Please comment on the verses in the Guru Gita *that speak of meditation on the Guru's form.*

If you want to understand it fully, you should read *Play of Consciousness* in which I have described this mode of worship. The Guru exists on two levels. There is the transcendental Guru, who is all-pervasive and all-knowing, and there is the individual Guru from whom you receive shaktipat and through whom you attain perfection.

One form of meditation on the Guru is meditation on the transcendental Guru. In the scriptures it is described like this: The Guru is not an individual; the Guru is pure absolute bliss, greater than any ordinary pleasure or happiness. The Guru's form is not made of flesh; his body is pure knowledge, the knowledge that all this is Brahman, all this is God. The Guru is the being who is behind all dualities, who is beyond the consciousness of differences. He is like pure outer space. All that you see around you is nothing but the Self. The Guru is That in "Thou art That." He is the one in many, he is everlasting and eternal. He existed before, he exists now, and he will always exist. He exists here, he exists there, he exists above and below, and he exists in everything. He is totally pure, and no matter where he lives, his purity can never be tainted. He remains immobile in his inner nature, like a mountain. The Guru is the source from which all creation has come. He is the witness of man, of plants, of animals, of all the creatures in the universe. He transcends all feelings of good or bad, positive or negative.

He is totally beyond the reach of the three *gunas,* the basic qualities of nature — purity, activity, and inertia. I bow to that Sadguru. He is the Sadguru who lives in Truth all the time and he also exists in us as the witness of our intellect.

The word *Guru* consists of two syllables, *gu* and *ru.* *Gu* means the one who destroys the darkness of ignorance which has enveloped one's heart, and *ru* means the inner light, the divine light. The Guru puts his disciples in contact with the divine light. This is the Guru as the cosmic Principle.

Then there is the Guru as an individual. That individual is a Guru who, by constantly contemplating the true nature of the universal Principle, has become just like the Absolute, just like the highest Being. Such a one is said to be a Guru in a physical form. A Guru is one who has attained total freedom from within and without. Though he lives in a body, his awareness transcends the body. After having drawn the power of God into himself, he functions just like Him.

Such a one is called a *Siddha* and he is totally free from all mental agitation. His mind does not move unless he permits it to move. His imagination does not work unless he permits it to work. His intellect is firmly anchored in the awareness, "I am the Absolute, I am everything." His ego has identified itself totally with the awareness of "I am That," so he is free from ordinary ego. His ego has become the universal ego. A Guru is totally free from the pull of external senses too. He has completely mastered all his senses; his senses are slaves to him.

A true Guru has saturated himself with the divine power of grace and has the power of transmitting grace into others, enabling them to become just like himself. A true Guru has the power of shaktipat; he can pierce all the spiritual centers of a seeker and he can stabilize the seeker's mind in the sahasrara. A Guru removes all the blockages in a seeker. He is totally serene and he transmits the knowledge outlined in the scriptures.

When you meditate on a Guru's form, you are not doing him a favor. It is not the Guru who will get something from the meditation. You yourself will experience the bliss that is the true nature of the Guru. When you worship God or the Guru with love and reverence, who enjoys the bliss of that worship? Who enjoys the calm that you experience? Is it the Guru or is it you? This secret cannot be grasped by people who are dull-witted. One who constantly meditates on the Guru and loses himself in that meditation becomes like the Guru. This is no favor to the Guru — this is a favor to yourself.

EVERYTHING IS MEDITATION

Only after I began practicing Siddha Yoga was I able to meditate, and then my meditations were deep and full. This lasted only one month. Since then it has been very difficult to go deep in meditation or even to sit for meditation. Please explain how to go beyond these obstacles to a constant experience of that Self in me.

It is true that obstacles will always exist. This is the way of the world. You just have to face every obstacle that comes before you. Although you find it very difficult to sit for meditation, you should force yourself to do so, and meditation will just happen. If there is any obstacle in meditation, the scriptures say to repeat the mantra, and the mantra will take all the obstacles away.

You say meditation should occur spontaneously. I have been attempting to meditate for a few years now, but it has been a big struggle. When will I meditate?

It is your great struggle that stands as an obstacle to your meditation. For a while you should give up struggling, and whatever you look at, regard that as an object of meditation; understand that everything is just meditation. All that you have to do is meditate on your own inner Self. So whatever you see outside, consider it as your own inner Self. Then you don't have to struggle. Otherwise, no matter how much you struggle, you will have to struggle all your life, and ages and ages may pass if you don't get the right understanding. To do sadhana it is true that you need a technique, but along with that you also need right understanding.

Whoever meditates should think about what he is going to meditate on. Are you going to meditate on the mind or on the source of the mind? You should meditate on that inner Being all the time. It is only when you miss the knack of meditating that you feel sad, you get into trouble, and nothing good comes to you. Don't meditate on the mind; meditate on the witness of the mind. But instead of doing this, you give up meditating on the witness of the mind, and you begin to chase after the mind. You try to control your mind. How can you control your mind? It can't come under your control. Through what force do you try to control the mind? Through what force does your mind think?

Meditate on that force, meditate on that Being. No matter how much your mind thinks about other things, you are not going to lose anything; and even if you sit quietly without thinking of anything, you are not going to gain anything. But everything will come to you only if you meditate on the witness of the mind, the inner Self.

Meditate in this way: whatever you look at, whatever you see, whatever appears, consider it to be Consciousness. Or you can meditate on the witness of the mind, the one that always witnesses the impurities of the mind, that always witnesses the fickleness of the mind, that knows everything about the mind. In the *Bhagavad Gītā* Lord Krishna says to Arjuna, "O Arjuna, what can I say about this universe, that this is this or that is that, because everything is Me. I have become this whole universe. This whole universe is part of Me."

Try to look at your mind with great respect, with great love. Tell your mind, "O my mind, please repeat the mantra *Om Namah Shivāya* — at least for a while."

Then your mind won't give you any trouble.

In my meditation I am plagued by the desire to have kriyās, to see lights, or to receive your touch. How can I handle this desire?

Well, if you keep on desiring, maybe your desires will be fulfilled. But why don't you try to free yourself from desire? The lights and the kriyas will come by themselves when they are needed. Only what is necessary will happen in meditation. So you should meditate without wanting anything. Everybody has one desire or another. Those people who get forceful kriyas want to stop them. They say, "Enough!" and yet the kriyas keep happening. The inner Shakti, the Kundalini, is all-knowing. She is intelligent and conscious. She knows exactly what your body needs at a certain time, and she causes kriyas according to that need. It is not necessary that everyone should have the same kind of kriyas, or even that everyone should have kriyas at all. In meditation you should be without desire and you should let the Shakti do whatever She wants to do.

What am I to do when I experience sadness or pain or unhappiness while meditating?

In meditation all the old tapes of one's personal history are played out in the *sushumnā*. There are impressions of all sorts embedded there — positive impressions and negative impressions. Sometimes feelings of dejection or unhappiness or sadness come up, but you should not worry about them. Just let them come up. They are coming up to be expelled from the system. This happens because of a certain impurity of mind, but you should not be scared of it. This morning I said that if the water from the spring is muddy, don't lose your patience. Wait for a while until it becomes clear.

Why do I get depressed after I experience deep meditation?

In the beginning this can happen, but don't worry. The experience of the joy of deep meditation is extraordinary; it is unique. When you come out of that state into normal consciousness and experience the difference, you will feel depressed. But this will last only a short time. As you meditate you reach the state of void, where it is empty. In this state there is no love and no joy. It is totally dry. Buddhism believes only in the void. But if you keep meditating, you will reach another state that is beyond the void. It is a very good sign if you feel depressed after meditating. You are meditating very well.

The *Bhagavad Gītā* says that our lives are governed and bound by the three gunas or qualities. Either we act according to *sattva guna*, the pure guna, or *rajoguna*, which makes us very active, or *tamoguna*, which is the quality of inertia. The *Gītā* says the entire world functions within these three gunas. When a meditator transcends these gunas, he feels disinterested and depressed for a while. It is a good state.

Why do I often become afraid when I begin to experience my inner Self?

It happens. There is a veil of fear between the inner Self and the individual soul. Many people give up meditation when they reach that state. At that time you need to be very courageous, very brave.

Why fear for no reason? You are going to die at the time that God has determined for you to die. You won't die before that time. So why fear? When I reached that state, I also became afraid. Everyone feels that. But beyond that fear is the state of fearlessness, and that state of fearlessness is God. So beyond this fear lies God's supreme bliss.

In Maharashtra there was a saint named Krishnasuta, who said that it is only because of the state of individuality that one fears. Beyond the state of individuality there is no fear. When the mind, which is like a piece of salt, sinks in the ocean of supreme bliss, it melts. So if there is a person whose mind has melted in the ocean of God's bliss, how can he have any fear? Give up fear, and with great courage keep meditating.

Something happens after about fifty minutes of meditation. It is as if someone comes along and corrects each vertebra in my spine, so that I stay perfectly straight. It feels as if I could stay in that position for months. My whole body tingles and feels charged. But I feel alarmed about such a powerful force, so I have stopped meditating.

That is a very good experience. It is a sign of deep meditation. It's a pity you didn't understand that it was the inner Shakti that was working on you. You should have sat quietly and watched what was happening. More would have happened. You might even have had the experience of leaving your body and going elsewhere. I can assure you no harm will come to you from such experiences. Your meditation was going the right way. You will have experiences that are even stranger than this. These experiences are not at all dangerous; they are very good, very positive experiences. Sometimes in meditation one can go to the world of the sun or the moon or some other world. You did not do well by stopping meditation. If you had persisted, you would have made phenomenal progress. Still, it is not too late to resume.

I've experienced leaving my body in meditation, but I also knew that I couldn't go very far because of my fear. Would you comment on that?

It is for exactly this reason that we need a guide. You should meditate again and again. If you leave your body in meditation or in a yogic state, you can be sure that you will come back to it. So don't have any fear. It is only when the time comes to leave the body forever that you will do so.

When I get into deep meditation, I get very frightened. I get the same uneasy feeling I had when I was a little girl and I thought I was dying.

The place of God lies on the other side of fear. It is just this fear that is the wall separating you from Him. This fear harasses everyone; it is a hurdle that a meditator needs great courage to cross over. You feel frightened because in deep meditation your *jīvabhāva,* your false state of limitation, is about to die. Jivabhava is a sense of separation from God, a sense of alienation from Him. It is this alienation that causes us all our agony and misery. When this sense of separation is about to die, fear occurs. Just meditate more and more and more. Let yourself die. Do not worry; I will bring you back to life. If you totally lose yourself in meditation, for an instant you will experience your own death. The great saint Tukaram wrote in one of his poems that he saw his own death with his own eyes, and that it was a very beautiful experience. He said that after dying, he came back to life forever. It was only his death that died. So let go of yourself. If you have to die, just die. In an instant you will attain perfection.

During meditation I felt all my personal qualities, as well as my defenses, falling away. All that was left was my soul. After meditation, I felt very frightened because I was just a soul with no physical body to protect me. I felt open and could feel people's energy coming right through me. What should I do?

You were in a very good state. You should not have been frightened; you should have celebrated with great joy. This usually happens. If it happens again in the future, have no worries. If you know how to live being the soul, being the Self, why do you need this inert body? Still, you should not worry; the body will remain with you as long as you are destined to have it. You will not lose your body the moment you attain the state of the Self. The Self will remain in the body as long as it is destined to. Nonetheless, your experience is very beautiful.

Many times I feel that I would like to get quieter and quieter. I would like to go inside deeper and deeper. If and when I go too far inside, how will you bring me back out?

Do not fear. I am responsible. I promise I will bring you back out. At least once, go inside. Then understand that God has bestowed His grace upon you. If you go inside, you will also come outside again. Once you go inside, going in and coming out will take place all the time — just as you come here to the ashram, go home, come here, and go home. Once you have the knowledge of the inner Self, you will not get stuck inside. You will come out, and you will live outside with the same knowledge that you have inside.

Every time I enjoy peace and a sattvic energy level, it is followed by a tremendous fatigue and lethargy, as though the tamasic forces are stronger. Is this common?

This is quite common. But it does not mean that the tamasic force has invaded you. On the contrary, it happens because tamas is dissolving away. Each state of consciousness produces intoxication corresponding to it. If you feel anger, you get intoxicated on anger; if you feel love, you get intoxicated on love; if you feel greed, that too intoxicates you. When you experience a pure emotion, a sattvic feeling, you become rather drunk and your previous tamasic state is dissolved. As a result of that, you feel as though you had spent all your energy. If you lie down quietly for a short while, you will return to your normal state.

I want to meditate but I need a lot of sleep too. I'm torn between wanting to do both things. How can I give up hours of sleep in order to be able to meditate early in the morning?

To get up early in the morning, wash your face thoroughly and wash your hands and feet. You will overcome your sleep. Now how much value do you give to meditation? Are you going to attach more importance to sleep or to meditation? Man spends his life sleeping. If you have a life span of a hundred years, you spend fifty years sleeping. The other fifty years, most of them, are used up in seeking sense pleasure, entertaining yourself, eating, drinking, playing around, enjoying sports, and doing various things. How much of your time do you use to remember God? So try to renounce some of your sleep for meditation. When you meditate, sleep will follow.

Kabir, the great poet-saint said, "O man, wake up! You have been sleeping for a long time. You continue to sleep. At least now, wake up." We consider this state, in which we are moving and talking, a waking state. However, wise people who are truly awake consider this to be nothing but a sleeping state. A person who has self-control is awake in the awareness of God even at night. But a person who lacks self-control is asleep even during the day.

The human body is very valuable. Inside this body there are things so valuable that you could not obtain them even if you paid millions of dollars. Therefore, Kabir said, "O my dear one, wake up. You have slept so much; at least now open your eyes. You have closed your eyes with the sleep of attachment. Open your eyes.''

If you count how much time you spend in the waking state, you will see that you really spend hardly any time awake. The individual soul is always in darkness, always in the ecstasy of his own sleep. However, the individual thinks he is awake and doing something. Lessen your sleep. Increase your meditation. Even in meditation you will experience the happiness of sleep. If you feel very sleepy while meditating, just allow yourself to sleep while sitting.

This morning in meditation, as usual, I was very resistant. I felt anger, frustration, doubt. How can I overcome that resistance? How can I stop fighting?

Sit quietly for a while. It will go away on its own. Don't try to stop it; don't do anything about it. This is also the work of the inner Shakti. It is called the *vikalpa shakti*. Just let it happen. Sit quietly and watch it taking place. It will happen and then it will go away and new things will arise. It is all right if you are resistant to this.

The *Bhāgavatam* says that the demon Kamsa was so afraid of Lord Krishna that he was always contemplating Him. Finally, he attained Him. It is not that he attained Krishna out of love, but out of fear. The demon Ravana was Lord Rama's enemy, and finally he attained Rama. So it is completely all right to be resistant to good things.

During an interview someone told me, "I feel so much resistance toward you.''

"Increase it,'' I said.

The person was amazed. I said, "Increase it with full force. At the moment, you are resistant toward me, but one day your resistance will become favorable to you.''

Whether it is out of good or bad feelings, whether out of laziness, envy, jealousy, anger, or hatred, just think of the Self, think of the Guru, think of the Shakti. It does not matter *how* you think of That — just think of That. It does not matter *how* you feel about That, you are still contemplating That.

I find the transition between the inner state and the outer world very painful. When the lights are turned on and the activity begins, I go from feeling peace and bliss to agitation. What should I do?

Now you should learn how to maintain the peace that you have experienced in darkness, even when there is light. If you experience something only in one particular place, it is not enough. A great being said that a person cannot be called a yogi who goes into a dark cave and meditates and experiences peace but cannot experience that peace out in the world. He is a true yogi who can meditate in a cave and remain in that same state even when he is out in the world. He is not only a yogi, but a king of yogis.

While you are in meditation, you should have that state. Even while you are not meditating, you should have the same state. The awareness of *aham* should continue even in your daily activities. Right now it is all right because you are at the initial stage. Later, you will practice it very well.

Should we stop reading—even your books—and just meditate?

Keep meditating. However, if you come up against any obstacle, any doubt, and if you don't understand anything that is happening inside you, you can read these books. These books are not books; they are meditative states.

WHEN THE BREATH BECOMES STILL

Whenever I experience kumbhaka in meditation, I have the sensation of being on the window ledge of a tall building ready to jump into space or I feel as if I am going to leave my body. How can I overcome this fear?

Sometimes you have this kind of sensation, but have no fear. In this kumbhaka, the inner unfoldment takes place instantly. *Sahaja kumbhaka*, the natural retention of breath, is very important.

Shankaracharya said, "I offer my salutations to this natural retention of breath, which has no exhalation or inhalation."

When the mind becomes completely still inside for a long, long time, natural breath retention takes place, and it is great. It is this inner kumbhaka that brings joy and bliss. Because you don't have enough understanding about it, you are afraid, but have no fear.

Is it safe to do a few hatha yoga postures with the retention of breath after your Shakti has begun to unfold?

If you practice a few simple hatha yoga postures, it would be good for meditation. But in meditation you get all the results that you can get in hatha yoga. Meditation is the greatest posture. If you want to do some hatha yoga, go ahead, but don't practice breath retention. If the retention of breath comes by itself, it's fine. If you try to do it on your own, something will go wrong inside you. When you are still, kumbhaka takes place by itself. Still your mind and sit quietly; then the kumbhaka will just come by itself. That is how yogis do it. Natural kumbhaka is very great. It has a lot of significance.

Why does my breath stop for a longer period of time on the outbreath than on the inbreath?

This is all right. There are two types of kumbhaka. Some people have outer kumbhaka and others have inner kumbhaka. Wherever the breath stops, either inside or outside, let it happen. Don't interfere with the retention of breath. If you have outer kumbhaka, the belly goes inside and you have a flat stomach. If inner kumbhaka takes place, you have a puffed belly. With outer kumbhaka, the stomach is cleaned, it becomes really pure and you become free of all stomach diseases.

Some time ago before sleep, I felt violent shuddering, but my body did not move. I felt a rush of energy through the body ending in the head. The pressure in the stomach and head was great. Then the breathing stopped. Fear came and the experience ended.

When such things happen, you should lie down very quietly. Don't try to stop them. Whatever was happening to you was very good; it was right. The inner kumbhaka was taking place and you got scared and woke up. At such times, don't get scared and stop the experience. If anything bad is going to happen, it will happen at the right moment. If you are going to die, you will die at the right moment. God will come to take you at the right moment. Why do you have to get scared and wake up?

When you have devotion for God, you can experience your own death before you die. It's very good if you can experience that death completely. If it is incomplete, it is not good. The prana stops and you feel, "Alas, I died!" But only then are you truly alive. After that, you never die. With great courage, you should face it. What happened to you was very good.

In meditation I often feel a pressure building in the top of my head. All the energy seems bound to this point, and I usually experience a shortness of breath.

Whatever is happening to you is fine. The pressure that you feel in your head is a particular kind of kumbhaka. You feel that pressure because the prana moves upward and is collected at the top of the head. You don't have to be afraid of this. There is nothing wrong; it is a very good state.

At times I experience breathing from the inside even without actually taking in air. What is its function?

This is very great. It shows that your sushumna has been opened up. It has great value. Only after doing a lot of sadhana does the sushumna open and you begin to breathe through it. I will demonstrate it to you, and I'm going to make a sound so that you can understand, but truly speaking you don't have to make that sound. The breath is not coming out — and that is the supreme joy. This is called the opening of the crown center. Once that center is opened, one obtains the bliss of Consciousness. I am very happy with your question.

THE GREATEST FRAGRANCES, THE GREATEST TASTES

This morning when you touched me during meditation, I felt as if I had only my head, and I could smell the quintessence of rose around my nostrils. How can I recall this wondrous experience of joy and also proceed beyond it?

Through meditation you can proceed beyond it. If your inner Shakti is awakened, that doesn't mean your spiritual journey has come to an end. It only means that it has started. Now you have to proceed on your journey and then, when you reach that state, become established in it. What you have experienced is an ordinary thing — really very ordinary. There is much more to it. As you go further, you experience the greatest things. Keep on meditating. Greatness lies inside man. The supreme Truth is within you. There is more in the inner world than there is in the outer world. Inside there is the greatest fragrance, the greatest music, the greatest beauty. When you perceive the inner beauty, you realize that the outer beauty is nothing but ugliness. Beauty lies within you. Delicious tastes lie within. The best of all music lies within. Therefore man should see that beauty, man should listen to that music, man should taste that flavor and smell that fragrance.

My breathing becomes still through mantra and I get a taste of nectar in my mouth. Can you explain this?

Yes, you will have the taste of nectar by chanting the mantra. In fact, people start chanting the mantra when they get that taste in their mouth. They don't need to buy liquor. What you are tasting is the taste of prayer. While chanting, kumbhaka takes place and from that you get that taste. You have reached a very good place. Keep increasing your chanting and japa.

A few months ago my tongue went back up my throat, but I tasted no sweet nectar, only something very bitter.

There is nectar in that bitterness. Chocolate has a bitter taste too. The body does not need only one rasa, one taste; it needs six kinds of rasa. One of them is bitter, but it is also a kind of nectar. A person receives the rasa that he needs. When the tongue goes backwards, it is very auspicious. It is called *khecharī* and it is a very good thing. It does not happen to everyone; it is very rare. People practice yoga for a long time before it happens to them. The nectar you tasted is very good. Don't think that nectar has to be sweet.

I used to have a lot of experiences, but now I don't.

Experiences don't continue forever. There is a limit to them. When the experiences stop happening, that is when you attain the state of God. It is said, "O Lord, Your glory, Your experience, is beyond speech, beyond the mind." For this reason, God is not something you will experience, not something you will just see. The *Brihadāranyaka Upanishad* says that when the mother becomes motherless, when the father becomes fatherless, when the experience becomes the nonexperience, that is when you really experience the Self. When the understanding is finished, when imagination is completed, that is when you realize God. It is not just an experience; you cannot call it anything. It is nothing but pure love.

YOUR EYES BECOME PURER AND PURER

Repeatedly in meditation I see a broad field blazing with blue flames, which turn into crowds of people in quiet motion surrounded by blue light. Is it important to know the meaning of this?

When the Kundalini is awakened completely, the subtle ears appear, the subtle eyes appear. It is called *bindu-bheda*, and after that you begin to perceive the blue light, the blue sparkles, scintillating and vibrating everywhere.

Truly speaking, this whole world is filled with that blue

light. I see that blue light all the time. The world is inside this shimmering blue Consciousness. With these everyday eyes we see the world full of differences; we see with duality. But after your eyes are purified, you see that blue shimmering light everywhere.

Keep on meditating. There are more things for you to see. After some time you'll begin to see this vision with your eyes open — but don't tell your eye doctor about it!

Why do you wear dark glasses? I would love to see your eyes more often.

Are they too dark? I can still see everybody. There are so many lights in this hall, and these glasses are very special. If there is too much light, they become darker; if there is less light, they become less dark. Nonetheless, I can still see everybody, even the ones sitting far away.

Why don't you start watching your own eyes? It would be much better. Truly, you should perceive your own eyes. The Upanishads say that a divine being exists in these eyes. Perceive Him. He is no one but God, so perceive Him. This is a great practice in Shaivism — to watch your own eyes.

If you look at the eyes of the great beings, such as my Babaji, you will know that their eyes are still and they are watching themselves. The eyes are not closed; they are open, but they are still; they don't see anything. The mind is still, it is not thinking about anything. The prana, the vital force, is also still without doing *prānāyāma* or kumbhaka. When the eyes become still, when the eyes watch the eyes, the mind stops thinking and becomes still. For a while the prana becomes still without your stopping it, without you retaining it inside. This is called *shaivi mudrā* or *shivadrishti,* the vision of Shiva, and it brings all attainments. In this you attain the Self, you attain God. So start gazing at your own eyes; it is a great sight.

I am a beginner in meditation and I took one Intensive. When I meditate, the area above the right eye begins to hurt. Can you explain this? Am I trying to push through?

While you are meditating, a particular kriya in the eyes takes place. It is bindu bheda, a piercing of the eyeballs. At that point the eyeballs begin to roll. Some people experience pain with this, but not everybody. After that, you begin to perceive the bindu, the Blue Pearl, within yourself. After this happens, you don't see any duality; you see everything as one. You see unity and equality. What is happening to you is very good. Continue to meditate.

After receiving your touch, I experienced a rolling of my eyeballs into my head and fluttering of the eyelids, followed by a burst of energy that seemed to lift me upward and settled in the top of my skull. It stayed there and then I felt a great peace. Could you explain this?

This is very important. The eyeballs will continue to roll upward, and then the gaze will turn inside and it will keep looking upward on the inside. This vision is very good. It looks toward the sahasrara. Contemplate this experience, and continue to meditate again and again. Your experience is very good. Shakti bestows supreme bliss. For this reason, we pursue Shakti — for the sake of happiness, for the sake of love.

I have felt sizzling electric light and for the past two days I have seen a tiger's eyes inside. What does it mean?

Those are not the eyes of a tiger; they are your own eyes. Sometimes in meditation you can't see them very clearly, so you are just imagining that they are a tiger's eyes. Really they are your eyes and this is a very good vision. This is called *pratīka-darshan,* a vision of one's own form. After you see your eyes for a while, you will eventually be able to see your entire body. Seeing your own eyes in meditation is an indication that your body is becoming purer.

I was wondering what is the significance of seeing one's double?

You see yourself in front of you during meditation? That's very good. That is pratika-darshan, when you see your double. When you see your double for a long time, that is very good. That shows that your inner body has become completely pure through meditation. Sometimes you see your double so clearly that you begin to wonder who is the real you — the one looking or the one in front of you!

God Has Granted Me this Vision

One day I was meditating on the bank of the river in
Ganeshpuri. As I opened my eyes, I saw that Swami
Muktananda was right there before me. I looked at this body
and I looked at the other body — and they were identical.

Another day I was meditating in the cemetery and there
was a dead body being burnt. I went on meditating. I closed
my eyes and then I opened them, and once again I saw
Muktananda sitting there. Then I gave up meditating and
I ran away from there. I told my Baba about it.

"Two Swami Muktanandas have started existing!"
I said.

"It's all right," said Baba. "It's pratika-darshan. You
see yourself."

So in meditation you do attain this state. In the final
stage of meditation you have the darshan of the inner Guru,
and he appears in the same form as the outer Guru. Therefore,
our scriptures say that the Guru, the Self, and God are one
and the same. If you understand this, you will know that your
Self, the Self of the Guru, and the Self of God are one and the
same. If you have this understanding, you have the correct
understanding.

Even after having attained ultimate knowledge, it is not
enough. You have to continue that awareness through your
sadhana. For example, when you eat food, it's not that your

*hunger is over. You get hungry again and you have to
eat again.*

*I still do external sadhana every morning for three
hours. Once you have an addiction to sadhana, it goes on
happening and happening and happening. Once sadhana
becomes established in the heart, even if I were to give it
up, it wouldn't give me up — it would continue. So every
morning it takes me three hours for my meditation, and
after that I go for the darshan of my Baba. Then I sit in
silence on the porch in the courtyard.*

*Sadhana goes on forever. It never gives a person up.
The technique of sadhana may change, but not the sadhana
itself. What is sadhana in the beginning becomes the object
of sadhana at the end.*

Sometimes when I look into your eyes, I see many irises,
and a warm loving feeling comes through to me. Is there
any significance to it?

*There is the blue light in my eyes, which appears and
disappears, and this is God's gift. It is through that light
that I see all of you. All of you seem to me to be made of blue
light. When you see things through a red glass, everything
seems to be red; when you see things through a yellow glass,
everything seems to be yellow. So God has granted me this
vision by which I see everything with a slightly bluish tinge.*

*In India there is a plant that grows wild in the field, and
it produces small, light blue flowers. That is the color in my
eyes. In the scripture this is called the lotion of Consciousness.*

Tukaram Maharaj said that when this lotion of Consciousness was applied to his eyes, he could really see. First his vision was limited, and then it expanded. When it expanded, he could not see the world as world any longer. He could not see people as sinners or as wicked; he could see only God's light everywhere, and everyone appeared to him to be the light of God.

The same light dwells within the eyes of all of you. You will be able to see it sometimes during meditation.

CHAPTER 7

A Mine of Nectar

*There are only two things: either you cry in the name
of the world or you sing in the name of God.
So choose what you want to do — whether
you want to weep or sing.*

*Is chanting God's name necessary for Self-realization? Is
chanting necessary for expressing love and devotion to Him?
Aren't good deeds alone enough?*

Chanting is the means of attaining everything. Through chanting, you are purified on the inside. Through chanting, love arises. If love arises, it means that you have attained God, because God's true nature is love. You sing His name so that love will arise.

No good deed can equal chanting. Tulsidas said that by chanting the name of God, everything becomes pure and auspicious. Your neighbors become pure, the atmosphere becomes pure, and even the sky and the earth become pure. To chant the auspicious name of God is to make the tongue, the ears, and the heart auspicious and pure.

The Name is the true form of God. Shaivism says that God exists in letters. From letters come words. From words, a sentence is composed, and from a sentence you get meaning. The meaning of the name is God. When we chant, the tongue is touched by the form of God, the ears are touched by the form of God, and the heart is touched by that too.

So don't consider chanting the Name to be a mere *sādhanā*. The name itself is God. A poet said that the name of God is the mine of God's nectar. So chant the Name with great reverence. No deed can equal the Name.

How great a part does chanting play in the practice of this yoga?

Chanting plays the greatest part in this yoga; it is a magnet that draws the power of the Lord. Chanting makes meditation easy. The Kundalini Shakti within becomes very pleased with chanting. To discover how effective it is, you should chant. When you become overwhelmed by pain and suffering, you begin to shed tears, and tears provide some relief. When weeping can provide relief, you can imagine what greater relief chanting will provide.

The first step in this yoga of meditation is to chant the divine Name. It has enormous power. It not only purifies the heart but all seven constituents of the body. So chant continuously. Chanting will not only awaken your Kundalini and thus bring spontaneous meditation, but it will also fill you with peace.

Please speak about chanting the divine Name.

If you chant the divine Name, you attain divinity. In *Kālī Yuga* the name of God has great significance. In India there are many scriptures about this. There were many, many saints and sages and Siddhas, and they all sang the Name.

The Name is full of nectar. To explain it briefly, I'll give you this example. If someone abuses you with only a single bad word, you lose your mind, your body begins to shake, your cheeks turn red, and you need ice to make your head cool. So the abusive term brings a drastic change in you. You stay in that condition for more than a while; even for ten or twelve years you remember that abusive term. You just don't forget it. After twelve years, if you happen to meet that person who abused you, the moment you see him your face becomes bitter and your teeth begin to clench, and you think, "He abused me a long time ago. I'll get even."

144

This shows that the abusive term has so much power in it. When this is the case, what can I say about the name of God? What can I say about its beauty, its power, its enthusiasm, and the bliss that you get from it? That is why a person should give up thinking about other things, and he should pursue the name of God.

In India there was a great Siddha called Surdas, who was blind. All the great Indian musicians, all the classical singers, sing his poems. He used to sing a poem that went like this: Blessed is he, fortunate is he, who remembers the name of God all the time, who sings "Govinda" all the time. In the world only he is a great person who sings the name of God constantly, ceaselessly. A sweeper is great if he remembers the name of God all the time. But if there is a millionaire who doesn't remember God's name at all, what is the use of his wealth? A beggar is better off than he is if the beggar remembers the name of God.

The name of God is completely charged; it is full of Shakti. You cannot compare the power of the name of God with anything. Whenever I go for a walk, I still repeat the name of God, I use my *japa mālā*.

You speak beautifully of the value of repeating the divine Name. Which name do you mean — Rama, Krishna, Hari, Gopala? There are so many of them.

They are all one and the same. Rama is that which dwells in everything — that is Consciousness. Krishna is the one who lives in the heart and attracts everybody and keeps everybody under control. Gopala is the controller of all the senses of this body. When you remember Hari, all your miseries are destroyed. So they are all the same.

Sometimes my mind wanders while I'm chanting. Does this destroy the effect?

In Sufism there was a great being whose name was Junaid. For a long time he stayed at a Muslim priest's house. The priest used to do *namaz*, or prayers, five times a day, and Junaid would just keep quiet. One very important day came along, and the priest said to Junaid, "You should come to the mosque with me today to do the namaz because people will tell me, 'You have such a great saint, such a great being, staying at your house, but he never comes here to do the namaz.'"

Junaid said, "I will come with you. However, I will do the namaz only if you also do the namaz."

The priest said, "Of course I am going to do the namaz!"

It was a big day, and many people went to the mosque. They were putting a lot of money in the donation box. The priest had wanted to buy a buffalo for a long time because he liked buffalo milk. Since he was the priest, he was going to get all the money in the donation box, so he thought, "Today I'm getting a lot of money. I can really buy a buffalo!"

The time came for the namaz. Everybody bowed their heads and started to chant the great mantra of the Muslims, just as we do *Om Namah Shivāya*. Junaid was just standing there, laughing away. Again the priest did the namaz, and from the corner of his eye he was watching Junaid. Everybody was bowing down except Junaid.

Because Junaid didn't do the namaz, because he didn't bow down, the priest felt terrible. What was even worse was that Junaid started to shout, "Buffalo, buffalo, buffalo!" It was forbidden to speak at all during prayer and it spoiled everybody's concentration.

After the namaz was over, the priest spoke up. He said to Junaid, "You didn't do the namaz. You know you didn't! I am the main priest in this mosque, and people are going to mock me because you didn't do it. Not only that, but while we were praying, you were screaming, 'Buffalo, buffalo, buffalo!' Is that your way? You promised me that you would do the namaz!"

Junaid said, "I promised that I would do the namaz only if you did. You were thinking of a buffalo all the time. You were constantly wondering, 'What kind of buffalo shall I buy and how much milk will it give and when should I go to the market and buy it?' You were thinking about a buffalo, and now you're blaming me that I didn't do the namaz. When did you do the namaz?"

We shouldn't do the same thing that the priest did. We should really chant; we should really do it. You experience bliss from chanting only if you go beyond the boundary of the mind. Otherwise, if you continue to think about a buffalo while you sing *Hare Rāma Hare Krishna,* you won't really enjoy anything.

Chanting is the easiest means in Kali Yuga. Not only is it sadhana, but it is also the object of sadhana. Not only is it bliss, but it is also the medicine for many different kinds of illnesses.

As long as you chant, don't think of a buffalo. You can think about a buffalo after the chanting is over. So chant with great absorption while swaying in bliss.

The other day during chanting, I had a beautiful experience of Consciousness. Thank you for this blessing. However, the experience soon faded away. How does one make such an experience last longer?

If you want to retain this experience, all you have to do is keep chanting within yourself, within your own heart. It is so simple. Then the experience will never leave you. Only the great beings knew the value of chanting. They gave up drinking, eating, and meditating, and became completely absorbed in chanting. There is so much nectar in chanting. If you chant with great respect and reverence, you will open your heart.

The Upanishads say that in the void a divine sound arose. The entire world came into existence from that sound. The Word has great power. For this reason, people ask for the *mantra.* It is due to the power of the Word that we become happy or unhappy, good or bad, ignorant or knowledgeable.

Sit quietly. Pay attention to where you experience happiness and unhappiness. Do you experience these things from outside? Do they come to you with the wind? No. They come from within, from the inner sound.

This is a great and sublime subject which is spoken of in Shaivism. An aphorism says that *mātrikā* is the source of all ignorance and knowledge. *Mātrikā* means letters. All our pleasure and pain are created from those letters.

For example, imagine that you are sitting very quietly. Suddenly, a fear arises. What did you experience before you had this fear? From where did it arise? With whose help do you experience this fear? It is experienced through the letters, and they are always created within. They are unfathomable. The mind thinks with letters and words. And they in turn create happiness or unhappiness.

Listen to this with close attention. You do not attain any happiness or unhappiness from outside. For example, you think, "I am small, petty, and weak." You experience pain while thinking these words. Then you think, "I am great, I am sublime." And while thinking these words, you feel happiness. Contemplate this. Understand this. See from where you experience happiness or unhappiness. Matrika is the mesh of letters created in the mind. Whatever you are thinking, that is what you are becoming right now.

This is why we chant the name of God. These divine words also bear fruit. Our inner bad words torture us, but the good words of the name of God give us a lot of joy. Therefore, chant all the time. The same energy that lies within God also lies within His name.

When you say chanting purifies the atmosphere, I'm confused because I think that everything is God. So how can what is pure already become more pure by chanting? Is it our perception that is being purified?

Our perception becomes pure, and that which is already pure becomes pure, and that which we saw as impure because of our impurity also becomes pure. So chanting makes the pure supremely pure.

Though we are totally pure inside, what does our mind keep saying to us? What does it keep putting us through? Chanting purifies the mind, purges the mind of all its chatter; it purges the imagination of its fantasizing. It purges the intellect, and it purges us of the tendency to see bad in good.

What is the place of music in the spiritual journey?

In the scriptures it is said that music is yoga. There are musical compositions called *rāgas* that have a definite effect on the mind.

They help the mind to become focused and centered. Western classical music is also very good from that point of view, and the violin seems to be particularly effective. It helps to a certain degree; if you listen to it with attention, it will help you to focus your mind for a short while. Music is loved by all evolved people; it is created by evolved beings. What we chant here, *Hare Rāma Hare Krishna,* is also a form of music that gives fulfillment to the mind, to the inner Self. However, we should sing for God. Our music should be inspired by love of God and be full of that love. If we meditate successfully, we are also rewarded with musical harmonies that are heard in higher stages of meditation. That is called *nāda,* the inner music.

In India there was a great singer called Tansen, and whenever he sang a raga, it would have its corresponding effect. If he sang a composition relating to rain, there would be a shower; if he sang one relating to fire, it would kindle a fire. He was a great friend of the king of Delhi. The king was always saying, "Tansen, please get me an invitation to listen to the music of your Guru, Haridas."

Haridas was a great teacher of music, and he was also a great lover of God. He lived in Vrindavan, which is the land of Krishna. One day, Tansen took the king to Haridas. At that time the Guru was absorbed in meditation. They sat there for a long time, and still he didn't come out of meditation. Then Tansen took a *sitar* and deliberately played a wrong note. Then he began to sing, and he deliberately sang a few wrong notes.

That immediately brought Haridas out of meditation and he said, "Hey, what are you doing? You're not singing the right notes!" Then he picked up his instrument and showed him how to sing the raga properly. Haridas sang beautifully and the king was very happy.

On the way back, the king said to Tansen, "You don't sing like your Guru. When he sang, it filled me with great love, it unfolded my inner Consciousness, and it made me experience tremendous inner joy and delight."

"Your Majesty," said Tansen, "one's music is affected by the person for whom one sings. My Guru sings for God, the king of kings, the emperor of emperors, the Self of all; that is why his music has sweetness and power in it. But I sing for you, so therefore my music is what it is. While my music pleases you, his music pleases God, so you can decide which music is superior."

If your music were played for God's sake, that would certainly help you in your journey. We sing here for the love of God, and that is why everyone enjoys it so much.

When we chant in Sanskrit, is it the sound that produces results, or is it our understanding?

Even sound alone produces results. However, if you have understanding, the results are greater — a thousand times greater. In Maharashtra there was a great being called Ramchandra Pandit who said that whether you know it or not, if your foot touches fire, that fire will always burn your foot. Therefore, if you repeat God's name, whether you understand it or not, how could it not bear fruit? Even if you don't understand what you are chanting, as long as He understands it, it's all right. It works.

We chant so much in the ashram. Could you say something about the necessity of chanting at home?

Chanting purifies the atmosphere. Before long the scientists are going to discover this fact. They will be able to tell you who said what in a particular place. They can even grasp the words that are in the atmosphere. Near Delhi there is a religious place called Kurukshetra. I visited all the holy rivers and all the holy places of India. It was my habit to keep wandering and to keep testing the Gurus without testing myself. When I went to Kurukshetra and sat down there, I could hear the entire *Bhagavad Gītā.*

Words have that much power. And words also purify the atmosphere, the environment. When our neighbors come here and see this place where we meditate and chant, they say, "My goodness! What happened to this place?" They really admire it now. So sound is very powerful. The sound of chanting cleans all the filth of the atmosphere, and the vibration remains in the atmosphere. It also affects our inner space, our inner sky. For this reason, if you chant for an hour or half an hour when you are home, your entire house will become clean and pure. Whatever quality a word has, it affects the atmosphere. Therefore, before we begin anything here, we say, "*Sadgurunāth Mahārāj kī Jay!*" Then we sing *Om Namah Shivāya* and begin the program. We do this because it makes the atmosphere pure and beautiful. Even while we are waiting in line for meals, we chant *Shrī Rām Jay Rām* to purify the food.

So chanting is very good, and if you chant when you are home, it will make your entire house very clean and pure. It is not just temples and churches and mosques that should be places of prayer. Every place — including your home — should become a place for prayers. Your home should become a temple. Then in this very world you will perceive heaven; you won't need another heaven.

How can I find the source of the ego when trying to do spiritual practices?

If you chant intensely, ego leaves you in peace. God's name and ego are sworn enemies.

When I chant Jyota se Jyota, *I feel an incredible urge to cry. I feel as if a weight is being lifted off my heart. It makes it difficult for me to function and it interferes with my sevā. How should I handle this?*

When they sing *Jyota se Jyota,* they play the drums and the cymbals, and they make so much noise. So you can go ahead and cry; nobody will hear it.

Crying is very good too. Sometimes just for a while a person has to laugh a lot and also cry a lot. Don't cry because of unhappiness — cry because of joy. Only he can cry with joy who has become immersed in the love of God. While remembering God, if you feel like crying, that crying is much better than happiness. The *āratī* they do with *Jyota se Jyota* is filled with devotion. So it's worth crying about. After *Jyota se Jyota* you should

151

stop crying and start working. Don't cry while you are working! The arati doesn't go on for eight hours — only for five minutes.

Please tell us about the origin and significance of the Rudram *and the* Shiva Arati, *which we sing every morning.*

While singing the *Shiva Āratī,* you are doing the arati of the *Rudram,* the arati of Parashiva or supreme Consciousness. The *Rudram* is a great *mantra swādhyāya.* If you recite it with understanding, you yourself become Rudra. If you recite it without understanding, still all your difficulties are removed. You become worthy of knowing the Truth and becoming Rudra.

The *Rudram* says that Shiva exists in this, Shiva exists in that, Shiva exists in everything. It recites the names of every object and says that Shiva exists there. Those who recite the *Rudram* should also read the translation of it. If you want to know in a nutshell, it means that whatever exists in this world is nothing but Shiva. It's very good to read it every day because then you make everything Shiva.

What is the value of the Guru Gita?

There is great power in it. We gradually become like what we chant; we become like what we study. So when you chant the *Guru Gītā,* you become like the Guru, and the Guru reveals himself in your heart.

Would you please talk to us about the Guru Gita?

What can I tell you about the *Guru Gītā?* It is such a sacred book that you cannot talk about it; you have to chant it, you have to read it by yourself. If it were something that could be talked about, I could talk about it at great length.

With one-pointed attention and respect, one should read the *Guru Gītā* and understand it. You must notice every day the verse at the end about how everything in the chant is very mysterious and is supposed to remain secret. You should become absorbed in the chant, immersed in it. The great beings give the analogy of a wish-fulfilling tree and a wish-fulfilling cow. The *Guru Gītā* is the form of the Guru. People who get tired of the *Guru Gītā*, of course, sit at the back of the hall so they can go to sleep and they don't have to read it. They are not aware that I can see them.

When we chant the *Guru Gītā,* we are not just reading it, but we are worshiping the Guru within ourselves. The *Guru Gītā* is the conscious mantra body of the Guru. Every letter of the *Guru Gītā* contains the Guru.

In the Guru Gita *we are told that by reciting it in a certain way, we can obtain money, charm over others, peace, etc. It is difficult for me to reconcile this with the principle of renunciation of all desires. Could you please explain?*

The *Guru Gītā* caters to all kinds of people — those who want to recite it for the fulfillment of desires can have their desires fulfilled and those who do not have any desires can recite it for the sheer joy of it, the sheer beauty of it. Whatever is said about getting money and charming others and peace is meant for those who have desires. There are two kinds of people: those with desires and those without desires, and the *Guru Gītā* appeals to both kinds.

One person goes to a temple and prays, "Lord, grant me a daughter." Another goes and prays, "Lord, help me to run my factory better." And if it is a priest who is praying, he will ask for more love for the Lord.

In the *Bhagavad Gītā* Lord Krishna says that there are four kinds of devotees: those who want to overcome their suffering, those who want material things, those who turn to the Lord out of genuine curiosity, and those who are truly enlightened devotees. The *Guru Gītā* is also recited by these types of devotees. With whatever desire you recite the *Guru Gītā,* that desire is fulfilled. There is really no conflict between those who read it for the fulfillment of desires and those who read it without any desire.

There is the state of sleep and the waking state. You have both in your life, and there is no conflict between the two. So you can read the *Guru Gītā* the way you like — for peace or for agitating the mind.

There was a parent who lost his son and he began to recite the *Guru Gītā* to recover him. Then there was a woman who hadn't found a husband, and she started reciting the *Guru Gītā* to get a husband. In both cases it worked. So you should read it for whatever you want.

During the Āratī this evening I had an unusual experience. Near the end of the singing, I felt very faint and I noticed vibrations inside my body almost like lightning. I thought I might fall down, and as I looked around, everything was just vibrating with light. I am wondering whether I'll have more of these experiences and whether they just happen during meditation and chanting, or if they can happen anywhere?

It's a very good experience. The Shakti is vibrating within you, and if you are not able to stand, you can sit down. This shows that you will get meditation very soon.

We have this *Āratī*, and it is not for mere fun. The *Āratī* is chanted to invoke the Shakti. It is not a dry, insipid, traditional thing. It has so much strength in it. In India when we do the *Āratī*, the Shakti becomes very strong and sometimes people shake so violently that someone has to hold them.

Is there a significant difference between japa and chanting?

Japa, or saying the mantra silently, and chanting are the same. Japa is a yoga and so is chanting. They are both equal. Chanting is given a very high place in the scriptures; the sages have said that by chanting the name of God, you are purged of all sins.

There was once a devout king who belonged to the dynasty of the Pandavas. His name was Parikshit. He was cursed by a sage who said that he would be bitten by a snake and die of that snakebite within a week. He was in great pain, not because he had been cursed but because he had just seven more days to live.

He didn't want to die just like that, so he sent out a proclamation that if there was any great saint who could bring him liberation within a week, he would be most welcome. So a lot of great sages appeared to help the king. Some of them were thousands of years old, and their hair was extremely long, down to their toes.

Millions of them assembled there and one of them said, "Well, it's ridiculous that the king wants liberation within a week. It took me a thousand years to win liberation."

And another said, "It took me a hundred years."

"It took me twelve years," said a third one.

"It took me a couple of years," said a fourth sage, "so how can you give liberation to the king within a week?"

Some of the others said, "We've been doing this for at least ten thousand years and we're still in the same plight."

Now the king was even more distressed. He said, "Look at all these guys! I have fed them, hundreds of thousands of them, and now, during the last week of my life, there is no one who can tell me how I can find liberation!"

The king's pain reached Narada, the divine sage who was conscious of past, present, and future. He went to a boy sage named Shuka and told him what was happening. He told Shuka that only he was capable of liberating the king instantly.

Immediately Shuka went to help the king. Though he was young, he was fully enlightened, and since he had completely mastered all his senses, he looked even younger than he really was.

The moment the sages saw this youngster, they all stood up and bowed to him. People were surprised to see old sages bowing to a mere stripling.

Shuka walked through the assembly and met the king who had been cursed.

The king said, "O noble sage, I have been cursed and I am going to die within a week. One day has already passed, and this is noon of the second day so there are only five and a half days left. Can you do something for me?"

Shuka said, "That's plenty of time. We don't need that much time for liberation." And he began to instruct him. He said, "Your Majesty, Kali Yuga is said to be a treasury of all defects. Kali Yuga, the present age, is the dark age, and it has been predicted that in this age people will not be able to lead a life of discipline and self-control; they will be too weak to follow ethical principles. All that may be true, but this age has one great quality, one incredible quality — people will be able to win liberation easily just by chanting the name of God."

The king said, "Is this really true? These other sages are telling me it takes millions of years!"

"O King," said Shuka, "to chant the divine Name, there is no limitation of time, of space or place, of occasion. You don't have to do it in any particular ritualistic fashion. Just by chanting the divine Name with love, you can easily cross over to the other shore."

Then Shuka recited the *Bhāgavatam* for a week, and the king was liberated. Since that time, *saptahs*, or seven-day chants, have been practiced.

While coming and going, while standing and doing different jobs, one should chant the divine Name with great love. In this way one will not only become liberated himself, but one will be able to liberate others too. Chanting should become an addiction from which you can't find a way out.

Just as fire purifies gold of all its dross, likewise the name of the Lord, once it takes residence in one's heart, purifies that heart completely from the dross of impurities and sins. And when chanting circulates through the blood, the vibrations purify all seven constituents of the body. Another name for chanting is devotion.

Partway through the Om Namah Shivaya *saptah, I began hearing voices at a pitch five tones above the group. It mesmerized me. My focus became these higher voices and I felt very, very peaceful. Now whenever I chant* Om Namah Shivaya, *I tune into this. Can you tell me what I am hearing?*

Very good! This is why we chant *Om Namah Shivāya*. This mantra has the power to make you become one with God. The repetition of the mantra is a great sadhana. All these great Siddha beings repeated the mantra and danced with great joy. If you don't have the right understanding, it seems very ordinary. Once you have the right understanding about it, this sadhana is really great. Mantra has divine power. It is only because the mantra contains such divine power that we spend so much time repeating it. Lose yourself in the mantra. Repeat it with your mind totally absorbed in it.

During the chants I hear beautiful high voices singing in harmony. Other people say they do not hear them. What are they?

That's very good. During chanting you do hear such high voices from the inner space within. Become absorbed and chant. Chanting has a lot of strength, a lot of nectar, a lot of joy.

I used to chant when I was very young. I was very fond of having saptahs. I used to hold saptahs for people in Yeola and in Kokamathan, and thousands of people would chant during the seven days. I derive a lot of joy from chanting.

"Just Play this Tamboura"

While I was doing sadhana, I went through a time when
I couldn't sleep. During that time I had a very bad headache.
I read a lot, I meditated a lot, and because of that I had a
continuous headache.

I used to visit Pandharpur, a holy place. Many, many
people used to visit that place, millions of them. One day I
was going back from Pandharpur to where I was staying, and
I was on the platform at the railway station. There were a lot
of people waiting for the train to come and I went over and
sat down on a bench.

There was an old man sitting near me. He was wearing
one coat over another. He had on three coats, but still they
didn't cover his body.

He pulled out a flute from his pocket and began to play
a certain raga on that flute. There must have been a thousand
people in that station. The moment he played that flute they
became very quiet, completely still.

When he started to play, I went to sit closer to him.
After he stopped, I said to him, "Play some more."

"Look," he said, "don't ask me to play anymore."

I said to him, "No, I won't — but just once more."

Then he played another raga, a different one. He was
a great scholar, a great sage, and he began to explain to me
about this music. He repeated the mantras of the Sama Veda.
He also said that music contains a lot of medicine.

I told him, "I have this headache. Can you prescribe

some medicine for me with this music?"

Then he gave me a tamboura, *and he taught me to play it right then. He told me, "Just play this tamboura for four months and listen to it."*

So for four months I played the tamboura, and one day while I was playing it, I just fell asleep. I slept for a long time, and when I woke up, my headache was gone.

When the war was going on between India and Pakistan, I used to listen to the radio. After the war was over, I didn't listen to the radio anymore. One day I turned on the BBC and the program was Radio Pakistan. The announcer said that they were going to broadcast a group reading of the Koran and that two thousand people were taking part in the recitation. I listened to them, but I could hear only two voices, and I began to wonder if they were telling the truth. Those two thousand people were reciting in such unison that the voices had become one. That is what it should sound like here. When we sing Hare Rama, *anyone who listens should feel that there are only two or three voices singing.*

CHAPTER 8

Let the Name Play in Every Cell

*The mantra is so juicy, so sweet. We repeat
the name of God and become one with it,
and the mind becomes still.*

*Could you give me a seed mantra that I could take with me to
guide me throughout my life?*

I have already given you the mantra. That is the seed of all
seeds.

*What is the relationship between receiving shaktipāt and
receiving the mantra?*

Mantra is for shaktipat. If a mantra does not awaken the inner
Shakti, of what use is it to you? The true mantra and the Shakti
are one. A Guru is one who can invest a mantra with life and
Consciousness. When you receive shaktipat from a Guru, you
receive it through the mantra. If you receive a mantra from a
true Guru, it will certainly cause shaktipat. Another mark of a
Guru is that in his presence yoga happens on its own; you don't
have to practice it.

*Is a mantra from a Master truly necessary or is it only for
certain people?*

Mantra is necessary for everyone. It is a kind of insurance that
makes up for all your losses. Mantra is the strongest flashlight

to illuminate darkness. It is the best friend who stands by you in misfortune. Mantra is also a great negotiator who brings the devotee and the Lord together.

Can an unrealized person give another person a mantra which works or must the mantra be "invested" by a realized being?

That mantra will bear fruit quickly which you receive from one who is aware of the power of mantra, the Consciousness behind mantra, and for whom mantra has borne full fruit. There are two kinds of mantras — those which are dead or unconscious and those which are alive or conscious. A dead mantra is one that you receive from a person for whom it has borne no fruit, and a live mantra is one that you receive from a person for whom it has borne full fruit. However, until you have found one who knows the secret of mantra, it is good to keep repeating some mantra.

I have been experiencing a lot of perfume and incense. One day I was with a patient and there was a strong fragrance of incense. Sometimes it happens when I recite the mantra you have given me. What is it?

That is the gift of the mantra to you. Whenever you get this fragrance, you should think that the deity of the mantra has blessed you. You should repeat the mantra more intensely, devote more time to it, and it will bear tremendous fruit for you. That is a Siddha mantra: it is extremely powerful and it begins to do its work immediately. It will help you in meditation also.

I am feeling more and more that I should leave what I am doing and spend more time doing the mantra and being with you.

If you were to devote more time to it now, later you could do much greater work than you are doing now. Then you could work for many thousands of people. You are a great soul.

The idea of a mantra deity is completely strange to me. Is there anything you can say to enlighten me on the subject?

The mantra deity is the One who is the goal of the mantra — the One who is Consciousness and Truth. The mantra deity is the One who creates a cosmos when He opens His eyes, and when He closes His eyes, the great dissolution takes place. He is most glorious, He is most powerful, and He is purest bliss. That is the goal of the mantra; that is Consciousness. He is subtler than the subtle. The mind is considered to be subtle, but He is subtler than the thoughts of the mind. He lives in the lotus of the heart, and from there He creates these diverse and manifold universes from His own glory. He completely fills this universe, becoming absolutely one with everyone.

If you add water to milk, the water becomes completely one with the milk; you can't tell the water from the milk or the milk from the water. In this way He is one with all the manifest creatures of the universe. He is the highest Being. He is the goal of the mantra; and if we repeat the mantra, being aware of Him, that mantra brings supreme peace.

Where shall we say He exists? He became rock and He permeates it both inside and out. He became fruit and He permeates it inside and out. He became human and He permeates humans outside and inside. He is the creator of everything; He became the entire universe. That is the deity of the mantra.

Could you tell me a little bit about how the mantra works?

The mantra can accomplish any kind of work. A mantra is that which takes a person across worldly existence. A mantra usually bears fruit immediately. However, if you cannot get the fruit immediately, you should keep repeating the mantra with faith and it will certainly do great work for you. A doctor can give the same pills to different people, but the results will depend on how deep-seated the disease is, how powerful a hold it has on you. Likewise, the mantra bears fruit immediately in some cases, while in others it takes a little time. The mantra permeates all seven constituents of the body; it also penetrates the *prāna* and cleanses the entire being. Therefore, the mantra has been called *Maheshwara*, the supreme Lord, the Self, the *ātman*.

There are different types of mantras. Our worldly life also depends entirely on mantras. Just as worldly mantras show their results right away, if you have faith in spiritual mantras, they too will show their results right away. I will give you a simple example. If you went to a fruit stand at the market and said, "Give me an apple," an apple would come into your hand. So you know that the mantra "Give me an apple" bears fruit immediately. This is a worldly mantra and it works in the same way. All our dealings in daily life are accomplished by means of these mantras.

The secret of mantra is even greater than the secret of meditation. It is even greater than what passes for knowledge. You can watch the process going on inside you: just sit quietly and you will see words rising from within. At first they arise as letters, and those letters combine to form words, and those words have certain meanings. Then your mind gets hung up on those meanings, which keep pushing it around and around. And these words never know any rest; ceaselessly they go around inside us, sometimes evoking lust, sometimes greed, sometimes anger, sometimes other emotions.

However, the great mantra constantly vibrates within us to destroy all that is evil and give rise to all that is good. Some mantras have been composed by great seers; others have been self-born. According to the Shaivite philosophy, *Om Namah Shivāya* arose of its own accord for Brahma, the Creator. So the mystery of the mantra is great. If we let lustful words vibrate inside us, our mind is overcome by lust. If we let angry words go on inside us, they fill our mind with anger. Likewise, if we let divine words go on inside us, they will fill us with God. So keep repeating the mantra with this understanding.

Even after repeating the mantra continuously in the ashram and in my daily life, bad thoughts still come to my mind. How can I get rid of them?

As you keep repeating the mantra, bad thoughts will be destroyed. From the same place where the mantra pulsates, bad thoughts also pulsate. There is a central nerve called the *sushumnā nāḍi.* All these thoughts and fantasies arise and subside there. The impressions of countless lifetimes are there.

You should repeat the mantra over and over again and try to purify the mind. If you pray to God with compassion, the mind becomes pure very quickly, and you have no bad thoughts. If you do not value time and if you do not respect God, then you let your mind wander here and there all the time.

In the *Rāmāyaṇa* this question is asked: "What is the fearful time?" The answer was, "The fearful time — which is like death — comes when the mind forgets about God and starts wandering here and there." The state that you are in is fearful; it is nothing but death. Therefore, you should immediately take refuge in God's name. Even after repeating your mantra, of course thoughts and fancies arise in your mind. But in between, just keep repeating your mantra, and the mind will become pure.

For the past few years I have been overcome with fear of violence. I have been meditating and it helps somewhat, but the fear is overwhelming.

There is a place of fear in the heart and if your mind touches that, you feel fear. The seers have described the heart *chakra* as a lotus with twelve petals. The mind keeps traveling from one petal to another. Whichever petal consciousness settles on for a while, it experiences the quality or characteristic of that petal. If consciousness were to light on the white petal, you would experience devotion to God. Likewise, there is a petal related to fear, and if your mind reaches there, it experiences fear.

In meditation also, this is what happens. Keep meditating and your consciousness will move from the place of fear to the place of fearlessness. Repeat the name of God. God's name destroys fear.

I am having terrible kriyās of jealousy and depression. I try to do my mantra but cannot get beyond these feelings. What can I do?

Keep repeating your mantra, and jealousy and depression will be transmuted. Depression will be transmuted into hope and faith, and jealousy will be transmuted into love. A poet-saint said that because of the power of the divine Name, when Mirabai drank poison, it turned into nectar. The divine Name has such potency. You should keep repeating your mantra.

Would you speak about the relationship between the repetition of mantra and kriyās? When kriyās arise, I don't know whether to just go with them or to repeat the mantra.

If you would continue to repeat your mantra, the kriyas would become even more enjoyable. All the kriyas become permeated by the mantra. The sound of each repetition fills the entire bloodstream and all the elements of the body. That is a very great practice. Then no matter where you go, you hear only the mantra. As the mantra vibrates more and more inside you, the goal of the mantra — which is pure love — begins to flow in the heart.

Can we do anything to increase our devotion to you, or is devotion itself a gift of grace?

To increase devotion, you can increase your affection. If you repeat the mantra constantly, after a while the mantra turns into devotion.

If one has little or no feeling when saying the mantra, is it still all right to keep repeating it right through the day — even when working?

Keep repeating it even while working. The mantra will bring depth of feeling in you. Repeat it any way you want to. If you sow seeds in the earth, sometimes they fall right side up and sometimes they fall wrong side up. Still, however they are sown, they grow straight up. In the same way, repeat the name of God any way you want and it will bear fruit for you.

Is meditation on the Guru the same as repeating the mantra? If they are different, can you do both simultaneously?

Meditation on the Guru, meditation on God, meditation on the inner Self, and *japa* — all these four are one. It is only when these four become one that your yogic practice will be consummated and your *sādhanā* will be fulfilled. If you cannot integrate these with your meditation, you will not fulfill yourself. If the mantra, the one who repeats the mantra, the Lord of the mantra, and the Guru are not integrated, the mantra will not bear fruit.

The mantra that we receive from the Guru is the Guru in the form of sound. The correct way of doing the mantra is to be aware of the identity of the mantra with the Guru.

Is it possible to have an understanding of mantra as being one with me, God, and the Self, and still not be fully aware of it?

It's a very good question. This is the right awareness — that the one who is the Guru is also the Self, and he is also God. Shiva says that the Guru is me, and I am the Guru. There is absolutely no difference between the two. Any difference is only in language. Mantra reveals its power only when you become fully aware that the mantra, the inner Self, God, and Guru are one and the same.

Mantra is true, God is true, and the inner Self is true. Worship of God is true. The word of the Guru is true. It is only Truth that brings triumph. You will become fully aware of this Truth and fully convinced of it when, through regular meditation, one day you will have a vision of the Blue Pearl. Then the Blue Pearl will expand, and within that light you will first see God and then your Guru and then yourself. Then you will become convinced of the total identity of the three.

REPEAT THE MANTRA OBSTINATELY

How can I transcend those times when I feel confused and unable to concentrate and find peace inside?

Keep repeating your mantra. Keep repeating it obstinately. If you keep at the mantra come what may, you will certainly transcend confusion. This is exactly what the mantra is for — to bring the mind to heel. The purpose of mantra repetition is concentration of mind.

How can one concentrate on the formless and control the mind?

First, concentrate on the mantra, and the mantra will take you to the formless One. As you pursue *Hamsa* more and more, it will take you to the formless One. As you meditate continually, there comes a point when you forget what is outside and what is inside. You also forget yourself completely. It is at this point that you are meditating on the formless One.

[*Hamsa* and *So'ham* are the same mantra; the syllables are reversed according to whether one inhales or exhales first.]

Should we use So'ham *in meditation?*

You should repeat *So'ham* until you become completely absorbed in meditation. If you were to get lost in meditation, the mantra would disappear by itself. You wouldn't have to try to leave it. *So'ham* is the gateway to the kingdom of meditation. Keep repeating *So'ham* as much as you can.

I notice that it is easier to repeat mantras in places where people have repeated them before. Should I seek to meditate in those places?

Yes, but you can create a place for meditation anywhere. It's true that in a place where many people have repeated the mantra, particles of Shakti permeate the atmosphere; that's why you can meditate very easily there.

In the Himalayas there is an ashram that belonged to the sage Kakabushundi. He used to repeat, "*Shrī Rām, Shrī Rām, Shrī Rām.*" The whole atmosphere there is filled with that mantra. As a result, everyone who goes there begins to repeat, "*Shrī Rām, Shrī Rām, Shrī Rām.*" In the same way, Lord Buddha practiced nonviolence, and anyone who went to the place where he meditated would also become nonviolent while there. Even a cow and a tiger would sit there together very quietly. This is not such a great miracle; it simply means that the atmosphere had become permeated with Buddha's nonviolence. In the same way, your heart should be filled with the feeling of the mantra, with the space of the mantra. Then you won't lack joy and peace.

Please explain the following. When I am in bed, I feel like restricting the mantra to Om. *I hear a constant sound like an electric motor and at times I concentrate on that.*

It's very good to concentrate on that sound. When a particular sound arises within, that is the mantra for you. Lose yourself in listening to that sound. That is a good and great *sādhanā*. Keep listening to that sound. That is a straight road; with faith walk on that road. As you listen to the sound constantly, you will begin to taste nectar at the root of your tongue. In the space of the *sahasrāra* there is nectar. A meditator, by listening to that sound, begins to taste that nectar. If you go to sleep listening to that, you will hear it throughout the night and you will have a sound sleep called *yoga nidrā* — the sleep of a *yogi*. Hearing that sound is a great attainment. Shaivism says that the divine sound is the greatest mantra.

I never used a mantra before this week and now that I am using it, I feel a tremendous pulling in the center of my forehead. Am I using the mantra wrongly or am I doing it right?

It is completely right. In the sahasrara, there is a pot of nectar. Its mouth is turned upward, and as you do more japa and meditation, it will be tilted downward. When that elixir falls on the root of the tongue, it goes to your heart, and you will experience profound peace.

Why is it that when I meditate, I quickly fall away from the mantra and into something I am not sure of? This morning I may have fallen asleep, but I felt conscious of my thoughts. Yet when I came out of it, I remembered nothing.

This is a high state of meditation. To get into the state in which you cannot do the mantra any longer — that is meditation. However, the mantra should not be replaced by all kinds of thoughts and fancies. If that happens, it means that you are not doing japa, mantra, or meditation.

There was a great devotee in Maharashtra who wrote in a song: "O Lord, while I was remembering You, I got into a state where I lost awareness of myself; nor was I conscious of the mode of worship. Everything was blotted out. Only Consciousness remained. O Lord, play Your flute again, so that I may come back to myself."

This is a good state to be in. It is not necessary that the mantra should go on all the time. In fact, you should reach a state in which the mantra disappears. If you can stay in that *laya*, that state of complete inner absorption, it would be high *tapasya*. It would be a state of total inner stillness.

Often when I lie down to rest, the mantra starts spontaneously and I see bright lights and visions. But when I sit to meditate, I get a rush of thoughts and no lights and visions. Why is this?

It's very good if the mantra starts spontaneously and you see lights and visions when you are lying down. When you are lying down, you are not worried about meditation or anything else; you are relaxed. But when you sit for meditation, you think about not thinking, and when you think of not having any thoughts, there is a rush of thoughts. Just as you relax when you lie down to sleep, in the same way when you sit for meditation, you should relax, and then you will get that state too.

Whatever modification the mind goes through, whatever thought the mind has, don't think about that. Whatever arises from the mind, consider it the world of the mind, and then you will have very good meditation.

The inspiration of the mind is not different from Chiti. Understand that Chiti, the Goddess, has taken the form of the mind; then you won't have any trouble. The *Pratyabhijñā-*

hridayam says that it is the same Chiti, the same Kundalini, the same Goddess, the same vibration, that descends from the level of pure Consciousness and mixes with objects and takes the form of objects. That is how it becomes the mind. Therefore, the mind is not the mind. It is Chiti.

Whatever world arises and subsides in the mind, consider that Chiti and sit in meditation. You will feel more blissful. This is true meditation. This is the meditation of wise people, of the highest people. How can the mind exist without Chiti, without Consciousness? Every thought, negative or positive, arises from Chiti. Therefore, change your understanding. Then you will enjoy your meditation.

LET YOUR LIFE BECOME FULL
OF THE MANTRA

How may I go about choosing a mantra?

The person who is going to give you a mantra has chosen it already. Why do you take the trouble of choosing a mantra? You need not choose.

Please tell me something about how to use the mantra.

You should be the repeater, and you should also be the listener. Listen to it from within as you repeat it silently. Use it like this and it will awaken your inner Consciousness.

Please speak to us about the importance of japa and how it is best performed.

Lord Shankara said, "O beloved one, if you do japa, if you repeat the mantra, you can attain everything." He said it three times: "O beloved one, if you do japa, you will attain everything, you will attain everything, you will attain everything." It is only because japa is taking place that a person lives. Once japa stops, a person dies. Japa is going on in all beings; you don't have to do it, it is happening. Just become aware of it. Once you become aware of it, you will be liberated from this identification with the *jīva* and then you will merge into God. In the *Bhagavad Gītā* in the chapter on *vibhūti yoga*, the Lord said, "In the *yajña*, in the fire ritual, I am japa, I am the mantra." So repeat the mantra with that awareness. There is a particular way of becoming aware of doing japa. If you want complete understanding of this, read *I Am That*.

What are the obligations after receiving a mantra from you?
What if the person has already received the Gayatri Mantra?

The *Gāyatrī Mantra* is a long mantra. It is very difficult; it won't help much in your meditation. It is meant for a different purpose. The sages have recommended shorter mantras for meditation. Anyone who receives the mantra from here should repeat it in his heart, combining it with his breath. Let your life become full of the mantra. No matter how you make your living, keep repeating your mantra.

Mantra yoga is great yoga. If you have received the mantra from me, you should repeat it all the time. The first step would be to go to sleep while repeating the mantra. After you lie down, be aware that the mantra is above, below, in front, and behind. Repeat the mantra and go to sleep. One who goes to sleep repeating the mantra will find he is repeating it when he wakes up. If it is not going on, repeat the mantra and then get up. When you wash your face, repeat the mantra; when you drink your coffee, repeat the mantra; when you eat your breakfast, repeat the mantra. Travel to your office repeating the mantra; enter your office repeating the mantra; leave your office repeating the mantra; come back home repeating the mantra. When you sit down to eat a meal, first repeat the mantra eleven times and blow on the food; that will purify it. It will permeate your food with mantric vibrations. This is the yoga of mantra.

Everyone should follow these instructions. When you drink, whether it is coffee or tea or milk, blow the mantra into it and then drink. In this way the mantra comes to permeate your being very quickly. While having a bath, keep repeating your mantra. This way the bath that you give yourself will become a sacred bath, and you will become your own deity. This is the way to make the mantra an active force inside of you.

Do you know that one who repeats the mantra intensely will find that even his clothes begin to vibrate with the mantra, and if anyone were to hold his shirt, they would hear the mantra? Mantra is a living force. The fact is that the mantra is vibrating in everything but we are not aware of it. If you strike the earth, the sound that it makes is nothing but mantra. Now I am striking the table, and the sound that is produced is the mantra of the table. While the wind blows, it repeats its mantra. When the water flows, it repeats its murmuring mantra. This is how you should repeat your mantra. Anyone who repeats the mantra will find that all the deities come and stand solidly behind him and support him.

When do you stop saying the mantra? Or do you just keep saying it?

You should keep repeating your mantra, and when the mind becomes completely silent and focused, the mantra will stop by itself. When the mind becomes totally focused, you will find it difficult to repeat the mantra.

At times when I repeat my mantra, it does not disappear but takes the form of light or of your face, and it remains unmoving in my consciousness. It takes an effort to make it go away. Can you please explain why this happens? Also at times my eyes go to the top of my head and I cannot tell the difference between the inside and the outside. This happens mostly when I am with you.

If you repeat the mantra with great respect, the deity of the mantra appears before you. This is certain. Therefore, we give a lot of respect to the mantra. For this reason a wise person repeats only one mantra and he does no business with the mantra. What you have said is true: as you repeat the mantra, a form appears that is the deity of the mantra, and the same deity merges inside you. Keep repeating it. The mantra is also divine light, the light of the Self.

A sage said that in this very body the self-born light exists. This light is very beautiful and very loving. However, this light appears before you or manifests before you only when you become free from faults. The mantra has great importance. As you repeat the mantra, the eyes move toward the sahasrara, the crown of the head, and there you see the Blue Pearl. There is divine light in the crown chakra. It is called the *sahasrāra* because the rays of a thousand suns are there. One day you will see it. To see it, your eyes turn upward toward the top of your head.

It is good to discover that the inside and outside are the same. It is not true that there is one thing inside and something else outside. Nanakdev used to say that what is inside is also outside, what is outside is also inside; it is the same Principle which pervades everything. This is called knowledge — the understanding that inside and outside are the same. With this understanding, man becomes the friend of happiness.

I have been repeating my mantra for a few months, but nothing seems to be happening. What is wrong?

Nothing is wrong. Keep repeating the mantra. When something is supposed to happen, it will happen. Your main duty is to focus your attention and to make sure that the mantra is going on in you. Your attention should not go to that place where you imagine that something should be happening but is not. The *Bhagavad Gītā* says to perform good deeds constantly. Never think about when your deeds are going to bear fruit or what fruits they are going to bear.

Somebody once said to the great *yogini* Rabi'a, "O Rabi'a, you are constantly moving your *japa mālā*. Do you ever have any experiences?"

She replied, "It does not matter whether or not I am having any experiences. It does not matter as long as He experiences that I am repeating His name." So repeat the mantra very quietly.

I am a coach and need to analyze situations quickly and to remember details. But my mind seems to go blank at times, and I have no answers for my team. When I use my mantra, I see only the mantra. Please help me.

At such times, give up repeating the mantra for a while and think only about the team. As you repeat the mantra for a long time, it begins to give you the fruit of that mantra repetition. Then you will not have to think about the team. The fruit of the mantra will make you so worthy that you will be able to give the answer very quickly. I never think very long about anything. Even while coming and going, I only repeat the mantra. If anyone asks me a question, I have an immediate answer for him. Every week I receive a thousand letters and I answer all of them. I have to give answers very quickly because I do not have time to think about anything. This is the power of the Name.

When I start seeing pictures in meditation, should I stay with the mantra or should I follow the picture?

It is the mantra that brings those pictures, so why look at the pictures? Stay with the mantra.

I am confused about how to do japa. Should I just pick one mantra and repeat it all the time? Sometimes I feel like thinking, Ram, Ram, Ram. *Sometimes* Om Namah Shivaya *pops up spontaneously. Sometimes* Guru Om *hops in. And sometimes I contemplate the nature of the Self. What is best to do?*

The best thing is to contemplate the nature of the Self. Whatever name comes to your mind, know that it is the name of the Self. In meditation you can repeat *Guru Om, Guru Om* — that is also very good. If you repeat a single name with one-pointedness, that will remain with you, and all the others will just go away. You should not focus your attention on the names themselves, but on the goal. Focus your attention on the goal of all the names.

If I do japa without complete understanding of the mantra, will it still be beneficial for me? Will repeating the mantra help me to gain understanding that Shiva, the mantra, and I are one?

First of all, you should have complete understanding that your soul is the Self, your soul is God. It is identical with God. If you repeat the mantra with this awareness, the mantra bears fruit immediately. If you have dual awareness that the mantra is one, the person who repeats the mantra is another, and the goal of the mantra is different from them, it does not bear fruit.

Just repeat the mantra. By repeating it, you will gain understanding. Even if you do not understand it, but you have devotion and faith, that is sufficient because the One for whom you repeat it knows that you are repeating the mantra. Tulsidas said that no matter how you repeat the mantra, even if you repeat it with laziness, with negligence, and with bad feelings, still it is all right. It bears fruit nonetheless.

There is a particular method of repeating the mantra, yet what you really need is love and faith. The mantra is the manifestation of God. The mantra is true, the Guru is true, the goal of the mantra is true, and the worship is true — all of these are true when you become true. If you are not true, nothing is true. If you are false, the mantra cannot be true for you. So first of all, you have to become true, you have to become honest. To become true is to have the awareness *aham Brahmāsmi*, "I am the Absolute." That is the right remembrance. If a person knows "I am the Truth, I am Consciousness, I am the Self," only then is he true. He speaks the Truth, he knows the Truth; otherwise he tells lies, and he does not know the Truth. You become true when you have the awareness in your heart "I am the Truth."

Look at your own mind. Always you are thinking and thinking. You have one thought or another in your mind about yourself. Sometimes you think you are petty, sometimes you think you are wretched, sometimes you think you belong to a certain class, sometimes to another class, sometimes you think you are poor, sometimes rich. In this way, you have one thought after another, one feeling after another about yourself.

Then why not have the awareness, *So'ham*, "I am That"? What is the difficulty? Tell me! Instead of having evil thoughts all the time, isn't it much better to have good thoughts? Your entire life will be transformed. In this way you become true. You become so pure. As long as you do not understand that you are *So'ham*, that you are That, you are false from the spiritual standpoint. You may be true from the worldly standpoint, but from the spiritual standpoint you are false. When you have the awareness, "I am not just a part of Him, but I *am* He," only then do you become true.

When I repeat the mantra, I sometimes reach a state where I'm not saying it anymore, but just observing it going on. Could you comment on this?

This is a very great state. While you repeat the mantra, you should get into this state. This shows that within a short time you are going to experience the inner Self, the inner peace, and also that you will experience happiness in your life. There is a poem by Kabir with a very profound meaning. He says, "My tongue does not repeat the name of Ram, these teeth are also not working to repeat the name of Ram. My tongue is very quiet. I am sitting here very relaxed, but Ram is repeating my mantra." This is how it should be.

The mantra should be going on within you, and you should be very quiet and listen to that mantra. Throughout your life you have been performing good and bad actions. You think, "I have done this; I am doing this; I am going to do this." The contemplation of these actions takes place in your mind, and sometimes you wonder why you are thinking about your actions without even making an effort. So these thoughts, good and bad, go on in your mind, and after that they permeate your vital force, your blood, and every pore of your body. You constantly think about these actions, and then these actions come out of your being; you begin to perform them.

In the same way, if you repeat the mantra constantly, the mantra burns up all your old impressions. Once you are purified, the mantra is being repeated within you all the time. After

177

that the mantra descends from the tongue to the throat. Then you begin to hear the mantra inside your throat. And after that you begin to hear the mantra in your heart. Very subtly, if you try to listen to the mantra within you, you hear it in your heart. When the mantra repeats in your heart, you attain supernatural powers, but these powers are nothing great. You also begin to know things that are going to happen in the future, or that are happening somewhere far away from you. Then the mantra descends from your heart to your navel. When it reaches the navel, you attain divinity.

On the spiritual path, miracles do not have any importance. I know how to perform many kinds of miracles. Someday I might reveal them to you, but if I did that, wise people would say, "He is a thief among *sādhus*." That's what they would say about me if I did that. This world itself is a great miracle. Even the tiniest birds fly in the sky. That is such a great miracle. So if a sadhu tries to show off his miracles, what is so great about that? Even the tiniest fish swims in the ocean. It continues to swim even when the big waves come, and it does not need the support of a ship or machines or anything else. Isn't that a great miracle? If you attain the state of a sadhu by chanting and by worshiping and by remembering God, but then you display your few miracles, do you think you will be greater than the tiniest fish and the tiniest bird?

The real miracle is to change yourself. To invoke the inner Shakti and to get the benefit of the inner Shakti is the great miracle. To burn your ordinary individuality in the fire of Kundalini and to attain divinity is the greatest miracle, and that is the miracle of God. It is completely valid.

Thank you for your question. You have described a very good state. And I also thank you for your sadhana.

THEY ARE ALL THE SAME

Why are there so many different mantras?

Truly, they are not different; they are all the same. Both *So'ham* and *Guru Om* emanate from the primal sound *Om*. You can chant any mantra because every mantra is the name of God. But you shouldn't be deluded about the mantra: no Guru repeats fifty mantras. He repeats only one mantra, and that mantra becomes conscious. He attains something from that mantra. Only then does he give that mantra to other people. *Namah Shivāya* has come down from the original Guru. There are no differences among these mantras: *Om, So'ham,* and *Guru Om* — they are all the same. If you start lacking faith in the mantra, it becomes very difficult to turn inward.

So'ham *is the gateway to meditation,* Guru Om *is the king of mantras, and* Om Namah Shivaya *is the great redeemer. Is that because they are all the same?*

You seem to have studied this very carefully. It is true that all three are one. He whom we call the Guru is also known as Shiva, so *Om Namah Shivāya* and *Guru Om* refer to one and the same Being. The only difference between the two is that while *Om Namah Shivāya* has five syllables in Sanskrit [not counting *Om*], *Guru Om* has just two syllables.

The mantra is called the redeemer because it protects and saves the one who repeats it. Keep repeating the name of the Lord at all hours of the day while coming and going. Direct your awareness inward to the Lord dwelling there. If you persist in your mantra, you are bound to see the indwelling Lord —if not today, then tomorrow, and if not tomorrow, then the day after. Whether you see Him or not is not of such great importance; what is important is the repetition of the mantra.

The desire to see God is nothing more than the desire to invite a person to come and visit you on a particular day. Let the Lord reveal Himself to you whenever He wants to; let Him visit you whenever He feels like it. But you should continually sing His name within you with love.

The truth is that God fills us completely within and without, and it does not matter whether we see Him or not. What matters is that we keep singing His name joyfully all the time.

If I feel drowsy while meditating, should I surrender to that state or struggle to stay with the mantra?

If you feel sleepy while meditating, then sleep. But also keep repeating your mantra. When you feel drowsy, repeat your mantra again and again. There is a kind of meditative sleep that gives great peace. As far as possible, repeat the mantra as intensely as you can. Even if you can't get into meditation, it will not matter as long as you keep repeating your mantra. Japa has enormous power.

All the great sages and saints achieved their divine power through japa. Lord Shiva says to Parvati, "By japa, realization. By japa, realization. By japa, realization." You may follow other spiritual practices, but you must do japa all the time. In India some people carry beads, small malas, with them all the time. This is to help them do continual japa. Japa purifies you totally inside and outside. Japa is the most effective method because you can do it no matter what else you are doing, no matter where you are.

There was a saint in Maharashtra who said that you should repeat God's name continually, whether coming or going, sitting or standing, giving or taking, speaking or chewing your bread. So give up your sense of shyness about it and keep repeating God's name to yourself everywhere, at every moment. In the *Mahābhārata* the Lord says that in Kali Yuga, the present age, japa alone, japa alone, japa alone, is the way to attain Him. There is no other way. There is no other way. There is no other way.

How should one repeat Om Namah Shivaya —*with the breath, at the point between the eyebrows, in the heart, or at the top of the head?*

You should focus on the mantra itself and try to discover the place from where the mantra arises. Sit quietly, look at what is happening, and start repeating your mantra. Try to see where it is vibrating, and focus your mind on that place. While you are repeating a mantra, do not direct your mind to any place other than where the mantra is vibrating. That is the quickest way of realizing its power. I will tell you the secret of realizing a mantra quickly: for one who sees the Self as the supreme Lord, the mantra bears fruit immediately.

One should repeat the mantra with absolute regularity for some time every day. While riding in my car, I repeat *Om Namah Shivāya* very intensely. For this reason I don't let anybody else sit in my car — because then my mantra repetition is interrupted. Intuition is developed through mantra repetition. You should talk less, but that doesn't mean you become indifferent. If you want to repeat the mantra, you cannot afford to be gossiping or talking idly. When you practice mantra, you do not have to struggle to combine the mantra with your breath; it will blend into your breath by itself in due course.

Hold the mantra within the heart. Then see what happens to the mind.

I notice that many of your devotees use a japa mālā. Would you please speak to us about the place of the mālā in sādhanā?

If you want a japa mala, you can have one. It will be very good; it will interrupt your gossip. I also use one. If anybody comes to meet me, I take my japa mala with me. If they speak well, it's fine; if they don't speak properly, I start doing my japa. Otherwise the time is wasted in gibberish and gossip.

I obtain a lot of joy from japa and chanting, but during meditation I have lots of thoughts in my mind. I cannot cool them down. What attitude should I have toward them?

If you derive a lot of joy from japa and chanting, why don't you do japa during meditation? Your joy will increase. Forget about meditation and do japa instead. That is also meditation. Joy, happiness, and supreme bliss are necessary for us — not some technique. The technique is not essential. Keep doing japa. It contains great bliss. An ordinary person cannot understand the mystery of japa. If there is something of great value, you need an equally great person to understand it.

Tukaram Maharaj said that japa is very easy. It is not at all hard to do. It is not strenuous. However, only a wise person can attain it, not a person who lacks understanding. Just as meditation is a yoga in itself, so is japa.

In the *Bhagavad Gītā* the Lord says that there are many different sadhanas by which one can attain Him, such as *karma yoga, jnāna yoga,* and *ashtānga yoga.* He says, "I am attained by people according to their natures." Speaking about mantra repetition, He says, "The mantra is not just the *means* to attain Me; I *am* mantra. Mantra japa is My very nature."

In the beginning japa is sadhana. At the end, japa itself is the fruit of sadhana. An Indian saint used to say that the name of God is so full of nectar, so full of joy and happiness, that only a sharp and penetrating intellect can know it. The name of Ram is so sweet that there is nothing sweeter. Whoever drinks it becomes Parashiva, God Himself. Therefore, keep doing japa.

While doing japa, you will get into the *tandrā* state. Understand that this is also a great yoga. As you do japa with the tongue, it descends to the throat. As you do japa in the throat, it descends to the heart. When it descends to the heart, you experience the intoxication of tandra. Generally, one receives fascinating revelations from within when this occurs. Various siddhis are also obtained. When japa descends from the heart to the navel, the inner Shakti Kundalini is awakened. One attains divine enlightenment and has the vision of God, divine and radiant in the sahasrara. Japa has so much power. But you should not do it with any desire. You should do japa for the sake of japa.

At the retreat you gave me the mantra Om Namah Shivaya. *Since then I have been repeating it in meditation. However, I realize that I do not know much about this mantra. Please speak a little about how I may best use it.*

You should keep repeating the mantra silently; don't let anyone hear it. While repeating the mantra, be aware that the deity of the mantra lives right in your heart. No matter what word it is, if we repeat it in our heart, it is bound to do its work. The sages say that your own Self is the goal of the mantra and that we should repeat the mantra with this awareness. *Om Namah Shivāya* is a mantra that refers to God. There is no other meaning. God lives in the heart; He is our best well-wisher, and He is the giver of peace.

Om Namah Shivaya is translated as "Salutations to Shiva" or "I bow to Shiva." In English "bow" can also mean submit or surrender. Does "namah" have this meaning too?

That's the right meaning of *namah*. It does mean to surrender. As you repeat the mantra continuously, you lose yourself in the mantra, which means that you lose yourself in surrender. A person who bows to God becomes one with God. You have asked a beautiful question. I am also happy because you have given the answer to your own question.

If I use the mantra Om Namah Shivaya, is it important for me to study Indian mythology and the literature about Shiva?

It is not necessary. You do need the knowledge of Shiva, but to become one with Shiva it is not necessary to depend on Indian mythology, scripture, or religion. He is Shiva who exists everywhere within everything at all times and who dwells within everyone in the form of Consciousness. The meaning of Shiva doesn't change when translated into the French language; it remains the same. What do you call water in French? In Hindi, we call it *pani*. Even though we use a different word in Hindi, still the water is the same as it is in France. Therefore, when we say *Shiva*, we are not referring to any individual being. Shiva is that Consciousness dwelling within everything; Shiva is the doer of everything. He is the Self of all. He exists within and without. Without knowledge of Him, this appears to be a mere world. With knowledge of Him, this world appears as God.

Please tell us more about the meaning of Om Namah Shivaya.

Om Namah Shivāya means supreme Truth, everlasting peace,

divine power. In the *Shiva Purāna*, there is a long dialogue between the great sage Upamanyu and Lord Krishna about the importance of *Om Namah Shivāya*. If I were to tell you all that is written there, it would take me at least two hours a day for the next two months.

Shiva is the same as the supreme Guru, the Lord, the highest Guru. His form consists of *sat chit ānanda* — Existence, Consciousness, and Bliss. Truth is the Being who never changes, who remains the same in all places at all times and in all forms, the Being who is pure, who never alters, even while dwelling in circumstances that keep on changing, decaying, and dying. And this true Being dwells in all of you, in me, and in every creature. When Shiva is Chiti, the Consciousness that illumines everything, He is throbbing in the heart as bliss. So this supreme Shiva is the goal of *Om Namah Shivāya*.

In another aspect, He is presented as the destroyer. He destroys all the sins and impurities of those who repeat his name with *Om Namah Shivāya*. Shiva is the Being who puts an end to all our inner changes. He is the supremely quiescent Being. In Him there is no such thing as the universe. Shiva is without any support. All of us have to depend on some support or other, but Shiva does not depend on any outer factor. He is supremely free and effulgent. He is always sparkling and shining from within. This is the meaning of *Om Namah Shivāya*.

When we chant Om Namah Shivaya, *I can clearly hear beautiful celestial voices. I don't hear them with any other chant. Is there a special quality about* Om Namah Shivaya *that reveals itself right away?*

It's fine. It seems that *Om Namah Shivāya* has become your friend — that's why this happens. So you should repeat this mantra more. Repeat it in your meditation; make it your dear friend. It should become your greatest friend, greater than all your other friends. Then it will give you great joy and it will also do a lot of work for you. It can do that because it has great power.

Why do we always chant the mantra Om Namah Shivaya *in the evening programs and the Intensives? Why not other mantras?*

Om Namah Shivāya is a great mantra. Other mantras are all right. There are mantras that were composed by great seers who experienced and perceived them. There are mantras that emanated from the ether; nobody composed them; nobody wrote them; they did not come from anybody's intellect. *Om Namah Shivāya* is a mantra that emanated from the sound of the ether. The Lord of Kailasa said to Maitreyi, "O Maitreyi, the practice of japa is greater than all sadhanas, greater than all other pursuits. Among all the mantras, the five-syllabled *Namah Shivāya* mantra is great." (Even though we say *Om Namah Shivāya*, if you don't count *Om*, then *Namah Shivāya* contains five syllables.) It does not matter whether one is a woman or a man, a child or an old person, good or bad, illiterate or educated — everybody can repeat this mantra. This mantra will redeem anybody who repeats it.

The sage Upamanyu repeated this particular mantra and explained its secret to Lord Krishna in this way: if the mantra vibrates in a person's heart all the time, that person has no need of austerities, meditation, yoga, or *āsanas*. For every mantra there is a particular initiation. Most mantras bear fruit only when you also perform rituals and ceremonies. Upamanyu explained that to repeat *Om Namah Shivāya* you don't need any rituals or yajnas. To give this mantra and to repeat it, you do not need an auspicious time or place. This mantra is ever pure; no matter in which state a person repeats this mantra, it will purify him.

So you call God with these letters, *Namah Shivāya*. The mantra has its own power. All the great beings sang this mantra. The sages said, "This is the great mantra, always repeat it, repeat it, repeat it." This mantra is very mysterious. I could talk for a month on each syllable. These five syllables are the form of the five elements. These five syllables destroy the five agonies or afflictions. Every syllable has its own supreme power.

I received Om Namah Shivaya *as my initiation mantra, but since I have been here, the mantra* Guru Om *keeps coming up in meditation. Now I am confused, and I would like to know which mantra I should use.*

All the mantras are the same, and the goal of all mantras is also the same. You should not have any confusion. You can repeat *Guru Om.* Shiva and the Guru are one, so *Om Namah Shivāya* and *Guru Om* denote the same thing. Before beginning our programs, we always recite the introductory mantras. The first of those mantras is *Om Namah Shivāya.* To whom does *Om Namah Shivāya* refer? It refers to the Guru, the supreme Guru. The scriptural authors say that this entire world is created by the trinity of Brahma, Vishnu, and Shiva. It is the job of Brahma to create the universe. Vishnu sustains it. Shiva dissolves it.

There are infinite creations that are nothing but inner thoughts, sometimes positive and sometimes negative. Because of them, we suffer. Thoughts arise and subside inside us, and in the same way, creation arises and subsides inside God. According to our own creation, we feel happy or unhappy. If thoughts do not arise, we will reach a state where there is no happiness or unhappiness. As long as the inner creations continue, man cannot have a good and happy sleep.

Only the Guru, who is also called Shiva, can destroy the inner creations of one's imagination through wisdom, through meditation, and through grace. When we repeat *Om Namah Shivāya* and offer our salutations to Shiva, we are also offering our salutations to the Guru. What is the Guru's true image? It is sat chit ananda — Existence, Consciousness, and Bliss. The Guru is completely serene and without thought. He does not depend on anything; he gives support to everything. He is a mass of light. If you repeat *Om Namah Shivāya* it refers to that Guru, and if you repeat *Guru Om,* it refers to the same Guru. Therefore, you have no reason to be confused.

Do you still recommend Guru Om *as a good mantra for deep meditation?*

Yes, of course it's a good mantra. You read the *Guru Gītā*, don't you? If you do, you know that it emphasizes this mantra. Shivaji said, "O Goddess, this word *Guru*, composed of two letters, is the greatest of mantras. According to the words of the Vedas and Smritis, the Guru is the highest reality itself." Therefore, it is a very good mantra. Even the two syllables *gu* and *ru* are truly great. A sage said that *gu* dispels darkness and *ru* reveals light inside you. Therefore, the mantra *Guru* is the sovereign of all other mantras.

Could you please tell us how to combine the mantra Guru Om *with the breath?*

You should repeat the whole mantra *Guru Om* once with your inbreath and once with your outbreath. While combining the mantra with the breath, you should also be aware of its meaning. When you combine the mantra with your breathing, it becomes natural japa or *ajapā-japa*. Saints have said that one who practices ajapa-japa is delivered from both sin and virtue and becomes completely pure. As you combine *Guru Om* with the inbreath and outbreath, you will find it quite easy to glide into the state of *samādhi* and experience the Self. Keep repeating *Guru Om, Guru Om*. It is a great mantra, it is a divine mantra; it is also called the king of mantras.

My devotion and right understanding are always coming and going. How can I achieve a steady state of gurubhāva? Is repeating my mantra Guru Om *the best method?*

Yes, to repeat *Guru Om* is the best method. Man becomes whatever he constantly thinks about. Therefore, gurubhava, or identification with the Guru, is very good. You don't really have to attain gurubhava. If you simply lose the identification with yourself, whatever is left is gurubhava. Therefore, give up your own *bhāva*. If you do this, you attain the steady state of gurubhava. The highest bhava has a lot of strength.

In Maharashtra there was a great saint and yogi called Kesarinath. He used to give great lectures on bhava, on feeling.

He used to tell people to have the kind of bhava in which you yourself become God. Great feeling has the power to turn you into God. He also said that no matter what anyone says to you, don't let it spoil your own feeling. Discard praise and blame, attain great love, and have the feeling of the Self. Give up identification with ideas of "thine" and "mine." In reality, there is no bondage, there is no ignorance. If a person gets rid of his ego and attains the awareness of So'ham, he becomes sublime. For that reason, bhava, or great feeling, is the divine mantra.

You see this world as a mere world containing sentient and insentient objects, but the truth of the matter is that this whole world is the bhava of God, the great feeling of God. The Lord Himself says that the whole world and all its creatures exist in His own feeling. So change your old bhava, and attain new bhava. Then find out how much happiness you have inside yourself.

THE GATEWAY TO MEDITATION

Can a man discover his own inner mantra?

Man is born just for that.
How can he recognize the sound?
Sit with a silent mind in a silent place and listen carefully to what is going on inside you. You will be able to hear that mantra. If you are repeating your ordinary mantra, you won't be able to hear the inner mantra. By "your ordinary mantra" I mean the chatter and the tapes that keep running in your mind all the time.

So sit quietly and let your prana become even, and empty your mind of all the old tapes. Then you can hear the mantra as the breath comes in and goes out.

I am using Om Namah Shivaya *for meditation and for japa but I find it easier, especially when I am working, to coordinate the* So'ham *mantra with my breath. It is more pleasant. Which mantra should I use?*

You should use the mantra that gives you joy. *So'ham* is a very well-respected mantra. *So'ham* japa is called *ajapā-japa*, the japa that you don't have to practice. It is constantly repeating itself within you. If you become aware of it, it has the power to destroy all your sins. This is a fact. The *So'ham* mantra is ancient and without beginning.

During the Intensive you said that the breath comes in with the sound ham *and goes out with the sound* sa. *Are you referring to a sound in the physical body or a sound in the subtle body or something else?*

It happens in all the bodies, in all four bodies—the physical body, the subtle body, the causal body, and the supracausal body. It arises from the supracausal body.

This morning in meditation I had difficulty being with the So'ham *mantra. Often* Om Namah Shivaya *would come. Sometimes in meditation the name of* Rama *comes. Should I let them be as they arise or become one-pointed on one mantra?*

If you want to pursue sadhana, you have to become one-pointed on one mantra. Convince Rama that He is also *So'ham*. Tell *Om* that He is also *So'ham*. Tell them to keep quiet and they will listen to you.

Must the mantra Hamsa *always be repeated in rhythm with the breath, or can I repeat it spontaneously during the day as I reflect upon its meaning?*

Ideally, one should not be repeating *Hamsa*. One should be able to hear it as it goes on inside. If you can get into the state in which you hear it, that is good. If you cannot, then repeat it.

Hamsa is self-born; it has been going on within you since the moment of your birth. It is not something new that you have to learn. When this japa ceases, you also cease. It is only highly evolved souls who understand its mystery. A sage has said that within all creatures the japa of *Hamsa* is going on all the time. You don't have to repeat it, but you do have to become aware of it. The moment you become aware of it going on within, you are liberated.

Sit still and inhale and see what sound your breath makes as it comes in — it makes the sound *ham*. Then exhale and see what sound the breath makes as it goes out — it makes the sound *sa*. A saint said that one who becomes *Hamsa* by repeating it doesn't see the world as the world any longer; he sees it as God. And although he lives in a body, he experiences a state transcending the body. Great saints and Gurus repeat *Hamsa*. Therefore, achieve awareness of this japa. When you are in solitude, notice how the breath comes in as *ham* and goes out as *sa*. That is self-maintained japa and it brings great realizations.

When is it appropriate to use So'ham *as opposed to* Om Namah Shivaya?

So'ham is the final japa. It is meant for Siddhas, for free beings. First, you must be worthy of it. By this I mean having the undoubting, certain, firm awareness: I am in Him, He is in me; I am He and He is me. Then you can repeat this mantra.

People are so foolish: if you tell them, "You are sinners," they will accept that. If you tell them, "You are fools," they will accept that. If you tell them, "You have sinned and you must pray to God for forgiveness," they will accept that, and if you tell them, "God is up there," they will believe that too. But if you tell them, "You are the pure Self," they will not believe it. If you tell them, "God is up there and He is all-pervasive; He is also inside of you," they will not believe that. They will wonder if they are being converted to Hinduism.

So'ham is the most natural mantra. It is the true mantra. In all these three mantras, *Guru Om, Om Namah Shivāya* and *So'ham*, it is *Om* which is the main element, because *Om* is the seed of all the mantras. If you take out the syllable *so* and *ha* from *So'ham*, what remains is *Om*, so repeat that.

Anyone who repeats *Om Namah Shivāya* and is worthy of it is asked later on to add another *Om* at the end of it, and then it functions in the same way as *So'ham*. The meaning is the same: Shiva is Consciousness, and the Guru is the same Consciousness, and *so* refers to this Consciousness. *So'ham* is good — repeat it. But to do so, you must be firmly established in a certain awareness; otherwise you may begin to feel nervous about it.

It seems that during meditation the space between ham *and* sa *is creating everything — physical, emotional, and so on — while the space itself is not any of those things. Is this true?*

All feelings and emotions come out of that space. Every person, according to his own individuality, creates his own feelings or qualities. The Shaivite authors say that the source of these feelings is the three *gunas* or qualities — *sattva, rajas,* and *tamas.* If you meditate very well and pursue sadhana very well, you become free of these three qualities. Lord Krishna said, "The entire world contains these three qualities. O Arjuna, go beyond them." It is that space between *ham* and *sa* that is beyond these three qualities. Become anchored in that space.

In order to experience God at the juncture of the breath, I want to retain my incoming breath and prolong expelling the breath. Is this cheating?

Don't try to do either. Let it happen naturally on its own. As you repeat the mantra for a while, it will automatically be retained inside and prolonged as it goes out. You don't have to do it. *Ham* will come in and be there for a long time without your forcing it. It would be better to repeat the mantra for a while instead of trying to stop the breath. Then *ham* will merge. If you have the awareness that it is merging, even for a fraction of a moment, that is more than enough. Just try to perceive what happens. Then try to perceive how *sa* arises and merges outside. Eventually, if *sa* merges outside for a long time, you will also experience that your belly will be drawn in; it will become flat.

This is a great mantra. This is the Siddha mantra. In the Siddha lineage, we repeat *Hamsa.* If you exhale *sa* and inhale *ham,* and watch Bhagawan Nityananda's face in the picture, you will know that he has become established in *pūrno'ham*, the perfect I-consciousness. Don't try to force it. The natural process of breathing should take place on its own. This is natural japa, natural *prānāyāma*. Kumbhaka takes place on its own. Give it some time. Then you will know how *ham* merges inside for a long, long time. When this natural retention of breath takes place, you experience a lot of joy. When *ham* merges and *sa* hasn't risen yet, the *madhyādasha*, the middle space, arises — and that is the state of God.

When I do the Hamsa *mantra, I experience what sounds like* Om *reverberating throughout my body. This happens when I stop to listen to myself. Would you talk about this?*

It is true. Every part of your body reverberates with this mantra. Every blood cell reverberates with it. You don't always realize this, but when you meditate and become very quiet and look within, you experience that every blood cell contains the *So'ham* mantra; it reverberates in this body. And not only in this body — it permeates the entire universe.

I Fell in Love with the Mantra
When I Heard It Coming Out
of His Shoe

Once I met a great Shiva yogi. He was a great Siddha. He was such a great Siddha that even his shoes repeated Om Namah Shivaya, Om Namah Shivaya. *If he put his shoes down somewhere, they would resound with this mantra. This shouldn't be a matter of surprise. The mantras and our feelings do have such power. I love this* panchakshari. *It is called "panchakshari" because it contains five syllables. I first received this mantra from my mother and then I received it from my Guru. I was very curious to know what it really meant. So I went to this Siddha to find out what it was all about. In India some great beings wear a certain kind of shoe with the front part curving up. When I went to him, he told me, "Pick up one of the shoes and put it against your ear. Listen to the mantra from there." And I heard it coming out of the shoe! When I heard the mantra coming from there, I fell in love with it.*

Then I said to him, "Please give me some understanding about God."

He sang a bhajan, *a devotional poem in the Kannada language: "O Knower, You are inside me. Since You are inside me, You know everything."*

Well, at that time I was very young, and when you are young, it is difficult to understand things. So he asked me, "Did you follow what I said?"

"Of course I understand the words," I said, "I understand the lines, but I can't get the meaning of them."

He had rock candy, and he gave me some and said, "Eat this." I ate it and he asked me, "How does it taste?"

"Very sweet," I said.

"The one who is inside you," he said, "the one who realized that it was sweet — that is God."

Then he said, "Now get out of here."

So God is the Knower. He is not the known. Consciousness is the experiencer; it is not the experienced. Consciousness is inside you. Since it is inside you, it knows everything, it experiences everything. If you want to know it, go inside and get rid of your wrong understanding. When you do that, you will attain the understanding of Consciousness.

If you could make friends with the divine Name even slightly, no evil spirits or demons or devils would have the guts to face you. They would keep themselves at a respectable distance, because all these beings are mortally afraid of the divine Name. These ghosts or evil spirits live only in places where minds are impure, where actions are impure, and where everything is tainted and polluted. In Maharashtra I spent twelve years in a small village. There was a three-story house in that village, and it was called "the haunted house," the house of ghosts. Nobody had dared to live in that house for eighty years. When I went to that village, I could not find any place big enough for me to stay. I always need a big place because so many people come. So I chose that house.

People did not want me to live there because they were scared of the ghosts. They begged me with folded hands not to go there, telling me that the ghosts, which were haunting the house, had tormented many people, had given them different kinds of diseases, and had subjected them to all kinds of suffering.

I just smiled their fears away and said, "Look, I'm ashamed of you because you are feeling scared of disembodied spirits, which find nourishment only in impurity, and here I am, a being whose life is pure and who is living in a body. Why should I feel scared of disembodied things? My life is pure. I continually remember the Lord and my body is quite strong. Why should I feel scared of these spirits, which are not visible and which can survive only in impure and corrupt places?"

I did not pay any attention to those people and I lived in that house for twelve years. For the first two or three days many people came to the house and stood there as sentries to protect me. I turned them away, telling them, "You are behaving like ignorant fools." They didn't understand that I was continually repeating the name of the Lord, Shri Ram, Jay Ram, Jay Jay Ram, *and that in my heart I was also carrying the sword of the divine Name, which can cut away these insignificant spirits. All inauspicious things flee when the divine Name is chanted, when your heart becomes permeated by the divine Name.*

CHAPTER 9

The Easiest Means

*It is possible that just by reading scriptures
or meditating or through japa, you
can attain something, but it is not so easy.
The easiest means is to offer service to the Guru.
There is no means as easy as this.*

What is sevā?

In Sanskrit one of the meanings of *sevā* is to imbibe something.
You make that thing yours; you take it into yourself. That is seva
or service. You serve God for a while and in this way you make
God yours; you incorporate God into your being. When you
make God yours, it doesn't mean that He doesn't belong to anyone else. Seva is to incorporate the Guru into your being. After
that, you give up your outer service. You incorporate God into
your being, and you give up yourself. Mira says, "I accepted
God, and then I gave myself to Him." This is seva.

The Guru Gita *says that a person cannot be liberated without
service to the Guru. What is the best way to serve the Guru?*

To follow the path that he has shown you is to serve the Guru
in the best way. You should understand what he teaches you.
Whatever understanding he has given to you, become established in that. This is the best way to serve the Guru — there is
no other way.

I would like to know your thoughts on service as a means of reaching liberation.

Service to the Guru has a very high place. A servant of the Guru does not have to chase liberation. Liberation chases him!

Will you please comment on the proper attitude toward Gurusevā?

Whatever work you are doing, understand that you are doing it for the sake of the supreme Principle. Whatever work you do for someone, forget that you have done it. All work is seva— it is for God, and that is fine. God Himself exists in all names, in all forms, and in all actions. If you attain this understanding, you will derive bliss from all work; you will experience that God is manifest in all work. Without this understanding, even a blissful bed will prick you like a thorn.

Will you please talk about Gurusevā in the ashram and Gurusevā in our personal, worldly lives? If one has a choice, which is more meritorious?

Why don't you pursue Guruseva with your mind, your speech, and your body completely absorbed in it for a while, and then see what happens? Seva is a very mysterious *sādhanā*. While you are doing seva, do not consider it a mere job. Consider it sadhana. In ancient times all the seekers attained the Truth while pursuing seva in a disciplined way.

What can exist in the world that is separate from God? What action exists where there is no Shiva? What is there where there is no Shakti? A great being said, "God Himself exists in all names, all forms, and all actions," so how can seva be separate from that? How can seva be separate from yoga, meditation, or *bhakti*? This is the mystery of seva. Shaivism talks about the two aspects of God—the immanent as well as the transcendent. Therefore, all seva is religion, is God's action, is meditation.

However, a person should have understanding and discrimination. First of all, understand that God pervades everything. Do seva with the feeling that God exists inside everything. Then you will experience joy; then you will be doing sadhana.

Tomorrow I go to Hawaii to set up the retreat. Please instruct me how to make this work all yours, not mine. How can I make this time away from you bring me closer to you in my heart?

You should regard your inner Self as me. This kind of question arises when you imagine your inner Self to be different from me. You should know that this work is meant for the good of others and do it with that awareness. You do not have to feel that you are going away from me. You should feel me very close to you because Consciousness is all-pervasive.

Would you please explain true Guruseva and its power? Does the Guru know and care about each person's work, however humble it may seem? Do the fruits of Guruseva depend on the nature of the work done?

It is not necessary for the Guru to know what kind of work you are doing. Your own inner Self always keeps the report of your work. Inside, there is Consciousness, which is also called the Guru. In the *Guru Gītā* every day you read that there is a triangle in the *sahasrāra*, and in the center of the triangle is the Guru Principle. This place is also called the heart. Whatever work you are doing, whether it is big or small, the inner Guru is watching you. Nobody else has to supervise you. So with this understanding perform your seva.

Can you give us some advice on how to distinguish between service to the Guru and an ego trip that we might think is service to you?

Ego is the thing that has been chasing after us for countless lives. Ego gives a lot of trouble even to great people. But one who wants to serve God, one who wants to serve the Guru, should not be aware that he is serving; he should forget the word *seva*. If you give something to your Guru, if you do something for your Guru, you should forget it. That means your ego has left you.

How can I know I am doing pure Guruseva?

You can understand what kind of Guruseva you are performing by the feeling you have inside yourself. By performing Guruseva, a person becomes very happy. Through seva, joy begins to well up within him. Not only that, he can attain knowledge from seva. The wisdom that arises from within is true wisdom. What you read in books is not true wisdom; it is just something that was written by someone else. Through seva, true knowledge and also bliss arise from within of their own accord. Just see what happens within you when you do some service for others with respect, with honor, and without expectations. The result of seva is seen within you immediately. Seva brings an immediate payoff. It is not that you perform seva for a while, and then after two or three lifetimes, you attain the fruits of your seva. As you perform your seva, you attain the fruit of it immediately. You perform the seva with one hand and with the other hand you attain the fruit.

With what attitude should one do Guruseva — out of fear of the Guru or out of fear of one's co-workers?

If you do it out of fear, it is not seva; it is mere work. If you do it by respecting the command of the Guru, that is seva.

There is a very good story about a Sufi saint named Musa Imam. Two seekers went to him and asked if they could stay in his ashram. The only reason you can stay in an ashram is to perform sadhana and to do seva; an ashram is not a hotel, not a place of pleasure. So the two seekers, whose names were Hameed and Tanduri, went to Baba Musa and they put in their application. They said, "Please bestow grace upon us so we can walk on the path of God."

There was a small garden in the ashram, and the saint told them to go and work there. There was no chanting, no meditation, no *Āratī*, no *Guru Gītā* — only seva in the garden.

So they worked there, and three years passed. Then Tanduri said to Hameed, "O brother, we have been working here for three years! We have been growing chilies and tomatoes and cabbages. We grow them and then we eat them. But what's going on? We haven't attained anything here!"

Hameed said, "Well, I've been working here for three years too. All I know is that he told me to work here, and I'm offering my service to him. I'm not thinking about anything else. He told me to work, and I'm offering my service — that's all I know."

Tanduri said, "I'm getting bored. My mind is going through so many negative feelings, positive feelings — all kinds of things. And I've been hearing about different courses. There is one particular course in which you attain something in just three days. There's another course where you attain something in eight hours! So I want to go there. I really want to attain something as soon as possible."

"If you want to go there," Hameed said, "then go. It's fine. But I want to stay here. I'm not really thinking about attaining anything. It's just that my Guru told me to work here, so I'm working and I'm enjoying it. I don't mind if I attain something or not, because I've spent countless lives without attaining anything. If I don't attain it in this life, it's fine because I will in my next life."

So Tanduri left and Hameed kept working, and as he worked in the garden, he began to get some understanding. He began to think, "This isn't just working in a garden; this is different. This must be some kind of yoga that I'm doing." His understanding began to change in this way. He began to see that everything was pervaded by Consciousness; that nothing was different from Consciousness. Then he realized, "This isn't just work — this is Guruseva! This is real sadhana!"

As his understanding developed more and more, he began to attain higher and higher knowledge. He began to have many experiences. He forgot his sense of time; he wouldn't remember that it was evening and he should leave. He wouldn't even think of resting or of his own comfort. He lost his ego in his seva. He even forgot whether his ego existed or not.

One day Baba Musa went out to check on him. He saw that Hameed was still doing his seva. For a long time Baba Musa stood right before him. Hameed didn't know that his Guru was standing there. He had become so completely absorbed in his work, so immersed in his seva. Then Baba Musa kept on walking, and as he was coming back from his walk, once again he went to see Hameed. He stood right in front of him, but Hameed was still absorbed in his work. The Guru could see the disciple, but the disciple couldn't see the Guru because he had lost himself in the work. Finally Baba Musa said, "O Hameed!"

Hameed looked up and said, "What?"

"How is your seva going?"

"Very beautifully."

"How many hours do you work?"

"I don't know. I don't have a watch."

Baba Musa said, "Good. You can go now. You have completed your sadhana. You have become perfect."

That was all. Hameed left. He just needed to hear that one word from the Guru: "You have become perfect." And he had become perfect. The Guru gave the command; the disciple did it. The disciple never doubted whether enlightenment would happen, when it would happen, how it would happen. He had no doubts at all.

So Hameed went to the town where Baba Musa told him to go, and he became a great Guru, just like his own Guru. Many people came to meet him. Thirty years went by. The news of Hameed spread to his old friend Tanduri. People were talking about a great being who was able to give grace. Now Tanduri had taken a lot of different courses, but he was still feeling dry inside. He was still wandering and wandering. All that he had done was to empty his pockets. But he was still searching. So he came to see this new Guru. When he got there, he saw that it was his old friend Hameed and he was very surprised. He saw the state Hameed was in; he saw the radiance in his face.

Tanduri stayed there for a day, and then with great love and humility he asked, "O brother, how did you attain this state? What did Baba Musa teach you? What *mantra* did he give you?"

Hameed said, "Whatever he gave me, he gave me when you were there. He didn't give me anything extra after you left. You left, but I stayed — that was all. I just stayed and worked. Knowledge arose in me, and I began to understand that I wasn't performing mere work, but it was my sadhana. The moment I realized that it was my sadhana, the impact of seva increased.

The notion that I was inferior, that I was small, was punctured. Within myself I began to expand and expand. I expanded so much that I reached the last limit of expansion. Before I was like a balloon, and the sky was so vast. But now I have become the sky, and compared to me the sky is as small as a balloon."

In ancient times in Eastern countries, this is the way they used to attain knowledge. And this is the attitude to have toward your seva.

GOD DOES EVERYTHING

I try to do my work as karma yoga, but I find it difficult.

As your understanding grows, attachment becomes less. If you could be aware of the fact that God alone is the doer, attachment would be gone immediately and you would laugh at yourself for being so attached. Noni has just put the window up and now the breeze is coming into the room. He might very well think it was he who brought the breeze into the room, but it has come in by itself. It is God who sets the wheel of action moving and who controls it all the time, but individuals think they accomplish things. They act and take great pride saying, "I did this," "I did that." If we could become aware that He is the doer, our false idea that we are the doer would be reduced. Your thoughts are moving in the right direction.

How can I get over my karma?

The bondage of karma will be cut asunder the moment your ego is dissolved. If you want to get over your karma, you should first get over this egotistical notion that you are the doer.

I am so used to doing things alone that I don't even know how to let my Guru do it for me. How do I accept your help?

You just do your work, and when your work is going very smoothly, understand that the Guru is helping you.

*How can I renounce the fruits of Gurusevā when this work has
a clearly stated objective and I am frustrated in not being able
to meet this objective?*

Keep doing seva, but do not expect the fruit. Your Guruseva
should be devoid of objective. Offer your service for the sake of
service; do not have any other purpose. If there is any objective in
the seva, it becomes like a business. Do not perform seva with the
intention of getting something from the person for whom you are
performing it. If you do seva but don't expect anything, that is real
seva. Ram Tirth says, "If you are aware of your love, devotion,
and service, it is not true love, true devotion, or true service."

*I don't understand how to offer the fruits of my labor to you.
In the ashram it is easy, but in my own business I don't see
how I can abandon the fruits to you unless it simply means to
be unattached to the outcome of the work. I am working for the
fruit, whether it is money, satisfied desires, or the enjoyment
of the work. How do I abandon that fruit?*

You have to abandon the fruits of your actions by being detached
from them. In mundane life you have to perform one action or
the other. Don't have the pride of your action, but do keep performing actions. For this you need a lot of understanding. The
Bhagavad Gītā teaches you to work while being detached. You
have the right only to work, to perform actions, but you don't
have the right to desire the fruit of your action. Generally speaking, when you work for your livelihood, it is not a bad action. The
scriptures say it is Brahman, it is God, who takes the form of
everything, who takes the form of names and colors and actions.
If you work with this awareness, it is very good for you.

THE WORK OF THIS WORLD IS
A DIVINE WORSHIP

Would you please talk about the value of Gurusevā?

Guruseva is invaluable. It's priceless. You can put a value on anything else, but you cannot put a value on Guruseva. Only after you do Guruseva, after you offer your service to the Guru, do you realize it and attain it. There are different kinds of seva. The foremost and the best seva is to follow the path that has been shown by the Guru. Shaivism says all beings and all inanimate objects are filled with Shiva. Not only that, even dust is filled with Shiva. So no matter what seva you do, no matter what service you offer, you obtain Shiva Himself. All actions, all activities, all religions, all names, belong to Him. Therefore, no matter what you do, you are offering your service to Him. In reality, the work of this world is a divine worship, a divine seva of God. A great being said, "Whatever I do, I am doing Your seva."

I have been offered a very good job, but I am afraid that it will interfere with my spiritual development by taking too much of my energy. I must decide tomorrow.

If you have a good job offer, accept it. Your job will not interfere with your spiritual evolution. The only thing that could impede it would be your own laziness.

All the deities presiding over the forces of nature are totally liberated. Take, for instance, the wind. The wind is blowing constantly, it is working constantly, yet the wind god is liberated. The same holds true of the fire god. Even while engaged in the task of heating everything, he remains liberated. Do your job well and at the same time remember God earnestly. Don't have any fear.

How can I — a householder with a full-time job — serve the Guru?

Do your job with great honor. That is also a great seva. And when you finish work, you can meditate. That is also Guruseva. If you really look at this with understanding, you will see that this whole world is the form of the Guru. The Guru is not just an individual being of a certain height and physical appearance. In the *Guru Gītā* every day we read that this whole world is the Guru. All the things that you see — sentient and insentient, matter and

Consciousness — they are all the form of the Guru. When this is the case, you too are the Guru. Without worshiping your own Self, without serving your own Self, if you serve others, if you meditate on others, it is not of much use. That is why I continually say, "Meditate on your Self. Worship your Self. Kneel to your Self. Honor your Self." The great beings make you worship your own inner Self; they don't make you worship the outer Guru.

Before I had spiritual awakening, I was working as a journalist. But now I have difficulty doing that work. I have lost confidence in my ability to do that kind of work.

Spiritual awakening should increase your interest in writing. It may not happen now, but it will certainly come later. There is a center of knowledge within, and when that center unfolds itself, inspiration floods you. Then you begin to write spontaneously. *I am nowhere near that now because writing for me is very much tied in with judgments of people and myself and ego, and I find it very difficult.*

Whatever has to happen, has to happen, so why should you worry about it? I never went to college, and in spite of that, people quote me these days. At no time did I think things would turn out the way they have, yet everything is happening the way it is happening.

Meditate a little with a quiet mind and also write a little. You should not lose your ease in writing. True meditation is total freedom from thought. Keep repeating the mantra and there will come a time when you will transcend this difficulty.

My work brings me in contact with many people who are in pain. How can I help these people without becoming involved in their suffering?

A person should work in the mundane world just as an actor or an actress works in a theater. Shaivism says that the Self plays all the different roles in this world. In India the *Rāmāyana* is often performed on stage. There are two main characters: Rama, the Lord, and Ravana, a demon with ten heads. Ravana is portrayed as a wicked, ferocious creature, and whenever he comes on stage, the children shriek, thinking that Ravana himself has actually appeared. But when the curtain is closed, Ravana removes his ten heads, and only the head of the actor remains. Once the play is over, the actor becomes his old self.

In the same way, when you are working, just consider yourself to be playing a role. Then you won't be troubled. Keep working and performing actions, but don't identify yourself with your actions. Identify yourself as the witness of the actions, and simply watch everything happen.

How can I keep you in my consciousness when I'm actively engaged in work — either sevā or my own work?

You don't have to maintain the remembrance of me all the time, but you do have to become aware of That. If you become aware that every work you do, every seva you perform, is God's, you will feel very happy.

Keep performing your actions, and in your mind keep repeating the name of Rama, of God. When I say Rama, don't look up somewhere to see Rama's photo. He is not in the photo. And don't look for a statue of Him. The One who has become this whole cosmos is Rama; the One who is within this cosmos is Rama. In this way, keep remembering Rama. This is more than enough.

Don't consider your seva just to sweep; don't consider the broom a mere broom. Don't think that you are cleaning a mere bathroom, and don't consider that you are just making chapatis. Also don't think that you are merely eating chapatis and dal.

Whatever work is there is God's seva; you are offering your service to God. If you become aware of this, it will be blissful for you. You will attain joy if you have the awareness that this whole world and all the people in it and all the actions belong to God. If you have the awareness that everything is God's, you will attain *samādhi* right then and there. If you consider that every work is a mode of worship, you will attain God even while you are sweeping the floor; you will attain God even while you are washing your clothes.

I work full-time and am exhausted at the end of the day. In this state, how can I do sevā wholeheartedly? Is it just the attitude that is important?

Yes, your attitude is very important. Before you fall asleep, pray to God; just say, "O God!" Even that is enough.

In whatever field you work, even in a factory, if you work with justice, with purity, with simplicity, and with a straightforward heart, that also becomes seva. God sees that work too. Even if you get exhausted at the end of the day, it doesn't really matter because you have done your seva. However, always remember Him in your heart. That is more than enough.

Please talk about how one's work can become true meditation.

It's not only that meditation is meditation — every work is meditation. Every work contains Shakti. What work is there where there is no Shiva? What action is there where there is no Shiva? What word is there where there is no Shiva? If you have this understanding, every work is meditation. The *Bhagavad Gītā* says that if a person works without any selfish interest, knowing that he is offering his work to God, he attains that great state.

Kabir was a weaver, and while weaving, he attained God; he did not have to go to a jungle. There was another saint called Gora, who was a potter. While making pots, he attained That. Sena was a barber who attained perfection while shaving beards. There was another saint called Sautamali, who was a gardener. While working in the garden, he attained That. Kanupatra was a dancer who attained God while dancing. So if a person performs his natural work and offers it to God with a lot of respect, he attains the same fruit that is attained in meditation.

As long as you are ignorant, as long as you lack knowledge, this world exists as a mere world for you and every action seems to be a mere action. When you attain true knowledge, you will know that your work is not a mere service to God — it is the worship of God. This is why Jagadguru Shankaracharya said, "O Lord, whatever action I perform is Your seva. I offer my service to You and it is Your worship."

How can service to one's family be transformed into service to the Guru?

The Guru is the Self of everyone. You should remain aware that when you are serving your family, you are serving the Guru, who is the Self of everyone, who lives within everyone. Who ever told you to become indifferent to the world? Who told you not to have any love and affection for your relations and friends and to give all your love only to the Guru? The Guru dwells within every person in your family, and if you are aware of this when you serve them, you are serving the Guru.

Sai Baba of Shirdi was a very great saint. I had great love for him. There was a disciple of his called Upasani Baba who used to cook for Sai Baba in a hut that was some distance away. He would bring the food over to his Guru and serve it to him. One day the sun was blazing red-hot in the sky, and Sai Baba said to Upasani Baba, "Don't bother bringing the food all the way here today. I'll come to your hut and eat my meal there."

Upasani Baba cooked a meal for his Guru. But Sai Baba didn't come, so Upasani Baba decided to take the food to him. He packed it in a lunch box, and as he was about to leave the house, he found a dog standing in the door. The dog was very hungry and it was obviously asking for food. Upasani Baba said to the dog, "I'm going to serve this food to my Guru; you wait here till I return, and then I'll feed you."

He left for his Guru's place with the food. The moment he reached there, Sai Baba said, "Look, you didn't have to come all this distance in the hot sun. I went to your hut, and if you had served me there, that food would have reached me right here."

So if you look upon all people equally and if you have love for things around you, that is another way of expressing your devotion to the Guru. Service to your family is service to the Guru. While feeding your family, you also feed your Self; while giving clothes to your family, you also clothe your Self; while putting them to sleep, you also give rest to your Self. Make the Guru a member of your family, and that will take care of it.

THE TRUE INNER SEVA

Is service to the needy sufficient to fulfill the purpose of one's life?

If you offer your service to the needy, that will help them, but how can it help you? What makes you think that the purpose of your life is only to serve the needy? Whatever you are doing is fine; at least it will help the needy. But the purpose of one's life is to know one's own Self.

In the state of Maharashtra, there was a great king called Shivaji. During his time there was a drought and famine. It didn't rain for two years, so he began to build a fort. You people who have gone with me to visit Rajasthan must have seen this fort. They used to spend a lot of money building forts and castles — more than you spend these days on nuclear bombs. While the fort was being built, the king wrote a letter to his Guru saying, "I am building this fort because people don't have anything to eat and drink. It hasn't rained for two years and I want to help the people. Will you come here and bless this place?"

His Guru was Samartha Ramdas. He was a great Siddha being; he could do anything. So he went there. The king welcomed him very warmly and showed him what he was building. He said, "It's because it didn't rain for two years and people have been starving — that's why I am trying to help them."

"Whatever you are doing is fine," said the Guru, "but along with this work you have a little bit of ego, and that's not good." Of course, the Guru wanted to remove this ego, so he was walking around here and there, and he saw a big rock. "Shivaji," he said, "call your laborers because this rock should be broken right now."

They broke the rock. It split into two parts, and inside there was a little bit of water and a frog. "O Shivaji," said the Guru, "who put this little bit of water inside the rock for the frog?"

"It must be God," answered Shivaji. "Who else could do it?"

Then the Guru said, "God does everything for everyone. He keeps everything for everyone. You are doing your work just on behalf of Him. You are just a means of doing His work." Then the Guru left.

So it is fine to offer your service to the needy, and it will help them, but in order to fulfill the purpose of your life, you have to seek inside; you have to attain the knowledge of the inner Self. And for that, you have to meditate.

How can we find out what our real work or mission is in this life?

Your real work in this life is to realize God in your own heart. The first priority is God; the second priority is your daily duties. Bhartrihari says, "As long as you are completely healthy, as long as you are far away from old age, as long as your senses are strong, try to uplift yourself." After the house is on fire, if you try to dig a well to extinguish the fire, what's the use? The house is going to burn down anyway. If you are very old, and if your eyes are sick of seeing things, and if your ears say, "No, no, we don't want to listen to anything anymore," and if your body is decrepit, how can you realize God in that state? So this is your main duty; this is your real work.

Is there anything you could suggest for Gurusevā?

Chant a lot.

All You Need Is One Word

When I was fifteen years old, I met my Guru. For thirty-five years, he told me, "Go here, go there, travel here, travel there." And I did what he said: I traveled everywhere but I didn't really leave him. I was fully convinced that I would not go empty-handed from this person. Sometimes my Guru would allow me to come close to him, sometimes he wouldn't. One day he called me close to him and said, "Go to Suki. There is a field there; go and sit there."

So I went there and sat under a tree. When I sat there, I attained everything there is to attain. I attained everything sitting under that tree.

This is the science of Gurus and disciples. Without the Guru's grace, no matter how much you learn, it amounts to nothing. And if you hear something from the Guru, all you need is one word — because everything is inside us. You don't need anything from outside. Every day we see That, but still we don't have knowledge. Every day we hear about That, but still we don't understand. We are surrounded by that divine pure knowledge; we are wandering in the midst of it, but still we are not aware. We are like a boat in the middle of an ocean. Inside us and outside us, above and below us, behind us and in front of us, that Consciousness is all-pervasive. Consciousness is just like the ocean, and we are all the waves and ripples of that ocean.

You don't have to worry about anything; you don't have to search for that Truth anywhere else. But through the grace of the Guru, through the love of the Guru, your real eye should open.

What is your work on this earth?

A meditation revolution. First, I worked for it in my own country and after that I came to the West.

I have heard that you had a vision of Bhagawan Nityananda dancing in the courtyard here in the ashram, and that in this way he revealed his blessings for your tours to the West. What was it like to see him dancing in the courtyard?

Beautiful. It was very beautiful, and the dance that I saw was just like this, just like the dance of the Shakti that is going on right now.

I was to transmit his Shakti to thousands of people; I was to impart his teachings to thousands of people, and I have done it.

CHAPTER 10

In the Presence

*When a person keeps watching God,
he obtains the right outlook in his life.
Then his own vision becomes darshan, and
wherever he looks he sees God.*

*What is the best way to relate to the Guru? There is not enough
time at darshan to really meet you. How can I develop a personal
relationship with you?*

You don't have to establish any relationship with the Guru; you
should develop a relationship with your own Self, and then it
will extend to the Guru also. The Self is the supreme Guru of
all. During darshan, if you can develop that relationship, even
at that moment, even at that instant, it is more than enough.

There was a great being named Tulsidas who wrote a commentary on the *Rāmāyana*. He said that if you are in the company of a great being for twenty minutes — if not twenty, then
ten minutes; if not ten, then five; if not five, then even for a fraction of a moment — that instant will be enough for countless
lifetimes.

So you don't need too much time. If you really know how
to do it, even an instant is more than enough.

*For me the most intense Shakti occurred not when you touched
me with your hand or with your feathers, but when you sang*

during your talk. Then I felt a wind of fire blow through me. What do you do when you sing?

When I sing, I sing. What else can I do? When I'm singing, I just sing with love. I become absorbed in the meaning of the song. These songs are not written by just anybody. I sing the poems of those great beings who have become one with God, who are inspired from within; they are commanded by God to write songs.

I always end up in the back of the hall. How can I sit close to you?

It is my habit to look at the back of the hall; I don't have the habit of looking here in the front. I never know who is sitting close to me because I am always looking to see who is sitting in the back. You shouldn't worry about this. As long as there is love in your heart, although you are far away, you are not far away. If there is no love in your heart, although you are close to me, you are not close to me.

I've come a long way to have your darshan, but when you are giving darshan, I can't keep my eyes open because of the inner dance. What am I to do?

You can have my darshan within the inner dance. The purpose of your coming here is to watch the inner dance — not to watch the outer decoration. If you just come here to eat and drink and to get a good rest and to watch this outer beauty, it's of no use. You should come here to watch the inner dance, the inner beauty.

Sometimes during darshan you don't bop me with the peacock feathers. Is there some reason for this?

Yes, there is some reason for this! People come up for darshan five or six at a time and so many of them have questions and problems. Some people ask about their work and some ask about their dogs. Some ask about their wives and some complain to me about how their husbands scolded them. I get involved with their problems; I am very intent on listening to what they have to say. So when I am doing that, the other person just comes and bows and goes away without getting bopped. There is really no other reason. You can understand it in this way: so I didn't get a bop today, I'll get it tomorrow! Or you can understand it in this way: maybe his arm is tired today — every day he bops fifteen hundred people.

Please talk about darshan and why we have it. For me it is a chance to look at you up close and give you something for your ashram.

Just as it is a chance for you to look at me up close, it is the same thing for everybody else. Everybody wants to look at me at close range, so darshan came into existence. It is said that if you really have the darshan of a saint with your body, mind, and speech completely absorbed in it, immediately bliss wells up from within. The Self is completely satiated. In darshan if you wonder, "Did Baba really see me?" — that is not darshan. If you wonder, What kind of hat is Baba wearing today? — that is not darshan.

True darshan is to see a great being and become totally absorbed in his state for a while. Tukaram Maharaj said that if you really have the darshan of a saint from your heart, coming and going cease to exist. Now he did not mean that you should not come to the evening program. What he meant was that your birth and death cease to exist.

Would you please explain darshan?

In darshan your feeling is the most important thing. Whatever feeling is strongest in you, you obtain the fruit of that feeling. When you meet someone — no matter who it is — and you have a particular feeling, you have to face the same feeling from the other person. When we are having the darshan of a great being, if we are filled with great feelings, if we feel holy, if we feel pure, that is what we become. So in darshan the feeling is most important. The greater the feeling you have, the greater the result will be. The smaller the feeling you have, the smaller the result will be.

Why do I feel such fear in your physical presence?

There must be some reason behind it. However, the fear of God, the fear of *sādhus*, the fear of spirituality, is not an ordinary fear. It is nothing but fearlessness. In the case of God, a person who is fearless suffers — not one who has fear. I am not saying that a person should have fear of people: he should have fear of God. I consider your fear to be very good; it is natural. But don't have this fear when you think of your past actions. Forget your past; you should not remember your guilty conscience all the time. That will burn you.

Why do you tease some people by obviously ignoring them?

It isn't like that. You don't see that I see you. I see everybody. Do you come to darshan for me to pay attention to you? Do you want me to say, "How are you? I love you so much?" Do you come for that kind of attention? This is just chit-chat. The true message is something else. I see the all-pervasive Self, I see Consciousness in everyone and everything all the time. And you are a part of it. It's very true. So with this understanding, know that I see you also.

I feel uncomfortable bowing. First of all, I am not sure who or what I should be bowing to. Also, you say that the Truth is nondual, but doesn't bowing assert duality?

Your flesh must be very dear to you. People who are very interested in their own flesh have a lot of difficulty bowing. Because of the weakness of your conviction, this doubt has arisen. When you are bowing, you become one with That which you are bowing to. This is not duality — it is nonduality. It seems you have never bowed — you have just made a pretense of bowing. From your question I can tell for sure that all this time your bowing has been phony.

To have a doubt about bowing is to pump air in the balloon of ego so that it immediately bursts. If you want your ego to last longer, don't bow. Bowing is the sign of a person who is free from ego. It is only when you have not understood what bowing

218

is that you have trouble bowing. When you bow down, the weight of ego decreases; it is not completely destroyed, but at least it is diminished. When you walk around with an over-loaded ego, you are bound to meet with an accident that will puncture it. This should not happen; you should continually try to decrease the weight of your ego by bowing down.

Are you so egotistical about the rotten flesh and body that you have? My Baba has given a new name to this body. When an egotistical person would come before him, he would say to him in the Kannada language, "Hey, you pot of shit!" Think about it.

Why do I feel so wonderful when I get in the darshan line and so terrible when I leave it? And why do I keep coming for your darshan every chance I get?

This is the tendency of your mind. When you come up for darshan, you think it is an auspicious time, a very good time. It is beautiful, so you feel wonderful, and when you leave the darshan line, you leave those wonderful feelings behind. That is why you feel terrible. Take the same feelings that you have in the darshan line with you when you leave it, and then you won't feel terrible afterward.

What is the significance of your prasād?

The significance lies in your understanding. If I give you something and you consider it prasad, it is good for you. The *Bhagavad Gītā* says that if you receive prasad, all your pains go away. If you receive prasad with a very pure heart, it becomes very effective. If you consider it mere sweets, it will be mere sweets for you.

Whenever I give you anything, you return it to me. Does this happen when I give you my ego? Is this the reason why I can't get rid of it? Please take away my ego — or at least show me how to give it away permanently!

It's not quite like that. However, giving and taking, giving and

219

taking — that's how it happens. I'm just sitting here for no good reason and being an agent for no good reason. People give me things and I give them away to somebody else. I always remain empty. I don't really take anything and I don't really give anything. But when it comes to your ego — no, absolutely not; I don't give your ego back. I do keep it. So don't worry.

I would like to give you this gold necklace.

You wear it for me. It will remind you of me. Now it is mine, so don't take it off again.

What should our attitude be toward darshan? I want to come up all the time, but I understand that you belong to everybody.

It's a good question. One should understand whose darshan one should have. Whose darshan does a Guru give you? He gives you the darshan of the inner Self, of the all-pervasive Consciousness. Therefore, have the darshan of that which the Guru gives you. Only when you have the darshan of the Being inside yourself will you become established in serenity and contentment. If you have this darshan, you won't have to go to the trouble of coming to darshan and going back. If you don't have the darshan of That within you, the darshan line will be a mere custom or habit; it won't be true darshan.

If you have a low understanding of your own inner Self, how can you consider others to be great? How you consider others is a reflection of how you consider yourself. Therefore, wherever you are, try to have darshan of That. There is only one thing worthy of darshan and that is the conscious inner Self. The right understanding about darshan is to become aware that That exists everywhere. If instead of having this understanding, you try to have the darshan of a great being by pushing and tripping over other people, by fighting with others just to get to the front row, you are insulting darshan.

As long as a person does not become pure, as long as he does not change in his heart, even if he comes for darshan, it is a mere show.

How can I keep the deep experience I have of you here when I go? I know that the mantra and my inner Self are you, but somehow it is not like looking at you.

Who said that it is not like looking at me? The inner Self is more beautiful than I am. The inner Self has real teeth; it does not have fake teeth like me. My physical body has wrinkles; the Self has no wrinkles.

The experience of the inner Self is something different: it has the form of shimmering blue light. Compared to my inner Self, I don't like my physical body, because the inner Self is so beautiful. Therefore, you too should like the inner Self. All the *tapasya*, or austerities, that we pursue are for us to have the deep experience of the inner Self; they are not for outer things.

No matter how beautiful external things are, still they are filled with the six modifications—one is born, one grows, one reaches middle age, one gets old, one gets very old, and one dies. These six modifications are in everything. However, the inner experience is always new. It is devoid of these modifications. Wherever you are, you should have this inner experience all the time.

If you are just sitting in front of me, watching my beard all the time, you are doing nothing but pretending; you are nothing but a fake. You know it too. So remember this: don't stare at me all the time. Try to enter inside.

When I have your darshan, or when I sit before you or live near you, I feel extreme joy and happiness. Is there any way that I can live in the same state of mind during your absence?

Yes, there is a way. Just as you sit in front of me with a certain attitude, in the same way when you are engaged in other activities, have the same kind of attitude, the same kind of feeling inside you. Then you will feel the same. You make yourself a particular way when you are around me, but when I am absent, you change the condition of your mind and heart. That's why you experience something else. All these things are nothing but the play of inner tendencies. If the tendencies are under your control, no matter where you go, the state of your mind will be the same.

I came without an offering — only my heart.

What could have more value than your heart? Mira once went to the Lord and said, "O Lord, I haven't brought any gift for You, I have brought only my heart. Please take it." So Mira gave her heart to the Lord, and then the Lord had to give her something in return, so He gave His heart to her.

IN THE COMPANY OF A SAINT

The aim of human life is to see God. When I see you, I think I have seen God face to face. Has my life's goal been fulfilled?

The aim of your life will be fulfilled when you see your own Self. See the Truth within yourself. I am outside. The success in seeing me is that you should be able to perceive your own inner Self.

I used to watch my Guru; I used to meditate on my Guru. The result of that was that I saw my own inner Self. Man should honor his own inner Self. At least once, he should try to please his own Self and perceive it. Inside man there dwells great Shakti, but it is concealed. Inside there is an ocean of bliss — not just a drop. But people never go there! So first of all, perceive your own Self and then God.

When a person becomes Self-realized, he realizes all the other gods and deities as well. The Self is the greatest deity. Shaivism says, Whatever is there — all the greatness of Vaikuntha and Kailas — is also here.

How can I get the most out of the time I spend with you?

Follow my discipline fully and participate fully in the schedule. Whatever programs are held here, participate in them —

not for my sake, but for your own sake; not because I will shout at you if you miss them, but because you love to participate. Then you will benefit a lot.

Even though you are with me physically, you should find out whose company you are really keeping. If you keep thinking about all kinds of things, imagining, and fantasizing in all kinds of ways, and if you keep doing whatever comes to your mind, that will not serve much purpose. If you participate and become one with all the programs that take place here, you will benefit from it fully.

What about Guruseva and staying in the presence of the Guru?

To really be in the presence of a Guru you don't have to be in his physical presence. You can feel him anywhere; you can be in his presence anywhere. The awareness of the Guru is right with you. The knowledge you receive from the Guru is with you, and with that knowledge you can experience your Guru anywhere and attain perfection.

There was a great Guru in our country — he is still alive and all the national leaders regard him with great respect. He walked through the whole of India on foot, living only on buttermilk, nothing else. Now it so happened that many, many disciples started following him, walking after him. And for a while they were following his discipline: they ate whatever they got to eat and they lived just as he did.

But as time passed, they started sending wires in advance saying, "Well, so many of us are in the Guru's entourage. You must keep hot water ready so we can wash our feet. We will need cow's milk to drink and you must keep it warm and fresh. Also have some fruit because we are quite accustomed to eating fruit."

Then in the morning these disciples would get up and they would go to anybody's house, wondering whether there was a tub there for a bath or whether there was a shower. Eventually people started saying to the Guru, "Please, sir, just come by yourself. Don't bring your disciples with you."

However, if you are not the type who would seek hot

water and fruit and milk and tubs and showers, there is no harm in staying for a little while. Who knows how much discipline the disciples follow by hanging around the Guru? Find out from those who stay with the Guru how much they participate in meditation and chanting and *japa*, or whether they just go from store to store and market to market and street to street.

It is much better to stay in one place quietly and live by your own work and remember God, than to be with the Guru and keep looking for ice cream or cake in someone else's refrigerator. Such disciples only create delusions and they can even act as death for the Guru. If such disciples were to hang around me, I would consider them shameless, with no discipline and no renunciation.

I wonder whether my disciples follow me or their own leanings.

Do those people who remain in the presence of a true Guru receive more grace than others?

It's not like that. Whatever feeling you have, that's what really matters. It's not that people who are close to me get more grace and people who are far away from me get less. It's not like that at all. You should not have the delusion of sitting very close to me. You should have that longing, that love, that burning desire for attainment.

I read a poem by a great Maharashtran poet-saint about a cow and a tick. The tick is always hanging right on the cow's udder. The cow goes to the forest to graze and the tick goes too. The calf is back home tied up to a pole, yearning for its mother. Although the tick is so close to the udder of the cow, it does not suck milk—it sucks only blood. The calf, who is tied up to a pole far away from the cow, gets to drink the milk even though he is far away from the cow most of the time. But the tick sucks only blood.

Therefore, if you don't have that feeling inside, it is of no avail. So have that longing, that burning in your heart, that love; have a great desire to attain That. Then, even if you are far away, it is still all right. If you don't have these feelings, even if you are sitting right here, it doesn't mean anything. People will say, "Oh, you are sitting right under the podium!" You'll attain that remark, but you won't attain anything else. So have that burning in your heart.

Will I be able to have your darshan after you have merged into the ocean?

Yes, yes, you will keep having darshan. It is your own feeling that takes on different forms. Even now many people have the darshan of saints who have merged into the ocean. It is your feeling that manifests those forms.

A saint is the Self, supreme Consciousness, and it is that supreme Consciousness that takes on different roles and dances in different forms. The Self wears different costumes; it plays different roles. Then it gets rid of those costumes and puts on other costumes. It is a very natural thing for the Self to do.

For this reason, if you remember someone with respect, that being will reveal himself to you. When you think of somebody, his name comes into your mind, his form comes into your mind, and the entire being of that person stands before you.

If it is not possible for me to make contact with a Siddha, is Siddha Yoga the right path for me?

It is possible for everybody to meet a Siddha. The entire world functions because of the Siddhas. The entire world stands on the teachings of the Siddhas. There were seven sages, *saptarishis,* and they made the rules for this entire universe. Asita, Devala, Atri, and so on — these are names of some of those seven sages, and they have always lived; they never died. Even now in the galaxies you see the seven stars together. In Ganeshpuri you can see these stars very easily because the sky is so clear.

So it is possible for everybody to have contact with a Siddha, because through the subtle influence of the Siddhas the entire world functions. A Siddha is not anybody's personal property. He belongs to everybody; he is for everybody. So over and over again you can have contact with a Siddha. If you have firm conviction, if you have total determination, just by remembering a Siddha, you can make that contact from within.

"Have Your Own Darshan"

Bhagawan Nityananda is my dear beloved, my highest Guru.
What else can I say? He is my beloved Guru. Once you say
"beloved," that's it. There isn't any other word to describe
him. He was a great Guru, a great being. You can understand
it in this way: it was God's supreme energy manifesting in
that form as a Guru.

He had many, many powers, countless powers. Still, he lived
a very simple life. Just like this, hundreds and hundreds of
people sat before him day and night. He didn't talk as much
as I do, but there was always a big crowd around him. He
might be lying down with his eyes closed or he might turn
over and show his back and then sleep. He could stay in that
state for hours, and some people would get fed up and leave.

My Baba was very fond of children. For the sake of
the children he had a playground built with horses and other
toys. In his presence nobody was allowed to talk; there had to
be absolute silence. But children were allowed to make noise;
he wouldn't say anything when they cried. Every day he used
to give out lots of sweets to the children, and not just one or
two of them—there were four to five hundred children in
the village.

If he ever spoke, he might say two or three words, and
those three words were enough for a person's entire life. He
was such a great being. Although he lived a very simple and

natural life, still he uplifted many, many people. He had
something for each person. Whoever asked him for anything,
he gave it to that person. He never moved away from his own
place, his ashram. When someone offered him something, he
never received it with his hands. He would just tell the person
to put it down.

He was a great being; he was unique. Whatever he said
would be true, completely true. It bore fruit. It never went
to waste. He was such a beautiful being. Now I can only tell
his stories.

My Guru didn't write any books. He used to speak a little
and people have collected his words and put together some
books. He spoke in aphorisms and mixed different languages
together. He might say just three words, "Give this there."
Give it where? There were so many places, so many people!

He used strange words. Sometimes he would say,
"Hmm" — that's all. The people who had been with him for
a long time could understand his words, so they interpreted
them to others. For instance, they would say, "Baba said you
should leave."

There were times when he would speak very straight-
forwardly and simply. Somebody might go to him and say,
"Baba, I came for your darshan."

Sometimes he answered, "Hey, you dimwit! Don't I live
in you? Why do you have to come here for my darshan? Have
your own darshan. I am in you. Why do you have to have my
darshan? Don't I live within you?"

That was his state. He was a Siddha. He was beyond your rules, beyond your customs, beyond your disciplines. Siddhas live a strange life.

The Worship of Consciousness

*If you worship God within, the results of that worship
will appear right inside of you in the form of
contentment and fulfillment.*

*To what degree should one pay attention to the rituals and
symbols in the ashram? What power do they have?*

These rituals contain great meaning and they have a lot of
power. The scriptures say that it is God, the Absolute, who has
become everything. He has become the rituals and the articles
that you use for rituals. He has become the worship and the one
who worships. These rituals are designed very precisely to
have certain effects.

During the *Āratī* we use particular instruments whose
sound purifies the outer atmosphere as well as the inner atmosphere. These sounds kill the germs of negativities. The sound of
the conch has the power to still the mind, and the sound of the
stringed instruments affects the fine nerves in the head, making
the mind very pure and free from sins. These instruments, which
come from the *Yoga Shāstras,* are used so that you can become
completely immersed in worshiping the inner Self. When you
meditate very deeply, you hear these sounds; they are going on
inside constantly. Inside there is a great music. In meditation you
will hear different kinds of sound, which are called the divine
sounds, or *nāda.* You will hear the sound of the strings, the conch,
the drum, and the various instruments that we play here.

During the *Āratī* we also burn frankincense, and that smoke contains great properties. Its fragrance overcomes negativities in the atmosphere. In all temples and mosques, frankincense is used. The Self is fragrant, but you haven't smelled the fragrance of the Self because you are always trying to smell outer fragrances. When the inner Shakti is awakened, it starts to move higher and higher. As it moves higher and eventually reaches the space between the eyebrows, the element of fragrance is unfolded. When a *yogi* smells this divine fragrance, he becomes very intoxicated. So we use fragrance in the rituals with the same awareness.

Then we sing *mantras*. Mantras are the divine prayers of the inner Self. There is one mantra in the *Āratī* that goes like this: "O infinite One, You have thousands of hands and thousands of legs; You have become all our hands and legs. You have thousands and thousands of eyes. You are very, very ancient; You will live forever. You are inside our hearts. I offer my salutations to You, who is infinite, who has no end." So this is the worship of right understanding; this is not a mere ritual. In this way, you are praying to the Truth, to the inner Self.

Now after performing these rituals, you can tell the difference. If you sit here for an hour and then go to a hotel and sit there for an hour, you will feel the difference.

During the saptah, the Guru Gita *was canceled, but not the* Arati. *Could you please speak about the significance of this ceremony?*

The *Āratī*, the *Guru Gītā*, and the saptah are all the same. There is no difference between them. During the saptah, we continue to eat three meals a day. *Āratī* is the meal for the Being who provides meals for you. Do you want Him to fast? Twice a day when they do the *Āratī*, they feed Him. So you can understand that the *Āratī* is the offering of food to God.

I was talking with a friend about the Arati, *the chant we do every evening. She said that in this practice we are actually calling Bhagawan Nityananda's presence into his photo or his statue. Is this true?*

We do the *Āratī* for ourselves, to purify our own selves, so that Nityananda can bless us to receive his grace. We don't do this *Āratī* for someone else's benefit, but for our own. A householder cooks food at his house. Why does he cook that food? For himself. In the same way, for our own peace, for our own happiness, we do this *Āratī*. Many people worship God with love. What makes you think that God is starving for love, that He doesn't have enough love? On the pretext of loving Him — and only to increase love within us — we love Him. Even though we do this prayer in front of a photo, you attain the peace of your own Self.

In the ashram we burn *dhūp* and we remember Nityananda. We put frankincense on the coals remembering Nityananda. Now who smells that fragrance? Nityananda or you? In temples in India there are people who offer food to God. They cook delicious food like *seera* with so much *ghee* and so many almonds and pistachios. They put the plate in front of God, in front of the statue, and they cover the plate. After that, the priest closes his eyes and repeats a mantra. Then he takes the plate and eats a little bit and also distributes it to the people as *prasād*. So people do *pūjā* for themselves — not for anyone else.

From ritual you get stillness of mind and pure feelings. From ritual the flame of peace arises from within. I do the same thing every day too. In the morning I get up and take my bath and I do puja — an arati and everything else. I don't use fragrant oil now, but I used to. I used to take a piece of cotton and dip it in the oil; I would show it to a picture of my Baba and I would put it inside the top of my ear — that was part of my puja. So everyone does his own puja.

People who have no understanding of these things may say, "What are they doing after all?" But if you love someone with great respect and honor, who enjoys that love? In whose heart does joy spring forth — in you or in the other person? That joy springs forth within yourself. So whatever you do, you do for yourself.

I loved my Baba a lot; even now I love him, but I love him not for his sake, but for my own sake. Just as an angry person suffers with anger, even though he is angry with someone else, in the same way, one who loves, enjoys that love in his own self.

Whatever we do here, we do for ourselves, we do for our own benefit.

WORSHIP THE GURU WITHIN YOU

Is it better to worship a Guru than to worship the formless?

Where is form? Everything is formless. You were without form before you were born, and after you die, you will be again without form. You have form only for a short while in the interval between birth and death. Form is like ice which lasts for a short time. But ice is really water. Worship of the Guru or worship of form is also worship of the formless. It is only that we are not able to understand it. Worship of the Guru is worship of God.

Is it true that the Guru is actually present wherever his picture is worshiped?

In our country a Guru's picture is installed in a certain manner; it is enlivened in a particular way. It is of course true that Consciousness is all-pervasive. Is there anything that is without Consciousness? We worship the Guru as Consciousness, everlasting and tranquil. The Guru is not a physical form; the Guru is the inner Consciousness. When the Guru enters a seeker, he does so in the form of Consciousness, in the form of Shakti. The worship that we do and the devotion that we offer — such things have results only for us. Worship bears fruit for the worshiper alone.

Please explain what is meant by the Guru's feet?

The Guru's feet should not be confused with physical limbs. The Guru is not a physical body; the Guru is really the inner Lord. The Guru is that inward state of profound absorption in which there is complete union with the inner Lord. The Guru's feet are like the foundation on which a building stands. The Guru's feet are *tat* and *tvam* in the phrase *Tat tvam asi*, which means "I am That." The Guru's feet are the two elements in *So'ham*, which also means "I am That."

234

True worship of the Guru's feet does not mean offering him a pair of broken sandals and putting a few flowers on them, and then the moment the Guru turns his face away, turning your face away from him. True worship of the Guru's feet is total awareness of one's identity with the Guru. Jnaneshwar says to his Guru, "I worshiped your feet by realizing the identity of myself with God."

Live continuously in this awareness and worship the inner Guru's feet. Whatever activity you do, first remember and worship these feet. God's divine Shakti lies dormant within man; keep yourself continually aware of it. Worship it, remember it. Have it awakened by the Guru's grace and you will discover how blissful life is. Discover this through direct experience.

Please explain the significance of the Guru's feet and his sandals.

The Indian scriptures do revere the Guru's feet a lot. However, you have to understand this with subtle intellect. In Maharashtra there was a great being who was the Guru of all Gurus. His name was Jnaneshwar Maharaj. He said, "I perceived the Guru's sandals, which were in the form of *tat* and *tvam* and I offered my salutations to the Guru's sandals." *Tat tvam asi* is one of the four proclamations of the Vedas. *Tat* means God, the Self of all. *Tvam* is the inner Self.

The *Guru Gītā* says that the Guru's feet are in the *sahasrāra* in the form of *ham* and *sa,* like the sound of our breathing. The great beings have said that when the Guru's sandals are nothing but the form of *ham* and *sa,* how can we forget them?

My Guru never wore any sandals. However, if anybody took sandals to him, he touched them and blessed them. Then that person would worship those sandals with the feeling that they belonged to his Guru, and this feeling would bear fruit. The great sages say that God exists in the depth of your feelings. He doesn't exist merely in an idol, in wood, in clay, or in images. For this reason, there are many people who worship sandals as the Guru's sandals. No matter with what feeling you worship, it is God who makes your feeling bear fruit. In

Maharashtra there was a great woman saint called Bahinabai, who said that it is the depth of your feeling that bears fruit, and it is your own feeling which brings about liberation. It is the Self of all that gives the fruit of all feelings.

In the meditation of Siddha Yoga we are taught to drop all techniques that we have learned in other types of meditation, for example, focusing our attention on an image or on the rhythm of breathing. I find myself quite dependent on these techniques of breathing and visualization. What should I do?

Here you are asked to focus your attention too, but you are asked to focus it on your inner Self. It is much better to focus it on your inner Self than to visualize something else. In Siddha Yoga we say, "Meditate on your own Self." If, through visualizing something, you can attain some peace, what makes you think you won't attain peace by focusing on the Self?

There was a poet-saint in Maharashtra who spoke about people who have idols made and then bring that idol to a temple, where they have it installed and enlivened. The worshiper imagines that that idol is God and he worships it every day. As a result of worshiping the idol, he receives blessings from it; the idol turns into a real God. So it is the awareness with which you do something that is extremely powerful. Your feeling or attitude or awareness will never go to waste. When a devotee worships any idol with tremendous feeling, with the awareness that the idol is divine, for him the idol becomes divine, for him the idol works as God.

Divinity resides not in the stone or in wood, but in the awareness of the worshiper. When through your feeling you can invest even stone with divinity, it is ridiculous to say that you would not be able to realize divinity by worshiping your Self — because your Self is already divine. You don't have to imagine it being divine.

I have suggested the truest object for meditation. But if you are interested, you can meditate on the swimming pool or on the kitchen — I have absolutely no objection.

I always feel torn between meditating on you while watching you and meditating on you with my eyes closed. Is there any difference? Which should I do?

It is always better to meditate on one's own Self, not on another. However, if you happen to develop a great love for another, you can make him entirely your own and you can become his. The *gopīs* were in this state. They used to meditate on Krishna, considering the entire universe to be Krishna. To them, even their children and households and the things around them were only different forms of Krishna.

In *Play of Consciousness* I have said that meditation on the Guru is really a form of meditation on the Self. The best kind of meditation on the Guru is to identify your own Self with the Guru, to feel the Guru within you. Why don't you worship the Guru within you instead of worshiping the Guru outside? Don't you think that would be much better?

The poet Krishnasuta said that for one who worships an idol, the idol turns into God. That is quite true. The idol does turn into God. After all, God is everything. Stone is God, and water and trees are also God. There are some foolish people who hold that there is no God in stone or water or trees. Such a person will not be able to find God anywhere. What is the entire animate and inanimate universe, if not God? One who sees God everywhere in everything will be able to see God within himself also. But one who thinks that God's presence is confined only to certain places or to certain things will not be able to see God even in those things, nor will he be able to have the experience of the formless, attributeless Being.

Everything depends on the intensity of your feeling, attitude, and devotion. Whatever object your devotion is attached to, that becomes God for you. The poet says that those who worship stone images of God experience Him through their images. However, first the image has to be made, and then it has to be infused with divinity. Or one has to imagine that God is in it. But that is not the case with a living human being. God is already in the heart of a human being. If you worship Him within you, there is no reason why you should not experience

God, why you should not become Him.

We find that from time immemorial, people have been spending their entire lives seeking love from each other. Two people begin to love each other intensely, but neither feels as much love for his own Self. When two people are in love, what happens? The lover projects the love of his own heart, the love that is inside him, onto his beloved, and as a result he experiences satisfaction and happiness. The beloved is doing the same: she is projecting her own love onto her lover and experiencing satisfaction and happiness.

But this is not what Vedanta or yoga teaches. Vedanta says to direct the love that you have within you onto your own Self, and find your own happiness, your joy, right within your own heart — not in someone else. Instead what often happens is that a person thinks that his happiness and joy are coming from that individual. However, this is delusion. It is not the teaching of Vedanta. Vedanta says that you yourself should become Nityananda. See what happens when you yourself become Muktananda. There is not much point in worshiping another as Muktananda.

The love that you receive from others is not going to last. It waxes and wanes. It depends on the other person. It is not a reliable support; it is feeble and temporary. You should experience the love that is in your own heart. Make an effort to have your own love arise from your own inner depths. Then you will experience true love, true bliss. The moment you become saturated with the flow of love that springs up from within, that love will flow toward every object you see.

Then you will not have to make an effort to love another person. You will not have to indulge in all the hysterics that you call love. You will not have to cry at the top of your voice, "I love you, I love you, I love you! My love is true!" That is nothing but a theatrical, melodramatic affair. You will really know what love is only when you begin to love yourself. These play-actors of love swear in the name of God, in the name of every other deity, that their love is true, but it remains mere falsehood.

You know from your own experience that whenever anger arises within you, it pours out on anyone who comes in contact with you — regardless of whether that person is dear to you or a stranger. When anger flows out of you toward others in a most natural manner, why won't love also flow out naturally toward others when it has been released in your heart?

A true Guru is not one who makes everybody his disciples and keeps them in that condition even after leaving his physical form. Only he is a true Guru who, having himself become a Guru, takes discipleship away from his disciples and turns them into beings like himself. All other Gurus are false. The view that only one person can become the Guru and all others must remain as disciples is held only because somebody has a vested interest in it. The true message of Guruhood is that no one is a disciple. Everyone is the Guru. All are one. All are equal. All are divine. That is the only genuine message. Every other message is false.

Therefore, make your own eyes the Guru's eyes, your own ears the Guru's ears, your own stomach the Guru's stomach, your own legs the Guru's legs, and keep repeating *Guru Om, Guru Om* to yourself. Feel that you yourself are the Guru. That is the one genuine state, the one authentic goal.

I was wondering why people in western civilization can't get the same feeling from their own religions if they follow them as intensely as they follow the teachings of the Guru?

You find people in this predicament not only in the West, but also in the East. However, in the West some religious thinking seems to have frozen into dogma which says that God exists somewhere up there, and if you worship Him as a Being up there, your worship will show results only up there. In our country all the true saints have worshiped God within. If you worship God within, the results of that worship will appear right inside you in the form of contentment and fulfillment.

How do we worship and invoke Chiti or Shakti? Why is She not given an external form like Shiva, or prayed to as much as Bhagawan Nityananda?

Isn't Bhagawan Nityananda also Chiti? What is there that is different from Chiti? Isn't Shiva also Chiti? To understand that this whole world is the embodiment of Chiti is the greatest worship. Tukaram Maharaj was a very well-respected Siddha. When he began to understand everything, when he attained divine realization, he said, "O God, O Lord of the world, I am going to worship You in this way: whatever direction I go, whatever I come across, whatever person I come across, I will not regard it as a mere direction or thing or person, but I will consider that it is also You. That is the way I am going to worship You." He also said, "I do not have anyone else's company any more because God is my company all the time."

This is the way you should worship Chiti. Meditation and *japa* are also the worship of Chiti. The greatest worship is to become aware that the great Chitshakti is living inside you. No matter how many names you give Chiti — God, Rama, and Krishna — they are all one and the same. Chiti is She who has given birth to this entire universe, so we are all Her creation. That Chiti is being worshiped everywhere. She is the Guru. She is the mantra. And She is the articles for your worship. She is worshiped as Durga. Shakti is nothing but Chiti, Durga, Kali. She has different names and She has various forms. She has so many names; the list is very, very long. These are all the names of the external forms of Chiti. Every morning when I take a bath, I repeat these names.

Would you please explain how one should worship his own Self?

Once the sage Ashvalayana asked another sage, "Where does God dwell, what is His temple, and how do you worship Him?" The sage replied, "God dwells in the human body, with its seventy-two thousand nerves, five organs of actions, five senses of perception, five *prānas*, and four psychic instruments."

So this human body is the best temple of God. The individual soul, the Self dwelling inside one's heart, is God. Dwelling within the body, the Self makes our minds, senses, and body function. Man is wearing the veil of ignorance. When he discards this veil, he becomes aware that he is That. Then he begins to worship his own Self, saying, "I am That." The awareness of *So'ham,* "I am That," is the best way of worshiping the Self. The *Mānasa Pūjā* that we chant in the evenings emphasizes the value of this awareness. After worshiping That on the outside in different ways, a person becomes introverted. He begins to repeat these mantras: "O Lord, You are my Self. My intellect is Your energy. The five pranas are Your companions and this body is Your temple. The eyes see, the ears hear, the mouth eats and drinks, the tongue speaks, and the senses are worshiping You in this way. Whatever the senses do, that is Your worship."

We usually say, "I do this, I do that, I eat and drink." In this way we are putting up a wall between God and our Self. Whatever we are doing is also the worship of God. When man removes his veil, he will see what is really true. Kabir put it very truly when he said to remove the veil from your face, and once you remove it, you will see Rama within you. God dwells in every heart. So don't speak harsh words to anyone.

Every philosophy has stated the importance of morning prayers as a form of worship. Hindus wake up early in the morning to offer their worship to God. Muslims also wake up before five o'clock in the morning and offer their prayers to God. Every religious person practices this kind of worship.

A great being said that every morning when you wake up, remember God who is effulgent in your heart, who is shining, who is vibrating inside you in the form of inspiration. He is of the form of *sat chit ānanda.* He is not destroyed by any state. He is awake in the waking state, in the sleeping state, and in the deep sleep state. All these states arise and subside, arise and subside, but He always remains. Shaivism also says one who has the full understanding of all these three states — the waking, sleeping, and the deep sleep states — attains the *turīya* state within himself.

Therefore, one should turn inward; all one's senses should turn inward. This is the greatest worship of God. When the senses become still, that is true worship. To do merely external worship is not real worship. Jnaneshwar Maharaj said that when you do nothing — that is true worship.

Now when you hear this, don't think you should not go to the *Āratī* tonight. True worship does not mean that you stop doing your practices. If you do that now, your mind will still be wandering, your senses will still be active. So that is not the true doing nothing. Real worship is to become one with the Self.

There Was a Time When I Used to Worship the Lingam

Would you speak about the *shivalinga*? It has a great attraction for me and appears often in my meditations. Could you mention some ways of doing puja to it?

If it frequently comes into your meditation, go to the upper garden where there is a shivalinga; keep staring at it and meditate on it. Keep watching it until it disappears. However, the scriptures say that the true shivalinga is inside and that the outer one is a symbol. The true lingam is inside in the heart and it is called the "jyotirlingam," the lingam of light. It is better to meditate on that. This lingam is the individual soul. In Shaivism when the individual soul merges in the absolute Soul, that is called "lingānga samarasya." Millions of people worship the outer lingam. These people attain either good or bad fruits from worshiping it. However, it is very ordinary. It is much better to worship the inner lingam.

There was a time when I used to worship the lingam all the time. I had a great interest in reciting the Rudram *and doing* abhisheka, *ritual bathing, of the lingam. Then I came to Ganeshpuri and I went to the Bhimeshwar lingam. That was when I stopped worshiping on the outside. I used to live in Vajreshwari and from there I would go to see my Babaji in Ganeshpuri. Before I went for his darshan, I would go to the Mahadev Temple and I would pour water on the lingam.*

One day, Babaji asked me, "Where did you come from just now?"

"I came from the temple," I said.

"That is the outer lingam," he said. "Worship the inner lingam in meditation. Worship the inner lingam — not the outer deity, but the true inner lingam. Worship the inner Self in your meditation."

God has no lingam; He has no form, no shape, and no gesture. He is nothing but Consciousness. We perform outer worship so that we can attain the inner worship. Once we start to worship the inner Self, we don't have to perform outer worship. Still, if you have a great attraction for it, you can go ahead and worship the outer lingam. Don't try to understand its mystery and fill your mind with doubts. Just understand that the lingam is nothing but God, and that is more than enough.

If a person tries to attain a lot of understanding about something, what often happens is that he attains incorrect understanding. You should try to achieve perfect understanding because imperfect understanding gives you pain. Just by having outer faith, man can swim across. Many people worshiped the lingam with faith and went across. Many more will go across in the future, worshiping it with faith. No matter what worship it is, you should become completely absorbed in it. Eknath Maharaj said that a worshiper and the deity of worship should not remain two; they should become one. Only then will the worshiper attain the object of worship, the fruit of worship.

There is a lot of power in a person's faith, in a person's feeling. With that faith and feeling you can attain anything, you can do anything. Shaivism asks, What place is there *where Shiva doesn't exist? What object exists without Shiva? What time exists where there isn't Shiva?*

No matter what you worship, what bears fruit is your faith, your feeling, and nothing else. Your feelings should be noble and high. Your faith should be very strong. Your trust should be very powerful. Then no matter what you worship, it will bear fruit. In the Panchadashi *it is said that everything is God. God pervades everything. If you worship anything with faith, everything will bear fruit for you.*

THE CONTINUOUS AWAKENING

CHAPTER 12

Love Is the Bliss of the Self

*What is God? God is the bliss that rages continually.
That is the Self.*

*What do you mean when you say, "God dwells within the
heart?" Do you mean a certain physical or subtle space inside
us, or that we must approach the Self through love?*

Through right understanding and love you can approach the
Self. There is a specific space inside the heart and it is divine.
Right in this space there is a light, which is the size of the
thumb, and that is Consciousness. Consciousness pervades
from head to toe; it pervades everywhere. No place is without
Consciousness. Everything is made of Consciousness. The scientists know this very well, although they speak of energy
rather than Consciousness. Whatever you give them, they can
turn into energy — whether you give them iron, copper, or
stones, they can put them through a process and change them
into energy. In the same way, the Vedantic philosophers consider everything Consciousness. Consciousness exists everywhere and in all beings, but specifically, it lives in the heart.

Could you reveal some secret about penetrating one's heart?

That is what meditation is for. *Shaktipāt* and meditation are
meant precisely for penetrating the heart. You go within; you
focus the mind and lead it toward the heart. It is something very

great if you can enter the heart. It is the most important center; there is no other center that can compare with the heart.

What is the relationship between the physical heart and the heart that you talk about?

They are the same — a person has only one heart. In scriptural terms the heart is in the chest as well as at the top of the head. However, it is the same heart that extends from one place to the other. A *yogi* who meditates on the *sahasrāra,* the upper heart, considers this thousand-petaled lotus to be the heart. The heart is the same for everybody — for yogis and for regular citizens. The breath goes out and comes in, and there is a space inside where it becomes still just for a second. The breath has merged inside, and it hasn't yet started to come out; it is still in the state of merging. The space where it merges is the true heart. That is called *hridaya.* You have asked a beautiful question and I want to thank you.

How can one learn to love?

I'm sure you love various things in your worldly life. Doesn't one love oneself? A person wears beautiful clothes, jewelry, and so on. Is this not taking refuge in love? People love one another as well. Sometimes this love is true and sometimes it is false. If one wants to love truly, one must meditate a lot. In the body there is a special place of love, and one must attain this place. When we attain this place, we experience love all around — only love. Hate disappears. In order to love, one must think about love, one must deeply contemplate love, one must create a bond of friendship with love.

I have some difficulty following the path of devotion; however, I do meditate on the heart chakra regularly. Would you speak about the difference?

Devotion and meditation are quite different. Meditation focusing on the heart chakra is fine, but devotion is supreme love for

250

God. Devotion is to feel great, intense love for God, so much that your heart opens by itself. Just as one feels love for one's father or mother or son or wife, or some people feel love for their dogs or cats or for their food — you feel all-consuming love for God. That is what devotion is.

How do you hold the pain that comes from loss of love?

Love is something that exists inside all the time. It is constant. You will never lose your love. Even if you think you have lost your love, you can attain it once again in the heart. If love is lost because you lost a person, because you lost that loving event, it was not true love. It was merely an illusion of love.

The nature of true love is existence, consciousness, and bliss. It is always there; it is always shining inside. The person that you love may go away, but love is always going to be there inside. Love is something that always resides in the heart.

If one turns within in hopes of finding love on the outside, can that be detrimental to turning within? If so, how does one turn within and let go of still wanting love and other things on the outside?

If you find love within yourself, you don't have to let go of your feeling of wanting love from outside. When you attain love from within, that inner and outer love merge into each other. They become one in reality. Once you attain inner love, the same love will pulsate in all your various actions and you will see it outside too.

Love is the source of this world. All religions, all actions, all names and forms exist in that love. Everything pulsates in that bliss, in that love. If you attain that love first from within, you don't have to wonder what to do.

I have the greatest fear that I will never be truly loved, nor will I be able to express my love truly without it being destroyed or rejected. Please speak to me about love and fear.

It is your own fear, so you can very easily renounce it and become fearless. You create your own fear in your imagination. Nobody else can love you; love is not something that is given or taken. If you think so, that is your wrong understanding. You have to make love well up inside yourself. Giving love and taking love are only outer forms; they are not the true nature of love. Have you ever experienced taking love? Is it tangible? Can a person who gives love measure how much he has given to someone? No. Love surges within.

Have no fear. Love is not an object that you can show. Man can talk about anything and everything; however, he can never speak about love because there is no language for it, there is no tongue for it. Love is indescribable; you can't catch it with words. It is free from desires, free from qualities. In a very subtle way it springs forth from within.

What is my path now and in the future?

Your path is to maintain mundane activities and perform them in a disciplined manner. Don't betray your life; don't betray your mundane activities either. Most of all, never betray your own Self. Always respect the divine flame that exists inside you. This is your path. As long as That exists in this body, respect That with love.

We spread our own fantasy by saying, "I love you, I love you." Do you ever think, "I love myself, I love me?" If you don't love yourself, how can you have any love within to give others? If a person says, "I love only you," isn't he spreading his own delusion everywhere? What is this giving and taking of love? When you say, "I love you," do you really give love? Does love depend on your speech? Is love going to sit in your hand so that you can give it or take it? Is it restricted to words? If you don't have love within yourself, if you don't know what love is, if you say that you are giving love to others, you are just saying pretty words — nothing more.

Love is the inner, sensational, pulsating, secret thing that takes place deep inside. You don't give or take love: love arises and manifests within on its own. When that happens, it just flows to others; it is not something you can give or take. You can experience that love by turning inside and using the inner senses. One thing is certain — when love starts surging within, your senses can feel it.

So your path is to love your own Self. Make your very heart the temple of God. In the heart there is love that is concealed. It also appears in the form of scintillating blue light, and that is nothing but God. Make that your love. This is the path for all humanity.

The kingdom of God is within. How does one find it?

Through meditation you can find it. It is true that the kingdom of God is within. Whoever saw anything saw it inside his own heart, not outside. Only after seeing That inside his heart was he able to see That outside too.

There was a great saint called Mansur Mastana, a great Sufi being. Always he used to say, *ana'l-Haqq,* "I am God." People who were blind to religion killed him, saying that he committed a crime. Even while he was being killed, still he said, *ana'l-Haqq,* "I am God." Those nails didn't bother him. Even then he said, "You can tear down a mosque, a temple, a church; you can break all those things, but never break anyone's heart, because this is the real shrine of God, this is where He dwells."

So never break anyone's heart. In a temple there is an idol and in a mosque there is only void, emptiness. But in this heart God dwells; this is the real shrine of God. The light of God is shimmering here, it is scintillating and vibrating all the time. Through meditation you can find this. And when the inner Shakti is unfolded, you get it. It is there for you to find; it is completely yours.

Will you speak about love?

People always use this word "love, love, love." Love is also devotion and devotion is love. In India there was a great Guru called Shankaracharya, who said there is devotion where there is no division, no differences. One who becomes completely one with God has devotion, because in devotion there is no duality. Shaivism says that to know the inner Self, to perceive the inner Self, and to become immersed in the inner Self is devotion.

First of all, you should have complete love for the Self, for God, for the supreme Principle. To have love, you don't have to know any category; you don't have to understand whether God has form or whether He is without form. If you have complete love for God, that is called devotion.

Love is nothing but nectar. The divine sage Narada said that having attained this love, one becomes perfect, one becomes a Siddha. One becomes nectar incarnate, the very image of ambrosia. One becomes completely satisfied in his own inner Self. He never has this desire: "I want more, more, more." This is called devotion.

After attaining the nectar of love, one doesn't have any petty desire. Nor does one wonder, "What will happen to me tomorrow or the day after?" Nor does one have any hatred, because for one who has attained this love, only love exists, nothing but love. Only God exists and nothing else.

While explaining the signs of a true devotee in the *Bhagavad Gītā*, the Lord said that only he is a true devotee who understands that the entire universe is the family of God. He doesn't dwell on the different things of this world. He never becomes depressed, dejected, or lacks enthusiasm; he never sits with his head in his hands. After obtaining this love, man becomes completely intoxicated, madly in love with God. He becomes completely still, completely stable, because he is fully satisfied in his own inner Self. Everything has been fulfilled for him. His mind, subconscious mind, and intellect take refuge in the inner Self, in that love. He begins to revel in his own inner Self, in his inner love. He doesn't look in various directions. He doesn't search for different subjects. He doesn't look for new talents or skills.

To have complete love for God is a great *sādhanā*. Among all spiritual pursuits, this is the easiest — still it is very difficult to follow. If your love grows very naturally and spontaneously for the supreme Principle, you get everything. You don't have to look for anything. The saint Tulsidas said that the river flows and flows continuously, and eventually it merges into the ocean

254

and becomes the ocean. In the same way, a person who continuously loves God merges into God and becomes God.

To have great and intense absorption in God is called love. In our everyday life we experience the shadow of love, but not the complete love — just a tinge of it. The world came out of love. The Upanishads say that God is supreme bliss, and the universe emanated from Him. All beings live in bliss or in the hope of attaining bliss. So love is truly a great sadhana. *Love* is such a small word, but there is a lengthy philosophy on it. Love means the inner intense feeling for Him.

We love our pets — our cats and dogs — and they seem to love us. Do they experience the same love we do?

They too experience love. They experience love while they eat and drink. They can also perceive the love of human beings. Trees can also perceive this love, and rocks too. If you read something good while sitting on a particular rock every day, you can tell the rock is changing; its feelings are changing. The philosophy of Shaivism was written on a rock. Lord Shiva inscribed the sutras of Shaivism with His trident on a huge rock in Kashmir. When I sat on that rock, I began to experience the wisdom that was written there. Love pervades everything. Along with Consciousness, love permeates everywhere.

Please speak on how I can hold on to love in my heart when I am in the presence of another person who is feeling negative and saying critical things about me.

You should love for your own sake, not for the sake of hearing sweet words from another person. There was a great poet-saint in our country who said to remember God and leave others alone. Keep intensifying your love for God. You shouldn't care about hearing good words or bad words from others.

How can I be free of my attachment to personal love for a particular individual?

It's all right. Sometimes you have this personal love. With this same love try to love the Self. In the world whatever love you feel — a little bit or a lot — is love of God, because there is nothing in this world without God. Whether you are eating, drinking, seeing, hearing, or speaking, if you feel a little bit of happiness, it comes from the ocean of happiness. What you feel is a drop, but it is of the same nature as the ocean of happiness. Even in the dealings of your mundane life, that little bit of happiness contains the joy of the Self, but only a trace. It is like the dust on the point of a needle. But the Self is an ocean of joy. To experience that in its fullness we have this Intensive, and we do this sadhana. Whatever happiness you experience in your daily life doesn't last long. It is like a shadow — it's there and then it's gone. But once you attain the happiness of the Self in meditation, it lasts forever.

I really like myself, but sometimes I wonder if it's my ego self or the inner Self that I am liking. Is it all right to like one's ego self?

It doesn't matter whom you love or how you love. If love opens up within you, that's fine. Love should spring forth from within a person all the time. One's heart shouldn't be dry like a dead tree. It should be filled with love. That love should come out from your eyes, ears, and speech. If you don't earn that love, what do you earn in this world anyway? Every creature has these things — sleep, food, and fear. If man also has only these things, what's so great about that? Man should be greater than other creatures, and he can be greater only if he has love.

To attain this love you should repeat the name of God, who is the embodiment of love. As your repetitions increase, your love increases too. This is the nature of the mind — if it thinks about something for a long time, it becomes like that.

Your touch on my forehead traveled to my heart, and I am experiencing an opening to you that surprises me in its intensity. How can I make this part of my work with my students and clients who are experiencing pain? How can I make it part of my everyday life?

Meditate more. There is tremendous love in the heart, and as you experience more of it, it will certainly help you in your life. That love is imperishable, it is endless. Being aware of that, you should function in the world. This love will chase after you and keep growing inside you, so don't worry. If you have pain, you keep feeling it all day long. In the same way, you will experience this love even in your daily life. Focus your awareness on your heart.

Very often we find ourselves falling in love with people who are not in love with us. What do we do when that happens?

You should have love without any expectation. In the *Bhagavad Gītā* there is a verse that says you should keep on performing your actions, but do not expect any fruit from them. In the same way, you can have love for someone, but do not expect any results from that love. Then it will be just like Mahatma Gandhi's yoga of detachment.

Why don't you bestow your grace on yourself? Why don't you love yourself? Have compassion toward your own Self; love your own Self; increase that love within you. That would be great. Then it would not matter if someone or no one gives you love, because you have that love within yourself.

THE TRUEST BLISS

I think it is good to remain separate from the Guru because in this way I experience devotion. This devotion gives me great bliss, but at the same time to be away from you gives me great pain. How can I get rid of the pain of separation and become one with you without getting rid of the bliss of devotion?

There are nine kinds of devotion. The devotion of the pain of separation is considered to be the best one. But can a person really become separate from the Guru? If you think you can, what have you understood about the Guru? Nothing but dust. What makes you think the Guru is only five-and-a-half feet tall, that he is only a bundle of flesh? The Guru is the grace-bestowing power of God; he is not this body. Is the power of grace so small? No! The power of grace pervades from north to south, from west to east. It stretches from above to below. When God's grace pervades everything, how can the Guru be small? This is the wrong understanding.

If you have the right knowledge of the Guru, no matter where you go, the Guru is with you — he is in front of you and he is also behind you. This is the measure of true devotion.

Is your teaching mainly for devotional people? What is the place of so much chanting for one who follows the path of knowledge, for one who asks: Who am I?

When I tell you to meditate on your inner Self, what does that mean? Doesn't it mean that I'm asking you to find out who you are? Meditate on your own Self, honor and worship your Self, kneel to your Self — that is the purest Vedanta.

What is the point of just making your heart dry and sterile by joyless, intellectual inquiry: Who am I? Who am I? Who am I? Devotional practices liberate *rasa*, joy, sweetness, nectar. True knowledge is not dry; it releases bliss. If it does not release bliss, it is not knowledge. It is for releasing the inner joy that we chant.

Our devotion is nondual devotion, and that too is a form of knowledge. It is only when knowledge and devotion, or *jñāna* and *bhakti*, come together that you have the ideal combination. Otherwise, to see the same Self in everyone is jnana, and to love everyone is bhakti. If knowledge has no love in it, it is dry and joyless. If love has no knowledge, the devotion is blind; it lacks understanding.

Devotion has immense power; it is full of knowledge; it is the ocean of love. A poet sang, "O Mother Bhakti, you are marvelous. You hold liberation in your right hand and enjoyment in your left hand. You fill all your votaries with bliss. You make the poor rich, you make beggars kings, and you make kings emperors. You destroy all evil and sins, you generate knowledge, detachment, and dispassion. You make fools knowledgeable and bring enlightenment to the knowledgeable. You reveal consciousness in matter; you reveal the real in what appears to be unreal. You show the existence of God in the beginning, in the middle, and in the end. You fill our hearts with love and bliss. O Mother Bhakti, your power is marvelous. You hold liberation in one hand and enjoyment in the other. You fill our hearts with sweetness and joy."

Sometimes when I am chanting or listening to you, a strong emotion of love comes over me — love for you, for myself and for the world. I feel a need to express it, but I feel frustrated because I don't know how.

Whenever you experience this rush of love in your heart for yourself and for everything else in this world, you should hold on to that state. That is the doorway to divinity; that is the key. Don't let go of it. The truth is that this world is full of love. This world is an embodiment of the bliss of God. Look at those trees — God's love is vibrating in them. Look at water — God's love is vibrating in water. Look at the faces of all the people — God's love is vibrating there.

If you don't feel any love in your heart, it is because you haven't turned within and found it within yourself. A poet-saint has said, "I see the root of all joys sparkling and shimmering everywhere. That is God's bliss; that is God's own being. In all states of consciousness, in waking, dream and deep sleep, in all the thoughts and feelings of my heart, I see only God's bliss and love vibrating. Since I became immersed in God's love, the distinction between these states of consciousness has disappeared. There is only one thing I know — and that is God's bliss and love. I am experiencing supreme bliss all around me, above and below, in front and behind. There is only one ocean surrounding me, and that is the ocean of God."

You should keep experiencing more of your inner bliss, even while you are engaged in different activities. Let your mind become soaked with That. If there was a time when you didn't feel love, you yourself were responsible for that. Now that you have started feeling love, it is your responsibility to unfold more of it. You can always find a way to express your love for everyone. Whenever you get into that state, try to find out how you got there.

My desire to love you is great, but I feel very separate from you, as I do from myself and nearly everything else. I even feel separate from my desire to love you, although I know it is there. Please speak about acceptance.

You try to love me — that is what separates you from me. If you love your own Self, you will love everybody. If a person wants to love somebody, but he thinks that person is separate from him, he just can't love him. Whoever has loved others, has loved them with the awareness that they are his own Self. A great being said, "O Lord, You are me and I am You. This is my worship."

What is the source of your love? How do you manage to love everyone all the time?

I continue to love my own Self, to increase love for my own Self. My joy permeates everybody. For example, if you are weeping, if you are sad, if you are feeling pitiful, others start weeping along with you. You don't have to tell them, "Cry with me." Automatically they weep with you. In the same way, I laugh with joy, and spontaneously you catch that and you start doing the same. Express joy on your face and another person will also start feeling the same thing. I look at everybody with joy. The vision of joy is great.

Your gift of love to each of us is indeed a great gift, but even greater is your teaching about how to love. This I feel is the greatest teaching that one being can ever give to another. How can one learn to do this?

Meditate every day. Don't be like Sheikh Nasruddin who got drunk and, rather than trying to find his house, sat in one place thinking, "Well, the world is spinning and sooner or later my house will come before me." Every day meditate; meditate continuously. Just open yourself. If you open yourself, love will surge forth; it will spring forth. You will find that all you have inside is love and you just can't help but love others. For this reason meditate in a disciplined manner. Try to reach the center of love at least once. First, you yourself should become very loving; then you can start thinking of others. What has happened to you is that you are already thinking of others.

Once Nasruddin inaugurated a big bank. When he was asked why, he said, "To help poor people." Many people became extremely happy; they thought it was great that they could get a loan from the bank and help needy people. So the next day some people went to the bank to ask Nasruddin for a loan. He said, "Well, I have opened the bank, but there is no money in it yet."

It shouldn't be like that with you. First of all, you should be filled with love. Then you can learn how to love others; you can think about others later. Once you find love within yourself, you won't have to try to love others.

Baba, whom do you love the most?

(*Points to himself*) In the Upanishads there is a very long conversation between Yajnavalkya and Maitreyi. Yajnavalkya was one of the great sages. He was the expounder of one of the Upanishads, the *Brihadāranyaka*. He was a king as well as a Guru.

In India there is a tradition of giving things to a great being, so people had given him great wealth. One day he brought out all his wealth and he divided it in half, and he counted the number of cows and divided that in half.

Then he called his wives, Katyayani and Maitreyi. Katyayani was the first wife and she was very old. Maitreyi was the second wife and she was still a young woman. When he offered the wealth to them, the older wife took her share.

The younger one questioned him, "Why are you giving all this wealth to us? Why don't you keep it for yourself?"

"O Maitreyi," he said, "the Self cannot be satisfied with wealth. Therefore I am renouncing all this. I want to leave. I want to renounce you too."

"If that is so," Maitreyi said, "you can give my share to

Katyayani. Even though you are so old, I married you, but not for the sake of your wealth; I married you to attain the Self. Now you are leaving to attain That, so please give me That for which you are yearning too. I don't want your wealth." She was a great *yogini*.

Yajnavalkya then began to speak, "The Self is very dear. Man speaks of love, but truly man loves for the sake of the Self. The Self is dearer than this physical body, dearer than a son, dearer than wealth and *prāna*. You may say, `I love you, I love you,' but when you say that, you don't really love that person, you love your Self. So it is not that I love you — I love me. The word *you* is wrong. I have two wives, and I love you both, but I do not love you for your sakes; I love you for my own sake."

The Self is filled with love; it is of the form of love. One who loves somebody else does so for the sake of this love, not for the sake of the other person.

Many people tell me, "I love you," and I also answer, "Yes, I love you." Truly, everybody does the same thing. Everybody says, "I love you," but the truth is that nobody loves you. Everybody loves his own Self.

The Self is filled with love, it is the embodiment of love. You love the Self.

I want to let you into my heart but my armor keeps you out. How do I make the first chink in the armor?

I have already entered your heart. What is this new idea that you want to let me into your heart? You are mistaken; you have the armor of wrong understanding. Even before your father, I entered your heart. So understand that I am already in your heart.

Sometimes I feel great love for you, and the feeling is accompanied by great bliss. Why do I not experience this love twenty-four hours a day?

Why are you talking about twenty-four hours? Just an hour or even a few minutes would be more than sufficient. Try to develop it slowly and gradually. Even though it is bliss, you

262

must have the strength to enjoy that bliss. Your body must be strong enough to take it.

What do you think of one who is attached to you, wanting recognition from you in some way? Is attachment to the Guru like other attachments—a source of suffering?

Attachment to the Guru brings suffering only when it is accompanied by desire. If there is no desire in it, there will be no suffering. Love for the Guru is its own justification, and if it contains no demand on the Guru, it will not cause any suffering. If there is some selfish interest involved in your attachment to the Guru, it is like any other attachment, like any other form of greed, like any business. Devotion to the Guru that has no desire in it gives the highest bliss and sweetness. Your sole concern should be to sustain your devotion. Even if I do not recognize you, it does not matter. What really matters is the purity of devotion without desire. That is its own recognition.

Since I have been here, I have been wanting to cry and cry, and it doesn't have anything to do with what you are saying.

A person generally cries for two reasons: one is pain and sorrow and the other is joy and happiness. Whenever you are in a situation where you experience purity or something elevating, you express your feeling of love through crying. When I look at your face, I think you are crying out of love. That is what I observe.

There is a center within the human being that is a reservoir of love. When it overflows, you cry—that's just how it is. When the heart is filled with love, there is no language. No language can communicate love. Tears are the only medium through which we can express our love. Because there is no technique and no language, peacefully we have to cry. There is no other way.

What is the best way for me to show you the love I feel for you?

First, love yourself and then you will be able to love me automatically. We seek love outside of ourselves—from others— and that is why we suffer. If you were to seek love inside, you

263

would find it and you would also be able to give it to others. Keep giving your love to your inner Consciousness, and I assure you, that love will come to me.

How do I know that you really love me?

When you become real, you will really know that I love you. Now you are unreal; in other words you are "uncooked." So how can you understand my real love for you?

The Lord has filled my heart with so much love for you ever since I first met you. Can this love lead me to the Self? Is it an experience of the Self? Or is it an attachment to you?

That love is the love of the Self, but you think that love comes because you see me. You accuse me for no good reason. Don't blame me — it is your love; it comes from you.

Since I have been at the ashram, I have begun to love you very, very much — so much so that at times it feels as though my heart is going to burst. Yet at the same time I am very frightened of you, so much so that I can't look in your eyes. Why is this?

Fear of God or fear of a great being increases love in your heart. It seems you have a very good soul. As the love increases, it doesn't mean it will burst your heart, but it will burst the fear that obstructs you in love. It will tear away your fear, and once this fear is torn off, you will be the happiest person in the world. It is this fear that makes a person deluded, that makes him do what he doesn't want to do. As love increases, your fear will burst. Become an image of love, become very beautiful. It is really very lucky to be like this.

I think of you with love all the time, but my love is not always the same. Sometimes it is so tender that I cry. Sometimes I love you with such joy that I laugh. Sometimes I love you peacefully. Sometimes I love you with fear and I want to hide myself from you. Sometimes I love you with anger. When I love you with anger, I feel more identified with you. Why? What should I do?

All these are signs of love. For true love to arise within you, you need all these symptoms. In true love, one laughs, cries, sings, and dances. The great sage Narada says, "When one is absorbed in true love, he becomes very still or mad with that love or delighted within his own Self."

Just as sometimes when you are in love, you laugh and cry, in the same way you also get angry. There are two kinds of anger: one anger is filled with hatred and the other is filled with love. The anger that is free from hate is better; it contains true love.

The ocean of love resides within everyone, but only in one who is very fortunate can it spring forth. The great saint Kabir said that every heart is filled with love, there is no heart that is not filled with love, but only in a rare being does this love come to life.

Love that is without expectation or desire is the greatest love. Truly speaking, if there is anything in this world to attain, it is that love. Objects don't contain love; they can only help in your mundane life. They can't become the means of giving you love. A person lives in this world just for the sake of love. He does all these things just for the sake of love. The One has become many just for the sake of love. You try to find love in different ways, but if you look inward, you find that love within you.

DRINK THAT NECTAR

How can I kindle the flame of love?

The flame of love is already kindled; it is not extinguished. You don't need a match to kindle it again. It is effulgent inside. However, you will have to reach that center where love exists. Meditate with great respect. This divine love is inside. If this love were not inside you, you could not live in this world with joy.

Love is God. He is shining all the time. However, He lives in the secret cave of the heart. Cool down the thoughts of your mind. Then you will know that love is already kindled; you don't have to kindle it again.

Recently I caught a glimpse of who I was and a few days later I was overcome by tears of happiness. Is this usual?

The second experience is greater than the first. In the first experience you just found out who you were, but that was your understanding, that was knowledge. Now you have gone beyond that and you have begun to cry because of that love, because you know who you are. Become immersed in that love; give up all other things.

Man has taken birth to attain love, to jump with love, to dance with love, and to swim in the ocean of love. He didn't take birth to fight with others, to be confused, to have conflicts. Give up thinking of others; give up looking at others. Look at your own Self; become immersed in your own ecstasy. Try to see how much happiness lies within you.

The ocean of joy, the ocean of happiness, the ocean of love and peace, is so large that compared to it the outer ocean is not big at all. Inside you, listen to God, talk to God, see God. Then you will become an ecstatic being. Give up looking at another's makeup, another's moustache, another's hair style. Look at your own Self.

The poet-saint Kabir used to look at his own Self. He spoke in this way: By listening to the divine music, by listening to my inner Self, my mind became immersed in That, my mind became ecstatic. The inner love is so great that the moment I attained it, I became still. I went mad with love, and I perceived the inner flame, the divine flame. Then I began to delight in the Self. When I began to experience that love, I went into *samādhi*, and I became Consciousness, I became God, I became Ram, I became immersed in the wisdom of my Guru's words. When I arrived at unity-awareness, I began to see everything as beautiful, as Consciousness, as God. My mind became completely absorbed in the wisdom of my Guru. My individual being became the supreme swan. As I began to listen to that music, the brilliant light began to blaze in its fullness, and the nectar of love began to flow. The pot of nectar turned upside down, little by little, and as I tasted that nectar, I became very intoxicated. O *sādhus*, I became so intoxicated just by sipping that nectar of love. While listening to that inner divine music, my mind became immersed in That.

This is the attainment of Siddha Yoga. Only when man attains this is he called a human being. Then his human birth has accomplished something. Otherwise, what is the use of this human body?

Everyone is great, everyone has that love, everyone has that peace. No one has any negativities, no one is inferior, no one is low, and no one is petty. Never commit the sin of thinking yourself ordinary or petty. Never commit the sin of considering yourself a sinner. That divine Self is blazing within all of you. It is true — in the mosque of everyone's heart the light of God is shining. That is the abode of God.

Love and devotion are such a big part of the path. I worry that I don't love you enough and that I am not devoted enough. How do I go about increasing my love and devotion for you, and how do I stop worrying about this?

The more you increase your love, the less you worry. This love and devotion are greater than any other sadhana. Love and devotion are not different; they are one and the same. It is only through love that you meditate and become absorbed in meditation; then your inner love opens up. It is only through love that you open yourself to another person. Love is the origin of this world. The universe was not created through anger or through other desires. This whole universe was created through love, the love between Shiva and Shakti. When their love joined together, this whole universe came forth. Through supreme bliss, Shiva and Shakti created this whole universe.

All beings are playing in this supreme bliss; they are born of it, and at the end, they merge into it. So bliss is at the beginning, in the middle, as well as at the end, too. But we don't get the sense of it; we don't get the knack of how to open ourselves up so that we can experience that joy, that bliss. We always praise other people by saying, "Oh, that person is so great, that person is a high being. Wow, wow! That person is really beautiful!" But you do not praise your own Self. You do not have the confidence that inside you, there is a great inner Self. We should have the greatest self-confidence.

Therefore, through meditation and through right understanding, we have to open up that inner bliss, that inner joy. Constantly think of that supreme bliss. Always contemplate yourself. Always smile at yourself. Always laugh within yourself. Always be happy within your own inner Self and always think that you are so good. Then you can see that the Self is not far away from you.

Is shaktipāt love? Is love shaktipāt?

Shakti is the form of love; Shakti is the embodiment of love. Shakti is nothing but the pulsation of the Self, nothing but the throb of the Lord. It is the embodiment of supreme bliss; it is the form of supreme effulgence.

When we say the Shakti is awakened within, that means it is awakened within with great joy. In the form of happiness it is awakened. That is called supreme bliss. People also call it the bliss of Consciousness, because Consciousness is the embodiment of bliss. So Shakti is bliss and bliss is Shakti. The Upanishads say that out of supreme bliss, supreme love, this entire universe comes into existence.

How can one bear so much joy? Can one drown in it? I remember feeling full of happiness and asking a friend if a person can be too happy? He said, "Never," but I don't know what to do with that feeling of overflowing.

Look at the pictures of these great beings. They lived in such great joy. Look at their faces.

The happier you become, the better the life you can lead. This world exists in joy. This world came out of the supreme bliss of the Lord. The same is true of a human being.

You have been addicted to unhappiness for a long time, so when you experience this joy, you become very afraid. Don't give up your joy.

268

Can love conquer the mind? How?

Love can conquer the entire world. Not only that, love can keep God in your pocket. It's true.

Mirabai was a great being, and she said, "I have bought God, I have bought God! Some people say He is very expensive; some people say He is very cheap, very easy to get. But I got a scale and I bought Him. I measured Him and I bought Him with love."

Love is very powerful. The only reason the world exists is because of God's love. When there is this divine pulsation, this divine throbbing, this divine movement of God, the world comes into existence. When it stops throbbing, the world is reabsorbed.

Through love, even poison turns into nectar. Mira was given poison once, but she drank it with love and it changed into nectar for her. For Mira, because of love, even a snake became a garland of flowers. So love has great strength. Make your love reveal itself to you inside.

What can I do to get rid of my childhood fantasies about God and the associated fears, doubts, chagrin, and sense of rejection?

Once you begin to feel love for God, your fantasies will go by themselves. God is compassionate and He will forgive all the wrong notions you might have had. Don't worry about it; they will go away on their own. Before true understanding dawns, everyone has fantasies about God.

Sometimes I love God as my parent, sometimes as my child, and sometimes as my lover. Would you talk about God as lover?

You can love God any way you want to. No matter how you love Him, He will accept your love. A devotee sang, "O God, You are my mother, You are my father, You are my friend, You are my wealth, You are my knowledge, You are my everything. You are mine and I am Yours."

God can become anything, He can become everything. Do not think that God is different from you, that He is far away from you. God is not different from your husband or wife, nor from your son or daughter. If you understand God, you will discover that everything is created by God. God has become everything. One loves God according to one's own feelings. He accepts your feelings and reveals Himself to you according to His feelings. God exists only within feelings. He is not in a stone or in an idol; He exists only in feelings. If you have intense feeling for God, He reveals Himself to you in your heart.

Who is Shiva?

A major question! Who is Shiva? Shiva is Shiva. There is no comparison, there is no analogy for Him. If you were to ask me, "What is that person like?" and if there were another person like him, I could say, "He is like this person." But there is nobody like Shiva. Shiva is Shiva, as Shiva is.

People describe Him in many different ways, but their description doesn't get anywhere close; it is far away from Him. However, I can say that Shiva is the embodiment of bliss. He is the doer of everything in this world. Shiva is the support of all. Shiva is the inner Self of all.

Shaivism says, When He opens His eyes, the entire cosmos comes into existence. When He closes His eyes, the entire cosmos dissolves; it ceases to exist. He is the source of all *shaktis*, of all powers. He is the Lord, He is Shiva. He is Consciousness, and in the form of Consciousness He pervades everything. He makes everything function. Not only that, He is the embodiment of bliss.

If you want to know more than this, I will say, "I am Shiva." If you ask me again, I will say, "You are Shiva."

GOD HAS BECOME EVERYTHING

I would like to know how to pray to God. I have heard that God can hear only those who are in a high state of consciousness. I would like someone to talk to.

Everyone is in a high state of consciousness. To God, all are equal. It is only we who think in terms of high and low. Distinctions such as rich and poor, white and black, learned and illiterate, high-born and low-born are all man-made, and they are of no concern to God. If God's view were not any different from ours, if He were only an ordinary human being, what would be the point of praying to Him? The Lord says in the *Bhagavad Gītā* that all beings are equal to Him. No one is especially dear to Him, and no one is especially hateful. He is not especially fond of those who are supposedly in a higher state of consciousness.

Either God listens to everyone or He listens to no one. The great poet-saint Kabir wrote that although God can hear even the footsteps of an ant, some priests shout at the top of their lungs when they pray to God. What makes you think that God is so hard of hearing? It is just your wrong understanding. Give it up. God is very close to you, right in your heart. Say whatever you want to say to Him with love and devotion, and He will certainly hear you. His kingdom extends everywhere.

If the Absolute, the supreme Lord, is my divine soul, does that mean there is no one outside of my soul whom I can regard as my God—to praise Him, plead with Him, and finally merge with Him? If my divine soul is all that exists—if I am God—do I need to pray to God?

Your understanding is quite correct. The truth is that it is God who has become everything. In fact, there is no other being except God. If you truly feel that, you will not wonder whether you should pray to God. But as long as you have a question about whether you should pray to God, you must pray to Him. Since God is our inner Self, to meditate on the inner Self is to pray to God. If you could be in that state in which you feel that everything is God, you would not have this kind of doubt.

If you think that God is not outside you, pray to the inner Self, meditate on the inner Self, and merge into the inner Self. This is exactly what devotion is—to worship God by becoming God. That is what God is doing: He has expanded Himself and He keeps on looking at Himself with great love. Without any doubts, you too should do the same, and that will be your great worship and meditation.

Why are some people able to achieve Godhood in one lifetime, while others are not able to in hundreds or thousands of lifetimes? If God's heart is open only to a few, where is His mercy, His compassion, and His love?

This question is very good, but it shows that you do not have full understanding. What a person attains depends upon his self-effort. It is not God's method to give grace only to a particular person and not to another. In the *Bhagavad Gītā* the Lord says, "I pervade all beings equally. Neither do I hate anyone, nor do I love anyone. Neither do I befriend anyone, nor am I inimical to anyone. I am not close to one person and far away from another."

One who has intense faith, subtle understanding, and love for God takes only a short time to attain Him. Swami Ramakrishna Paramahamsa had a Guru whose name was Totapuri. To experience the supreme Truth, Totapuri pursued very austere spiritual practices for thirty years. When Ramakrishna went to receive initiation from him, he attained realization immediately just by listening to his Guru. He did not have to go anywhere to meditate.

Whatever takes place within you takes place through the inspiration of God. What place is there where there is no God? What time is there where God is not? What person is there in whom God does not dwell? God is always with you, but you do not have the understanding of that. You only have the understanding of worldly life. To have interest in God is a matter of great fortune. All you have to do to attain God is to develop an intense interest in Him.

Just as mountains and forests and oceans are open to everyone, God is open to everyone. He is not partial. He does not have any favorites. He does not belong to any one caste or party or sect. God's mercy, compassion, and love exist equally everywhere for all. But how are you receiving God's compassion?

You should become God and bestow your compassion on Him. Why do you expect God's compassion when you are not compassionate to Him? Have mercy on God. Forgive Him a little bit. You are merciless. If you were even a little bit merciful to God, if you would bow down to Him even once, He would bow down to you twice. You should learn how to imbibe God's compassion by becoming compassionate. You should attain God by becoming God. He is yours.

What is the ultimate unchanging reality?

It is the Self. The ultimate reality is the Self, which never changes; it always remains the same. It does not undergo any effects. It never increases or decreases. Nothing can taint it. The heat of the sun cannot reach there. The wind does not blow there. Pain does not enter there and death does not enter there either. The Self is always blissful, the embodiment of supreme bliss. It never changes. It is always the One. That is the goal of yogis, and after liberation a person becomes That.

If the Self is beginningless and free from time, why did it become bound inside this human body?

You think it has become bound within this human body, but it is not bound. The Self is free, not only in this human body but in other bodies. It is never bound. Neither does it do anything nor does it do nothing. It remains completely pure and true to its own nature. The nature of the Self is Consciousness. There is no bondage in it. It is bound only in your understanding. The Self is always pure, it is purer than the purest. You will know this when you perceive That.

You talk about the Self without perceiving it. This is what we do constantly: we teach people what we have not read and show people what we have not seen.

Even though the Self lives in this body, it is not touched by the good or bad actions performed by this body. It is supremely pure and supremely free. Although the Self is completely pure, because of our wrong understanding we think that it is impure, that it is tainted. Therefore, we should change our understanding.

What is this quality that attracts people to you?

I don't know what quality I have that attracts people, but there is one thing I know — I love my Self. I only know that I love my Self. A person cannot tell what virtues he has — only others can tell that. But I have deep faith and confidence in my own Self and my Guru, and I don't chase after desires. For that reason, I am happy.

What is the Self?

The Self is the light of God. The Self is God.
When you say "Self," I think of the body or the ego or the mind — but you are not talking about any of those?
No. The body, the mind, the ego, and so on are just instruments which allow the Self to be in this body.
But the Self itself is God?
Absolutely.

I understand that the Self is the essence of everything, but could you explain why the Self expresses itself in so many different forms?

It is its play. You too must think sometimes of becoming two or three instead of being just one.

Baba, are you everywhere at once?

Why not? How can the Self be in one place and not in some other place? The Self is present in every place, in all things, in every object, and at all times. The Self exists in everybody. You sing the *Guru Gītā* every day. Do you ever read the English translation? Do you ever think about what it means? The Guru is nothing but the Consciousness pervading every sentient and insentient object. There is a triangle in the sahasrara at the crown of the head. In the center of the triangle there are two feet, *ham* and *sa,* and these are the feet of the Guru. So the Guru exists everywhere and in everybody. There is no individual in whom the Guru does not exist. In the many He is the One, and in the One He is the many.

He Was Always Absorbed in Love

What can I really say about my Guru? He was a being who had attained everything. Most of the time he was absorbed in his own Self. He had attained such a great meditative state that when he ate, he was in that state; when he drank, he was in that state; when he walked, he was in that state. Just as when the river Ganges merges into the ocean and becomes the ocean, in the same way he had merged into the supreme Principle and become That.

He was always absorbed in love. He was completely rapt in the intoxication of love. If a worthy person went to see him, he would offer him love. He was a great renunciant and very generous. He loved giving things away to poor people; he would give them clothes and food. He lived in a jungle where there were mountains all around and there were adivasis, *tribal people. He changed the jungle into a beautiful town.*

He was omniscient: he knew the past, the present, and the future. Nonetheless, he remained very simple. He didn't like people coming too close to him. He did not allow them to touch his body. Thousands of people would be sitting in front of him, but they had to be very quiet. Nobody could make any noise. Just by watching him, people would attain something. They would experience that Shakti.

He was such a great being. His state was so strange. Sometimes he would speak, but if he didn't want to, he wouldn't. He would use one or two words, and those words were enough for people. He would say, "Follow the right path," and that was it — a person would start following the right path. He was such a great being; the stories about him are marvelous.

He performed so many miracles but he did it very quietly. His miracles were meant for his work, for his mission. On the stage people mesmerize other people; they show off their powers. But my Guru did not display his powers. He had attained self-control. He had also attained the siddhi of knowing what is going on in another person's mind or heart. Even though he knew it, he wouldn't let you know that he knew it.

He had equal vision for everybody. He did not take any interest in religions; all religions were the same for him.

He would put a shawl around his shoulders and wear a loincloth around his waist. If it was very hot, he would just wear the loincloth. His body was very beautiful. He had a big belly because of kumbhaka.

Just by being in his company, you could attain everything.

CHAPTER 13

The Ultimate Relationship

Remembrance will exist between you and me — it is the sign of God. If we have good understanding, you are with me and I am with you. There is no separation.

Baba, would you please talk about developing the inner relationship with the Guru?

There is already an inner relationship with the Guru, so just understand it. There is no room inside to develop a new inner relationship with the Guru. God, the Self, and the Guru are one and the same. Therefore, that inner relationship exists already. How can you have any more room inside for another relationship? The Guru is the Self of all, God is the Self of all, and you are also the Self of all. So the relationship is already established — you just have to understand it. Every day I tell you this. First of all, you should understand it, and then practice it.

I have the feeling you could help me, but I have a tremendous aversion to asking for help or putting myself in a dependent position. I feel I would rather remain more limited and achieve all I can on my own than become heavily dependent on a Guru. For me, dependency seems equivalent to personal failure. Please comment.

What you say, if you were to think about it coolly, shows that you are suffering from an illusion. In God's world you don't

279

mind depending on the earth; you don't mind depending on air and other natural elements; you don't mind depending on the food that grows on the earth. You never say to yourself, "I am not going to depend on any of these things." So why should the Guru stick in your throat?

You remind me of an ancient saint whose name was Vishvamitra. He was a very great being. He had acquired powers through practicing the hardest austerities, and as time went by, he developed a strange attitude. He spoke like this: I am not going to depend on God for anything; I am not going to take anything from His world; I am going to create my own new world.

You are behaving just like him. Once there were two friends — one had full faith in God and he depended completely on Him; the other did not believe in God, but he depended on everything in God's world, denying His existence all the time. One day they met. The one who did not believe in God, who did not want to depend on Him, and who did not even want to have anything to do with Him, said to his believer friend, "I am full of praise for you. You have such tremendous devotion and faith. You remember God all the time; your life is sublime and divine. You are very great."

The believer friend snapped, "Look, you are much greater than me. I accept God, who is all powerful, but you have rejected Him and have thrown Him out of the universe. How much greater than me are you!"

Your attitude seems quite considerate. You don't want to give any trouble to the Guru. If you were to depend on him, he would have to worry about you. Besides, you are also leaving poor God in peace.

Do you literally watch over and protect your disciples who take refuge in you? Even the ones you don't know personally?

There is a special protector of all, and I am just an instrument. I don't have to do anything. I speak to you about the One who is inside everybody's heart. He is there just to protect everybody. Still, sometimes a person has the feeling that the Guru protects him. So if you have this kind of feeling, understand that the feeling itself has its own power; it has its own strength.

When I first met you, you were in my thoughts constantly. Now it seems that your presence in my mind has become more subtle. Is this true or is it my imagination?

This is a sign of great progress! I will become more and more and more subtle and then merge with you. No matter what you do in your daily life, how you conduct yourself, what your work is, keep reminding yourself that you are a portion of supreme Consciousness, which lives in its fullness inside you. This is the awareness that you should maintain all the time. Cultivate this awareness over and over again. When this Shakti is transmitted into someone, no matter what he does, he becomes perfect at it. If a thief were to receive Shakti, he would become a first-rate thief.

There was once a thief who came to be known as Shyam Chor, or Stealer of Krishna. He kept stealing and stealing, and his desire for more and more booty increased. He was always trying to find out what greater treasures he could steal. Even though he had stolen a vast amount of wealth, because of his anxiety to find out whether there was anything greater to steal, he could neither sleep nor rest.

Whether you are a thief or a businessman, you cannot earn inner joy by wealth. I come from a very wealthy family. I did not become a renunciant because I did not get any food to eat or because nobody would give me any work. I became a renunciant for the sheer love of it. I was born into such a wealthy family that they would make me eat from a silver plate with silver utensils. But no matter how much you have, it cannot give your spirit enthusiasm; it cannot give you peace.

This thief was going from place to place to find what greater treasure he could steal. Once he went to a temple where a great seer was teaching. That day the lecture was on Krishna's crown and necklace and the other ornaments that He wore. The seer was rhapsodically describing the beauty of Krishna's crown, studded with sapphires and rubies and emeralds.

Around His neck Krishna wore a necklace of jewels and diamonds so bright that when He walked, He would light up the darkness. Then the seer went on to say that Krishna still plays in Vrindavan, holding His divine sport in the form of a child and that He still wears those precious ornaments.

So Shyam Chor said to himself, "I should steal those ornaments. If I could only steal them, I would be the greatest thief. No greater treasure could be stolen. I would become very famous."

He listened very carefully to the lecture because of course he couldn't ask any questions. Then he began to visualize the form of Krishna. He thought to himself, "He is dark; He wears a crown that is studded with most precious jewels. On His neck there is a necklace and on His arms there are bracelets."

He became totally absorbed in this contemplation and he began to walk toward Vrindavan. In those days there were no cars, and even if there had been, he would not have used one because he had to be stealthy. So while he walked, he kept contemplating all the treasure that Krishna wore. The more he walked, the more he became absorbed in the form of Krishna, so much so that he even began to see Krishna in his imagination. Whatever takes seat in your mind, you also see in your dreams. He kept walking and walking, and his contemplation on Krishna became more and more intense.

No matter how you relate to God, His love is bound to transform you. There was a seer who used to sing, "No matter how you contemplate God, whether with a good feeling or a bad feeling, whether with a good motive or a bad motive, even out of sheer laziness — it is bound to elevate you, it is bound to purify you."

Shyam Chor had to go across the Yamuna River in order to get to Vrindavan. Just as he crossed the river, he saw a being who fit the image of Krishna in his mind. He ran toward Him and hugged Him. The moment he received Krishna's touch, he forgot what he had come there for. Then he became a great friend of Krishna and got his name, Shyam Chor, Stealer of Krishna. Tukaram often said, a great Guru, by his mere touch, by his mere company, makes a person like himself. The glory of a Sadguru is great, and such Sadgurus are rare.

It is necessary that you think well of yourself and not put yourself down because of certain deeds you may have done or certain thoughts you may have thought. Even though Shyam Chor had been such a thief, it did not stand in the way of his becoming a very great saint. Anandi, who was a dancer and a prostitute, became totally transformed after receiving the touch of her Guru, Ranganath. So do not make yourself smaller and smaller by remembering all the bad things you may have done in the past.

Keep worshiping your Self every day with great honor. The sacred water is inside you; it will cleanse you. The Guru is within you and That will awaken your inner Shakti. Within you is the *mantra*, which will one day become active and draw the fullest power of the divine. As your meditation becomes deeper, you will hear a new mantra from within. This is the true mantra. Then you will see a most holy body of water inside and when you bathe in that, you will become supremely clean. Have complete faith in yourself. Put all your trust in your inner Self and honor it. This is neither Hinduism nor Christianity — this is the true religion of man, this is the religion of the Self. And this is what you should attain.

How can I take you back with me in all your fullness? Either take me with you or let me take you with me completely.

It's better if you can take me with you. In this ashram there are so many people that I'm wondering where to put them all. The experiences that you have had here, you will experience at your home too.

The Shakti that has entered you is inside you. It will never leave you; it will always pursue you. You should respect that Shakti. To take that Shakti with you is to take me with you. Your condition is very good. The Shakti is with you, it is in your company, and even when you go away from here, it will be with you; it won't decay. Man weakens his Shakti only through lack of faith and understanding, through ignorance.

Who knows how many people have received my touch? And who knows how many more I will touch in the future? Still the Shakti doesn't become less. But don't consider yourself low; remember this.

My earliest memories, from four years old to the present day, are of inner despair, even though there is no reason for it. I have been surrounded by all that I could want materially. I would like to know if there is any way I could learn to love more. Apparently I am not loving enough.

There was a great saint in our country whose name was Jnaneshwar. He composed a hymn of love for the Guru in which he says, "You may have horses and elephants and be very powerful, you may be able to compose the highest poetry, you may have tremendous strength and many friends, but if you haven't offered your heart at the feet of God, what is the use? What is the use?"

Now you should befriend Him and your heart will open. Befriend Ram and Krishna. See how your heart opens up from within. Then it will never close, it will keep on opening and opening.

Would you speak about the importance of being near you physically?

It's not like that. The importance lies in a person's feeling. You don't have to stay with me physically. Everything depends on your feeling. Many people live very close to me, but if they don't live in their own feeling, what's the use? If you have the feeling of being close to me, that's what will make a difference. Still, if you live very close to a great being, you are affected by him; his vibrations flow to you, and one day or another, you will be affected by those vibrations. Nonetheless, if your true feeling reveals itself to you, no matter where you are, you will experience the same thing.

The great woman saint Bahinabai said, "If you have feeling, only then does God exist for you; if you don't have any deep feeling, God doesn't exist for you." Even if God were to manifest here in a human form and you didn't have any deep feeling, what would be the use? How could you experience Him? Whether you stay close to me or far away from me, you should experience me in your feeling. Feeling is very powerful.

Bahinabai also said, "Your feeling bears fruit. Whatever you want, it gives back to you. Not only that, it is your feeling that brings about your liberation."

We live in the power of this feeling; we live with other people in harmony due to the power of this feeling. When this feeling disappears, there is no more relationship, there is no more friendship.

In the *Bhagavad Gītā* the Lord said, "All beings and all worlds exist in My feeling." When the Lord's feeling disappears, the world also disappears; it is reabsorbed in Him. So no matter where you live, have deep feeling.

How can one become a better disciple? How can one overcome the feeling of loneliness after leaving you? I cannot be away from you for more than three months.

Even for a minute no one can be away from me, so why talk about three months? It's only because you haven't acquired the right understanding that you feel you are away from me. I am the Self of all and everyone is the Self of me.

You should consider me Consciousness, which is all-pervasive. And you should also consider yourself that Consciousness. Then what can be far away and what can be near? Just correct your understanding.

If you discard all your bad qualities, you are a better disciple. The main thing is to imbibe the teachings of the Guru. The Guru says: "You are That." If you imbibe that teaching, you are a better disciple. Being a disciple is not a matter of being close to me or giving me wealth or doing a lot of *sevā*. The true disciple is the one who has become like the Guru. The Guru is always immersed in *So'ham*. When the disciple becomes that *So'ham*, he is a true disciple.

After hearing Krishna's instructions, Arjuna says, "O Lord, after Your Shakti has removed all my ignorance, now I have gained the right understanding, and my wrong understanding has gone away. That is why I will do Your bidding." One who is like this — he can be the best disciple.

Jnaneshwar Maharaj called the disciple one who washes his mind with the water of the knowledge of the Guru. One who holds the knowledge of the Guru in his heart, one who is always in the awareness of the inner Self, he is the best disciple and he is the best servant of the Guru.

How is it that we are able to experience your presence and your grace even when you are not physically present?

The Shakti that has been transmitted into you is who I am. It cannot be different from me. In the same way, when my Sadguru Nityananda transmitted his Shakti into me, he himself entered into me. When a Guru gives you the mantra, it is not only a mantra. He is actually entering into you in the form of the mantra. In meditation you will experience your own inner Shakti. So understand that that is me.

Since forming a relationship with you, I have felt a force working within me in the form of inspiration and guidance. Now, since coming into contact with your physical form, I do not understand that aspect of our relationship. How can I reconcile the two?

Have a relationship with your own Self; don't try to have a relationship with somebody else. My teaching is not that you should have a relationship with me. My teaching is that you should have a relationship with your own inner Self.

If a Guru teaches you something, it doesn't mean you have to have a relationship with him. What he says is that you must have a relationship with your own Self — and that Self is what he reveals to you.

The power of the supreme Truth lies within everybody. As you get close to it, you experience that force more and more. That is the only proof you have. That experience bears testimony that God is inside and functioning through you. The Upanishads say that there is nothing greater than the Self. Everything exists for the Self. For this reason, have a relationship with your own Self.

Do you know who your disciples will be ahead of time? Do you know about our past lives and everything that is currently taking place in our lives?

What is the use of this understanding? You tell me! Why should I try to look at others' lives rather than being immersed in the Self? Why should I wonder, "Where was he born? What kind of life did he lead? How many times did he weep? How many times did he scream? How many times did he beat his head with miseries?"

Tell me, what will I gain from this? What is the use? The inner Self can find out everything; however, meditation exists to erase this kind of understanding. I do not really have to find out who my disciple is going to be. But it is necessary for a disciple to find out who his Guru is going to be.

Please speak about the nature of the Guru and the relationship with the disciple.

A true Master will communicate a vision to a disciple in which he will see the entire universe. We should honor such a Master with the greatest devotion and reverence, because the one who is working within our own being is the real Guru, and he is much closer to us than any outer teacher. A disciple will be able to see his Guru again and again within himself, and then he will no longer have any doubt about who his Guru is. After you have received a Master's Shakti, you will constantly see him in meditation, in visions, in dreams. Remember that the Guru has tremendous power, and the greater your reverence for him, the greater your devotion to him, the higher you consider him to be, the more you will receive from him. There is not the least doubt that you will receive in the fullest measure all the Guru has within him to give if you have full devotion, full reverence and love for him. But you must be free from affectation and pretense.

There are many who come and tell me, "I love you very much. I worship you all the time. I remember you." I listen to them quietly and tell some of them, "Look, if you are worshiping me, you are doing it for your own sake. That worship will yield benefit to you; I have nothing to do with it."

For instance, my Guru's picture has been placed here and incense sticks have been burned in front of it. This is not going to do any good to him. By installing his picture and doing *pūjā* to it, I am not doing a favor to him, I am doing a favor to myself. In this way I am hoping to receive his grace.

So worship the Guru within your inner being for your own sake, for your own welfare, for your own good, and don't think you are doing a favor to the Guru. If your devotion to him is genuine, you will receive all his knowledge.

How can I give up my attachment to the outer Guru and create an attachment to the inner Guru?

For this you should attain *gurubhāva*, that is, total awareness of your identity with the Guru. Have you read *Play of Consciousness*? In that book I explain gurubhava. You should install the Guru in the different parts of your body, and in meditation become your own Guru. If you were to practice this, the outer Guru and the inner Guru would merge into each other. This is called *parabhakti,* or highest devotion. There is no higher devotion. As a result of this, you look upon the inner Guru and the outer Guru as one and the same.

There was a great saint in India whose name was Keshava. He used to say, "I prostrate myself at the feet of one who worships God by becoming God."

You should worship the Guru by becoming the Guru yourself. Without becoming the Guru yourself, there isn't much point in worshiping a Guru. This is what *surrender* means: to be able to cast off a sense of separate self and fill yourself with an awareness of your identity with the Guru. The true mark of devotion is discarding a sense of separate existence and becoming one with the Guru.

The scriptures say to remember Shiva by becoming Shiva. You cannot worship Shiva without becoming Shiva. One should know what true devotion is and how it is manifested. The Guru should be worshiped by you yourself becoming the Guru.

Will you still work for your devotees when you leave the body or will we need another Guru?

I won't leave the body. When my gross body leaves, it doesn't mean that I leave. There are four bodies — you know that. This gross body will leave when it becomes old, but I will stay in the inner body and I will always be swaying in ecstasy.

Today a lady brought me a vest. Now I'm going to take off this sweater and put on the vest. What makes you think that when the sweater is gone, I will also leave? That's how this body is. When the body leaves, I won't leave. I'll just stay where I am. I will be with all of you, and whenever you remember me, I'll be there.

A Self-realized person doesn't go anywhere; he doesn't vanish. He is all-pervasive. Here many people have experienced that Bhagawan Nityananda comes to them and talks to them. He can come to you only because he has an inner body. So the gross body will go away, but the inner body is very beautiful and that won't go away. And I will always meet you through that body. Have this understanding.

In the event of your physical death, how do you continue passing on shaktipāt to devotees?

Even when death occurs to this physical body, the Shakti won't die. It will remain as it is. It will always be alive.

When Sai Baba was ready to leave his body, he let his devotees know. He had many, many devotees — many intellectuals, many scholars, and many kings too. When he told them what was about to happen, they felt miserable.

He asked, "Why are you crying? Even if I leave this physical body, I won't go anywhere. I will still be in the same place. Where you bury me, if you go there and call for me, from inside I will say, `Yes?'"

So *chidākāsha*, the space of Consciousness, the inner space, pervades everywhere. Because of this chidakasha, even *prāna* goes out and comes in. And prana merges into the same space. A river keeps flowing and one day it merges into the ocean. The

289

river ceases to exist, but the ocean still exists. The river becomes the ocean. The river disappears — not the ocean. In the same way, *jīvātma*, the individual soul, merges into the supreme Soul, into God. So even though the individual soul ceases to exist, God still exists.

Therefore, have no worries. Whenever you want to meet him, Muktananda will appear. Right now, I am in the form of a river, and afterwards, I will be the entire ocean.

THE WORLD IS THE FORM OF THE GURU

Reverently and respectfully, who are you? When the question comes, "Who am I?" how do you answer?

I am that I am. What other answer can one give?

I read a dialogue in the *Rāmāyana* that is good for the person asking this question. After explaining the knowledge of Truth for a long time, Ramaji asked Hanuman, "Who are you?"

Hanuman said, "From the ordinary point of view, I am the son of Anjana and the Wind. From the point of view of a servant, I am your servant. From the feeling of devotion, You are my Lord, and I am Your devotee. From the perspective of the knowledge of Truth that you have explained to me, I am Brahman and everything."

This is the answer he gave. I am wondering what answer I should give to you; I am still thinking about it. Certainly I can say one thing: I am that which people call That.

Is it true that a real devotee makes no demands on his Guru? Not even to ask for his grace?

It is not necessary for a true devotee to ask for anything at all. He knows that when he works in a factory, his employer calls him at the end of the month and pays him money according to his work. God is so great — why should He be in debt to anyone? Why wouldn't He pay the fruit of one's action? So when you perform good actions, why would you have to ask for the fruit of those actions? You get the fruit without asking.

I didn't ask the Guru for all these things — like meeting with you and being in America. I don't remember ever asking for all this. If you are destined to get something, you get it without asking.

Tukaram Maharaj used to say, "O God, I should not ask You for anything, but still I am asking for one thing — that I should never forget You. And I have a second thing to ask from You — that good people should never be hindered by their thoughts or their imaginations. Please keep them free of all these things."

He is a true devotee who doesn't ask the Guru for anything except devotion. Everything comes to you according to destiny. Did you ever imagine that somebody like me lived in this world and that you were going to meet me and come to love me? Did I ever think that I would meet all of you and love you too? Never! However, the meeting between you and me did take place. That is why a true devotee does not have to ask for anything.

A saint once said, "O man, you call yourself a true devotee. Then why do you pray for a little bit of food, clothes, and wealth?" One of the names for God in our language is *Vishvambhara,* "He who fills this universe." Won't He give you everything since He fills this whole world? Why would He leave you aside? He gives everything to the whole world. Can't He give you just a little bit? So you don't have to do this asking for something. If you want to ask for something, ask to be free from expectations.

In the *Bhāgavatam,* the Lord says, "One who is free from expectations, one who doesn't ask for anything, one who is completely satisfied in his own Self, one who is free from hatred and enmity — I always follow him; I always walk behind him to protect him." A true devotee doesn't have to ask for anything because he becomes absorbed in love. In the *Bhagavad Gītā* the Lord says, "Keep on performing your actions; never think about when you are going to attain the fruits of those actions."

So it is very good not to ask for anything, not to demand anything.

The twelfth chapter of Jnaneshwari *talks about how worship of the Absolute is better than worship of the form. Will you speak about that?*

It is true that it occurs in the twelfth chapter of *Jñāneshwarī*. This is a commentary on the *Bhagavad Gītā*, and it is called *Jñāneshwarī* because it is the very image of knowledge. One of the verses contains only six syllables, and Jnaneshwar Maharaj has written five hundred verses of commentary on those six syllables.

Jnaneshwar describes worship of the formless Guru and worship of the form. This is the greatest worship — to worship the Guru thinking that you yourself are the Guru, that the Guru is within you. But without grace you can't achieve anything; everything is empty without grace. If you haven't received grace, you keep changing the name of your technique. In America I have seen the people who haven't received grace, and they keep changing the names of their techniques.

Jñāneshwarī is very long. Read it many times, particularly the twelfth chapter. It says that you yourself have become the materials for worship. There is a secret meaning here: when you yourself become the materials for worship, you expand into this whole universe, you become Consciousness. You become the water to bathe the Guru and you become the cloth to dry him after the bath. You yourself become the bed on which the Guru sleeps. Whatever the Guru needs, you yourself become all of those things, and that means you have become everything, you have pervaded everything. This is the secret significance.

After this, you establish the Guru right inside your heart, and you consider him as the Lord of your heart. Then you don't worship the Guru, but you yourself become like the Guru. After you finish this mental worship, you see that you yourself have become the form of the Guru; you see the whole world as the form of the Guru.

Jñāneshwarī is a very great text.

What is the correct attitude for a true disciple to have toward the physical body of his Sadguru?

A true disciple considers the physical body of his Sadguru the embodiment of Consciousness. He considers that his Guru's body is filled with Consciousness. He does not consider it a mere body. Even though they may appear to be mere bodies to other people, the bodies of Gurus are filled with Consciousness. Not only their bodies, but everything in this cosmos, whether sentient or insentient, is filled with Consciousness. So what can you say about the Guru's body?

How much time do I need in your presence for better gurubhava, identification with the Guru? Do I need to live with you?

Gurubhava doesn't get better either by being in my presence or by living with the Guru. It will increase the moment you become the embodiment of the Guru. Even if you live with the Guru, but you continue to identify with yourself in the usual way, what will you gain? You read the *Guru Gītā*, don't you? It contains a verse that says, "Every sentient and insentient object is nothing but the Guru." That is true identification with the Guru. If you just sit in front of me and stare at my face, that is not gurubhava — that is "cult bhava."

All the moving and unmoving objects in the world are nothing but different forms of the Guru Principle. The world is the embodiment of the Guru and the Guru is the embodiment of the world. You become the Guru when you pervade all sentient and insentient objects. So if you see all sentient and insentient objects as the Guru, your identification with the Guru will become much better.

Once the relationship between Guru and disciple is established, will it always exist even if the student no longer practices Siddha Yoga?

Yes, the relationship will always exist. Even if the disciple does not pursue Siddha Yoga, it will stay with him, because it is a true relationship. Once you are born in this world and as long as you live, there is a relationship between you and your breath. As long as you are alive, the breath is with you. In the same way, once this relationship with the Guru is established, it stays with you; it doesn't leave you.

BEAUTY AND GURUBHAKTI

Will you please explain true gurubhakti and the feeling of oneness with the Guru?

There are two kinds of gurubhakti. One kind is developed through understanding, and the other is developed without any understanding but with feelings of love and faith. Understand the Principle of the Guru, develop devotion for the Guru, and feel oneness with the Guru. The *Guru Gītā* says that having devotion for the Guru is understanding that all the things you can see and not see are the same as the Guru. With this awareness become one with the Guru. By understanding the Guru continuously in this way, one becomes the Guru.

Tukaram Maharaj said, "I went to perceive God. While I was perceiving God, I myself became God." This is absolutely true. The truth of the matter is, according to the scriptures, whatever you see is Consciousness. In the same way, when you realize what the Guru Principle is, you discover that you are a part of the Guru Principle. You are not just a drop of that Principle, you are the ocean of that Principle. You are in the ocean.

You are so beautiful and I love you so much that I don't want to take my eyes off you. Did you say yesterday that you are even more beautiful inside? Please reveal yourself inside to me.

I am an old man, well over sixty, so how can I be beautiful? It seems that your vision is beautiful. My inside is inside you, so turn within and meditate. The beauty that is inside me is also inside you, so meditate on that.

At your age how do you manage to stay so beautiful?

I don't know. I also wonder why I look so beautiful at this age. The Upanishads say that man is what he thinks. Man becomes whatever understanding he has.

Swami Ramakrishna Paramahamsa observed many, many practices. He did not really have to do all those practices, but he wanted to understand the goal of those practices. He followed

Hinduism, he followed Sufism and Christianity and so on. In all these practices and religions ultimately he saw the same One; he did not see many different things. Whatever *sādhanā*, whatever practice he followed, he would become that. In India there was a great woman devotee named Radha. For a long time Ramakrishna practiced the devotion of Radha; he practiced her worship, and he began to act like Radha, he began to move like a woman.

Therefore, the Upanishads say that man is what he thinks. For this reason your understanding should be good, it should be sublime. You should keep your thoughts clean.

Since I was very young, I have practiced one thing: to be happy constantly. It is my firm belief that God is within me. I do not believe that God exists here or there or somewhere else. I believe completely that God is within me. It is not that I *assume* God is within me — I have experienced it; I have directly seen God within me.

So there could be two reasons why you think I look so beautiful. The first is that since I follow the beautiful One all the time, I am totally immersed in the beautiful One and therefore I look like that. The second reason is that there is beauty in your eye. If you also follow that One, if you practice how to be happy, you will look the same. The goal of a human life is to attain that joy.

What can we do to really please you?

I'm already pleased. I'm always pleased. You don't have to do anything to please me because I'm already pleased. Do something to please yourself.

I don't really know how to love you, and sometimes I feel I'd like to give you something from within. Please help me to understand this feeling.

If you must give me something, give me the blocks to knowledge that you may have inside you. And if you want to love me, love yourself. One who does not love himself — how can he love others? First, love your inner Self, then that love will come to me. When a child laughs and laughs, the father automatically becomes happy. If a child were to go out and try to buy happiness for his father, what could he get? What could the child give to him? So you should first make yourself happy.

Do you know how much your devotees love you?

I don't have to know how much they love me because their love bears fruit for them — not for me. For instance, if I love you, you might feel that love, but it is I who am experiencing that love within myself. Still, I understand if your love is true or just a display. But the fact is that love bears fruit for you. You can try to love someone else, but you will find that happiness is increasing within you even though you are loving someone else.

Would you explain gurubhāva?

We identify ourselves with so many different things in our life. Identifying yourself with the Guru and thus filling your heart with love for him — that is gurubhava. When we love a child and then the child enters our heart, that is "child bhava." If we want to identify ourself with somebody, that person's soul possesses us. If you feel anger against someone, you are possessed by anger. The same is true of love for the Guru. If you feel love for him, the Guru comes into your heart. That is what gurubhava is.

Only when I am in deep meditation do I experience gurubhāva. It seems difficult to maintain this identification at other times. Will it happen spontaneously or is there anything I can do to be always immersed in gurubhāva?

The experience you have of gurubhava in deep meditation should be maintained in your daily activities also. After pursuing sadhana for a while, you will be able to maintain it. Whatever man feels inside about the Truth, that is also what he sees outside. Everyone exists because of his own feeling of what is real. The whole world exists in feeling. It is your feeling that is your world, and that becomes your own heaven and your own hell. It is your own feeling that gives you pain or pleasure.

One feels that he is smart, another feels that he is dull, and yet another feels that he is a man of knowledge. In the same way, this world exists in God's feeling. In the *Bhagavad Gītā* the Lord said, "This world is My own cosmic feeling and nothing else." But we impose our own feeling on it and we look at this world with our own attitude. When this feeling merges in the inner feeling of the Self, then a person sees the Truth. This Truth is called Consciousness or God. The world is nothing but Consciousness, and if you can maintain this feeling effortlessly, your feeling is truly consummated.

A man feels that he is a man. Does he have to make any effort to maintain the feeling? A woman feels that she is a woman. Does she constantly have to tell herself she is a woman? She doesn't have to meditate on it, she doesn't have to contemplate it, she doesn't have to gain any particular understanding to know it.

It is very good that in meditation you experience this *bhāva*, this feeling. Understand that this feeling exists outside also, that it pervades outside; then it will be very easy to maintain it.

Would you talk about the Guru-disciple relationship? It is my extreme desire to open my heart and fully receive your grace, but something is in the way.

The heart is already open! However, what happens is that when you examine your heart, you close it. So what you should do is improve your outlook. Then look at your heart and you will see that it is open. The Guru-disciple relationship has a long tradition. It exists in the East, but the West takes hardly any interest in the subject. Some people become very unhappy when they even hear about this relationship. It gives them a headache, but that's understandable because there are some bad gurus around. So choose a good Guru.

The relationship between a Guru and a disciple is divine. It is so great that as time passes by, the disciple becomes the Guru. Whatever bundle the Guru has, the disciple attains that.

But don't become a disciple in order to attain this bundle from the Guru; have true discipleship.

A disciple has to surrender to the Guru, to lose himself in the Guru, to bow to him completely. Then when he gets up, he himself is the Guru. Just as a devotee loses himself completely in the Lord and then experiences that he is the Lord, in the same way the disciple experiences that he is the Guru. If a disciple has completely imbibed and incorporated the teachings of the Guru into his being, he is a true disciple.

This subject is very mysterious and significant. In this modern age, people say that you can read a book and attain knowledge. People say that a professor can give you knowledge. However, when it comes to this subject, it is different. The Guru has this mysterious wisdom, this knowledge, which comes from his lineage. A Guru should be a true Guru, not a Guru in name only. He should be someone who practices what he says. A Guru should not bind you more and more in worldly things; he should not tempt you with the sense pleasures of this world. He should be able to separate you from these worldly enjoyments and make you free. A genuine Guru makes you establish this love for the inner Self and makes you merge in the inner Self.

Tukaram Maharaj said, "The glory of the Guru is unfathomable. Even the analogy of iron and the philosopher's stone is mediocre." The philosopher's stone can change iron or base metal into gold, but it cannot turn them into itself; it cannot make another philosopher's stone. But the Guru makes the disciple like himself. He doesn't give only *jīvanmukti*, liberation in this very life — he makes a disciple just like himself.

WHY IS THERE FEAR IN MY LOVE?

I want to feel that I am special to you but you never seem to notice me. Should I give up?

Now how do you know I don't notice you? Should I make you sit on my table and meditate on you? I notice you all the time,

I look at you all the time. Every day I say that everyone is my Self, that everything is my Self. Constantly I contemplate that Ram is in all these people, and that all these people are in Ram. I notice you in this way. Isn't that enough?

Truly speaking, I meditate on you all the time. Instead of giving up hope, you should begin to understand what I do feel about you.

When you ignore me, does that mean I am not ready to receive your grace? Why do you have favorites?

What makes you think I am ignoring you? Do you think that to laugh and exchange a word means anything? If you came to me and I smiled, would that mean recognition of you? Should I show you the front of my teeth?

It may seem that I don't talk, but I am always speaking to you. It may seem that I don't notice you, but you are constantly under my eye. I may not seem to give you anything, but I am constantly giving to you. It is because your eye is defective that you think I have favorites. I don't have favorites. I have nothing to take from you and I have nothing to give you. The Lord says that all beings are equal to Him; He loves none and hates none.

Still, if a person relates to me in a certain way, I relate to him in the same way.

I am often troubled by the feeling that I am just another face in the crowd to you, that you do not know me personally the way you know some others. Can you comment on this and tell me how to deal with this feeling?

I know not only you, I know everyone. I know that everyone's body is created of five elements. I also know that in your body the vital force, the prana, goes out and comes in. Everyone has a stomach, legs, hands, nose, mouth, and head. In everyone's heart the pure, divine flame is blazing. I know this much about everyone — there's nothing more to know. You think that I don't know you, but from this point of view I do know you.

If you were around me every day and played the harmonium

or were my secretary, I would call you by name. But I know you through and through, because everyone is the Self, everyone is the pure and clean Self, everyone is the divine Self. If I didn't know this, how could I tell you all the time that you are the pure Self? If you want me to know you more than this, when you come up for darshan, just shake my hand and say, "Thank you."

Why is my relationship with you filled with so much pain as well as so much joy? I love you with all my heart.

This is a very good kind of relationship, and truly speaking, there is pain as well as joy in love. One suffers pain just to enjoy love. If you don't see me for a while, you feel pain. Many people complain to me saying, "You haven't even looked at me!" But every time I speak, I look around me and then I talk. Even when I look at everyone, still people complain, saying, "Baba never looks at me."

I want to worship only you. You mean everything to me, so why am I afraid of you when I am in your physical presence?

That fear is a good fear; it is very good for you. It comes from devotion, from love. Your understanding creates this sort of fear in you. Even now, when I look at my Guru's picture, I get scared. But this is not an ordinary fear — it is the awareness of his greatness.

Is fear of the Guru parallel to devotion?

The fear and respect that you have for the Guru are not only devotion but transcendental devotion, parabhakti. Ordinarily, people have different kinds of fears: is this man going to eat me up? Is he going to take away all my wealth? What is he going to do with me? These kinds of fears are not right. But if you have fear and awe of a Guru who is real, who has given you the Shakti, that is transcendental devotion. And that devotion is the greatest and the highest.

Will you please speak about fear of the Guru and the right kind of love a disciple should have toward him?

I have a lot of love for my Guru, and even though I have so much love for him, still I am afraid of him. When I look at my Guru's picture, I am afraid of him. It is fear that keeps you pure and keeps you away from bad actions, that makes you perfect in your sadhana. It is only because I had a lot of fear of my Guru — more than my devotion — that I could achieve so much in my life. The Upanishads say the fire burns only because it is afraid of God. The wind blows for the same reason. The fear that you have of your Guru or of God — that is great devotion. Even now I have fear of my Guru, even now. The more of that kind of fear I have, the more I am fearless. The fear I have of my Guru makes me fearless and brings me happiness.

I have been coming to you for the last thirteen years or so. Still I hesitate to talk with you. Why such shyness or fear? I do get answers to all my questions and I get my problems solved when I speak with your picture in my house, but I feel some gap or vacuum. Please lead me and guide me so that this vacuum will disappear.

There is no gap, there is no difference — it just seems like that to you; it's just like clouds in the sky. Without talking to me, all your problems are solved. Then what's the use of talking to me? It's not necessary because your work is done anyway. The veil that you see — it isn't there. Truly speaking, there is only One. It is because of your awareness of your individuality that you feel this way. Through understanding and through meditation that will go away. When it goes away, it is called nonduality. You have been coming here for a long time; it's very good, and I am surprised that I haven't spoken to you. But it doesn't mean that you lack something and that other people have something. Sometimes I speak and sometimes I don't. Wherever my face turns, there I speak; and wherever my face doesn't turn, I don't speak there. So whether I speak or don't speak, it doesn't really matter.

In twenty-five years I spoke to my Baba only a few times. The night before he left his body, that night he spoke to me for half an hour. So something came into my life on its own; it's not just that I attained something.

You are fine whether I speak to you or not. Your work is going very well.

I continue to relate to you with feelings of guilt. How do I stop having these feelings and start relating to you with an open and loving heart?

Forget your past actions. They are not worth remembering at all. Whatever action a person performed today or yesterday or the day before that, he should forget it immediately. Whether it is good or bad, it is not right to remember it.

Lord Buddha was once sitting with his disciples. An angry person went up to him and spat at him. Buddha just dried his face with a blanket. Then he asked, "Do you have anything more to say?"

The disciples were puzzled and Lord Buddha explained, "Language is so small, so narrow, that it cannot really explain what you feel inside. Just as I feel such tremendous love inside that there is no word that can express it, and just as people embrace each other to express their love, this man was filled with so much anger and abhorrence that no words could express it, and when his feelings surged up from inside, he spat at me. He could never explain those feelings. So by spitting on me, he expressed something to me of what he felt inside. For this reason I asked him, `Do you have anything more to say?'"

After listening to Lord Buddha's statement, the man was filled with embarrassment and he left. Afterward, he could not feel inner peace. He kept burning inside. The next day Lord Buddha went to a different town. He was traveling from one place to another giving spiritual teachings. The man who had spat at him went to the town where he was and threw himself at his feet saying, "Please forgive me."

Buddha said, "What kind of a man are you? You still remember the action you performed yesterday? Look at the water of the Ganges. The water has been flowing since yesterday and it has traveled for miles and miles. It has gone so far. Why have you become so inert? Why have you stayed in the same place? Do you know that even this minute has passed by? In the same way, yesterday's time has passed by."

The man was sobbing and sobbing. Once again he said, "Just forgive me."

Buddha said, "I forgave you the very moment you spat at me. I forgot what you did right then. How can I forgive you again? If I had not forgiven you, I would be in the same place I was yesterday, just as you are. Let your life keep flowing like the water of the Ganges. Whatever happens, forget it. Don't ever remember what happened in the past. In the future, be alert. See what is happening at the moment."

In the same way, why don't you forget your actions? Why do you have this guilt? Why do you remember those things? Time has passed by. So many other thoughts must have created their mansions in your mind. Discard that feeling.

Your family is becoming so large, and it will grow even more. Some of us have been spoiled by the sweetness of being close to you physically. Will this be possible in America? Will there be time for questions and for private darshans?

Meeting and having private darshans will depend on the place, on the country, on the time, and on other factors. From here I cannot decide what will happen in other places. It is true that my family is growing larger and larger; however, if you compare my family to God's family, it is only a fraction of an inch. It is very small. Jnaneshwar Maharaj said that only he is a true *sādhu*, a holy being, who considers this entire world the family of God. So the entire world should become one's family.

Do you feel that something is lacking? It all depends on your experience. If you still feel that you lack something, discard the understanding which makes you feel lacking. The minute you discard that understanding, you are complete. The idea that you are incomplete is your imagination. All your ideas come from the mind — your ideas of good and bad, superiority and inferiority, good people and bad people, a king and a beggar, a smart person and a dumb person, pain and pleasure, heaven and hell, honor and insult, liberation and bondage. All these things depend on your mind, and they all exist because of your mind.

Shaivism calls this *vikalpa*, your own imagination. Compared to what is perfect, to what is eternal, to what is always in the form of liberation, all these things are untrue. So discard your understanding.

What should we do when the Guru gets angry?

You should laugh with great joy. Then you will cool down his anger. However, remember not to commit foolish actions that will make him angry. Does he become angry with your vanity? Does he get angry because you are trying to attract more and more boyfriends or girlfriends? Maybe he gets angry with you because every day you make more and more mistakes. If you are not disciplined, if you are a fake, and on the outside you appear to be meditating but on the inside you are really not — of course he's going to get angry.

Nonetheless, he doesn't really get angry. What happens is that he mirrors your feelings and you see your own reflection there. So whatever you do, whatever action you perform, that is what you experience, that is what comes to you through the Guru.

The Guru is like a mirror. You perform some actions and you look at yourself in that mirror. Then you yourself see your own actions. You think that the Guru gets angry, but it's not so. You should improve.

Baba, I want the attention of a personal relationship with you and with God. I want visions and powers. Will you please talk about this?

If you meditate very deeply, you will have a constant relationship with me. If you sit very close to me, what makes you think that that is going to establish a relationship? That is not a relationship; that shows separateness. The deeper you enter within, the deeper will be the relationships you have with people. In meditation you will have the darshan of God, the vision of God, and you will receive everything. You will have many visions. There is a center of visions inside. However, you will have to reach that center.

You should really meditate on the Self. You should not meditate like a heron — it is always absorbed in meditation with one of its legs in the water and the other leg folded up; it is always watching the water, it does not move a bit. For hours on end it is absorbed in meditation, but it is not meditating on the Self — it is meditating on fish. If the heron moves and does not concentrate, no fish will come. But the moment a fish comes, it grabs it and eats it. Then once again it is in meditation.

Your meditation should not be like this. Meditate truly on the inner Self. Lose yourself in meditation. Then you will receive everything. Visions are not so unusual.

THE PAIN OF SEPARATION

Why do people often experience you more strongly when they are away from your physical form?

This is very good; it is due to the pain of separation. Even if a person is physically far away, he is not truly far away from his beloved, about whom he always thinks. If a person does not have any feelings for another, if he does not respect that person, no matter how close he is with somebody, he is still very far away. If somebody dwells in your mind, it does not matter how far away that person is, he is still very close to you. Sometimes a husband and wife are close to each other physically, but they have turned their backs on each other. Although they are in the same house and they appear to be very close to each other, they are incredibly far away from each other.

You should fill yourself with That, with complete love and complete affection. Then no matter how far away you are, you are very close to me. For me, my Baba is not far away; he is very close to me — very, very close to me. For me, he hasn't left. He is still with me. He has permeated my entire being from head to toe and is in every pore of my body, in every blood cell.

If I am not in your heart, if you only use the word "Baba," so what? It doesn't really mean anything if you don't have it in your heart.

After practicing mantra repetition and identification with Shiva, my awareness becomes detached, remote, and very dry. So then I dwell upon your physical form. This creates adoration and an intense longing for you, but also a sense of separation from you, emotional outbursts, and a lack of self-restraint. How can I experience detachment and devotion simultaneously?

Devotion is nothing but detachment. In devotion you get rid of all other kinds of attachments and you are attached to devotion only. It's not that you become dry.

It seems that you like your mind to think all the time. If the mind becomes still, that is the fruit you achieve from mantra repetition. For the mind to become stable, the bundle of positive and negative thoughts must go away. If different kinds of thoughts are in your mind, that's not a good sign.

From your question, I understand that you are in a very good state, but I don't know if you realize it. Separation and non-separation — don't have either of them. You should not become attached to anyone except the Self, but you should also become detached from the Self.

If you have the right understanding, will you really feel separation and longing? If you consider me as this body, it's fine, but if you consider me as *only* this body, it's not fine. If you consider me the Self, then I am in you also — so why the separation?

This is just a mental concept, but you can develop good understanding from it. Quiet the sense of separation and become peaceful within yourself. The truth of the matter is that you are perfect within yourself. So you should be satisfied within yourself.

In the scriptures it is said that you must lose yourself. If you worship Rama, it's fine, but lose yourself in Rama. If you worship Shiva, it's fine, but lose yourself in Shiva. If you are worshiping Allah, I am completely happy. But no matter whom you worship, just lose yourself in that. As long as your existence is separate, how can you attain anything?

A great being has put it very truly. He said, "If you want to attain anything, first of all lose your individuality." You are trying to strengthen your individuality rather than destroy it. In ancient days enlightened people tried to lose themselves. They didn't try to attain God, because they knew God was within them already.

Another great being said, "When I met a pure being, I myself became pure. When I met God and lost my individuality, I myself became God. I did not *attain* God, I *became* God." A seed merges itself in the earth, in the soil, and it loses its individuality completely. Afterward, it sprouts and grows into a big tree with beautiful flowers.

First of all, you have to burn yourself into ashes. You cannot keep yourself alive and attain That. You have to burn yourself. When the longing is over, then see the Truth standing before you.

How can I make a personal connection with you and have some indication that a Master-student relationship exists between us? I am concerned that my three weeks here will be over, and you will leave, and once again I will be searching for a teacher.

The Guru neither leaves nor comes. He always stays inside constantly. Don't you read the *Guru Gītā*? It speaks of a mantra in the *sahasrāra*, at the crown of the head. Inside there is a triangle and there are two syllables, *so* and *ham,* and the mantra *So'ham* arises from there. Right in the center of this triangle the Guru dwells. For this reason, you don't have to continue to search for a Guru. If you see that Guru, you will receive messages from him. If you experience this relationship between a Guru and a disciple, even for a moment, it is more than enough.

The relationship between a Guru and a disciple is not like a relationship between a husband and wife, where you rub your bodies together all the time, where you have to have that friction constantly. This kind of relationship does not need that. Even a moment of true relationship is more than enough. You have asked a very good question. Thank you very much.

Does sādhanā progress without the physical presence of the Guru? Exactly how much is the devotee's spiritual growth accelerated by constantly being with the physical Guru?

Once the Shakti awakens through the Guru's touch or grace, your sadhana always progresses, because the Shakti, which is within you, is also the Guru. Have this kind of understanding. The Guru is not just a human body who wears nice clothes or hats. The Shakti that has been imparted to you, that has been transmitted to you, is the Guru. So the Shakti will always be within you. It will help you to progress in your sadhana. And if you are with the Guru physically, spiritual growth will accelerate. You don't have to worry about your sadhana, but you do have to think about it.

All you really need is love — just love. That is enough. Then your sadhana won't take long. If you are with the Guru physically, but you have anger or you increase your negative feelings, what is the use of being with the Guru? You need love for your Guru. If you have love for the Guru, you can imbibe all the Shakti from your Guru and that Shakti will take you to the highest state. And if you can be with the Guru physically with great love, that's fine. The greatest sadhana, the greatest mantra, the greatest means, the greatest *yoga mudrā*, is love and nothing but love.

The more I experience you as my inner Self — that you are everywhere and so always with me — the less attachment I feel for your physical form. I love to see you, but I don't pine for it. Is this good or is it a trick of the mind?

If you attain the vision to see me in everyone, you don't have to pine for me. There are people who see the Self in everyone, but still they like to see a particular form of the Self. Tulsidas and Namdev had attained the knowledge that the Self existed within everyone; still they worshiped the form. This was the state of Radha also. She had attained the formless completely; still she pined to see the form of Krishna. When Uddhava tried to convince her, she gave him the following answer: "You can do yoga or not, you can even babble that God is not different from me, you can also practice all the rituals and ceremonies, but as long as the form of Krishna does not stand in front of my eyes, everything is useless. Whatever you say is useless. It may be useful for you, but not for me."

After attaining the formless, the devotion that arises within for the form is the highest devotion, the best devotion, the greatest thing on the spiritual path.

When I need advice but the Guru is far away and it seems hard to reach him, what should I do?

The Guru gives you the seed. When you sow it, on its own and without your effort, it gives you the leaves, fruit, shade, and everything else.

Sometimes there is a need for specific advice. Whom should I ask if the Guru is far away?

When there is a necessity, even though the Guru is far away, still on the inside he is very close to you. He will give you advice right away. The Guru is not his physical body; the Guru is the grace-bestowing power of God. The Guru bestows Shakti. Once he bestows the grace of Shakti on you, that will give you the answers to your questions.

Sometimes I wonder if my ego is taking on the guise of the Guru.

It is not so. The ego cannot do the Guru's work. If the ego could do the Guru's work, why would you need a Guru?

Sometimes I hear the inner voice and I think it is the Guru. How do I know it isn't the ego?

If you have the knowledge of the Guru, certainly you'll know if it's the voice of the ego. Man should become free from ego. Ego is the worst enemy, the most wicked thing. First of all, consider what you have to be egotistical about. You aren't the Prime Minister of India, Morarji Desai, nor are you the French DeGaulle, nor are you the American Carter, nor are you the Russian Brezhnev, nor do you belong to a wealthy family like the Kennedys, nor are you a great musician like the Beatles — so what is the basis for your ego? Are you egotistical about your shirt, your beard, or your hair?

If you contemplate it in this way, your ego melts. If the ego melts, what is left is God. Become free from ego just for a second. Then see what answer you get from within. It is due to ego that a person is far away from the Truth. It is due to ego that instead of experiencing peace, a person burns in the agitation of the mind. The success of every sadhana lies in getting rid of the ego. The enemy is within man — and that is the ego. It is ego that has brought about all the difficulties.

In India there is a great philosophical work called the *Yoga Vāsishtha*. In it a very strange story occurs. There were three demons, and they couldn't be defeated even by thousands of gods. So the gods went to meet a very wise being and asked him how to conquer them.

The wise being said, "They are free from ego, so it will be very difficult to conquer them. But if you want to conquer them, I'll show you a way. Send one of the gods to them and tell him to give them the knowledge of ego."

So the gods sent a very sensible person to the demons. He met them and offered them his respects and began to praise them. He said, "Wow, wow! There is no one in the world like you at all. There are no warriors like you. You have been fighting for so long. Even though there are only three of you, none can defeat you, even thousands of gods. What bravery, what strength, what greatness!"

As they listened, they became aware of their own greatness. Along with that, pride and ego were aroused. The strength they had from lack of ego was depleted. The weakness of ego increased. The person noticed this and left.

Once again there was a war. Immediately the three demons were defeated and died. That was that. It was ego that defeated them.

The company of the ego is the company of death. The company of freedom from ego is the company of immortality. It is due to ego that all countries fight and fight and become smaller. It is ego that makes you feel, "I'm greater, I'm greater," and for that reason you have lots of weapons and ammunition. Man should get rid of the ego. For a second, be free from ego and see how much bliss and peace surge forth.

What determines the type of relationship a disciple will have with his Guru? What role does karma play in this relationship? Is it necessary for a disciple to live in an ashram with his Guru all the time?

If a disciple is with his Guru, he will relate to him as a disciple. There is no other way. So where does karma come in? Once you form a relationship with a Guru, all the karmas which you have accumulated are destroyed; they are all burned up. New karma is not created after this relationship is formed.

It is not necessary for you to live in an ashram all the time. After you attain something from the Guru, you can go back to your home and pursue your sadhana. It will be better if you can live in an ashram for a while, but it is not that you have to live in an ashram. If you really become aware of your Guru and if you stay with your Guru even for a second, you will attain what you are supposed to. Even a short time with the Guru can be very powerful.

BECOMING ASHES AT THE FEET OF THE GURU

Is it true that people give their lives to you?

Many people say that. Maybe they give their lives to me, but I have my own perfect life with me. So that means I also give my life to them — as much as they are able to hold.

Please speak about the importance of a disciple's obedience to the Guru's command.

The more the disciple follows the Guru's command, the more experience he gets of the Guru. The more he obeys the Guru's command, the more the impurities go away. If you receive even one word from the Guru, and if you take that word into your life, it will help you throughout your whole life.

311

I know that the direction of my life is about to change. How am I to know in what direction to go that will cause the least hardship to my family? I feel I cannot keep running to you to ask you what to do.

It is not necessary for you to stay with me all the time. If you stay with me, either you will fly or sink. It is better for you to stay away. But always follow the path that has been shown to you. It is not that a plane will come for you from heaven only if you stay with me. It is not that people who stay with me will receive a big bundle and other people will receive a small bundle. You attain something according to your heart's disposition. Therefore, stay away, meditate very well, and chant. Your faith will keep increasing. If a person stays in my company, either he will climb the steps or he will fall off the steps. You should meditate on the inner Self, very privately. Keep following the same direction and put forth your own self-effort. Don't put your burden on someone else; then you won't bring any hardship to your family.

My Guruseva requires hard work with long hours, and I often experience intense resentment. Then I feel angry with myself and I experience distance from you and from my inner Self. What can help me to get through this and to feel love?

You are so close to me, but you experience that you are far away from me. This is the delusion of your mind and nothing else, so give up this delusion. There is nothing far away and nothing very close. No one is very far away from me, nor is anyone very close to me. The more you understand me within yourself, the more I am close to you. When you feel that I am far away from you, that is nothing but the play of your mind. This is called the devil — there is no other devil. So first, discard your devil. Then I am very close to you, not far away.

Resentment is also a devil. Understand that and let it be. This is the nature of the mind. Why do you have to give so much importance to it? Why do you value the mind so much? If you give value to it, you're trapped. If your mind wanders

312

here and there for a moment, you also wander here and there with your mind. Meditate more and repeat the mantra more; then your resentment will go away. Keep on working, and when you feel very far away, repeat the mantra; then you will feel me very close to you.

The people who spend a lot of time with you seem to get lots of personal teaching and work on their egos. How can people who don't have a personal relationship with you get the benefit of that kind of teaching?

A person should not try to have a personal relationship with the Guru to get the benefit of the teachings. The Lord of all beings dwells within everyone's heart — that is why you should meditate on Him and remember Him. Then you attain what you are supposed to attain. Without trying to attain it, it comes of its own accord.

Nowadays you can get these teachings wherever you want. There is no lack of shops. It's not that you have to study a lot, it's not that you have to read many books, and it's not that you have to put forth so much effort. If you can imbibe only two words, they are more than enough to cross the ocean. For one who has intense longing to attain That, for one who is thirsty to attain that supreme Truth, it reveals itself in his own heart.

Where is that place where there is no Self? Who is that person without this Self? The scriptures say God is apparent. So the Self — which dwells in your own heart and is everywhere — can be seen by everyone. To attain this which already exists within, why do you have to put forth a lot of effort? All you need to attain it is intense longing and tender devotion.

How can you distinguish between spiritual authority and authoritarianism, that is, controlling people's lives?

The true Guru will teach meditation, he will teach the technique but he will not control a disciple's life. He will make the disciple become established in the technique, but he will not control his life. You know, it is not difficult to become a certain kind of guru. They are innumerable. They put pressure on their disciples and they loot their wealth. But that Guru is rare who quiets a disciple's mind and brings peace into the disciple's life.

A true Guru will not try to control a disciple's life, yet he will make the disciple control himself with that technique. A true Guru does not need many people around him all the time; he teaches the technique and he lets them go free. The Guru has everything within himself. Does a Guru's life depend on the disciple? Doesn't the Guru's life depend on himself?

That was my next question. Isn't there something in you that says you must teach?

Yes, spiritual teaching — and over and over again. It is very important that the wisdom be tested.

Do you want many disciples?

It is not that I need so many disciples. Now you are speaking to me and I am speaking to you, and only two of us are necessary for each other. Yet there are so many other people sitting here listening to what we are saying. It does not really matter whether they are here or not. What is important is that I am speaking to you and you are speaking to me.

So if there are seekers, it is very important for me that I do teach them.

Since the Guru knows everything, is it necessary for a disciple to initiate conversation or interaction with him or should the disciple always keep quiet?

A good disciple, a complete disciple, doesn't have to speak to the Guru. There are some disciples on a smaller scale and they have to speak to the Guru. But a good disciple doesn't need any conversation, any experiences, any liberation, or any attainment. He doesn't need anything except the Guru. He doesn't want anything except the Guru, and then he becomes the Guru. For him, any *siddhis*, any supernatural powers, any liberation, any miracles, are mediocre.

There is a beautiful story in the *Rāmāyana* about a Guru and a disciple, Bharadwaja and Sutikshana. Sutikshana was the disciple and Bharadwaja was the Guru. He was a great sage, a great Siddha. Sutikshana was following his teachings very well, and he led a very good life. Lord Rama was wandering around the universe and eventually He visited Bharadwaja's ashram. Bharadwaja welcomed him with great respect and took him to the hut of Sutikshana. Sutikshana was meditating in his hut. They knocked on the door and Sutikshana came out. He saw Lord Rama, the Master of the world, and he also saw Bharadwaja, his Guru. Sutikshana was very happy.

The custom was that if a Guru came to a disciple's hut with other people, the disciple would always bow to the Guru first and then to the others. However, Sutikshana was in a fix. His Guru was there, but also the Lord was there. "To whom should I bow first?" he wondered. Discrimination is, after all, discrimination. He thought about it and thought about it, and then he said to himself, "It's my Guru who has uplifted me. For this reason I will bow to my Guru first and then to the Lord. My Guru has shown me the Lord, so I will bow to him first."

If a disciple attains complete discipleship, it is much better to remain quiet. However, if you are weak, you had better talk to the Guru. Otherwise, you will be neither here nor there.

Would you explain the meaning of becoming ashes at the feet of the Guru?

To become ashes at the Guru's feet means to lose yourself at the Guru's feet. When your ego is destroyed, when your separating individuality loses itself, at that very moment you attain God.

Brahmananda showed a true path when he said to become ashes at the Guru's feet, to lose yourself completely at the Guru's feet, to destroy your ego at the Guru's feet. If you do so, it won't take too long to attain God. If one is far away from God, it is due to one's ego. God is not really far away; we are far away from Him. The scriptures say that God is all-pervasive, and it is absolutely true.

In Karnataka there was a great philosopher, a great being, called Nijaguna Shiva Yogi. He used to say, "If anyone says that Lord Shiva is there and not here, don't listen to him because that is a lie. If you learn how to perceive, wherever you look you will see Shiva, you will see the Lord."

There was another great Siddha being called Tikanath. He used to say, "In every pore of your body Rama dwells. Why are you going to look for Him far away?" This is true understanding. This is the right outlook. If you see something other than this, you have cataracts in your eyes; you don't have true vision. Otherwise, in every pore of your body, in every blood cell of your body, in every particle of your body, even in every particle of the dust of this earth, He pervades. Therefore, this poem was written and you have asked about it.

To become ashes at the Guru's feet means to destroy your ego completely at the Guru's feet. Then you will attain God. Now this doesn't mean that you haven't attained God; all it means is that right now you don't know whether you have attained God.

Vedanta says that you attain that which you have already attained. It is not that you are going to attain something new. You are going to attain that which you already have. What you are doing now is removing your ignorance — which isn't really there anyway. This you can grasp only if you have subtle understanding. You obtain this subtle understanding only from a Guru and only when you become ashes at the Guru's feet, only when your ego is destroyed at the Guru's feet.

You don't have a Guru to attain God, because you already have attained God. The Guru turns your ego into ashes. That is the only reason you have a Guru. This is the only job of the Guru — to destroy the disciple's ego. That is all he does. But one must have God's grace in order to have a Guru. Along with God's grace we should also bestow our own grace upon ourselves. The Lord says, "To such a person I give subtle understanding, subtle intellect." With that subtle intellect, immediately you become aware of God, who pervades inside and outside. It is a person's prime duty to perceive the all-pervasive God.

I Felt that My Heart Was Going to Burst

When I was doing sadhana, I came across a person who was teaching riddhis and siddhis — how to attain supernatural powers, so I studied under him for a while. He had the power to materialize a train or bus ticket. Of course, it was a fake ticket. He could also tear a piece of paper and it would become a five rupee bill — for five hours. Afterward, it changed back into plain paper. He could transport a piece of apple from one place to another. Or if someone had something in his pocket, he could transfer that object into somebody else's pocket. So I studied these things under him. It was all fake, it was phony. It wasn't God's grace, it was just a mediocre skill. It meant nothing.

Having learned all these tricks from this person, I went to see my Baba. The moment I entered my Baba's place, he took out a long stick and began to scold me. He said, "You thief, you traitor, you rogue! What are you doing here? Get out of here!" I fled.

After I ran away, I began to think about it. He called me a thief? He called me a traitor? I never stole anything. I never betrayed anybody. Why did he say that? I just couldn't understand why he would say such things about me.

Again I peeked in because I really wanted to go inside to be with him. He got the stick out again, and he said, "You unworthy fool! Get out of here."

I went out and I began to think about it. I hadn't done anything like that. Why would he say such a thing about me?

I was really upset; I felt that my heart was going to burst if he was going to be like that with me.

But my right understanding told me it did not matter what he did. The Guru's anger, the Guru's curse, the Guru's blessing — they are all the same, they are nothing but a bestowal of grace.

So I gathered myself and with great courage I went inside again. He had already thrown the long cane in my direction, so it wasn't close enough for him to reach. But he still had one more — a little one — and he hit me very hard with that, saying, "Will you ever do that again?" He hit me so hard you can't even imagine.

With great humility, I said to him, "I don't understand what mistake I made."

"Didn't you learn those phony supernatural powers?" he said.

"Oh, yes." Then I promised, "Never again, never again."

He said, "In your entire life, will you ever use those supernatural powers? Will you ever try to fool others with those phony powers?"

And I said, "No."

Then he told me, "He is a sadhu, he is a holy being, who is totally absorbed in his own Self, totally immersed in his sadhana."

The behavior of such great beings is unique. They remain very secretive. Even though they know so much, they act as though they know nothing. When people who know a lot go to them,

*they act as though they know very little. Even though they
are so divine, they still conceal themselves by pretending to be
very small. Now I talk to everybody and meet everybody, but
still you all complain that I don't talk to you. But it took my
Baba three years to say one word to me. Even though he did
not talk to me, I was pleased. Even though he did not speak to
me, still the shower of grace was there.*

*He is still with me, just as he was before. In America too
I saw him many times. Especially when I had a heart attack,
I saw him a lot. He is all-pervasive. No matter where you are
when you think of him, he stands there before you.*

*When you think of him in your meditation a lot and
merge in him, only then will you know something of him. His
wisdom was very secret. He was such a being that you could
receive instructions from his inhalation and exhalation.*

*If you remember him, no matter where you are, you can
experience That. There are many people who have experienced
him. Sometimes during shaktipat you experience him. He has
given me Shakti. This is the same Shakti I transmit into you.*

CHAPTER 14

The Mystery of Surrender, the Magnet of Faith

*You draw into yourself the Shakti
or the power of one you love.
All you need to do is have love and faith.*

*In America and in the West, there is generally great emphasis
placed upon the individual and on the importance of expressing
one's individuality. Some people say that in giving yourself to
a teacher, you give up your individuality, you give up your
individual responsibility. What do you have to say about that?*

Would you say that I don't have my own individuality?
No, I couldn't say that.
I am a person who has surrendered to my Guru, yet I still have
my individuality. Do you see on that wall the picture of the
ashram in Ganeshpuri? I am the architect of that ashram. I also
administer it. It's a big place. When I'm there, more than a thousand foreigners come and stay there. Even though it is out in
the country, there is electricity, water, all facilities. I'm not talking from ego. Without individuality, could I run that place?
People have this feeling that they have to give up their individuality, but it is not so. You have to understand that there is
a mystery in surrender. In surrender a person loses himself;
however, he attains that person to whom he has surrendered.
If you surrender to a great person, it is not that you lose your
individuality — you too become a great person.

Isn't there a contradiction in the idea of submitting dynamically?

First, you should submit and then find out whether there is a contradiction or not. This is just idle speculation. Do you know that if you were to submit dynamically, you would become God Himself? I have submitted myself completely to my Guru. Do you find me dull or passive? How do I seem to you?

Submission does not mean that you give everything to God and then remain passive. What happens is that you submit your sense of self to Him and in return you absorb His vastness. Arjuna submitted himself to Lord Krishna, and after that he fought a violent war. All the *gopīs* — the milkmaids — had submitted themselves completely to Krishna, and yet they were living their family life, taking care of the children they had, and having more children.

Are you saying that the freedom you get when you surrender to the Guru is much greater than the freedom of parties and worldly life?

Yes. You get the freedom of the Self. To surrender to the Guru means to surrender to your own inner Self. The Guru is not an individual being to whom you surrender physically. The Guru is the Shakti, which is all-pervasive. You surrender to the Shakti, which is within you, so that means you surrender to your own Self — not to anyone else.

Generally speaking, Westerners have the wrong understanding about this. There is a Shakti within you that is the form of the Guru, and when you surrender to that Shakti, you become your own Self.

Self-delusion prevents me from being completely open, thus blocking true surrender to your grace. Can you suggest a process or technique, or will this happen automatically in its own time?

Do not entertain any self-delusion. Surrender is essential. Surrender is deliverance from bondage; surrender is the attainment of God. Meditate more and surrender will come. Don't be miserly in your understanding of yourself; don't be miserly in giving yourself to the Guru. Why should you hold back? Become generous. Give yourself generously and then your delusion will leave you.

How can I practice surrender and stop believing I am separate from God?

The moment you stop feeling separate from God, surrender comes automatically. That is surrender. Discard *aham* or ego, and grasp *So'ham.*
Is there anything I can do to start letting go of the "I"?
Keep repeating *So'ham, So'ham.* Give up "I" and take up *So'ham.* That is the way to surrender.

Why do I experience conflict when I try to simultaneously honor myself and surrender myself?

You never honored yourself before; you always dishonored yourself. Now when you try to honor yourself, it becomes an obstacle. I honor myself by thinking, "Wow, wow! O God, You live within me!"

But you never practice in that way, and that is why you experience conflict. Give up surrendering, and just love your Self; then surrender will come of its own accord.

Surrender means to become one with That, to merge with That. The Self has already merged in the Self, but you are not aware of it. You don't have to surrender something new because it is already surrendered to itself. The Self is one with the Self.

Will everyone who comes in contact with you and really surrenders be able to get off this wheel of life and death and rebirth?

Why not? But don't make a show of surrender — really surrender. Then you will certainly get off the wheel of life and death. What do you understand by *surrender*? To come and live in the ashram? To say, "Baba, I give myself to you"? What is it?

True surrender is to leave yourself, to lose yourself, in the space between *ham* and *sa*. Don't show the wrong kind of surrender.

When you surrender falsely to a Guru, you lose everything. The *Bhagavad Gītā* says that true surrender is to become established in the Self. The Lord said, "O Arjuna, in every way surrender to Me. Take refuge in Me."

To surrender does not mean to feel you are so poor, so little, so wretched, that somebody should take care of you. True surrender means to lose yourself in the inner Self and in what the Guru has taught you.

If I am not a surrendered disciple, can I still hope for your help, energy, and compassion?

Yes, if you accept compassion, you will receive it. If you accept help, you will receive it. When I come to put candy into your mouth, don't close it — let me do it! Then it will work.

You once said that I should let my heart expand. How can that happen? How can I surrender and let go?

Keep meditating, and as you meditate, your heart will expand. When your meditation reaches its consummation, the ego will dissolve and you will be in a state of surrender. You don't have to achieve surrender deliberately — it comes by itself.

How did you draw your Guru's grace so completely?

To draw his grace completely, I gave myself to him completely. In that way, I received him completely. I pursued my *sādhanā* exactly the way he told me to. I did not do less or more — I did exactly what he told me to do.

I had this custom: whenever I approached him, I would sit down only if he told me to. Otherwise, I would keep standing in front of him. One day I stood before him all day long. He did not tell me to sit down, so I did not.

In India there is this fruit called mango, and it is a wonderful thing. It is revered in our country. One day my Baba told me not to eat mangoes. So I didn't eat mangoes for twelve years, but I had to do sadhana under the mango trees. I accomplished everything under the mango trees. Afterward, when I got the ashram, I planted mango trees everywhere. One day, twelve years later, he gave me a mango. I ate a mango on that day, and that was it — never again.

So I did sadhana in a very, very disciplined manner. When you follow the Guru's words, you attain everything. Not only this, when you follow his words, he enters into you completely. The Guru's grace is also called the lotion of Consciousness. Once this lotion is applied to your eyes, you accomplish everything.

A Guru looks like a human being to the physical eyes, and it is very difficult for an ordinary person to see God in that human body. Ordinary people say, "He eats like us, he drinks like us, he sleeps like us, he laughs like us and has fun like us." My Baba loved to play with little children. But in a Guru's body, there is this Shakti, this divine force, which is completely alive. That is what makes him a Guru. Therefore, as you follow the words of the Guru, the Shakti enters you more and more and more and more, and one day that Shakti transforms your being into the being of the Guru.

How can I deal with the tenacious idea that to give myself over to the Guru would mean a major change in my life? I am very afraid of change.

Are you afraid that if you gave yourself, you would become good? Usually in this world people are afraid of becoming bad! Don't give yourself all at once; give yourself little by little, just gradually. Then the change will happen little by little, and you won't feel it.

I want to surrender everything to you, but last night my father got very angry at me for not coming to his dinner party to meet his friends. I wanted to stay with you much more. Please help me to understand surrender and how I can keep from hurting others, like my parents.

It would have been great fun if you had gone and shared the dinner party with them. If you had gone, your surrender wouldn't have been spoiled. You should surrender yourself to your own Self — not to others. The individual being should merge into the Self and be in the state of the Self. Give up your understanding of surrendering to one person or another. Through meditation open your own inner Self and perceive That. Through words it cannot be opened; through listening you cannot get That. No matter how much you prattle, no matter how many lectures you give, you cannot attain That. For That you must meditate. Meditation is a kind of surrender. To see your own Self within is to surrender to your own Self. To surrender to others is not real surrender.

Please help me to understand your saying that we are totally responsible for all our actions, when at the same time the Guru is the root of all actions.

Rabi'a was a great Siddha *yogini* who lived in Basra. She had miraculous powers. Once she had a high fever and it stayed for a long time. In Basra everybody loved her, as she was a great saint. Many people visited her and gave her their suggestions. A great being called Hasan went to her and said, "O Rabi'a, just pray to God, and your fever will go away."

"O Hasan," she replied, "you want me to get rid of this fever, but what makes you think that I have invited it? Has God sent my fever or have I invited it? Which idea do you like? Tell me."

Hasan began to hem and haw. He did not know what to say. Then she asked, "Do you accept that God sends everything?"

"Yes, yes," he said.

"Do you want me to insult God's gift by praying to Him that he take it back?"

Finally he said quietly, "I ask your forgiveness."

"The One who has sent pain also sends pleasure," explained Rabi'a. "I just accept whatever comes and I experience it."

So accept either one of the statements. If you accept that the Guru is the root of all actions, then just become quiet like Rabi'a and accept whatever comes, whether it is pain or pleasure, wealth or difficulties. If you think you are responsible for your actions, you will have many chances to say that you are sorry, to ask for forgiveness, and to feel pain. Just decide which way you like.

How does a Guru take on a disciple's karma?

A Guru doesn't like to take on a disciple's karma; it is the disciple who likes to impose it on him. A Guru will have to take on the karma of a true disciple who has completely given himself to him, but he is under no compulsion to take on the karma of a false disciple. When a disciple completely surrenders himself to the Guru, he becomes the Guru's responsibility, and everything about him — good or bad — is transferred to the Guru.

Every now and then I get very strong feelings of revulsion against worship and the idea of surrender. I just don't know how to handle it.

You feel negative toward it because you don't understand the real significance of worship and surrender. The truth is that it is the worshiper who gets the results of the worship. Who experiences the contentment that arises from worship? Is it the worshiper or is it God? We should determine whether the worshiper is worshiping himself or God. When you appear to be worshiping someone else, you are really worshiping yourself.

When you don't understand the secret of surrender, you don't feel like surrendering and you can't do it. If a gutter full of filthy water falls into the sacred river Ganges, that water also becomes sacred. However, if the gutter were very much attached to its filth, it might not like to surrender itself to the Ganges. When the Ganges flows into the ocean, it becomes the ocean. What does it lose?

What does anyone lose through surrender? We are scared of it because we don't understand its secret. Surrender does not imply slavery. In fact, surrender frees you from slavery and brings you total freedom. Most people confuse surrender with slavery and that is why they are afraid of it. To explain it, great *yogis* such as Jnaneshwar use this analogy of the Ganges surrendering itself to the sea.

A few days ago I asked you for shaktipāt, and you told me to meditate more. I then had an experience and I knew I had your blessings. Yet somewhere in me, I doubted that. Most of me has surrendered to your love, but part of me still clings to not surrendering. I am very torn by this. Have you any advice for me on how to surrender fully?

It doesn't matter. Even if you can surrender just twenty-five percent, that's enough. You seem to have surrendered seventy-five percent. Wherever the greatest part of you has gone, the remainder too will be drawn there. Love God dearly and honor the inner Self. Meditate and do *japa*.

My fear seems to be of losing something, rather than realizing what will be gained.

You lose to gain. There is an ecstatic verse from a poet-saint that goes like this: If you really want to achieve the divine state, you must annihilate your separate consciousness. It is like a seed annihilating itself in the soil and growing into a tree that bears beautiful flowers and fruit. Unless you surrender your selfhood, you cannot attain Godhood.

Who says that you cannot find God if you keep remembering Him constantly? If you were to lose yourself in Him, you would certainly find Him. One seed annihilates itself and the result is countless seeds.

I certainly believe that idea in my head. But why do I have such difficulty accepting it in my inner being?

Don't get upset about it. Your inner being, your heart, will accept it naturally in due course. All you have to do is meditate a little and enter within. Try it just for fun. You lose waking in order to get sleep. But after you wake up, you recover what you lost.

How can I get rid of the fear of going crazy and let myself surrender fully?

You must have surrendered yourself to all kinds of things before and they didn't make you crazy. If you were to surrender yourself to God, how would that make you crazy? In your daily life you surrender yourself to different things: you surrender yourself to sleep, and when you love a child, you surrender yourself to him. These forms of surrender never made you crazy. When your mind is filled with anger, you surrender yourself to anger. When your mind is filled with lust, you surrender yourself to lust. If you were to fill your mind with God, how could that make you crazy?

It is because of wrong understanding that you have this fear. What makes you think that God will make you crazy in return for your surrender? He will make you God!

NO PERFUME MORE FRAGRANT
THAN FAITH

How can I learn to trust myself?

How did you learn to distrust yourself? Instead, you should learn to trust yourself. Just change a little bit. If you simply reverse your lack of trust in yourself, you will trust yourself. It is not so difficult; you can do it very easily. It is you yourself who has learned self-distrust, and now with the right understanding, you yourself can learn self-trust.

The scriptures say that a person who does not trust himself, a person who insults himself — what sin hasn't he committed in his life? If you trust everything else, but do not have trust in your own self, you are only killing yourself. You go to a doctor and you trust his pill; you go to a hotel and you trust the food they serve you. You go to a barber and you offer your neck to his sharp razor, and you are not afraid that he will cut your neck. You trust everything and everyone else, but you do not trust your own self. What kind of predicament are you in? To have distrust for yourself only makes you fall.

There was a great yogini named Jayadevi who said that the Self is the real deity. You do not have to doubt it; you do not have to question it. So have trust in your own Self. The man who does not trust his own Self cannot trust this world. His nonbelief spreads everywhere. Do not let this happen to you. The Self is very great, and you should trust yourself. To understand this, you should meditate and see the Self within.

I had several questions but now I realize the answer revolves around faith.

Faith has tremendous power. It is faith that compels the absolute Being, who is without form or attribute, to take on form and attribute. Faith brings close the One you think is remote. There are great scriptures in India called the Vedas. They are revealed scriptures; they do not come from the intellect. The Vedas say that faith can kindle fire without any matches. Faith is the ladder to heaven; it is a most beautiful thing. Our scriptures teach us to give with faith, to speak with faith, to act with faith. Faith is a strong cord that unites God and his devotees who have become alienated from Him. So let your faith grow.

Is there anything I can do to open up to your grace?

All you need to do is have love and faith in the Guru. That is all —nothing else. Even slight love for the Guru will draw his Shakti to you. The greater the flow of love for the Guru within you, the more the Shakti leaps inside you, and the greater the force with which it will work. You draw into yourself the Shakti or the power of one you love. All you need to do is have love and faith.

Is it not enough to have perfect faith in oneself? What else do you need?

It is great to have faith in yourself. People find it quite easy to put trust in everything else but very difficult to put trust in themselves. If somebody were to tell you that the highest energy dwells in water, you would rush toward water. If somebody were to tell you that the highest energy dwells in fire, you would rush toward fire.

But if somebody were to come and tell you that the highest energy dwells within you, you would say, "Now how can that be? I am inferior, I am a sinner."

The whole purpose of meditation is to give you this faith in your own Self. It is not for the attainment of God, because God has always been there inside of us. It is because of this lack of faith within our own selves that we have not been able to experience Him.

Is pure faith enough?

All you need is that — nothing else. But that faith must be real. One of the key words in Vedanta is *brahmanishtha* — one who has faith in the Absolute, in the supreme Being, one who is established in Brahman. Brahman is your own inner Self, so it means faith in one's own Self. Faith has great power. If you have such faith, you are doing the greatest good for yourself. When a disciple gives his grace to the Guru, the Guru's grace flows naturally into him.

I feel that you have given me so much already, but I find I hold myself back from you and it troubles me greatly. Can you help me to understand this?

Just renounce your hold and then you will become great. A person holds himself back and then he falls. When mothers want to feed their children, sometimes the children hold their lips together so tightly that they don't allow the mothers to feed them. I am in the same position! So don't shut your lips so tightly — make them loose.

I have experienced the outside world as very destructive, and it is difficult for me to open my heart because there are forces out there that make me feel afraid.

If you can't trust things outside, at least trust things inside of you. There is a lot inside to trust. There is Consciousness in your heart — trust that. There is the supreme Being in the *sahasrāra*

331

— trust that. In the *mūlādhāra* at the base of the spinal column, there is the Kundalini Shakti — trust that. In everyday life you put your trust in many things, like food and medicine. So when it comes to putting your trust in other beings, why should you stop short there? Learn to trust others.

Be aware that it is your own soul that is manifested outside as well as inside. It is you yourself who are responsible for your restlessness, for your alienation from the everlasting peace within you. You are responsible for your alienation from other people; you yourself are responsible for being what you are. Those people who have no faith in themselves, in others, in God, in inner Consciousness, harm only themselves. They uproot themselves and they keep pushing themselves around. They don't get anywhere and they only suffer more and more.

I would like to ask how discrimination relates to faith and doubt.

As faith increases and doubt is destroyed, discrimination arises. Doubt is of no use. If you have no faith either in yourself or in anything else, that will produce only delusion. People who are without faith cannot get anywhere in this world. If they were to go to some other world, they would not get anything there either, because wherever they go, they carry their lack of faith with them. To have faith means to be really alive, to have life in you that is alive. To have no faith means to have life in you that is dead.

Will the fact that I have no faith prevent me from coming in touch with my inner Self in meditation?

Keep on meditating, and you will have faith. One should have faith. It seems your faith must be hiding somewhere. It has not left you. It will come to you. The brother of faith is nonfaith. So if the younger brother is there, the older brother must be there too. Just keep on meditating, and someday you will find this older brother. Don't give up meditation because you don't have faith. Meditate for a while; see what meditation really is.

How can I be assured of receiving your grace?

If you become worthy of receiving grace, why shouldn't you receive it? Even before becoming worthy of receiving grace, why do you have to feel unworthy? The *Bhagavad Gītā* says that a doubting person destroys himself. His doubt brings about his own downfall. Why don't you have the opposite feeling — complete assurance, complete determination? The *Bhagavad Gītā* assures you that if you have supreme faith, not only do you experience great joy, but you buy God. Faith has so much strength. In the same way, lack of faith is very weak.

Yesterday you said something about "Baba-dependence." What does it mean? I have very rarely depended on others because I have not found many people who can be depended upon. You seem pretty dependable, but I still find it hard to depend on you. Do you have any suggestions?

I must have said it in the context of sadhana, in the context of God-realization. By "Baba" I mean my Baba, and I must have asked you to depend on him, saying that he would certainly help you. He has enormous power. What I mean by "Baba-dependence" is the faith that Baba will certainly give you Shakti, the faith that God will never let go of you and will always protect you.

In the *Bhagavad Gītā* great stress is laid on dependence on God. Lord Krishna tells Arjuna, "Take refuge in Me alone. Give yourself completely to Me and I will protect you from all evils."

You should learn to depend on the Guru with the faith that you will certainly receive something from him. This is devotion of a very high order, and it brings meditation. You must have the faith that you will be awakened, that you will be able to see the divine light within yourself, and that you will be able to attain God. No matter what task it is that I undertake, I rely completely on my Guru and that task is accomplished.

There is no better path than this faith. There is no makeup more adorning than this awareness. There is no perfume more fragrant than this awareness. Therefore, meditate with reverence on the Guru within.

Does an aspirant have to have faith in the Guru or have some karmic link with the Guru in order for shaktipāt to flow?

You have always had a karmic link with the Guru. Life is without beginning. All of us have been related to one another through countless incarnations in one way or another, so you don't have to form a new link; that link is already there.

All beings proceed from the same supreme Truth. The Bible says that the entire human race has sprung from Adam and Eve, and our scriptures say something similar. So all of us are related. However, you need to form a relationship of love with the Guru right now for the awakening of the Shakti within you. Yes, faith in the Guru is badly needed. It is faith that draws the Guru's Shakti into you. Even ordinary things work in our daily life because we have faith in them.

How can I learn to give love freely and also to accept love without suspicion? Can I receive shaktipāt even though I cannot attend an Intensive?

First of all, lose your suspicion; discard this suspicion from your heart. Remember God more and more, and ultimately you become like God. Once you are filled with this love, it flows to others of its own accord; you don't have to try to give love to others. But first of all, remember Him, more and more and more. Have a lot of love for yourself, a big mountain of love. He is inside you, That is inside you — so first of all release the knot that you have.

If you can't come to the Intensive, have firm faith. Maybe you have some obstacles; maybe you don't have enough money. But you don't need money to have this faith; you can have firm faith. If you repeat the *mantra* with great faith, it will work within you; it will work the same way it does in the Intensive. I receive so many letters from people who were reading *Play of Consciousness* and received shaktipat from the book. They put the book against their hearts and began to meditate. Afterward, they would come here just to check out the person who wrote that book.

The *Bhagavad Gītā* says that a person who has faith attains everything; wherever he may be, he attains it right there. Faith is a magnet. It pulls God toward you. So don't have any obstacle to this faith.

Will I get something from you if I keep coming here every night?

Whatever action a person performs, it doesn't go to waste. When the right time comes, it bears fruit.

A person should engage himself in performing good actions. He should not wonder whether they are going to bear fruit or not. The Lord in the *Bhagavad Gītā* says, "O Arjuna, keep performing good actions. Never wonder what kind of fruit you are going to attain and when." No action will go to waste. When the right season comes, the trees blossom and bear fruit.

In the same way, all your actions start bearing fruit within you. When you are performing any action, don't lack faith. The *Gītā* says that if you lack faith, you don't attain anything. In your heart you should create firm faith, firm confidence. You should know: I will do this, I will attain something, I will get something. Firm determination and firm trust have a lot of power. Because of this force people make the formless God reveal Himself in a form. Faith is a great thing. So with great trust, keep coming here.

You tell us we are Shiva, but we still don't become completely aware that we are. Is this a lack of pure faith in you?

It's not that you don't have pure faith in me, but the fact is that you don't have pure faith in your own inner Self. You do have faith in me. But you don't have faith in yourself; you don't believe that you are pure and that your inner Self is the pure Principle.

It is just to raise that faith in you that we have these programs. The main purpose of this Intensive is to raise that faith. That is why we meditate. Shaktipat is also meant for that.

You should remember that the touch given to you in the process of transmitting Shakti is not a modern touch. It descends from the lineage. It is an ancient touch. Even though this flame is here now, it is an ancient flame. This fire has existed since the beginning of time. And so has the Shakti.

It seems that Western philosophy is filled with judgments and that Eastern philosophy has a more accepting way about it. Do you feel this is true?

Judgments are everywhere — in the East as well as the West. It is not that the philosophy of the West is full of judgments; it is just that the mind of the Westerner is always trying to analyze everything. A mind that always analyzes becomes an obstacle.

In the East if you are pursuing a certain philosophy, you read it completely and solidly, and you accept it totally. However, in the West, you read one philosophy a little bit, and then a second philosophy a little bit, and you try to merge all the philosophies together. If you could know one philosophy completely and thoroughly, you would become totally satisfied. You wouldn't be in search of other things. You would realize that what you have learned encompasses all other things.

Don't have this doubting mind. There should be firm decisions about whatever you do and whatever you read. The doubting mind does not allow you to become established in anything. And that doubting mind does not allow you to reach your destination.

Any knowledge that I may have attained comes more from feeling than from thought. I would like to know the difference between thoughts and feelings — if there is a difference.

They are not really that different; they are related. In a feeling there is faith; but in a thought there is no faith. Instead, there is this desire for argument. You want to debate.

There are people who talk about the gloom and doom that lie ahead of us, especially since the development of nuclear weapons. What do you have to say about this?

Many people ask me this question, and many people believe

we are doomed. However, I have complete faith in God. Who knows what God has planned for us?

In the Puranas there is a story about a demon called Bhasmasura. He had performed many austerities and as a result had obtained a certain supernatural power through the grace of a deity. If he placed his hands on someone's head, that person would immediately be burned to ashes. After attaining this power, Bhasmasura went searching for some heads to place his hands on. But a sage found out about his power and realized that Bhasmasura was going to do some very wicked things, so he went to see him. Bhasmasura started to place his hand on the wise man's head, but before he could do so, the wise man said, "Wait. Have you really tested your power?"

"No," said Bhasmasura.

"If you want to see if it really works," the wise man said, "go to the deity who gave you this power and place your hand on his head."

So Bhasmasura went to the god who had given him the power. The deity was terrified and ran for help to another deity. The second deity said, "Don't worry. I'll take care of this." He took the form of a beautiful woman and appeared before the demon. When Bhasmasura saw the woman, he fell madly in love with her and forgot himself completely.

"Marry me, marry me," he begged her.

"I won't marry you just like that," she said. "I am going to dance, and I want you to dance exactly as I do. Imitate all my movements. If you do it correctly, I might think about marrying you."

The demon agreed. The woman began to dance, and the demon imitated her. As she was dancing, she placed her hand on her head. The demon also placed his hand on his head, and he was burned to ashes. He had attained this power to kill others, but he destroyed himself.

Who knows what God has in mind? God is the Maker, and He will always protect His universe.

Please tell me how I can overcome the habit of rejecting myself.

337

There are many people who always reject themselves; they consider themselves very low and they insult themselves. It's not good — it's very bad. A person creates his own heaven and hell; no one else gives him heaven or hell. One person understands himself and expands his consciousness and becomes great. Another doesn't understand himself and thinks he is very, very low, and then he becomes a small creature. There is no greater fault than considering oneself small, considering oneself little, insulting oneself. No one has taught you to consider yourself low or ordinary.

The sage Vasuguptacharya says that supreme Shiva's attitude is this: He sees that this entire cosmos has sprung forth from Him. He looks at all things, sentient and insentient, as his own Self. So look at yourself with great respect. If you reject yourself and insult yourself, you can't respect others, you can't love others.

Once someone said to me, "I can't believe what you're saying."

I asked him, "Be honest, do you believe your own self?"

"Yes," he said.

"Then how can you not trust me?" I asked. "Do you *really* trust yourself?"

And he said, "No."

So I asked, "Then how could you possibly trust me when you can't even trust your own self?"

You must have faith in yourself first.

I Had Full Faith
in My Self and in God

Patience is very much connected with discipline, and patience results from deep faith in God, from the awareness that I am God's and God is mine, that He will not forsake me in any situation, that He will always protect me and guide me. For patience what you need is faith in your own Self.

I do not know what fear is. I would feel afraid only when I saw my Guru. Otherwise, right from my early days I didn't know fear because I had full faith in my Self and in God. One whose inner Shakti has been awakened — and who is aware of this fact — knows that God is looking after him, that the Shakti is doing its work in him. He will never know fear or impatience. Once you have full faith in God and you have become fully acquainted with the inner Shakti, fear vanishes, and patience and courage take its place.

There was a great woman poet-saint who sang, "How can there be any fear for a yogi who has experienced the spirit, who has become acquainted with the inner Shakti? A seeker who follows the path of yoga overcomes his doubts through yogic practices. If he is following the path of knowledge, this knowledge burns up all his karma. Once that happens, is there anything in this world that can frighten him? Now that I have become aware that my own Self pervades everywhere, and that there is nothing other than my Self, what can frighten me? What can frighten me?"

The cause of fear is lack of faith in one's Self, in God, and in spiritual contemplation. It is also a mistaken understanding of reality. The seers have said, How can there be grief or attachment or fear for one who sees the same One everywhere, for one who has had the direct experience of his inner Self?

CHAPTER 15

Death of the Ego

The ego knows that if your sense
of smallness were to go, it too would have to go.
The ego shows you to yourself in a wrong light.
It functions like a screen between the real you
and your understanding.

What is the difference between the ego and the Self?

There are two types of ego — pure ego and impure ego. The pure ego is the Self. Saint Francis said that the pure ego is God. The impure ego is an obstacle that creates so many boundaries. It is the impure ego that gives you the wrong understanding about meditation. The role of the impure ego is to make you believe that what is good for you is bad and what is bad for you is good. The entire world is in the fist of the impure ego. But the great beings have grabbed this impure ego and have put it in their pockets.

I have read many definitions of the ego and I still don't really
know what it is. Does the mind create it? Where is it located in
the body?

The mind itself becomes the ego. Just as there are great actors and actresses who play different roles, in this way the same power plays different roles. Sometimes it is the mind, sometimes it is the ego, and sometimes it is the subconscious mind. When it is contemplating, it is *chitta*. When it is thinking, it is *manas*, the mind, with its various thoughts and doubts. When it is trying to analyze or judge a particular subject, it becomes *buddhi*, the intellect. When it starts saying, "I, I, I," that is the ego. If you stop at "I am," it is the pure ego. But if you add different things after "I am," that is bad. If you just say "I am" or *aham*, that is very good. But after "I am," you wonder, "Who am I? What am I?" Then you think, "I am Peter." When you add this name to the "I am," that is bad. The pure I-consciousness that arises is the Truth. Truly speaking, when the pure "I" throbs and pulsates, that is the Truth. But when you become somebody else, that is your death. Ego destroys everything.

If the Self does not engage in action, who is the doer?

The ego is the doer. The ego is a link between the Self and the body. The ego does the work. The Self is completely pure; it is the nondoer and it is pristine. In the *Bhagavad Gītā* the Lord said, "O Arjuna, although I live in the body, still I don't cause any action; I don't make anyone perform actions."

The principle that connects the body and the Self is the doer. Sundardas said that the body experiences no pain. Of course not, because the body is made up of the five elements, and once that life-force leaves, it is a dead body and you burn it in the fire. It doesn't feel anything. In the same way, the senses and the *prāna* don't feel anything. When you enter into the *samādhi* state, you don't experience either pain or pleasure. And of course the Self doesn't experience them either because the Self is so pure; it is Consciousness, and neither pain nor pleasure reaches That. In the *Bhagavad Gītā* the Lord said, "Weapons cannot cut it, water cannot wet it, fire cannot burn it, wind cannot blow it. It cannot come under anybody's control. The Self is free and pure." Sundardas said that there is this ignorance, this link between the body and the Self, and it experiences either pain or pleasure. This link, this ignorance, is nothing but ego, and it is the ego that undergoes everything.

Since ego seems to be such a block to man's spiritual evolution, what is the cosmic reason for ego? What is the purpose of ego?

If you know how to use the ego rightly, it can be a great help. Instead of attaching the ego to Tom, you can attach it to God; instead of having the awareness "I am Tom," have the awareness "I am God," and it will help you on the spiritual path. That is the purpose of ego.

How can I learn to act and express myself clearly and without hesitation, knowing that the ego isn't influencing my actions?

God has no ego, yet He creates this entire universe, He maintains this entire universe, and whenever it is necessary, He makes changes in this universe. The universe is so big. So many creatures live on this earth, so many creatures fly in the sky, so many creatures live in the water. There are so many infinite creatures, and God has related to all of them without any ego. And we have to relate to maybe three or four people or sometimes nobody — just ourselves.

It seems your understanding is off a bit. You don't relate to other people through your ego; you relate to other people with understanding and with the love that arises from that understanding. There is a particular understanding between you and the other person, and it is this understanding that creates any kind of knowledge and maintains the relationship. This understanding can make another person your enemy or your friend. If a person becomes free from ego, he can relate to other people very well, very beautifully.

Because of the weakness of our understanding, we are deceived and we have no knowledge of how to deal with the world. What is ego? Ego is this awareness that arises within you, the awareness of "I." When you wake up in the morning, you are free from ego. Later this awareness pops up: "I, I." This ego is not great understanding; it can bring you very close to death.

Once there was a great *tapasvin,* a person who observed austerities, a *yogi.* He had done *tapasya* for a long time and he obtained a supernatural power to make himself many. He did so much *sādhanā* that eventually he could multiply himself into forty identical forms. So one day he just stood there and he became many. He counted himself. "One, two, three . . . forty."

Time went by, and he forgot what he was supposed to do. A person becomes so deluded with just one ego, you can imagine what it must have been like to have forty! Eventually his final time came. Whether you are one, forty, or forty thousand persons, death embraces you. Death doesn't spare anybody; it doesn't come early or late. In this world, death is the one thing that is very punctual.

Only a wise person thinks in the following way: "I am born in this world; death is following me. What should I do? How should I prepare myself?" If one forgets his own death, understand that he has forgotten everything. So the yogi's final time did come, and the messenger of death brought the warrant. When the yogi realized that the messenger of death was coming, he multipled himself into the forty identical forms. The messenger just looked at them. He was supposed to take only one person but he couldn't figure out which one. So he left.

The yogi said, "Well, he left! That's it!" He had only forty egos, but now it was as if he had four hundred egos. He was very happy.

The messenger went back to Yama, the god of death, and said, "I could not catch him. He was not one, he was forty."

Yama said, "Oh, that is the cleverness of ego. I have something for it." He called another messenger and whispered a *mantra* in his ear and sent him off. It wasn't *Om Namah Shivāya* —it was a mantra of ego.

So the new messenger went there. Once again the yogi realized that somebody had come to take him away. Once again he multiplied himself into forty identical forms. The messenger looked and looked at them. He walked back and forth and said, "Wow, wow!" and kept shaking his head. Finally he said, "Even God couldn't do this! Since the beginning of time He has been only one. But you—so many! God can't even become two. Until now God is one and the same. He never became two, but you—forty! Everything is absolutely perfect. *Almost* everything—however, there is one tiny thing wrong."

The real yogi jumped up and said, "What's that?" And the messenger dragged him away.

That is the ego. That is its worthiness. That is its value. It delivers you into the hands of death.

You don't need the ego to perform any action. You do need the senses. You do need the intellect, which is the source of all understanding. To think, you need the mind and also the subconscious mind. But ego is completely valueless.

Is the bliss experienced by the Guru's grace the same as that experienced in early childhood prior to ego development?

Yes, what you are saying is true. A baby is nourished by that inner bliss before ego begins to vibrate in him. As he grows older, and as ego begins to vibrate in him, he becomes alienated from that bliss. If we could become like a child — that is, if we could become free from attachment and aversion — we too would experience the same bliss. A child lives much of the time in his natural state and that is why he is quite contented.

How closely related are ego and fear?

Fear, embarrassment, hatred, and hostility are the children of the ego. Once ego leaves you, your fear leaves you, along with the ego. It is ego that makes you fearful.

How can I know God's will from my own mind or ego?

God's will is to exterminate your ego. The ego exists not to bring you any happiness, but to let you suffer the consequences of your past *karma*.

I want to give myself totally and yet I hang on to my own selfish ego. I feel the grip loosening. What can I do to let go?

Selfishness will remain a little bit in worldly life, but you don't have to be too selfish because everything is destined. Whatever is going to happen comes before you, so remain free from selfishness. Even so, a person should put forth self-effort. Through self-effort you become free from selfishness. Not only that, you will fulfill your desires.

Ego is not selfish; it is your desire that is selfish. Ego is different. If you consider yourself to be something that you are not, that is ego, that is wrong identification. In reality, the body is not you, the body is not different from Consciousness, but you think the body is you and different from Consciousness. That is ego.

I never realized that the ego made you weak. I always thought it was a strengthening force.

If ego had real power, you wouldn't need the atom bomb. Ego is a very good way of dying.

Is it because of our ego that we cannot see the Guru as Consciousness?

Ego is lack of understanding. Ego is not a tendency in the mind. The ego is only a feeling of "I" and "mine." It's only a feeling, that's all. Ego makes man a ghost and keeps him far from the Truth. It prevents him from attaining the Truth. Out of every one hundred people, ninety-five of them are controlled by their ego. Only four or five have the ego under their control.

Why are we born with a sense of physical attachment and why must we change that attachment?

It is because we die with attachment to the body that we are born again with attachment to the body. You are reborn with the same attachment with which you die. Did it begin in you or in somebody else? It is you who must find out how this all began, but you are only talking about it. Stop asking these questions. Just repeat God's name. You will find God through remembering Him and repeating His name. You won't find God through these questions.

There was once a wealthy man who had a huge mango orchard. During the mango season he put up a sign saying that people who wanted to partake of his mangoes could come to his garden and eat as many mangoes as they wanted — for one hour. So people came and looked at their watches and ate mangoes, and after an hour they would leave. One day a fellow who seemed to be very highly educated happened to come there. He was full of questions and he went to the office and started asking, "When was the orchard planted? How many trees are there? How many varieties of mangoes do you have? What is the age of each tree? How many people come here and eat mangoes?"

Finally the owner said, "Your time is up. Get out."

All that fellow got was words — no mangoes.

THE PURE EGO

Are you an individual at all?

I am what you see. If you see me as an individual, I am an individual. If you see me as a human being, I am a human being. If you see me as a fool, I am a fool. If you see me as a yogi, I am a yogi, and if you see me as a realized being, I am a realized being. It all depends upon you.

What do you see when you look at yourself?

I look at myself being aware that I am — I am.

Is that all you see?

Yes. I am That. That "I" has a great meaning, that "I" is Consciousness.

Certain teachers have said that "I" is a very fine mantra.

There are two kinds of "I" or *aham.* One *aham* is filled with ego and the other *aham* is free from ego. I look at myself being aware of the "I" that is free from ego. The Vedas say *aham Brahmāsmi,* "I am God, I am Consciousness, I am That."

But are there two kinds of "I"?

Yes, one is ego, the ego that you have in the mundane life. And this mundane "I" binds you.

Isn't the I-consciousness the same in both cases?

Even though Consciousness is one and the same, still its work is different. From the same Consciousness, the snake is created and from the same Consciousness a human being is created.

What's wrong with a snake?
The snake doesn't have the same intellect that a man has. The snake bites you; it has poison in it. In the same way, this mundane ego contains poison. But that pure ego, that pure "I," doesn't have any poison in it. It is pure Consciousness.

But isn't the same "I am" being expressed in the snake?
No. It has the impure "I." Only a human being has pure understanding.

What is the role of the ego in our lives? I want it to serve me and those around me, yet if I do well for others and feel good, I quickly lose myself.

You cannot serve others with ego; you can serve them only with the *So'ham* awareness. *So'ham* awareness means awareness of your identity with the inner Self. The ego makes sure that we are afflicted endlessly and born again and again and again. This is the ablest function of ego. It shrinks what is great into what is small. It shows what is pure to be impure and hellish. One who should have been laughing joyfully is compelled to weep all the time, to complain and lament. It makes the fearless frightened. This is the role of ego. If *aham* or ego goes, what remains is *So'ham*. *So'ham* means "I am That," and it can do infinite work.

Please ask Shiva to step on my ego.

You should consider Shiva to be your ego. You should experience the ego as the inner Self and then it will not bother you.

Would you show me who I am?

You are you; you can't be anything else. You are that supreme Truth. When I-consciousness becomes attached to other things, it becomes limited. The pure I-awareness does not attach itself to anything; that is the light of God itself. When your ego becomes attached to a particular name or form, it becomes bondage. Through meditation you should get to the pure I-awareness within you.

This pure "I" is nothing but a vibration of the inner Self. If you are not aware of the pure "I," you know yourself as, "I am the body" or "I am a man" or "I am a woman." The pure "I" that has no attachment in it — that is the true Self. That is Truth and that is Consciousness.

What is the simplest way to deal with the ego?

Instead of having the ego that says you are this body, that you are this individual being, have another kind of ego that says, "My Self is beautiful, my Self is loving, my Self is pure." So let your ego remain, but change it into the other attitude. Just change the face of your ego. The ego that is meaningless makes you suffer, but the ego that is meaningful gives you happiness.

What is discrimination? How do you discriminate between someone's ego and the Truth?

Discrimination is the awareness by means of which you can tell the true from the false. Discrimination helps you embrace the true and reject the false. Once you become aware of what is ever-lasting and what is not, you will know that ego is perishable. It is not eternal. If you must have ego, attach it to God. Feel proud of the fact that God is within you. Get high on this egotistical awareness, "I am the pure Self, I am God Himself." The Sufi saint, Mansur Mastana, and another saint, Bistami, proclaimed all the time, "God is within me and God is outside of me. I am no different from God." Have that kind of ego. The ego that says, "I am the body" or "I am so-and-so," is the cause of bondage. But the ego that says, "I am the pure Self, the Truth is within me, and I am divine" — that is liberating. That is the true ego.

First, know the difference between your ego and your own Truth, and then you will be able to know the difference between somebody else's ego and the Truth. If you know yourself, you will be able to know everybody else, and if you do not know yourself, how can you know anybody else?

What should my daily actions be when I begin to see that almost everything I do, say, or think is proceeding from my ego instead of from God? I get nauseated by my own ego.

The clear perception that whatever you are doing or saying or thinking is rising from your own ego and not from God is its own solution. That is enough. As far as your daily life is concerned, keep on doing whatever is necessary. If you keep on practicing *sādhanā*, your ego will be transmuted into God. *Māyā* is different from knowledge. Maya is unreal, whereas knowledge is real. Similarly, there is the ego and the true I-consciousness, which appear to be the same, but are really different. Egotistical consciousness — "I am the body," "I am a limited individual," "I am enchained," — is false. The consciousness "I am God, I am divine, I am eternal" is the true I-consciousness. The I-consciousness that is the result of ignorance keeps you bound but the true I-consciousness makes you free.

YOU CAN ALWAYS CHANGE

Please explain why after years of meditation, I seem to be on a slow boat to China in my search for the Blue Pearl, whereas along comes an atheist who is on a supersonic jet with one touch from you!

Even though another person may seem to you to be an atheist, he may really be a great believer. It is your own tendency to be an atheist that has put you on a slow boat to China. If you have great belief, that belief will put you on a supersonic jet. So give up your nonbelief.

By now you all know that once upon a time Sheikh Nasruddin was a great physician. One day a man went to him to get some medicine. Nasruddin asked him, "What is your problem?"

"I have constant headaches; they are really intense," he said.

Nasruddin said, "You must smoke cigarettes."

He said, "Oh, disgusting! I never touch them."

"Do you drink alcohol?"

"No, I'm really pure, I don't drink at all."

"Do you roam around with girls and boys at night?"

He said, "No, no, no. I'm so pure. I observe so much celibacy. I just don't commit those sins."

Nasruddin said, "Now I understand what's wrong with you. You have this difficult disease of ego. Because of this you have a headache. You have the heat of ego; you feel that you are so pure, you are so clean, you are so clear, you are so great. Because of the heat of ego, you have these headaches."

In the same way, you think you are so pure and so clean; you have that same pride. For this reason you are on a slow boat to China, which will take at least forty years to get to the destination. Otherwise you would be on a supersonic jet.

Anyway, there is plenty of time; don't get scared. You can always change.

What is the ego? How can I make maximum use of it?

Instead of using the ego to go to a bad place, it would be much better if you could use the ego to go to a good place. The ego is called *aham*. Inside, "I, I, I" vibrates. If you use the ego in the right way, it will take you close to God. If you use the ego in the opposite way, it will take you right to the center of hell.

Instead of saying that you belong to the West and hate the East, instead of saying that you are black or yellow or red, it would be much better if you say, "I am the Self, I am Consciousness, I belong to God." Then you will be using the ego in the higher sense. If you say, "I am a great person, I am an old-timer," and you look down upon other people, you are nothing but an insect of hell, an insect that gives birth to many other insects.

Tukaram Maharaj has shown the practice of using the ego in a good way. He made very good use of his ego, saying, "I am God's, and God is mine." If you are egotistical about your body, about your color, about your skin, you should know that even a scoundrel who cleans toilets does not have that much ego. You are egotistical about the pot of shit that you carry everywhere. Isn't that true? What are you egotistical about? Become free from ego. That becomes the very path to God, that is the ladder to God.

Why does the ego fight so hard in its battle against death?

The ego rears its head so that you may really crush it. Jnaneshwar Maharaj says that a yogi is one who throws out the ego, who transcends all karma and all *gunas*, and who sits secure in the inner Self.

Ego is a real nuisance. Death is much better than ego because death comes and grabs you only once, but the ego makes you die every single moment of your life. It misguides you and tells you that there is sorrow in the Self and that there is happiness in what is really a source of suffering. The ego projects hardship on what is really easy; it projects anxiety on what is really free of it. It pushes the mind around and around until it loses its sanity. It is to expel the ego from our system that we repeat God's name all the time. If one were to live without pride, one would be able to go very close to God.

When you get closer to ego, you get far from others; when you get far from ego, you get closer to others and you also get closer to God.

Talk to your ego like this: "What are you so proud of? All you have done for me is to alienate me from God, from wisdom, from humanity. So what is there for you to get inflated about?"

The ego hasn't done anything good. It has made the great small, and it has only caused struggle and conflict inside you where there should have been peace. It has dried up the heart, making it sterile — the heart where love should have been throbbing all the time.

Even after experiencing the great peace and joy of the Self during meditation, my mind and ego still have the upper hand and make meditation confusing and depressing. How can I eliminate expectations and avoid this battle?

Because your ego and mind have taken residence within you for a long time, they don't want to leave you, but they will leave you at the right time. You will have to fight with your mind and ego for quite some time. But you have Shakti, and with the help of the Shakti, you can conquer them.

Is it possible for the Shakti, along with increasing the divine force inside me, to also increase the ego?

When Shakti increases, ego decreases; when Shakti decreases, ego increases.

How can a disciple help the Guru do his work of ego surgery and defect removal?

The disciple does not have to help the Guru. When the Guru does his work of ego surgery, he does it very well. However, you should allow yourself to have that operation. To destroy this ego, great beings have found many methods. If you go through all these methods, you have made it. In the entire world there isn't any other disease; the only disease that really exists is ego. It is because of the effects of ego that we are unhappy. Gurus use many different means to destroy this ego. Some people allow themselves to have the operation. Other people, however, see the scissors and run away.

How does one distinguish between the inner guidance of the Guru and the workings of Shakti on the one hand, and the ego and old habits on the other?

The Guru's guidance and the workings of the inner Shakti are meant to destroy your ego. If you have no ego, you don't need these things. This ego is like the Great Wall of China between you and God. To break through this great wall, saints and Sadgurus give you meditation and they show you how to do sadhana. When you become free from ego, you become God's.

I want you to sweep me out, but I feel very impatient. During your talk I felt like I was on an operating table waiting for the surgeon to cut my ego out.

The surgeon's problem is to see whether there is a disease or not. If there is no disease, what will he operate on?

Once there was a priest who was quite old. One evening he drank a little, then he drank a little more, then he ate too much, and soon his stomach felt quite heavy. But somehow he managed to lie down and sleep.

In the morning when he got up, his stomach was hurting. All of a sudden he said to his wife, "I'm having acute stomach pain. Cook an omelet for me."

Now he used to put his dentures on the table next to his bed and he looked for them but they were missing. "How terrible!" he said. "I forgot to remove my dentures last evening and I must have swallowed them. That's why I'm having this pain." He felt his stomach and it felt quite hard because there was a lot of gas in it.

Somehow he managed to pour some coffee down, but he didn't eat the omelet. Then he called the doctor and said, "Send an ambulance at once. I have swallowed my dentures and I must be operated on immediately." The doctor sent an ambulance and special arrangements were made for emergency surgery. As the priest was lying on the table, the doctor asked, "What happened?"

"Don't say a word, just operate on me."

"At least tell me what happened."

"Well, I was eating and drinking last night and I forgot to remove my dentures. I swallowed them and they are bothering me and you must take them out."

The doctor said, "Father, your gullet is not that wide. You couldn't have swallowed your dentures!"

The priest shouted back, "Don't act like that! I'm a priest and I know what I'm talking about. I've taught so many people! What do you know? Now open up my stomach."

The doctor was in a fix and he wanted to kill some time, so he gave the priest two pills to get rid of the gas in his stomach. Then the doctor began to feel his stomach and said, "First, I must find exactly where the dentures are." The pills soon began to work; the gas passed and the man began to feel some relief.

In the meantime the man's wife called and said that a rat had carried off the dentures and they were found in another room.

When the man heard that, he said, "Now I'm okay! I don't need an operation."

That is the Truth. You think there are dentures inside you, but are there really?

I would like guidance in solving the conflict between my sādhanā and my career. I am a filmmaker, and my work involves tremendous ego and high pressure. I do not know how to do this work and lose my ego.

If you lose your ego, you will be able to work better than before. You will be able to meet many people. When you lose your ego, it means that instead of letting your ego work, you yourself are working. So if you were to put your ego aside, your work would become great. Some people become great devotees of ego. They do not realize that the ego is their greatest enemy.

In Karnataka in South India, there was a great Siddha being whose name was Kanakadas. One day a number of *swāmis* got together and invited him to their place. One by one they began to ask him, "O Kanakadas, will I go to Vaikuntha?" (Vaikuntha is the abode of the Lord.)

Kanakadas replied, "You will go if I go." He gave everyone the same answer.

Finally, the most important swami asked, "Will I go to Vaikuntha?"

Once again, Kanakadas replied, "You will go only if I go."

All of these swamis were very smart, so they asked him, "Will *you* go to Vaikuntha?"

He replied, "I will go only if my 'I' goes."

"What do you mean?" they asked.

He explained, " 'I' means the ego, so I will go to Vaikuntha only if my ego goes."

Ego is really a big nuisance. It is much better to become free of it. What makes you think that God created this entire universe through ego and that His ego makes Him powerful? It is only because God is free from ego that He is so powerful, so full of Shakti and pure intelligence. It is only because He is completely free of ego that He is able to do anything. If He also had a limited ego, He would lose His Godhood. That is why you should keep your ego away from you and do your work. Then see how much you can accomplish.

How can I get rid of my ego?

You have to take the help of discrimination. It is the ego which is the world; it is the ego which is the chief threatening force. If one were to think very carefully about it, one might find out how to discard one's ego. You should think again and again how to expel it from your system. We may be hung up on our ego, but do we ever bother to find out what is the basis of it? Is there anything inside us which could serve as a basis for our ego? What shall we attach our ego to — the hair that grows on our head? Our hands or feet? You are not a great artist, you are not a great dancer, you are not a great yogi who can fly in the sky. What then is the basis of your ego? Are you a king? Even if you had some great talent or position, that would not be a basis for your ego because there have been much greater kings in the past. There will be greater kings and greater artists and greater singers in the future.

That is how you should talk to yourself to get rid of your ego. Remember God a little and He will certainly help you get rid of it.

It seems I am so close to being fully awakened that I can almost feel it, but there is a barrier, a block. How can this barrier between my mind and my real Self be dispelled?

It is true you are very close to it. It is only the thin wall of ignorance, or the ego, which is standing between you and the Self. If that veil were to be torn, you would find that neither you nor the world is there. Only God is there. Keep meditating, and the fire of knowledge of Kundalini will burn up that veil. This is a screen that you yourself have created. It is as if you are holding up an umbrella against the sun and cannot feel its heat. This is a veil of your own creation.

What is the quickest and surest way to get rid of ego and pride and open my heart?

The moment ego leaves you, your heart opens. It's not that you have to wait to open your heart. Once the ego leaves, that's it — your heart is open. Man considers himself different from the Self. Once he gets rid of this idea, his heart is opened.

I Was a Person
Who Was Too Proud

When I was still a child, I saw my Baba a lot. I used to go
very close to him. However, after I grew up, I didn't go so
close to him. He visited us when we were children and he
used to yell and run, and we would also yell just as he did,
and we would run after him. If he sat anywhere, all the
children would climb on him and hug him.

I left that place and wandered across all of India.
However, I was still the same as I had been before I met him.
I met two great saints—one in Ahmedabad, who was called
Jaganath Baba, and another one in Dwaraka called Shri Ram
Baba. He used to repeat, Shri Ram, Shri Ram all the time. He
lived on the beach and he was an ecstatic being. When I met
them, I thought I was smarter than they were, so I couldn't
attain anything, even from them.

One day I met a saint who said, "O Muktananda
Swami, it's useless for you to keep wandering like this. You're
wasting your time. Once again, go back to Ganeshpuri.
You'll find something there."

Baba was in Ganeshpuri so I went there. I began to
stay in the temple of the Devi in Vajreshwari, and from there
I went to visit him every day. In this way, eight or nine years
passed by. I would visit him, but then I would go to Yeola; I
would visit him, but then I would go to Kokamathan. What
happened was that when I went to him, I didn't like it, but

when I went elsewhere, I became restless. Let me tell you that the main reason for this was ego. The ego is really bad; it is the worst hell in the world. So I kept coming and going, coming and going. No matter how many times I left him, I would start missing him and I would come back.

Now he was a being who loved to insult others, and I was a person who was too proud. People used to line up there waiting for years to receive prasad from him. Sometimes he would pick up something and call somebody saying, "Hey, come here," and he would give him that. During different seasons he gave out different things. If it was mango season, he gave out mangoes. Whatever prasad he gave people was like a wish-fulfilling tree. It fulfilled any of their desires. I waited to see if I was going to receive anything, but I didn't get anything, not even a glass of water.

I'm telling you, our ashram is much better. At least you get water at the right time and food at the right time; we wake you up at the right time. I used to go to him and stay there for a few hours; however, to get some water to drink I had to go back to Vajreshwari. And there was no water or food along the way; only later did things begin to spring up here.

He would pick up something and say, "Hey, come here." I would go running. Then he would say, "Not you! I'm calling somebody else." Believe me, he would insult me in front of everybody again and again, and I would die right on the spot. The bigger my ego was, the worse the insults were. Now you are listening to me and laughing at this, and in those days people were also listening and laughing. This went on and on. Twelve years, thirteen years. As this happened

more and more, as he worked on me like this more and more,
finally he gave me something.

No matter how many lectures you give, no matter
how many things you do, no matter how many sadhanas
you pursue, none of them are of any use. Nothing helps you.
Only when you receive the prasad *or the grace of such a being*
do you attain something. A great being has a great amount
of prasad. Why doesn't he give it away? Because people don't
understand the value of it. Unless you become worthy, a
saint will never give you that invaluable prasad.

CHAPTER 16

Grace Is God's Prasad

A Siddha student's heart must be very vast, so that he can hold a Siddha's grace inside it.

I understand that it is through the Guru's grace that the longing for liberation is awakened. What must one do to receive the grace of a Guru?

It's not quite that. One should first be a real seeker with a longing for liberation. And once you have this longing, you will feel the need for the Guru's grace inside. When you feel that need, the Guru's grace comes.

When you feel that longing, do you have to be in the physical presence of the Guru?

Even if the Guru were at a distance, it would work. However, if you were in his physical presence, it would be better.

If you do not have this longing, what can you do to begin it?

Spend time with the right sort of people, read the right sort of books, try to understand things — these will all build up the longing for liberation.

Sometimes you refer to a knot in the heart. What does it mean?

There is a knot in the heart that makes you experience yourself as small though you are great. This knot makes you experience suffering even though you are nothing but bliss. It is because of this knot that you consider yourself to be made of matter though you are made of Consciousness. The knot in the heart gives rise to this kind of understanding over and over, and after giving rise to it, it fosters it and keeps it firm.

In meditation this knot must be cut out through the surgery of Kundalini. It is not a physical knot — it is a psychological knot. It is called *māyā* or illusion. The knot in the heart can be burned up by the fire of Kundalini. When this knot is gone, all of a sudden the inner being is filled with light and you begin to laugh. It is this knot that causes everyone to suffer. The purpose of the Guru's grace is to burn it up.

What is grace? Do I earn it, or is it available to everyone for the asking?

Grace is nothing but God's compassion. You experience God's grace inside yourself. The inner unfoldment takes place and that is called grace. You have to earn it with a generous and open heart, having firm faith and confidence. When this happens, your entire life is transformed. Then you attain a new life.

What is grace?

Grace is the result of the good actions you performed while being free from expectations. It is the result of the *sevā* you performed while being free from expectations. Grace is the gift you obtain for having devotion to the Guru. It also arises when you pursue *sādhanā* to attain God. The great sage Narada said that only through the grace of a great being can you attain That. Grace is God's *prasād*. God's love arises within you forever. That is called grace. Nothing else is the grace of God.

What exactly is Guru's grace? Is it something you are giving all the time, or do you give it to some people when they deserve it?

It is not that I give grace to those people who deserve it. Those people who deserve it take it. When they become engrossed in the Guru's work, when they become engrossed in the Guru, they obtain a kind of power through which they receive the Guru's grace.

A Guru will never have any sense of differentiation about his own people. You should never even imagine that Gurus are like that. The Guru is the ocean of compassion.

The authors of the scriptures have used an analogy: they say the Guru's grace is like the milk of a lioness. You can carry the milk of a cow or a goat or a donkey or any other animal in any kind of pot, but you cannot hold the milk of a lioness in just any pot. It is so strong that it will corrode any container except one made of gold. Only a golden vessel can hold the milk of a lioness. The Guru showers his grace on everybody, but not everybody is a golden vessel; not everyone can hold this grace.

Does your grace flow more toward those who are closer to your heart, or does it flow equally to all who love you and try to practice your teachings?

Grace is the same for everyone; there is no difference in that. It is not that people who are close get more or people who are far away get less. The sun is far away yet its light falls on everyone equally. However, it is up to you to have devotion, faith, and trust so that you draw that grace toward you.

How can I strengthen my heart to hold your prasād?

Don't make your heart too hard. It should be soft and malleable. It should be filled only with prasad and nothing else. It is not unusual to receive prasad, but after receiving it, it is very difficult to maintain it. Without complete discrimination nothing can be retained. You should attain worthiness. Vedanta calls it longing for liberation.

Is grace connected to karma?

Grace is the karma or the action of God. It is said that God performs five actions. One of the actions He performs is the bestowal of grace. You have asked a beautiful question. Grace is essential. *Will you bestow grace on me?*

If you can take it! The grace is not given — the grace is taken, it is received.

I wish to know and understand what Guru's grace is.

First, receive the Guru's grace; then understand it and become worthy of it. Just asking this question without receiving the Guru's grace doesn't make any sense.

Your question is like this: how do you get rest in your sleep? You have to go to sleep; only then can you find out how you get rest in your sleep. In the same way, you should first receive the Guru's grace. The Guru is the one who bestows the grace of God; he is the bestower of God's Shakti — he is not an individual being. Through grace, the Guru transmits God's energy into you. After transmitting that energy into you, he awakens your own inner energy and then spontaneous yoga begins to happen. That is the Guru's grace. The Guru applies the lotion of his grace to your eyes. Then the veil of ignorance is destroyed. Afterward, there is great delight in watching the world — you see the world as it is.

There was a great being who said, "My Guru applied the lotion of his grace to my eyes, and after that I experienced so much, it was such delight. How can I explain it to you? All that I can see now is Ram, the Self. It is Consciousness and nothing else. After I received the lotion of the Guru's grace, I see only Ram, only Consciousness, inside as well as outside." This is the Guru's grace.

THE DISCIPLE'S GRACE

Could you please talk about the disciple's grace?

This is a good question. Everybody always asks about the Guru's grace but nobody ever asks about the disciple's grace. It is disciple's grace when a disciple learns completely what his Guru teaches him. There is the teacher's grace and there is the student's grace. The teacher's grace is to teach the student with respect, and the student's grace is to study what the teacher has to say with respect and with faith in the teacher.

Without your grace I cannot be a good disciple. Please shower me with your grace. I cannot do anything without it.

This work is all yours; you have to become a disciple. Of course I will be a Guru; however, you yourself have to become a greater disciple. You have to become generous. Whoever wants to become great, there is no hindrance for that person. However, if you want to become smaller, there is hindrance. Become worthy of receiving grace. Grace is spontaneous and natural. Infinite grace from God is always showering; we call it the grace of the Guru. However, we don't have the understanding of it. We understand grace only when we become worthy of receiving it. In front of that Truth, in front of that great Shakti, we have to become humble. Therefore, become humble within yourself. Immediately, you will be worthy of receiving grace. Become free from ego; that is the only key to awakening the inner Shakti.

Can the grace of a Siddha cut through intellectual and emotional superficiality or is some special technique needed?

For that you don't need any other technique. A Siddha's grace can take you beyond that. Grace will not leave you midstream; it will perfect you.

What must one do to be entitled to this grace of the Lord?

We should offer our heart with love to the Lord. Just as we want His grace, we should also give Him our grace — namely love.

Sometimes I have many experiences in meditation, but not always. Is there any way I can earn your grace to have more steady experiences in meditation?

In grace there is no such thing as more or less. Just as you see the light of the sun, in the same way there is grace. It depends on your faith and your understanding — that is why you sometimes experience more and sometimes less. A person's faith is very important.

How does one develop love for God?

When you relinquish all other kinds of love.
You can't have both?
Yes, if you could really get love from others, if there were real love elsewhere. If there were love in things other than God, why would you need God's love? How can you sing and eat at the same time? You should either sing or eat.
If I understand it correctly, you have to have grace to do this. How do you earn this grace?
You should give your grace to me.
You have all my love, such as it is — as much as I have.
Before a Guru can give his grace to a student, the student should give his grace to the Guru. Then the student will receive the Guru's grace more quickly.
You have my love and my grace. What else can I do?
Then you should take it that you have my grace.
By faith, without feeling anything?
If you haven't felt it, if you haven't experienced it, it means there is something lacking in your grace to the Guru.

Is it possible to refuse the grace of God?

Yes, it is possible. When your mind turns away from grace, you are refusing it, you are rejecting it. Stop refusing grace — accept it. Use the wealth of God's grace for His sake. God gives out of compassion. He has given you a beautiful body. Use this body for His love, for His work.

How does a person know when his Guru has accepted him completely?

The moment a person accepts his Guru, at that very moment he realizes that his Guru has accepted him. The moment your heart is filled with devotion, faith, and trust — at that very moment you can understand that the Guru has accepted you. What is the use if the Guru accepts you and you don't accept the Guru?

Will you please comment upon the relationship between self-effort and the Guru's grace?

The effort that you put forth uninterruptedly to receive the Guru's grace is called self-effort. Once you receive the Guru's grace, you never encounter failure. You are never defeated. When you receive the Guru's grace, that live, divine flame is kindled from within.

Recently I was interviewed by a very good reporter who said, "Many gurus come to this country and they fail." I told him, "I studied in a school where there was no failure. If you went to that school, all you did was pass."

It makes me sad to think that you have showered tremendous gifts on me, but I haven't been able to open myself to your grace. Why is this? How can I change my understanding?

If you have received anything from me, understand that you have received it from your own Self. Then you can have peace of mind. Whether in meditation, or at an Intensive, or during *shaktipāt*—whatever it is, you will attain everything from your own inner Self. I am an instrumental cause—just a pretext—but you get everything from your own Self. Whatever you attain is due to your own effort. If you want to offer something in return, forget it.

Does self-effort bear any fruit without Guru's grace?

It is essential to receive the Guru's grace. But don't you think that even to receive the Guru's grace requires great self-effort? Only after you put forth a lot of effort can you attain the Guru's grace. As you keep putting forth effort, you come to a point where you can't go any further. Then it is the Guru's grace that helps you. So even to receive the Guru's grace, you have to pursue sadhana, you have to keep your mind under your control, you have to put forth great self-effort.

Does man have free will or is everything destiny?

Man does have free will; he can put forth his own self-effort. Whatever action you performed before becomes your destiny now. Whatever action you perform now becomes your destiny in the future. Therefore, in the *Bhagavad Gītā* the Lord says to perform action with your free will, to always put forth self-effort. Devotion to God comes from this free will.

Destiny cannot make your mind still. Destiny cannot make you meditate. Destiny cannot enter into you and make you become quiet. Therefore, put forth self-effort. It is not good to depend on destiny all the time.

Always remember the Self. Always see your own Self. Look at others less. Always contemplate your own Self. There is nothing greater than you. The *dharma* of a human being is to meditate on your own Self, to respect your own Self, and to honor your own Self. A person who has lost his own Self has not attained anything. However, a person who has attained his Self has attained everything.

IN RETURN FOR YOUR BONDAGE, I GIVE DIVINITY

Someone told me that it is as hard to lose the grace of the Guru as it is to take a lamb out of the mouth of a lion. Is that true?

After you have received Guru's grace, you can't give it up that easily. Grace is so compassionate that it must do its work of purifying you. Once you have received the nectar of the Guru's compassion, it never leaves. A saint's grace is very great. It is not only human beings who benefit from this grace. Even animals and birds would benefit if they were to receive that touch of grace; even they would be redeemed.

*I must go back to my everyday life after the retreat and I plan to
continue doing japa and meditating. What else must I do to keep
the Shakti alive and growing? I don't want to lose what you
have awakened in me. I'm afraid that without your physical
presence I might get discouraged. Please help.*

Pandardas, a great saint, said that once you have received the
Guru's grace, it will never leave you; it will always chase after
you. The sages have compared the Shakti to the teeth of a crocodile, which are shaped so that if you try to pull away from
them, you get even more hopelessly caught. You can find
release from the teeth of the crocodile only when you surrender
to them. In the same way, to escape from the Guru's grace you
must become divine like the Shakti.

Once somebody complained to me about various gurus
charging a lot of money for initiation. But they charge less than
I do, because I take a person's whole life. I charge you your
bondage and in return I give divinity.

*When one is under the guidance of a Siddha Guru, is it possible
to fall from the path? Or does shaktipāt mean that against all
odds one will definitely be liberated? Does the Siddha Guru
protect the aspirant from falling?*

Generally speaking, the Guru does protect the devotee from
falling. The *Guru Gītā,* which you sing every day, says that if one
is the child of the Guru, if one truly belongs to the Guru, even if
that person is a fool, he will attain liberation. However, a person must really belong to the Guru.

In Karnataka there was a saint who said that once you receive
the Guru's grace, it chases after you all the time; it just doesn't
leave you. It is like the new weapon that Russia has invented:
once it goes after a rocket, it won't stop until it finds that rocket. So
once you receive the grace of the Guru, it follows you all the time.

Please tell us more about what grace is.

Grace is the inner awakening. Truly, grace belongs to the primordial Lord. However, through a different channel, this grace
is bestowed upon others.

The Shaivite philosophy says that the Lord performs five actions. The first three are creation, sustenance, and dissolution. He creates this universe, He sustains it, and then He dissolves it. He doesn't destroy it, because after dissolving it, once again He creates it. If He were to destroy it, there would be no more creation.

The fourth action is concealment. For example, when there is garbage, we collect it and take it to the municipal dump and throw it away. However, God doesn't discard the world in that way. After dissolving the universe, He imbibes it again into His own being. That is called concealment; He reabsorbs the entire universe.

The fifth action is the bestowal of grace. Whoever wants to see Him, whoever wants to attain Him, whoever wants to understand Him, whoever wants to get closer to Him, on such a person He bestows His grace. This power of grace is called shaktipat.

If you accept this grace, it is bestowed upon you, but you can't just depend on the other being to bestow his grace upon you. You have to become receptive; you have to bestow your grace upon that being for him to bestow his grace upon you. More than the Guru's grace, the disciple's grace is important. Now you should become worthy of receiving the grace of the Guru.

Grace means shaktipat, the transmission of the energy, the inner awakening. If you really want to understand this in a very simple way, understand that shaktipat means opening the gate that leads to the heart of God.

Will there always be great beings in human form to serve as Gurus?

Yes, there will be. This is a law of nature. There will be many great beings as Gurus to serve the world. God performs five actions and one of them is the bestowal of grace. Only a Guru can do that; therefore the Guru will always exist. The five actions are creation, maintenance, dissolution, concealment, and grace. Shaivism says that Lord Shiva continuously performs all these five actions. He creates new worlds and maintains them and then dissolves them when they get old. He reabsorbs them and then conceals them. When it is time to create everything again, He creates it. In this way, creation, maintenance, dissolution, and concealment happen over and over again. When you finally have your last birth, He bestows grace, the fifth cosmic function — and He does that only through a Guru.

Nobody can erase God's original creation. It can never happen. A Guru will always be there, and a disciple will also be there.

How can I purify myself so that I can attain Guru's grace?

Devotion to the Guru is the greatest purifier. There is no action more purifying than affection for the Guru. Devotion for the Guru is the supreme sacred practice; all other holy practices are futile. Just as for a true devotee there is nothing higher than his Lord, for a true disciple there is nothing higher than his Guru. I am talking about a true disciple, not a fake disciple, not one who is just a mockery. A true disciple is totally devoted to his Guru.

There are two kinds of disciples: one is nonpromiscuous and the other is promiscuous — in a spiritual sense. If a disciple is completely nonpromiscuous, absolutely devoted to his Guru, the Guru takes on full responsibility for him. However, a Guru should also be a true Guru, not just a person who is only good at running practical affairs. If a Guru is not a true Guru, the kind of people he will attract toward himself will not be true disciples either.

Just as we expect a disciple to be high and ideal, we should expect a Guru to be high and ideal. The Guru should have the power to cause an inner awakening in his disciple. He should be well versed in all the scriptures, he should be able to see the inner spiritual centers and to transmit knowledge directly. He should have extraordinary skill in instructing his disciples. This is what a true Guru is like.

When a true disciple and a true Guru come together, enormous Shakti is generated between the two of them.

Then I Realized the Value of the Guru's Grace

There was a time when I believed in the sufficiency of self-effort alone. In my younger days I was very strong and well built. I practiced ashtanga yoga at that time with full devotion, following all its rules and disciplines. As a result I could reshape my body according to the ideals of yoga. I also practiced hatha yoga and spent various periods of time with great Vedanta teachers. I met at least sixty very great teachers. I learned a lot from them but I did not have the certainty that my inner being had been opened.

Although my body was well-shaped and people admired me for my strength and appearance and various other qualities, although they considered me to be highly evolved at that time, I always felt a certain inner lack. Even though people praised me, I knew I had not really attained the highest Truth that is spoken of in Vedanta. This feeling of lack often tormented me. Now I have become old, but there was a time when people had just to see me and they would gather around. But even so I did not feel at all satisfied within. I often wondered, "What is the use of praise? They may call me an aristocrat, but the fact is I don't have a single penny in my pocket."

This inner dissatisfaction compelled me to keep wandering on foot, and I thought I would spend my entire life that way. During the course of my wanderings, I came upon a saint whose name was Zipruanna. He was the *strangest of all the saints I had ever seen. He would lie on heaps of rubbish or in the most unwanted corners of town where nobody would expect to find anyone.*

But his body had become so purified by the fire of yoga that the garbage on which he was sitting did not affect him at all. There was a sweet fragrance emanating from his body. He was very old and like a skeleton, and he didn't have any teeth. He was omniscient; he knew the past, present, and future of any person who came to him. He always threw out mysterious hints, but he never gave a clear explanation of anything.

He was obviously neglecting his body; he let it lie anywhere. He hid his inner powers and did not let anybody have the slightest idea of them. The moment I met him, he said, "Stop wandering around and go straight to Ganeshpuri." I was astonished. But I did what he said, and the minute I reached Ganeshpuri, my Babaji did something to me.

When I met my Guru, I was without any worth, without inner realization in spite of the fact that I practiced many different forms of yoga with complete devotion and had followed various disciplines perfectly. I had fasted for long periods, too, but I was still without any satisfactory inner state.

One day my Guru put wooden sandals on his feet and then gave them to me. Then he said something to me. It seemed as though he entered into my inner being with his words. Although from the outside Muktananda appeared to be the same — his body was still the same, his senses were still the same — deep down within him, he was completely transformed.

That day I discarded the doctrine of the sufficiency of self-effort which I, along with many others, had held. I realized the value of the Guru's grace and started emphasizing the role of grace to everyone I spoke to. Self-effort and the Guru's grace are like the two wings of a bird. The bird needs both wings to fly. If it is without one, it cannot fly.

DON'T SLACKEN NOW!

CHAPTER 17

Life Is Beyond Your Mind

*The mind has become one with its habits
and must be set free.*

Who or what is God?

That is a very good question. Once all the sages and seers met in a conference and they asked an enlightened being, "Who is God?" He answered in one sentence: "God lives within everyone as the witness of the mind."

Just as God is the witness of the mind, He is also the witness of everything else. He is the witness of the earth, of water, of air, of fire, and of space.

Once King Janaka asked the great seer Yajnavalkya, "What kind of being is God? And where is He?"

Yajnavalkya said, "O King, God is the One who lives within the mind, but who cannot be known by the mind, because the mind is His garden. The One who makes the mind known is the indwelling Self. He is God. He is immortal."

A sage wrote this poem: "I bow to the Being who holds all the powers in His hand, who controls all those powers, who creates a cosmos when He opens His eyes, and when He closes them, the cosmos dissolves. That is God. God is the One who lives within the earth, but who cannot be known by the earth because the earth is His body. It is God who activates the earth and brings all the plants and trees to life."

The chief purpose of meditation is to attain this indwelling God, the One who is the witness of the mind, the One who is pure bliss, the One who is immortality.

What is God? God is the bliss that rages continually. That is the Self. Meditate on That.

The term "go within" is not a common term in our Western culture and philosophy. What does it mean? How does it differ from introversion?

You may not have studied Western philosophy, but if you did you would certainly find something similar. In the Bible Jesus said that the wisdom of God is within you and that you must seek it there. Even in our daily life we go within many times. How do you go to sleep? By staying without or by going within? Meditation is a little beyond sleep. When you think, where is it that you think? Outside or inside?

Going within is not the same thing as introversion. As you go deeper and deeper within yourself and reach the place where the mind arises, the mind becomes transmuted into pure Consciousness. It is only when the Shakti works outside that it becomes the mind. When the mind turns within, it becomes a ray of light of the Self.

So many of us want to stay in our minds and won't allow ourselves to go beyond.

Yes, that is the mistake you make. Your life is beyond your mind. Where there is true life, your mind is not there, and where there is no life, that is where your mind is working. Where there is true laughter, there is no mind. True laughter is even deeper than the mind. Therefore, you have to meditate.

What is the relationship between the individual soul and the mind? Can the individual soul stop the mind from wandering and committing bad actions?

Yes, it can. Once the individual soul becomes aware of itself, it can stop the mind from wandering here and there. The mind is an instrument of the individual soul. If you understand the nature of the mind, it can be in a very good state. The mind is nothing but Chiti, or pure Consciousness, mixed with *prāna*. Once it becomes aware of itself, it becomes pure Chiti once again.

The mind is under the control of the Self. However, it has become our habit to follow the mind. We do not make the mind follow the Self. If you still the mind even for a few moments, you will want only a quiet mind; you will not want your mind to wander. Truly speaking, you should respect the mind. Pain and pleasure are in the hands of your mind. One whose mind is clean, clear, and immersed in the Self — for him there is peace. One whose mind is not under control, one whose mind thinks of negative things and wanders here and there — that one always suffers. The scriptures say that the mind is the source of bondage and liberation.

If you want to know what the Self is, what Consciousness is, you will have to know that through the mind. Consciousness has become the mind and it creates all thoughts, fantasies, and various inner worlds. It makes them arise and subside. All our difficulties are due to the mind; happiness too is due to the mind. For that reason, make the mind Rama. One who comes under the control of the mind is flown right to the ocean of pain. One who brings the mind under his control, through chanting the name of God or through right understanding, climbs the ladder to heaven.

No matter how much wealth you have, no matter how many possessions you have, no matter how much power you have, if your mind is not pure, clean, and quiet, all those things are of no use; they don't matter. For that reason, give more importance to the mind. There are so many things in mundane life. Among all these, the most valuable thing is the mind.

Help me to distinguish between the mind and the inner Self. I get too caught up in my emotions. These feelings begin as thoughts; then they surface as what I believe to be me.

Should I help you to distinguish between the mind and the inner Self, or should I help you to erase the duality that you have created between the mind and the Self? There isn't any difference between the mind and the Self. Just as there are rays of the sun, in the same way the mind is one of the rays of the inner Self. Shaivism says that the mind is not just the mind, it is the light of Chiti, of Consciousness. But Consciousness forgets its own true nature and becomes the objects perceived. Then it becomes completely one with them; it imbibes their qualities and becomes the mind. However, once it discards those notions of name and form, it regains its own true nature. When it returns to its own true nature, it is once again Consciousness.

Therefore, with great subtlety try to understand the mind. When Consciousness becomes contracted, it is the mind. The moment it gives up its contraction, it evolves, it expands, it becomes free, and then it is Consciousness again. You are not your thoughts: you are the witness, the knower of your thoughts. You are the perceiver of thoughts; you understand them. That knower is Consciousness. Understand that you are that knower.

Sometimes when I perform an action, it seems to come directly from my Self. But at other times there is confusion. Where is the Self that knows during indecision? What is the relationship between the mind and the Self? Why does the mind give us such trouble even though it is a product of the Self?

The mind is the product of the Self. However, when the mind separates itself from the Self and begins to identify itself with the non-Self, that is when it starts giving us trouble. When Consciousness gives up its lofty state and comes down, when it begins to move among worldly objects, when it becomes them, that is when it becomes contracted and becomes the mind. When it turns within and reaches its pure state, once again it becomes That.

Why did God give us the veil of ignorance? What is it composed of?

There is no veil of ignorance in God's creation; it exists in your

creation. It wasn't necessary for Him to create a veil of ignorance. This is how people are — they create their own veil and
then they blame God. Because we have created it, we do *sādhanā*
so we can get rid of it.

Kabir sang about it very beautifully. Moslem women wear
a veil over their eyes. They make the veil with their own hands
and then they wear it. Because of the veil, nobody can see them,
nor can they see anybody else. Kabir said, "Remove the veil.
Then you will see your own Beloved." So we are wearing our
own veil of ignorance.

In the *Shiva Sūtras,* the second aphorism says that knowledge is bondage. Now you will be wondering how can knowledge be bondage? Knowledge is supposed to liberate us. But
we have this knowledge: I am this body. I am a man; I am a
woman; I feel this; I feel that.

People wear this veil of ignorance. This kind of knowledge
is called bondage. Because we have this knowledge we are
bound. But God did not make it; we did. Don't blame God —
He is innocent.

*Please teach me how to be honest before you and not to hide
or run away.*

This is your wrong understanding; this is the understanding of
your mind. The Self is very honest and open. Before a person
opens himself to somebody else, he must be open to his own
Self. If you are not open to your own Self, but you keep talking
about being open with others, you can't do that. If you have
become honest with yourself, you are honest with the entire
world. Through meditation, through high understanding, and
through love for God, a person should become open and
expanded. This human body is not meant for you to close and
contract yourself; it is meant for opening. For this reason
through meditation and understanding, just become open. God
has kept His own energy inside all of us. The Upanishads say
that after creating everything, it is He who entered everything
and made everything conscious. He injected Consciousness into
everything. Man can contract so much that he can make himself

feel as small as a worm or an insect. But man can also expand and make himself as great as God and even merge with God.

Therefore, the *Bhagavad Gītā* says man becomes his own enemy and his own friend. If man thinks only bad things about himself all the time, he is being unjust to himself. Don't do that. Keep expanding yourself all the time. The purer the mind becomes, the clearer it becomes, the more the light of the Self will reveal itself to you.

I have done some inner work and I feel that my mind is dissolving and disappearing. Is this a cleansing process? What is happening?

This is the exact purpose of true spiritual discipline. The mind should merge into its true nature, the inner Self. Any discipline that enables the mind to become one with the Self is commendable. All spiritual practices are meant to fill the mind with peace and strength.

Do we create the universe with our mind, and thus create all that happens to us? Or are we an effect of a pre-existing universe? Are we the cause or the effect?

You are the effect, and the One who created this universe is the cause. This entire universe is created by God's expanded mind. It is only through His mind that this whole universe comes into being, and that all these people and creatures are created. Our minds are also a part of His mind. That is why the scriptures say to purify your mind, clean your mind, and respect your mind. Make your mind God's mind. You impose your own creation on God's creation when you say, "This is my house" or "This is my car." To say "I" or "mine" is to be deluded by ego. God did not create these ideas. God's creation is helpful, and an individual's creation is harmful. That is what Vedanta says, and it is absolutely true.

Do such things as mental kriyās exist? If so, please explain.

When the mind has different kinds of thoughts all the time, that is called a mental *kriyā*. When those kriyas in the mind become stronger, when they flow through the senses, you perform the outer actions. The mind is always engaged in mental kriyas. When does it sit quietly? It will sit quietly, it will become stable, only when it becomes satisfied in the inner Self. Otherwise, the mind wavers all the time, it moves all the time. Either it will have good thoughts or it will have bad thoughts.

Once there was a man who wandered into a forest, and in that forest there was a beautiful tree. He sat down under that tree to rest for a while. As he was sitting there, he thought how great it would be if there were a nice cool breeze. Just then a beautiful cool breeze sprang up. So he was quite happy. Then he thought, "Well, I'm sitting here all alone. If only I had a partner, if only I had a friend." The moment he thought that, a beautiful woman appeared. She walked toward him swinging and swaying. He was very happy when he saw her, but then he thought, "Well, it would be so great if there were a house." Immediately the house appeared. Then he thought, "Well, we need a butler and a servant." All of a sudden, they were there too. The man told them to prepare a delicious meal. So after a while he and the woman began to enjoy the food.

Now he hadn't even finished his food when he began to worry, "Well, first I just sat down alone and now there are two of us, and then all these things started happening. What's the matter?"

The mischief of this monkey-mind was so bad that it didn't even let him finish his food. His mind began to think, "Whatever I thought came true, so . . ." He looked around. Then he thought, "There must be a devil around here!" Just then a devil appeared in front of him.

"Wow," cried the man, "he's going to eat me up!" And that was that. The devil ate him up.

That is the mind. That is the worth of the mind. That is a mental kriya.

Baba, you are the wish-fulfilling tree. Thank you for your grace.

Is it all right to remember and relive the experience I had of your inner love?

This experience should be with you all the time — and it will be! I am not the only wish-fulfilling tree. When God created this entire cosmos, he created everyone without duality. He doesn't have any sense of duality, of high and low. He doesn't know how to give a little bit to one person and a lot to another. We are much smarter than God in these matters; we are the ones with duality, but He is equal for everyone. He has made everyone a wish-fulfilling tree. It is only because you are not aware of this that you cannot make good use of it, and you experience sadness rather than happiness. It is the supreme Principle, God, who is sitting inside everyone's heart in the form of the wish-fulfilling tree. So I am not the only wish-fulfilling tree; everyone is a wish-fulfilling tree.

How does meditation purify the heart and mind?

After *shaktipāt* occurs, the Shakti purifies the mind and heart. When the mind becomes free from all thoughts and doubts, when it becomes still, then know that the mind has become pure. The fewer thoughts you have, the purer you become. Ultimately, the mind merges into the Self. The mind is not destroyed, but it becomes absorbed in the Self. When the mind becomes pure, it will still exist; it will be with you as long as the body exists. But then the mind will act as a friend to you — it won't be your enemy. It will play and sport within you with great joy.

Since your mind is still, even amidst action, what is your relationship to the play that goes on? Do you feel like a spectator, an actor, or what?

I am everything. Whatever is going to happen, happens. Why worry about it? This entire world is nothing but a play. Shaivism says that the Self is a great actor. Everybody has taken a different role; so I also play my part. In the play of the Self, there are many different roles. Even though I live amidst people, even though I am right in the center of all the actions that go on, still I do not get involved in them. Because they happen, they are supposed to happen. Even though so many actions are being performed, I do not get trapped in the awareness of performing them.

If a person conquers his senses and becomes established in his own inner Self with great serenity, he becomes the witness, the spectator. No matter what happens, he just watches it. Then he is not bothered by the pairs of opposites such as heat and cold, pain and pleasure, honor and insult. So man should learn how to live with the awareness of being a witness. Even though I did so much work this morning, I am still in the serene state. This morning there was the finale of the *saptah* and the weddings, and now I am meeting you all for the third time today. But I do not absorb the *bhāva* or the feeling of an action in my mind. So when a person is doing something, he should not absorb the feeling of that action; he should not have the feeling that he is performing it. He should become absorbed in the feeling of his own Self.

At night you go to sleep. Suppose somebody asks you, "Why do you go to sleep at night? What is the use of going to sleep?" You may say, "Well, I want to sleep so that I can feel rested." After you sleep, you do feel rested. This rest you could never buy from a shop, nor could you pray to someone for this rest. You yourself have to go to sleep. In the same way, you can never buy or beg others to give you the state of your own Self, the feeling of your own Self. You have to meditate. Your happiness lies within your Self. However, you are looking for it outside.

So I have no relationship with what goes on outside. It is supposed to happen, so it happens. I am just the witness. An actor plays his part. Sometimes his part is to be married to a woman who dies all of a sudden, and he just cries and cries. Does he really cry? No. He is just playing his role. A person should live his life in the same way.

LET THE MIND DROWN IN THE HEART

Why does man fear going into his heart?

It is the nature of the mind. If man attains knowledge, true wisdom, he knows that whatever is going to happen, happens. Man's understanding is weak in the sense that his understanding dwells on outer things, and he is afraid that if he goes inside he will have to lose everything he has on the outside.

There was a great *swāmi* named Siddharudha Swami. I took *sannyāsa* initiation in his ashram. Somebody once asked him, "If everybody became great beings, what would they eat and drink?"

He said, "You haven't become great beings yet. This is why you still need food. If you were all to become great beings, the entire ocean would change into milk and all the sand would become sweet pudding. You could eat anything you wanted."

Man just fears to enter inside. If you go inside, you can lead a beautiful life. But if you try to go inside while depending on drugs or drink, you don't go where you are supposed to go; you are in a trap.

Everything in life seems so well-designed. Why is enlightenment designed to be so far away from us?

It is just that we always turn outside, we never turn within; otherwise there is no difficulty. Do you find difficulty in going to sleep? No, it's natural. Just beyond the sleeping state lies the state of God. However, we accept it very slowly. We give it a very fearful, weird form. But it's not so — it's very, very natural, it's very close, it's the inner state. Man can go inside very naturally. He can meditate very spontaneously. Now, did you become so big within a day? Did you grow up just like that? Did you learn how to operate that video camera in three weeks? Did you become a psychologist in three months? Why do you want to attain God just like that? Is it cheaper than all these things? *If we all become enlightened, would this plane of existence just disappear?*

No. It will become heaven. Why should it disappear? It will become heaven.

What is the correct relationship between the heart and the mind?

The heart is the dwelling place of God. The mind is an instrument like hands and legs; the mind is just for understanding things. But the mind arises from the heart. Wise people understand that the mind is inspired by the heart; they don't consider the heart and the mind to be different. In meditation they make the mind merge into their own Self. Then nothing is different from the Self. The Upanishads say the mind has arisen from the heart, the intellect has arisen from the heart — everything has come out of the heart.

Please speak about the heart, how it becomes open, and its relationship to the mind.

The heart opens through love, through devotion. If you have intense love for Consciousness, for the supreme Principle, the heart becomes open immediately; it doesn't take any time at all. The place of the mind is far away from the place of the heart; there is no relationship between them. The mind is not the heart's brother or uncle; it is separate. The mind is an instrument. For instance, we have this microphone so that our voices can be heard at a distance. In the same way there is this mind; it is an instrument that expresses your thoughts and your feelings. And if your mind doesn't help you to remember the Self, to love the Self, to meditate on the Self, to contemplate the Self, then your mind is a great nuisance to you. All it can do is make you think about one thing or another.

So there is not much relationship between the mind and the Self, because the Self is so pure that nothing can enter into it. Nothing can touch the Self. The Self is supremely independent and self-existent and it dwells in everyone's heart all the time.

My heart wanted to come here but my head is resisting.

This kind of conflict is not unusual. Everyone has a conflict going on between the heart and the head, between stillness and mental agitation. For some time you will have to brave it.

There is a hard rock in my heart. How can I enter my heart and begin to feel?

It is not as hard as you think. The heart is already open. You have only to enter it with interest. We exist because the heart exists. How could it be closed? So meditate calmly and with interest. Using the legs of your mind, walk right into the chamber of your heart.

How can I integrate what I feel with what I think?

Though they may appear to be different from one another, thoughts and feelings arise from the same place, from the place in the heart. You should go past those thought-waves and try to stay in a state without thought. If you could see what is at the root of thoughts, it would be very good.

Can you tell me how I can turn the knowledge of the mind into the experience of the heart?

Let the mind drown in the experience of the heart. With discrimination, make the mind mindless and free from thoughts. This is the greatest attainment. Unless the mind becomes mindless you cannot attain anything. When the mind becomes free from thoughts, it attains the knowledge of the heart. In the heart divine knowledge always pulsates. But because the mind does not let you know the pulsation of that divine knowledge in the heart, you do not understand it. One who loses himself in the mind should understand that he has gone far away from Rama. Therefore, we meditate to still the mind. Meditation does not exist for any other reason. You have already attained the Self, but the activity of the mind conceals it from you. Therefore, make the mind pure and free from thoughts.

How can I open my heart?

The heart is already open; you can't ever close your heart. Once it is closed, either you go into *samādhi* or you take *mahāsamādhi*, you die. The understanding you have about your heart is mistaken. Remove that wrong understanding and everything will be fine.

The heart is a divine place. Kabir says, "I found the supreme Lord within my own heart, the supreme Lord of the entire universe." Your heart is God's temple. How can it be closed? So change the understanding that you have about your heart. Meditate at least a little bit, being aware that it is a divine place, and then you will find that your heart has been open from the very beginning. It has never been closed. The heart has been open since the beginning of time. It is God's temple.

In the *Bhagavad Gītā* Arjuna asked the Lord: "O Lord, if I want to meet You right away, where can I find You? Where do You dwell?"

The Lord said, "Arjuna, if you want to meet Me right away, come to the heart, because I dwell in everyone's heart."

The heart is pure and great. There are many people who say their hearts are closed; you are not the only one. It is not true though. The heart is always blazing within, and the knowledge of that brilliant light is always blazing.

How can I actually experience this inner reality rather than just think about it?

The One you are looking for is beyond thought. He is experienced when thought ceases. That is God where the mind cannot reach, where speech cannot reach, where the intellect cannot reach. Where the mind merges all its thoughts, there God begins to shine. When the mind becomes completely still, then God reveals Himself with all His love. You can know Him only by going into your inner being. That is why it is necessary to turn within, to turn all your thoughts to the inner Self.

There was once a great saint of India who sang, "Why are you looking for God from forest to forest, from place to place, when He is right in your heart? Look for Him within your heart and there you will see Him as you see a reflection in a mirror." One person looks for Him in the East, another in the West, yet another looks for Him elsewhere, but the truth is that He cannot be experienced unless you experience the inner touch.

Just thinking about it won't help, but when thought ceases, the mind ceases, and what is left is nothing but pure God. God is not something that will come from outside and meet you. He is ever present in your heart, but the paradox is that we have to attain what is already there in the heart. If He did not exist, neither would we.

When Nachiketa asked Yama, the god of death, "Who is God?" Yama answered, "God is the One who draws your breath inward and pushes it out. He lives in the junction between your inbreath and outbreath." That is the supreme goal of our quest.

WHY CARRY THESE FEELINGS ON YOUR HEAD?

What are we to do with the various feelings that arise?

Within all feelings lies the supreme Truth. A feeling arises within you and it is there for a while. Then it merges somewhere, and you don't know where. Then you have another feeling. It is there for a while and once again it merges. In the same way, from the center of the Self all feelings arise and they subside right there. When they subside in the Self, they completely merge there; they become the Self. Feelings are like the waves in the ocean — they come from the ocean and they merge in the ocean. If you contemplate the Self in this way, you perceive it instantly.

So you don't have to do anything with the feelings that arise inside; you don't have to look at them. However, you should try to understand one thing — where do these feelings arise and subside? What is that? Focus your attention on the root Principle, the basic Principle. Then you will know the Truth.

How should one deal with feelings of loneliness and depression? Must they be endured passively?

These feelings just arise, but you are not necessarily undergoing them. They are the creation of the mind. You should just understand them. Shaivism explains it very beautifully, saying that all these feelings are the creation of limited knowledge. Infinite thoughts arise and subside, arise and subside; infinite creations arise and dissolve, arise and dissolve in the mind.

Sometimes the mind marries somebody, sometimes the mind kills somebody. Should you laugh? Should you cry? A wise person understands that everything is the creation of the mind, and he keeps quiet. Why do you carry somebody else's burden? Why do you carry these feelings on your head? Let them fly away.

Vedanta calls this process *abhinivesha*, "wrong identification." Abhinivesha is when something does not really belong to you, but you say, "That belongs to me," and you start crying. All your life the mind has done that to you. What have you really lost and what have you really gained?

The mind is like soap bubbles. Why do you pursue the mind when the bubbles just vanish? So give up these feelings and don't worry about them. The mind is just playing with you. The mind blows soap bubbles in the form of feelings and you get agitated, and then the feelings vanish. So why worry about them if they are going to disappear anyway?

Please tell me how I can witness the mind without becoming emotionally involved.

In reality you never get involved in your emotions; you *think* that you do. Being apart from your emotions, you think you are involved in them. But who is it that knows your feelings? It is the witness of the mind, the witness of your emotions. There is no conscious knowing in emotions. Emotions cannot know themselves. The knower of the emotions is different from the emotions. Whatever feelings you have, whether good or bad, the knower of these feelings is different from them. To know the witness is realization.

*Does a person ever become free of the negativity of his
own mind?*

If a person were to understand the nature of his mind, he would
become free of negativity in that very moment. The many negative thoughts that arise from inside cannot do anything to the
Self. And just as nothing wrong can be done to the Self by those
negative thoughts, nothing good can be done to the Self by positive thoughts. Since the Self is just the pure witness of all those
thoughts, they cannot affect it.

Does the time ever come when negative thoughts stop?

When you become perfect in meditation on the inner Self,
all those thoughts merge into the Self.

*How can I overcome feelings of unworthiness and inadequacy
that arise during meditation?*

You should not attach any importance to these feelings. You
should try to transcend all feeling. You are not your feelings;
you are the place where feelings arise. Just as in the sky, clouds
appear and vanish continually, in the space of the heart endless
feelings and thoughts rise and set. So why should you attach
any importance to them?

*When I am disturbed by negative emotions, I concentrate on my
sahasrāra until the Shakti moves up from the emotional center.
Is it right for me to impose my will on Her actions, or am I
interfering with the Shakti working on my emotions?*

What you are doing is all right. But how long will the negative
emotions last? They will only turn into postive emotions. So
change your understanding. Whether your emotions are negative or positive, they are nothing but *vikalpas*, mere thoughts.
They arise from within and have no meaning. Neither good nor
bad emotions affect anything. It is only your pride that has an
effect. Understand that a positive emotion can arise as a negative emotion, and a negative emotion can arise as a positive
emotion. Become their witness; then see what they can do to
you. The value of your inner thoughts, your inner vikalpas, is

nothing. They are just like clouds. In the sky, the clouds come and go, come and go. Your thoughts too just come and go. When the clouds appear, the sky does not undergo any change. In the same way, whatever emotions arise in meditation can neither help nor harm you.

My mind sometimes seems to be full of negativities and impurities. Why is this, and what can I do?

The mind itself is not impure. External thoughts come into the mind, so you should discard them and then make the mind Shiva. The mind is like the waves of the ocean. Whatever garbage falls into the ocean, the waves throw it back onto the beach. The ocean does not keep anything within itself. In the same way the mind is very clean and pure. Don't let the garbage stay there. Throw it away. Then Shiva will reveal Himself to you. Your heart is already pure because God dwells there. You can't make your heart impure at all. This is the disease of a weak mind; you lack understanding. The heart is completely pure and God permeates it completely. There isn't room there for any garbage. Because of our wrong under-standing, we betray ourselves. Because a person does not have the right understanding, he is afraid. He eats fear. If you don't know how to eat knowledge, you eat fear.

If I accept myself as I am, will I also have to accept my own fears, doubts, and insecurities? If not, how can I eliminate them? I am confused!

These feelings will leave of their own accord. When you find your own Self, you will lose them. Jnaneshwar Maharaj said, "O supreme Principle, when You are concealed from certain people, then the world is manifest for them. When You reveal Yourself to those people, then the world disappears for them." So let the supreme Principle manifest. Don't worry about your feelings.

I feel very detached from my emotions. Some say that this is not good. Is it?

It is very good to be detached from your emotions. If you are, you will have the great emotion of the Self. In the *Bhagavad Gītā* there is *anāsakti yoga*, the yoga of detachment. What this yoga of detachment means is that you don't expect the fruits of your actions.

Now that I'm pregnant, I cry a lot, even though I try to be cheerful.

If you were to cry out of love, that would be good. If you could stay cheerful, chant, repeat the *mantra*, and laugh, that would affect the baby. It doesn't matter what has happened. Now you should be simple and pure and remember the Lord intensely; that is what is important. When you were in San Francisco, did you see a baby named Krishna? His mother came to the ashram when she was pregnant. She prayed to the Lord and remembered Him intensely and that baby is most wonderful.

Don't worry about anything; forget what has happened. Don't let past memories come into your mind. Let this new life begin.

Why is there such a thing as fear?

Fear is natural to the mind, and other negative feelings too emerge naturally in the mind. Don't attach any importance to them. Just as cold and heat, dry weather and rains, keep alternating with one another, in the same way the mind keeps passing through different phases. If it gets too cold, you turn the heater up. If it gets too hot, you turn on the air conditioner and it cools you down. If it rains too hard, people drink strong coffee. In the same way, when negativity arises within us, we should be able to make ourselves aware of the existence of God everywhere and in everyone, on the basis of the Guru's words and the scriptures.

All the negative thoughts that appear are like vapors or fumes that rise up into the sky. Don't attach any importance to them. It is these thoughts that are our most formidable enemy; they are the angels of death; they are hell. It is the mind that makes us restless and agitated, and it is the mind that sometimes lets us have peace.

A wise person must not attach any value to the various thoughts that arise in the mind from moment to moment. Just stay full of joy and be aware that the Self is pure, the Self is blissful, the Self is ecstatic.

Just as there are so many different parts of the body — there is the hair that keeps flying in the breeze, the legs that keep moving, the beard that keeps growing — in the same way there are many parts of the mind, and all kinds of things keep happening there. Don't lose yourself to them; don't consider them to be real; don't attach any value to them.

The peace and bliss you are going to experience in the future are experienced as agitation at this moment. Look at it all as the fruit of your *karma*. Keep remembering God, and stay calm.

When you were doing your sādhanā, what was your greatest psychological obstacle?

The mind will always put up some resistance against your sadhana, no matter who you are. But there was nothing with me to encourage that hostile tendency of the mind. Before I could have accumulated things around me, I left home and I possessed nothing. I was not addicted to anything and I didn't have any friends, so my mind did not have anything to really hang on to. And in my younger days my body was totally free from disease, so how could the mind torment me? However, the mind did yearn for perfection in yoga.

It is natural for the mind to be filled with attachment and hate every now and then, because those tapes have been running since time immemorial.

The Vedas say that the mind should be stilled. What about emotions?

As the mind is stilled, the emotions are also stilled. All this is a play of the three *gunas*. These three gunas are the basic forces or modes of manifestation: *tamas* is translated as ignorance and inertia; *rajas* is activity and passion; *sattva*, purity and light. Through the spiritual practices laid down in the Vedas, the mind can be freed from these forces, and it is possible to live in purity and light all the time.

Will that mean no feelings or emotions?

No, you will still have feelings, but they will be purified and positive; they will be divine emotions. In ancient times the seers and sages, some of whom were great teachers, found divine energy rushing up after they had stilled their minds. They gave expression to that in their literary and artistic works such as poetry and sculpture.

What are some examples of divine emotions?

When the heart opens and there is an outflow of pure love, that is divine emotion. There are different stages of the yoga of meditation. There is a stage when you become so filled and possessed by pure love that you laugh and dance in sheer ecstasy. That is divine emotion. That emotion can sometimes be experienced by listening to great classical music.

According to the Upanishads, man is, to a great extent, made up of emotions. He keeps identifying himself with whatever emotion wells up from within him, whether it be anger, jealousy, greed, or love.

Would you comment on the difference between emotion and devotion?

Devotion is the emotion of love; it is another name for love. When you don't have love, you have other emotions. The mind keeps passing from one emotion to another, from desire to lust to greed and then back to love. When other emotions rush into the mind, try to transmute them into love. Let love reign supreme in the mind.

I have heard that there are specific connections between the emotions and the heart chakra. Is this true?

Within the body there are such divine places. In the course of my sadhana I explored them very deeply. Amidst all the different energy centers of the body there is the heart center. It looks just like a lotus and each petal has its own unique quality. As soon as a person reaches the heart center, he has many different kinds of experiences; he gains a certain satisfaction — but still not a perfect satisfaction.

There are twelve petals in the heart lotus, each with a particular quality. I came to understand each and every quality of those twelve petals. Just as a honey bee is constantly moving around a lotus blossom, in the same way the individual soul constantly moves around the different petals in this heart lotus. During the time that it remains on one petal, it absorbs the qualities of that particular petal and identifies itself with those qualities.

You can experience this process without much difficulty if you sit quietly and contemplate for a few moments. Suppose a person contemplates someone very deeply and tries to imbibe the qualities of that person. He feels love for that person, but after a few minutes, he suddenly experiences an outburst of anger, and he feels perplexed. How did this feeling arise with no reason? After a few minutes, this feeling is gone and he experiences something like fear. Then a few more minutes pass and there is a feeling of greed. This doesn't last long, and next he feels excruciating pain because he is remembering his past sinful deeds. In a few more minutes he feels very peaceful and blissful because of his past good actions. Then he enters into the next petal and feels completely disgusted with everything, and he develops such dispassion that he wants to leave everything immediately.

This change of inner experience is due to the peculiarity of these petals of the heart chakra. Eight of the petals are facing upward and four are facing downward. When a person identifies himself with a petal, he experiences its quality. This is particularly true of the eight upward-facing petals. But it is very difficult to identify with the qualities of those other four petals that face downward.

If one is established in the first of these four petals, he will become a renunciant. He will be very steadfast; nothing can shake him or move him. When one identifies with the second of the four petals, he becomes a very great poet. When he enters into the third petal in deep meditation, he can visualize the whole cosmos. The fourth petal is such that if one is established there, he will be filled with knowledge and universal love. The specialty of skillful *yogis* who are mature in their spiritual practice is that they can constantly remain in that particular petal, and that is why they always revel in that experience of divine love and wisdom.

I spent a lot of time in meditation analyzing the different qualities of these petals in the heart chakra. Then I achieved steadiness, and I developed the ability to stay for a long time in the petal that gives the experience of divine wisdom and love. One can control the mind and remain in the heart lotus for a long time, but that is not sufficient. One has to know the technique of staying in these four petals, and then one experiences complete freedom. When one reaches that space, he is not afflicted by the pains and sorrows and pleasures of the physical body.

We experience pleasure from sense objects outside, because in the process of enjoying them, we get a shadowy glimpse of that petal of love. We feel that we are experiencing love or joy from those objects, but it is not a real experience. We get glimpses of joyful moments when we eat or drink or have sensual pleasures, but they are only fleeting, like lightning. These experiences come from that particular petal, which is the abode of great bliss. If one manages to get into that particular space, he will be able to experience joy not only during joyful moments, but also during painful moments.

Sit quietly and notice how emotions change for no reason. You will experience what I am talking about. You will come to know that what I am telling you is true, and you will wonder why the soul is constantly moving like this from petal to petal. The movement is caused by one's own past actions. But by the force of one's spiritual practices and also by the force of the Guru's grace, if one manages to get into this particular petal of subtle understanding, there is nothing that can attract you in this world and there is not even the slightest fear of death.

I did a lot of meditation on that particular place, and I always remain steadfast there, even while attending to all these activities. That is why when people come and give me things, it is fine, and if something is gone, that is also fine. It doesn't affect me much because, compared to the inner experience, these outer things are like dust.

Just by looking at this picture of my Baba, you can understand that he was firmly established in that particular center. You may notice that his eyes are open but his real focus is inside, not outside. There is such a center in each one of us.

When I first met you, you told me, "If you do your sculpture, you will become world-famous." Is this what you want me to do?

A person can become anything that he wants to in this world. What hasn't a person become in this body? In this body one became a yogi and another became God. In this very body one became sick and another became a slave of sense pleasures. In this very body one became brave and another fearful. And of course, even after becoming something, you can always change.

This world exists in feeling, so through your own feeling you become something. The Upanishads say that man becomes what he thinks, according to his intellect, according to his feeling. You can become whatever you want to. You can become a great artist, but for that you need faith and trust.

This body is not a thing; it is held in its position because of your feeling. The Lord says that this whole world and everything in it exist only because of the feeling of His mind. When this feeling is gone, then there is the great flood, the *mahāpralaya*. You also create your own world through your own feeling and then live in it. A doctor has the feeling that he is a doctor; he lives in that feeling and performs appropriate actions. An artist lives in his own feeling. The whole world is made of feeling.

When I meditate, I experience the Self. How can I maintain this feeling the rest of the time?

After you practice it for a while, you will be able to maintain it. Whatever a person feels about the Truth inwardly is what he also sees outside. We look at this world with our own feeling or attitude. When our feeling merges in the inner feeling, the feeling of the Self, then we experience the Truth. That same Truth is called Consciousness or God. This world is nothing but Consciousness, and if you have this feeling, it bears great fruit.

A man knows he is a man. He does not have to make any effort to maintain that feeling. A woman considers herself a woman. She does not have to meditate on the understanding that she is a woman; she has the feeling that she is a woman and she is. It is the same with the feeling of the Self. In meditation you experience this feeling of the Self. If you consider that this feeling exists outside also, it will be easy to maintain.

THE WORLD IS AS YOU SEE IT

How many different realities can there be of any given situation?

Everyone's reality is real for that person. But it is not really real. First of all, you have to attain the Truth from within. Only then can you perceive the Truth properly.

Now ten different people will have ten different understandings, ten different ideas, but that does not mean that they are the Truth. The Truth is when you see many as one. According to your own imagination, your own fantasy, you look at it in that way; you put it in the frame of your own fantasy.

For example, this person is sitting here: I see him as a noble person; she looks at him as a cheat, and someone else looks at him as a thief, and yet another person sees him as an embodiment of God. So what is true? Which perception is true? Is everything true?

To attain the true reality, you have to turn within and meditate and attain the inner vision of the Truth. The yogis say that a human being has three eyes. Two of them are physical, and the third is subtle. Through the physical eyes you see the world and through the subtle eye you see God. Therefore, meditate and have your Kundalini Shakti unfolded and then, through the third eye, see the Truth. Then you will perceive true reality.

How can I learn to see the beauty in everyone?

Unless your own heart has become pure, it is very difficult to see another's beauty. It would be very good if you could look at everyone with love. That is the true attainment of yoga; there is no other. Everything and everyone should look beautiful in your eyes. If anything seems ugly to you, it is because of a defect in your own eye, in your own understanding.

In the *Yoga Vāsishtha,* one of the greatest Indian scriptures, there is a significant statement: The world is as you see it. It is your own vision that creates your universe. What you see is your own thought perception, and your inner experience of the world is the result of how you see it. Through your own outlook you create your own pain and pleasure. For your own joy, you should see everyone as beautiful. If you see everyone as pure, the feeling of purity will grow in you.

The purer you become, the more beautiful the world will look to you. Then you will begin to feel happy, and in time that happiness will lead you to the final attainment. Eventually, you should be able to see everything as an expansion of your own Self. In the *Bhagavad Gītā,* the Lord says that one who looks upon a scholar, a humble person, an elephant, and a dog as equal is an enlightened being and is also truly human.

You have mentioned that meditation depends on the worthiness of the person. Please explain who is worthy.

It depends on the ability and strength of a person's understanding. And his understanding depends on his actions, his qualities, and his own nature. Whatever kind of life he leads affects his understanding.

Once three beings — a man, a demon, and a deity — went to see Prajapati. Prajapati saw all three of them and said, "Da, da, da." This was the only instruction he gave to them. (If I were to do the same, you would say, "We don't need this!") So he said to them, "Da, da, da. Now leave." One of them was the leader of demons, the second was the leader of men, and the third was the leader of all deities. Now demons are rather violent, so the leader of the demons thought that "da" meant *dayā*, or have compassion, don't be so violent. Therefore, the demons began to bestow compassion onto others.

Since men are very greedy for money and are always accumulating wealth, the leader of men thought that "da" meant *dana*, or to give money away in charity, and that is what the men began to do.

The deities were celestial beings and they lived a very luxurious life, enjoying a lot of subtle sense pleasures. So the leader of the deities thought that "da" meant *dama*, or self-control, that they should control their senses. And they did.

Man elicits his own meaning from everything according to his nature, according to his actions, according to his qualities. Otherwise, the moment you hear about the Self, you would know it, you would experience it.

Would you speak more on the mātrikā shakti, especially in relation to liberation?

The matrika shakti is the power of letters. The waves of thoughts that surge from within arise from the letters. From letters, a word is formed with its own meaning. From words, a sentence is formed with its own meaning. That meaning carries an image. Once an image is formed, you begin to feel good or bad. When you feel good or bad, you begin to experience the fruits of these feelings.

If you divide the letters in a particular word, those letters have no meaning in themselves. For example, take the word *fool*. Now if you just say these letters— F-O-O-L —one at a time, in themselves they don't carry any meaning. But when you combine these letters and say, "Fool!" it really has its own power. It has meaning, and it bears fruit too. The fruit of words is either painful or pleasurable; sometimes it is sweet, sometimes bitter, sometimes sour. This is a brief explanation of matrika shakti.

In the realm of our feelings matrika shakti gives us a lot of trouble. Look within and see what causes sadness, what causes pain from within. If you watch, you will realize it is the letters, the matrika. Without any reason the matrika gives pain to us all. But when you understand the five-fold activity of God, the matrika shakti cools down.

Why do negativities arise? How should we deal with them?
How can we stop them from arising?

It is very difficult to stop them from arising. Nonetheless, even before they arise, try to understand why they arise. One of the *Shiva Sūtras* says that the matrika shakti, the mother of all letters, is the cause of all these negativities, and this Shakti is very strong. It is this power which makes a person burn in the fire of agitation, jealousy, pride, and various other emotions. If something is worthless, matrika makes you believe that it is priceless. If something is priceless, it makes you believe that it is worthless. Without ever resting, this matrika shakti creates innumerable letters and words and thoughts. And these thoughts have their effect — either positive or negative feelings.

Does the matrika shakti have previous karmic thoughts in it?

There is everything in matrika shakti. However, the previous karmic thoughts are not exactly in matrika shakti. Matrika shakti begins in the third level of speech, while karmic thoughts are dormant in the fourth level. Just as there are four bodies — the gross body, the subtle body, the causal body, and the supra-causal body — in the same way there are four levels of speech. Usually we are aware of just two of the bodies. Yogis can see the other two bodies in meditation. The four levels of speech are *parāvāni, pashyantī, madhyamā,* and *vaikharī.* Karmic thoughts dwell in the paravani.

If you look at it from the point of view of Shakti, all these thoughts exist in the central nerve. There is this relationship of oneness between the Kundalini and the paravani, the fourth level of speech. The matrika shakti throbs and pulsates according to a person's karma of many lifetimes. The paravani is worth knowing.

At that level matrika shakti gives up its name and form and

all its work and it is very quiet. Just as all the waves and ripples and bubbles are quiet in the ocean before they arise, in the same way all these words and letters and speech are quiet in the fourth level. When pure knowledge, *shuddha vidyā,* arises, the work of matrika shakti subsides. You experience the rise of pure knowledge a long time after you have received shaktipat.

Will you please talk a little about the nature of the Guru's words?

The nature of the Guru's words is just like the Guru. Every person's words carry his inner feeling. In the same way, the Guru's inner feeling flows out through his words. For this reason, it is very effective. For example, a little child may use the same abusive term that an adult uses. But when the adult uses the abusive term, you roll up your sleeves and you want to fight. The child's heart is free from faults; no feeling of faults will flow from his words. No matter what, the child's heart is filled with love — whether it is love for God or love for somebody else — and that feeling flows through the child's words. So when a child uses an abusive term, you are not bothered. But an adult's heart is filled with anger, greed, and wickedness. For this reason, when he uses an abusive term, those feelings flow through that word. Words have their own power; they carry the power of your inner feeling.

How can I become a more perfect disciple?

You are already perfect. If you are not perfect, it is due to the poverty of your understanding. Get rid of this understanding and you will become rich; you will become really perfect. It is the poverty of understanding.

Lately I feel as though everything is a memory, and it feels very strange.

Yes, that's what it all is — it's a memory. And when all memories disappear, God alone remains.

TAKE THE UTMOST CARE OF YOUR MIND

Before liberation, how much free will does a person have?

If you had right understanding, you would realize that even though you may not be liberated, still you are completely free. But if your understanding is not right, you are a slave of everything. One has a birthright to total freedom, to total bliss and liberation. It is by means of that birthright that one becomes liberated. And it is as a result of this awareness — I am free, I am the Self, I am pure — that one goes beyond the struggle for freedom.

You once told me to teach my mind to love myself. What is the best way for me to teach my mind to do this?

Teach the mind good things about your own Self. Talk to the mind about the love of your own Self. Tell the mind it has been wandering here and there according to its own wishes, but it hasn't found anything, it hasn't attained anything, and for this reason it should try to enter the Self. Also question your mind. Ask it where it finds happiness — in fickleness or in stillness?

What are some basic ways to improve my mind?

Love your own Self. Love is within you. Regard everyone with respect because the rays of God are within everybody. Respect yourself, do not put yourself down, do not make yourself weak with bad thoughts. Perform actions with justice and put forth your own self-effort. Live in that way. Stay away from injustice. Stay very close to God.

I try to do what is right, but sometimes I just can't. What about when I fail?

You should try harder. Continue to put forth effort. It is a struggle; it is a war within you.

When I have a negative thought, how should I fight it?

Fill yourself with positive feelings. Think well. Pray to God. Use your discrimination. Why have a negative attitude toward others? You should work on your negativities from within.

Using the will?

Yes, the will is very strong; it has a lot of power. If you do not want to do something, you do not do it. If you do not want to think about something, you do not think about it.

So having good thoughts does not come naturally?

In the beginning you have to create good thoughts. You have to explain things to your mind over and over and over again.

I would like to know your techniques for keeping the body and mind in good shape.

You can keep the body in good shape through *āsanas*, meditation, and regular habits, such as sleeping regularly, getting up regularly, eating good and nourishing food regularly. It is regularity and discipline which are most important — in food and drink, in sleep and waking. And it is essential to have positive thoughts. Far more important than food and drink are your thoughts. All kinds of unnecessary thoughts pass through the mind, all kinds of negative thoughts. They have a very bad effect on the body. No matter how beautiful your dress or how beautiful your complexion, if your thoughts are not beautiful you may look beautiful to others, but you won't look beautiful to yourself. What is the point of wearing a beautiful dress and having a fashionable hairstyle and wearing cosmetics if your heart is impure, if it is full of negativity? Therefore, take the utmost care of your mind. Keep your mind fragrant; make it fragrant.

What can one do with negative thoughts such as constant self-criticism?

That is just a trick of the mind. Don't attach much importance to this mental process. Talk to your mind and tell it, "I am very good. Chitshakti, cosmic Consciousness, is blazing in me." Keep telling your mind, "My inner Self is a flame of the divine Self, it is a flame of God."

Through your grace and love and Shakti, I have had a long period of ecstasy and bliss, but now I am having experiences of dying and a period of darkness. Am I falling down in my development or am I breaking through another layer?

This is a step forward. A new layer is being revealed. To see your own death is part of the yoga of meditation. Once you see your own death in meditation, death dies and you become immortal. There is a region of darkness in the mind, and after you pass through it to the other side, you will find ecstasy and bliss. This experience of death is most valuable.

How does one strengthen the mind?

Combine the mantra with the mind and still the mind in the Self. Truly your mind is very strong. You don't have to make it stronger. Aren't you aware of the strength of your mind? Doesn't your mind make you wander here and there like a monkey all the time? Doesn't your mind make you roam all the time? How could the mind do that to you if it weren't strong?

In India there are people who take monkeys out on the street and make them dance. A man ties the monkey to a pole with a long rope, he plays an instrument, and then he tells the monkey, "All right, now jump!" And the monkey jumps. After the man displays all the monkey's tricks, he tells the monkey, "All right, now go and ask for money." Then those who were watching give money. That is how those people live.

In the same way your mind makes you dance like a monkey all the time, so isn't your mind very strong? Now you have to become stronger; you have to make the mind dance. Make it dance on the stage of *So'ham*. For that, meditate and repeat the mantra.

When my mind is experiencing fear, anger, or any negative emotion, should I just observe it without expressing it or acting it out in any way?

Sometimes psychotherapists want you to express these feelings in order to get them out of your system. When you do this, it may work, but the feelings may also become more firmly grounded in the system. You know what happens as the mind contemplates something over and over again. So when you try to act out these feelings, as you remember them, they may become more firmly anchored in your system. Our philosophy says that the impressions of countless lifetimes are stored inside. You can get them out of your system not just by remembering them, but by burning them in the fire of meditation, by rooting them out completely. The seed must be rooted out. And the seed of these impressions exists right in the central nerve, the *sushumnā nādi*, the passageway of Kundalini. Once Kundalini unfolds in meditation, all these feelings are discarded; they just leave.

How can I avoid negative thoughts without repressing them?

Instead of repressing negative thoughts, why don't you try to transmute them into positive thoughts? The mind keeps thinking all the time. It is very difficult for it to become steady right at the beginning. Therefore let it think positive thoughts.

Once there was a man who did not get any food for many days, although he tried, and the pangs of hunger were gnawing at him. He sat down under a tree and he wanted to deceive his stomach, so he decided to cook some food in his imagination. He took imaginary flour and water and made a dough for bread. He also made a cake. Then he made some chutney. Apparently he had just come back from India because he put some hot spices in the chutney.

There was a reasonable man sitting under a tree nearby, and he was watching this fellow quite closely, as he was making food that wasn't there. After he had cooked the food in his imagination, he started eating in his imagination. He ate some cake which he enjoyed very much. Then he started to eat the chutney, which had far too many chilies, and he began crying, "Ah, ah!" The man watching wondered whether the hungry man was freaking out and he asked him what was happening.

The man said, "Nothing happened; it's just that I'm a victim of my bad karma. For the past four days I have been starving, and this morning I was really tormented by the pangs of hunger. So in my imagination I made bread and cake and then chutney. I enjoyed the cake but the chutney was much too hot, and the moment it touched my tongue it burned it."

The observer said, "You idiot! If you were cooking food in your imagination, why couldn't you make ice cream? Why did you have to make hot chutney?"

The best thing is not to think at all. But if you must think, why don't you think thoughts like this: I am pure, I am God's child, I am sublime, I wish everyone well, and I think well of others. Or you could start worshiping your own inner Self mentally with great feeling.

The mind is the root of all evil. The sages have said that the mind alone is a person's heaven or hell; the mind alone is a person's bondage or liberation, his happiness or misery. For this reason, all the saints and sages and spiritual philosophers have urged that we should continually engage our minds in thoughts of God. Whatever there is, is due to the mind.

It is for cleansing the mind that we give shaktipat and transmit energy. It is for the mind that we have yoga, and it is for the mind that we have devotion. All sicknesses are caused by the mind and all pleasures are meant for the mind. When the mind ceases to move, you get into a state of spiritual stillness.

How can you repress negative thoughts? They have repressed you! You are already under their thumb. Now you should transmute them into positive thoughts.

You say that the mind is nothing but the play of Chitshakti. Sometimes I feel that my mind is blocking the flow of Shakti as it does its work of purifying me. How can I enhance this process through my mind and attitude?

When your mind is blocking the flow of the Shakti, at that time stop blocking your mind. Leave the mind alone. Leave it free, then the mind will flow with the Shakti. Convince the mind over and over again that it is a part of the flow of Shakti.

You believe that everything else is the play of Consciousness, but you don't believe that your mind is also that same play. If you do believe that, you can keep quiet, being aware that the mind's blocking the flow of Shakti is part of the play of

Consciousness. Whether the mind is moving or not, still it is the play of Consciousness.

When I remain a witness to myself, I peacefully watch the positives and negatives of my mind go by. If I try to increase the positive thoughts and decrease the negative ones, conflict arises since I am no longer a witness. What should I do?

Stop increasing or decreasing the thoughts — just be a witness.

I think so much that I get tired. Sometimes my thoughts go around and around in circles. What should I do?

Truly speaking, if you think in a correct way, you will not get tired. Instead, you will become more and more energetic. A sage said, "O my mind, always think well of yourself and others." There is no need to get upset. The result of thoughts is great. If you think of your own Self and contemplate your own Self, the same awareness will spread everywhere.

In ancient times there was a great sage called Kakabushundi who always used to think about God and repeat the name of Rama. He had his own ashram, and the power of his thought spread everywhere for miles and miles. Whoever entered that atmosphere would automatically start repeating the name of Rama. This is the result of one-pointed thought.

Lord Buddha observed nonviolence. Some people did not like his behavior. But even when people came to attack him, as they got close to him, they would automatically become silent. They could not fight with him. When they left, once again they would regain their power, and they would oppose him mentally. But if they went close to him, they would become silent again.

A person's thoughts pervade the atmosphere. Therefore, always have good thoughts. If you want to think, why don't you think well of the world? Why don't you wish for everybody to become happy? Why don't you think about attaining God?

Instead, you spend your time thinking about others, wondering, "How is that person's hair cut? How has that person trimmed his beard? What kind of lipstick is she wearing? What kind of color TV does that person have? Where did that person buy his car?" You are always thinking about others. Isn't this a disease?

The source of all the calamities in this world is one's own thoughts. Thought is the source of all quarrels and the origin of all diseases. If you go to a psychic who tells you that you have a disease, you will get sick whether you have the disease or not. When the mind can make you sick, why can't it also make you well? Therefore, think well of yourself and look at others with a good attitude. This is the medicine that will give you a good mind.

The mind has such great power that it can create another world within this very creation. In the *Bhagavad Gītā,* the Lord said, "This entire world and all the creatures in it are nothing but products of My own mind." It is very true. The cosmic mind pervades everything and everywhere, and the same mind exists within us.

When the Lord created this entire universe with His mind, we should at least be able to use good thoughts to keep our own creation fit. Therefore, have good thoughts about yourself. Always think that the beautiful effulgence of God dwells within you. All the scriptures and all the great beings say this. If you have this awareness, it will become your medicine.

I sit in meditation repeating Guru Om, *but all the while an inner voice keeps talking to me. I keep saying, "I want to surrender!" But the voice says, "You haven't made it yet, you're still thinking!" until I want to beat my head and scream, "Shut up!" Can you help me calm my mind and keep the voices quiet?*

You shouldn't resist that voice. Honor that voice. If you were to honor it, it would change. Honor all the thoughts that arise in your mind. If you try to resist them, you will find it difficult, because thoughts are very powerful. You can change them only by love and prayer and by honoring them.

*How should I surrender my mind to you — specifically the
analytical part?*

Stop saying, "My mind." Think that it belongs to somebody
else; then you won't have any trouble. The reason you should
stop saying, "It is my mind" is that your mind is different from
you. The one who knows the mind is different from the mind.
The one who realizes the mind is other than the mind. If you
can attain this understanding, it will be much better.

If I give you my negativities, does it affect you negatively?

No, it won't affect me negatively. All those negativities will
turn into positive feelings. If you put things into the furnace,
they change; they don't remain the same.

*I have done many bad things. Is it still possible for me to become
realized in this life? If so, will you help me?*

Forget the past. You must have eaten many bad things in your
life, but they are not inside you now because you have excreted
them. In the same way, throw away your remembrance of the
past. My Baba used to say, "Why do you remember those
things? You excrete what you eat. You don't remember what
you ate. It's gone." In the same way forget the past. Remember
only the new things.

*When I reach a meditative state like yours, will I have no
thoughts, or will I have thoughts but not be attached to them?*

By meditating more and more, you learn the knack of stilling all
your thoughts. However, even if a thought-wave were to arise,
it is only the thought-free Being who is becoming that thought.
An intelligent person knows it is water that becomes ice. He
doesn't have to melt ice over a fire to see the water. He sees the
water even when it remains ice. In the same way, an enlightened
being knows it is Consciousness beyond thought which becomes
all thoughts. He sees thoughts as waves and eddies in that ocean
of Consciousness and he remains drunk on inner bliss. He does

not try to sort them out, nor does he try to increase them. He is aware that if more thoughts were generated, it would not help in any way, and if fewer thoughts were generated, it would not help either, because the Self, his true nature, remains the same all the time whether or not there are thoughts in the mind.

You say that one should contemplate the Self through the mind, but the mind can think only of concrete objects. The Self is formless. How can it be contemplated through the mind? Please clarify.

Because you have read a lot, you have this disease. If you had read a little bit, it would have been much better. You have read too much about the form and the formless. That is why you have this disease in your mind. Instead of only reading what others have written, first contemplate the Self and see if the mind can do it. Afterward you can reflect on the matter.

The mind can think of everything, of all the objects that exist in the world, and it can also contemplate the formless. You haven't tried it, that's all. The mind is great; it is not inert. The mind is inert only so long as it moves among worldly objects and takes on those forms. The moment it turns within, it becomes Consciousness once again, and Consciousness knows everything. According to one of the aphorisms of the *Pratyabhijñā-hridayam* — a scripture of Shaivism — Chiti, or Consciousness, the formless Self, descends from its lofty state and becomes one with the worldly objects. At that point it is called the mind. Otherwise, the mind is not the mind, but Chiti. It is formless Consciousness that you should meditate upon.

Make your mind free from thoughts, and then see whether it is inert or conscious. Then see whether or not it can contemplate the Self.

Did you read a lot during your sādhanā? I wonder about the place of reading in my sādhanā.

I was like you, I was your brother. I was very fond of reading. I used to go and see my Babaji with a book under my arm. For a long time he watched me. Then he got tired of seeing me like that. One day he said, "Muktananda Swami, come here." He asked me, "What is that?"

I said, "Baba, this is a book. It's a good book on Vedanta."

"Bah!" he said. That was the worst insult. After saying that, he didn't have to use any swear words or call me a so-and-so. Then he asked, "Do you know how a book is created?"

"No, Baba." I would always say, "No, I don't know," because if I ever said, "Yes," he wouldn't give me the answer. If I had said, "Yes, this book is written by a sage and it was published in a certain place and everyone knows who wrote it," he would have turned his face away and gone to sleep. So I said, "I don't know."

He said, "It is the lies of the brain. A book is created by the mind. A book cannot create a mind. You are reading someone else's mind. Where is your own mind? Where has it gone?" Then he said, "Throw away the book. Throw away the book and meditate."

If you read many books and teach others a lot, what do you get out of it if you haven't read the inner book, the inner scripture? Through meditation, embrace the inner Self; then see what great scriptures arise from within you. Shaivism says that when pure knowledge arises from within, you attain Godhood. You don't attain it by devoting yourself to outer studies.

Without peace and love a *sādhu* is zero, a yogi is zero, a wise man is zero, a lecturer is zero, and a scholar is zero. Therefore, one should have this uninterrupted awareness all the time. What is this unbroken awareness? It is to become established in "I am That," having attained the right understanding of it. Without this ceaseless awareness, just by reading and teaching, you can't attain anything. If you attain this continual awareness through a Guru, you don't need to read nor do you need to teach. A person should focus his attention on the lord of prana —when the prana goes out and when it comes in. He should contemplate it and try to perceive what the prana is saying. This is the final step in sadhana.

Just by reading a lot, just by knowing a lot, nothing really happens.

When I meditate, my mind forms a description of what I am experiencing as if I were talking to someone else. This is annoying. What can I do?

Your mind is contemplating your experiences, and it's not bad; let it do it. During your meditation you should not pursue the mind. Once I read a story of a fisherman who was going out to catch fish. Meanwhile he saw a dog, and he forgot about the fish and began to pursue the dog. The fish were waiting but he was running after the dog. So you have to meditate on the witness of the mind. Instead, you are meditating on the mind. Don't chase the mind; try to pursue the witness of the mind. The goal of your meditation is not the mind; it is the Self. Let the mind go in the air. Why do you have to remember the mind?

I am confused about how emotions relate to the Self. If feelings constantly change and the Self is constant, does that mean that feelings must be suppressed? Won't suppressing feelings lead to panic and psychosis?

Many people feel that if you suppress your feelings you become a mental case, but today there are so-called gurus who have let their feelings run free, and now they have become mental cases. If you do not suppress your feelings, if you let them run free, what can you attain? Sometimes a person has the feeling that he wants to kill another person. Many people have the feeling that they want to steal someone else's wealth. When you have these feelings, if you do not suppress them, you get into real trouble. If you let your feelings run free and go anywhere they want, you will never achieve what you desire. You can achieve your desires only by controlling your feelings.

I also have feelings. However, I control them with self-restraint, and as a result I am able to use them for my own benefit. Nothing has gone wrong with me. I am not a mental case. I am going to turn seventy, and I still have a lot of strength, happiness, and a strong memory.

Feelings know no bounds, no limitations. If you always chase after them, how are you going to live in this world?

Therefore, the *Bhagavad Gītā* says that a person should control his emotions and feelings. It is not true that if you suppress your feelings, you will have mental disturbances. You are more likely to have such disturbances if you let your feelings run out of control.

Would you please speak on why one falls back into ignorance even after seeing one's true nature?

Because your true nature exists within you, you can experience it easily and spontaneously. However, to become established in that requires practice. After seeing your true nature, you should become established in it. Otherwise, you will fall. For example, you experience happiness so many times during the day, even if only for a few seconds. But that experience of happiness slips away. You never practice any sadhana to make it last. Patanjali's *Yoga Sūtras* say that after you experience the happiness of your own true nature, you should become anchored in it. Don't forget it. Practice it. Learn how to make the mind still in the inner Self. Once you have seen That, if you make the mind still there, happiness will arise within you. If the mind once again starts wandering outside, it takes on the form of what exists outside and happiness vanishes. If you do not have firm determination and firm practice, you will fall.

Due to attachment, aversion, anger, and greed, a person falls back into ignorance again and again. But be steadfast. Once you see your own true nature, learn how to become established in it. As long as you do not attain the state of witness-consciousness, you will rise and fall many times.

Therefore, the great beings do not give much importance to just seeing their true nature. The real attainment is the state of witness-consciousness, of steady wisdom, in which a person becomes established in his true nature, in which the seer becomes still in the seen. When a person attains this state, he is complete.

Would you speak a little bit about willpower and desire?

Desire is behind will. If you direct your desire into the right channel, your will also will be directed into the right channel. Let your desire take this form, "The supreme Truth is mine, and I am the supreme Truth." Let this desire grow inside you, "I will meet Him, and He will meet me."

Desire is good when it is directed toward God. If you empty your mind of all thoughts, your willpower will be enhanced. The more your mind is crowded with thoughts, the weaker it becomes. If your mind were without thoughts, your will would become extremely strong. This entire universe has arisen from the "no-thought" of God, from the supreme "no-thought." So if you too were to be without thought, from your "no-thought" something would arise.

The different miracles that some holy men display have nothing to do with God. They are miracles only of the mind, of mental power. God is beyond that. There was a mountain where I used to meditate. A priest lived on that mountain. He used to materialize a currency note and pull it out of his pocket, but the note would last for only eight hours. He would insist that we buy something with it within that time. He could also materialize various other nice things. Once he said to me, "You too should learn this skill." I have a strange temperament and also a ready wit. I asked him, "Do I have to study in order to steal? One can learn that naturally and simply."

As soon as there is no thought behind your will, no desire behind it, your will becomes very strong. Then miracles happen of themselves. When your willpower becomes strong, if you use it to purify other hearts and to bring them peace, God becomes very pleased. If you use your willpower in the marketplace, if you use it to materialize goods for display, you are using it in a very ordinary way. Once your mind is emptied of thought, tremendous love rushes in the heart and it becomes very easy to do work among others.

I Swim in the Ocean
of that Brilliance

When I became a monk, I traveled all over India by foot. I was very fond of traveling and walking. This was my habit — to just walk and walk and walk. During that time I met many great beings. I would visit them and hear what they had to say. One of these great beings said to me, "God's creation is so beautiful and everything is fine. Do you ever wish that it had been created differently?"

I replied, "Everything that God has created is just fine. But it would have been so great if He hadn't created the mind."

He said, "Oh no, no, no! It's only because of the mind that you have become a monk. If you didn't have a mind, you wouldn't even come close to God. If the mind didn't trouble you, you wouldn't think of getting closer to God."

I have read many scriptures, I have read many philosophies, and all of them say that their own philosophy is the greatest of all, that there is no other as great. They all claim to be the Truth itself. But there were so many of them — from India and from elsewhere too. So I read these philosophies, and after reading them, I lost all my devotion, I lost my feeling, and I began to wonder, "Is there any God?" Then I thought to myself, "I will give up these philosophies because they are nothing but a heavy load on my head."

So I gave up reading philosophy and scriptures, and I

went in search of saints. I began to look for great beings, beings who had lost themselves in God. And in my search I found these great beings and I wandered among them. I was in their company for a long time. I listened to many things from them, and after listening to their words, I put those words into action according to my way.

Then the doubt that I had about whether there was any God went away; it left me. I became convinced that God dwells within the heart.

I never think too much about anything. If I am confronted with a problem, I don't have to brood about it. The solution arises from within at once. The moment I attend to a problem, the mind becomes so completely focused on it that the solution emerges right away. This is the advantage of keeping the mind free from thoughts all the time. I have a very big ashram in India and I have supervised every construction project there. I haven't made much use of engineers or architects. I go around giving instructions to workers, and that is how the new buildings are built.

One year I was in a hill resort where I wrote my autobiography, Play of Consciousness. *There was a judge with me who sometimes watched me while I was writing. He was amazed to see me write so fast without thinking about it. He said when he had to write a verdict, it took him at least two weeks to think it over. But it took me about three weeks to finish my autobiography, which covered my sadhana of fifteen years and also some earlier years. Then it took other* people a year to get it ready for publication.

I don't let anything stay in my mind. I don't keep any wife, any children, any house, any horse, any elephant, or any dollars in my mind. I only keep Nityananda and Muktananda in my mind. That is all that I keep within. If I have to speak somewhere, Nityananda himself becomes the talk; he talks and talks and talks and I hardly know what is happening. When questions are put to me, Nityananda answers them. If somebody comes for a message, Nityananda utters the message.

There are lots of people in the ashram; my family is quite large, but I do not feel any burden in my heart. There are people who become weighed down with care because they have a small family — just a wife and two children. But I have thousands in my family and I am never weighed down.

I am most regular in my food and drink, and I do not tolerate any unpunctuality. At the ashram all the meals are served on time. Sometimes on weekends we have as many as three to four thousand guests in the ashram, and all of them are served food at the same time. Immediately after the Guru Gita, people go for tea and we never ask anyone how many people to expect on a particular morning. They all line up, and everybody is served tea, no matter how many there are. Then at 11:30 the bell rings for lunch and all the people move in an orderly line and the servers are ready with different items of food. For this I don't have to think or plan, and all these things are accomplished without any hindrance.

The ashram runs very well even when I am traveling in

foreign countries. Wherever I go, I am surrounded by a large number of people, and all of them eat and drink together peacefully. I live together joyfully with my large family. In Indian philosophical works they talk about the family of God or universal brotherhood. I put this into practice at the ashram.

If you want to live happily, and if you want to meditate peacefully, to sway with ecstasy all the time, meditate on your Self, honor and worship your Self, kneel to your Self —and at least once see the Self who lives within you in a hidden form.

The state that I am always in is a state that everybody has. However, everybody lives in the state of his own understanding. I live in my own understanding. Most of the time people live in the thoughts of their mind or in the subconscious mind. According to their thoughts, so they become. They experience either pain or pleasure; they experience enmity, jealousy, pride, or something else. I don't attach any importance to this kind of state. No matter what thought arises in my mind, I don't value it at all. I don't identify myself with these thoughts. I don't even think that they belong to me. I remain a witness to all the thoughts that arise in my mind. For example, I am sitting here watching you all. In just the same way, I watch all my various thoughts. If I have good thoughts, I don't become happy. If I have bad thoughts, I don't become unhappy.

Most of the time you may feel that you are your body; however, I feel that I am different from this body. A great Sufi saint said that the moment you think you are this body, that is when the mind undergoes trouble. The mind is deceived. Instead of thinking, "I am this body," I turn within. If I go beyond the mind, the subconscious mind, and the intellect, I realize that I am nothing but that effulgence, I am nothing but that brilliance, and I begin to swim in the ocean of that brilliance.

I always live in this state: I am not this body; I am Consciousness. I lose myself in this awareness most of the time. Sometimes I may come out of this awareness, but I know how to get back into it. Some of you may welcome your own ego. A great saint said that if you want to attain the Truth, if you want to become an ideal being, if you want to become divine, give up your ego. Lose your individuality completely. Often people are very afraid to lose the seed of their ego. If you sow a mustard seed into the earth, it loses itself completely. However, after a while it sprouts and grows into a plant. It blossoms and flourishes.

So I live in this state. I live in this body, but I am separate from this body. I live with my understanding, but I am different from my understanding. I live right in the center of pain and pleasure. For this reason I am extremely happy. I always remember Him, remember Him, remember Him. I don't remember anything else. If I forget Him, then I become something else.

CHAPTER 18

When Obstacles Arise

It is only your own home everywhere. Then why should you worry? You can only meet yourself. There is no one else.

I always feel that whatever I do for God is not good enough. When will I pass your tests?

It is you who feels this way; God does not feel this way. The scriptures say that God becomes pleased very easily. You can please Him with a little bit of love. If you praise Him a little, if you love Him even just a little, He becomes very pleased with you immediately. God does not feel the way you do. He is totally satisfied. With great contentment continue to love Him. Give up the feeling that whatever you do is not good enough. If you give up that kind of feeling, you have passed my tests.

What makes a person fall from yoga? What becomes of him afterward?

If a person makes a mistake while pursuing yoga, he falls. Sometimes this happens because of the number of obstacles. Sometimes the past impressions, the *samskāras*, become strong. When these overtake a person, he falls. However, a *yogi's* fall is not a total fall because later on he can rise higher. Even after his fall, he can pursue yoga once again, provided he has the interest. The virtues that he accumulated in his *sādhanā* bring him back to the yogic life. They do not allow him to go anywhere else. The *Bhagavad Gītā* says that a fallen yogi takes birth in his next lifetime in a very pure and wealthy family where he can pursue yoga again very easily and attain the ultimate state.

Do you ever test your disciples the way your Guru tested you?

My Guru tested me — it's true. But here I don't have to test anybody in any special way because when people are together, their temperaments spring up and they test each other. For example, if someone is sitting here and someone else says, "Just move a bit," the first person gets really angry. So they test each other. Why should I impose my test on them? But if it is necessary, I can give a test.

In the Indian tradition the search for a Sadguru is often long and arduous, and frequently much testing of the would-be devotee takes place. Here in America, one may walk in, receive a mantra, go to an Intensive and receive shaktipāt, and immediately one is placed in relationship with a Guru. Is the relationship between you and your devotees the same as the relationship between you and your Guru?

Yes. Once you receive shaktipat, the relationship will be the same as mine with my Guru. Once you receive shaktipat, the relationship grows, it never decreases. I do not have to test all of you because you test yourselves. You know what you have attained; you know what is within yourself. From your own attainment you can tell how far you have come. Through your own discipline, meditation, and *sevā*, you find out what you have attained. These things test you all the time. Therefore, I do not really need to test you.

How can I contain my anger, jealousy, and lust when I am away from you? When I am with you, you contain them very well.

Don't direct your anger to others; direct it to yourself. When you have lost devotion, when you have left equality-consciousness, when you neglect your spiritual practices, then be angry with yourself. Tell yourself, "Look, others are full of devotion to the Lord, others are chanting and meditating. Why should I neglect all these things? Why can't I do my practices regularly?"

Instead of having lust for petty and trivial things, direct it toward God, who is everything.

There was a woman saint whose name was Rabi'a. One day a priest asked her, "Rabi'a, how is it that you are not tormented by the monsters of lust and greed and anger?"

She replied, "O priest, my heart is full of God only. I feel love only for Him and there is no room in it for anger, jealousy, lust, greed, or infatuation."

If your heart were to turn toward the Lord, these passions would not be any problem for you.

Do you ever cry? Do you experience sadness when you are in touch with human suffering? If you do, what is the quality of that sadness?

I have a lot of self-control; I am very self-disciplined. There were times when I had to fast for four days and I wouldn't cry. I would tell myself that it was my destiny, my *karma*, not to eat for four days. But I wouldn't cry. When I see human suffering, I do feel sadness. I wonder, "Why are they suffering when there is so much joy inside? Why do human beings still want to suffer? Why this predicament? When God is inside, why look for Him outside and cry all the time? Why suffer when He is inside?" So I do have this kind of sadness.

Although I have followed many teachings and experienced much bliss, I have not been able to resolve the hate and anger I sometimes feel for those I respect and love. I don't understand how love and anger can exist together. Can I reverse myself in the cycle of birth and death in this lifetime?

It is nothing unusual when your love no longer remains love and becomes anger. If the people you love happen to go against your wishes, the same love turns into anger. However, keep developing more love. That will take care of hate and anger. As far as possible, try to stay away from anger. You should be aware that you yourself have to endure your own anger and hate first. It is only then that they will act on somebody else. It is your own heart that is first vitiated by hate and anger. The other person may or may not be affected, but the hate and anger are bound to have a bad effect on you. Hate, anger, greed, attachment — these are your own enemies, not somebody else's.

You have received the touch of grace from me and that will ensure that you are delivered from the cycle of birth and death. You won't have to be born again.

How can I overcome fear?

Just as you don't need to smoke, but because of the force of your addiction you keep smoking, likewise you don't need to fear, but because you are addicted to it, you keep on feeling frightened. There is absolutely no need for it. There is no fear in the inner Self. You feel frightened only so long as you do not know the inner Self, only so long as you have not seen it and are not aware of its immense power. Once you experience the power of the Self, fear leaves you. Explore your inner being, and you will realize that there is no such thing as fear.

I always worry about what I am going to do and who I will be with.

If you were to be aware of things as they really are, you would come to know that it is only your own home everywhere. Then why should you worry? You can only meet yourself. There is no one else. There is a limitless ocean of Consciousness, and all of us are just like waves or bubbles in that ocean. When these bubbles burst, they merge into the ocean. Even if they don't burst, they are still in the ocean.

I want so much to believe that God is within me and that everyone is good, but I am plagued with so much skepticism that I cannot, and it causes me great pain.

The *Bhagavad Gītā* says that one who doubts suffers. Don't see your doubt as doubt; see it as a form of Consciousness. See it as emerging from Consciousness. Stay calm, keep repeating the mantra, and remember God. Don't consider skepticism to be different from yourself or different from Consciousness.

I too have a problem with skepticism and my fear keeps me from experiencing God.

Why should you have any fear? You are in the kingdom of God. Your fear is nothing. Fear hasn't done you any good, has it? Pray to God and repeat His name all the time. That gives you tremendous help and tremendous power.

I feel that I can see the Truth around me, but to accept it is too painful and I fight with myself a lot.

If you can see the Truth, why should you fight with yourself? Stop fighting. If you were to stop fighting, you would no longer suffer, you would experience peace. It is fighting with the Self that obstructs peace. One who sees whatever is willed by God as God, is himself God. It is a pity we don't realize that whatever He wills is good. It is because of this lack of understanding that we suffer.

I want to come to you with happiness and joy, but I feel such shame. I feel strong in your presence but so weak when I am away from you. I truly want a simple life filled with the love of God, yet I find myself a woman of such desires and fantasies. Sexual lust seems unending and my will so weak. I need your help.

It's all right to feel joy and happiness, but why should you feel shame? Discard shame. It's good that you feel strength here in my presence, but when you leave, why should you think that you have gone away from me? Why can't you experience me within yourself and thus experience strength all the time? All kinds of desires, including sexual lust, torment you only as long as you do not become familiar with the inner love. So why don't

427

you transform your lust into love? If the lust could become love, it would be very enjoyable. Meditate more. Through meditation your lust will turn into love.

I have been feeling very scared. The only thing that helps me is coming here, but I get scared if I have to make a decision about my life.

You shouldn't worry. In meditation you pass through a stage in which you feel scared of everything. Since you meditate a lot, it must be that. There is a center of fear inside, and when your mind settles there, you get scared. It won't last long.

I'm afraid that when you leave, it will get worse and I won't be able to handle it.

Even when I leave here, you should keep me close to you; then it won't get worse. Don't worry.

People say that I am pure, yet I feel anger or hatred at times. I wish to understand this contradiction. I would also like to eliminate a feeling of conceit.

The only thing impure in you is conceit, nothing else. And that conceit is extremely faulty. Everything else about you is pure. Through meditation and prayer to the Lord, expel conceit from your system. Lust, anger, and hatred are mental phases. They do not last forever. They arise and subside. The phases of the mind, which come and go no matter how impure they are, cannot make the inner Self impure.

Who are you? Are you lust? Are you anger? Are you hatred? Are you greed? Are you ego? Or are you a being different from all this? Which of these are you?

You are the one who knows that all these passions are impure. The one within you who is aware of your anger is not anger. The one within you who is aware of the stirring of lust is not lust. The one within you who is aware of the stirring of greed is not the same as greed. The one within you who is aware of the ego strutting all the time and saying, "I, I, I" is not that ego. That being is different from all these.

Try to find this one and see whether you can detect any impurity there. I would like to know in which corner of the inner Self impurity dwells. The Self is the knower of all the thoughts and passions that pass through the mind. This concept of impurity is purely a mental construction.

I have so much fear about my body, but there is nothing really wrong. I am a singer and performer, and sometimes my fear is so great that I cannot get up on the stage.

To a certain degree fear is after everyone. Just as there are centers of anger, greed, desire, and ignorance inside the heart, likewise there is a center of fear. There was a king who said that one who is seeking fulfillment through all kinds of pleasures and enjoyments is subject to the fear of disease. One who wants a long life fears death. One who is from a high family fears losing his status, and one who is a scholar fears competition. One who is wealthy fears a king, and a king is frightened of his enemies. The body is subject to the fear of old age. If there is a person who keeps silence, he is afraid of being ostracized by others. Everything in this world is subject to fear.

There is only one thing free from fear — that is meditation on the inner Self. That alone can make you fearless. The inner Self is totally fearless. Take refuge in that and all fears will go. If you were to seek the support of the inner Self, even your music would become better. The sages say that music is a form of yoga, a form of spiritual pursuit, if it is followed properly and in a disciplined manner. Music is so great that in meditation yogis hear music inside themselves, reverberating in their inner spaces. Become absorbed in your music, become absorbed in your singing. That fear will go and your music will acquire a finer quality.

How is infatuation born? Where does it come from and why?

Infatuation is born from greed, and greed from desire. They are all linked to one another. If you have a desire for somebody or something, automatically infatuation arises.

There is this mother called Maya and she makes you forget everything; she is the mother of forgetfulness. She has six children who keep you away from God all the time. These children are desire, anger, greed, pride, jealousy, and infatuation. They make you bored with chanting and they make you very excited when it comes to gossiping. They make you tired of good actions and they make you cultivate a lot of interest in bad actions. They make you hate becoming free from addictions and they make you love addictions. They make you become indifferent to the Self, which exists in this body. They make you even doubt the existence of the Self and they make you identify with this body. In this way, they bring down the glory of a human being. They make a human being very tiny, very small. You do all the tricks commanded by the six enemies, the children of Maya. The scriptures have called them enemies — not friends. So save yourself from these enemies. To escape from them you should have positive thoughts. Wherever your mind goes, bring it back and tell it to think about the Self. Tell the mind to understand exactly what it is.

Tukaram Maharaj was a sattvic person; he was a pure being, yet he used to say, "Day in and day out, I fight. There is warfare between me and the mind." So even he was fighting with his mind, with the six enemies.

ANGER IS A GREAT ENEMY

How do I get healed from the inner rage?

With careful thought, with great understanding, get rid of the inner rage. It is your inner enemy; don't think it is your friend. But the same thing can become the source of either great peace or great misery. Anger destroys the subtlety of the mind; it kills the tenderness of a person's heart. The Lord instructed Arjuna, saying, "This is the worst enemy. O Arjuna, conquer it."

If you can't renounce this rage, at least try to use it in a good way. Get angry with your anger. Say, "Hey, you anger, why can't you worship God? Why can't you repeat His name? Why don't you read the *Guru Gītā*?" Just get angry with your anger; make use of it. You should learn how to use everything in a good way. In this world nothing is useless; however, man doesn't know how to make good use of things.

The scriptures say there are six enemies; however, these tendencies can also become your friends if you know how to use them. Don't have the desire to become king of this entire world. There were so many kings, but where are they now? Have this desire: I am going to experience God right inside me, I am going to meditate and make God reveal Himself within me. This is a great desire. In this way change all the bad qualities into good qualities. Then you will have only happiness, nothing but happiness.

Even though I meditate and often feel great love for myself and others, I still carry angry feelings. How can I stay focused on love when this happens?

Slowly but surely get rid of your anger, and your anger will turn into love. Anger is against love — remember this. It is not good for anybody. Anger and other poisonous things, such as marijuana and opium, delude man. In the *Bhagavad Gītā* the Lord described the two worst enemies of man as desire and anger. It is desire that later turns into anger. They go against wisdom too.

It is not just that the scriptures say this; you must have experienced it yourself. When you are angry, there is so much agitation inside yourself. Do you know that? The rest of your day is destroyed. Even the food you have eaten is not digested properly. This is your own experience. Some people have to put ice cubes on their heads to cool down their anger. So it is much better if you don't allow this poisonous thing to enter you. It affects your blood; it makes your mind become deranged.

I've had an aversion to the same person for the past four years. How do I overcome this?

Forget it. Four years ago, you had this hatred toward someone.

Now so much time has passed by. Why did you write this abhorrence so deeply, so clearly, in your heart? A person should be like a child in the sense that he should have hatred only for a short time. It shouldn't last too long. The scriptures say that a superior person has anger only for a short time and then he forgets it; the middle-quality person remembers anger for two or three hours; the inferior person remembers anger for a day and a night. However, a sinner never forgets anger until he dies. So a good person should forget anger very quickly.

You should understand this: if you have an aversion to a person, it is making a hole in your heart. Therefore, aversion is not good. Forget it and shake hands with this man. God will be happy with you.

If one feels very intense anger, is it true that one should not repress the feeling, that such repression is harmful? On the other hand, might it mean that one could strike another person? Is this a contradiction?

Those people who say that you should not control your anger are wrong. You should control it. In fact, you should try to control your anger the moment it arises. If you were able to do that, it might turn into love. Anger, lust, greed are all the same feeling. If you could control them, they would turn into love.

If we were to give expression to every wave of anger that arises in us, what else would we be able to do in life? Indian philosophy emphasizes self-discipline and self-control. Eventually, anger is going to subside on its own. But if you were to control it, it would subside right now. You must not let your body express the feelings of your mind. Find out what the root of anger is. You don't have to deal with anger itself: what is more important is to deal with the root of anger.

What is the root of anger?

Ego, self-pride. Don't attach any importance to that.

Trying to do anything is an expression of ego, so why isn't repressing anger an expression of ego?

There are two kinds of ego — proper and improper. It is proper ego to try to subjugate the improper ego.

What is the best way to get rid of anger?

Look for the source of anger. The *Bhagavad Gītā* says that when there is a relationship between two things, desire arises. When a desire is not fulfilled, it turns into anger. So the source of anger is the desire for something. It can be desire, expectation, attachment, or any impression. For instance, a person has a donkey and you want it. That person isn't going to give it to you, so you say, "I'll get him!" This is how one's life falls apart. Divorce can take birth right in the center of these things. When a person's desire is not fulfilled, it turns into anger. When a person gets really angry, he wants to hurt someone, and when this happens, he loses his discrimination. If a person loses his discrimination, understand that he is destroying himself.

For this reason anger is called a great enemy of a man, no friend at all. The Lord said, "O Arjuna, O brave one, try to conquer desire, because once it turns into anger it destroys you. Therefore, conquer it." Man should really try to calm his anger, to cool down his anger. Understand that anger is very harmful and get rid of it in your heart. If you get rid of attachment and desire, you won't have any anger either.

In the *Gītā* the Lord said, "O Arjuna, this anger arises from the *rajoguna*." The stomach of desire is so vast — no matter how much you put into it, it is never satisfied. There is so much beauty on this earth, but it is not enough to satisfy desire. Now they have reached the moon, and they want to go to Venus. They may say that they are discovering many important things. No. It is nothing but desire, nothing but expectation. Its stomach is vast. It is the father of all sins. It is the enemy of knowledge of the Self, the enemy of the bliss of the Self.

If a man is angry or threatens violence against me or someone close to me, how should I respond?

Have courage. Don't be afraid of anyone's anger. Even if someone threatens you, let him threaten you. Many people threaten in a dry way. There is a saying, "Dogs that bark never bite; clouds that thunder a lot never give rain." So you should just keep remembering God. There is no meaning in most people's threats.

However, if someone tries to beat you up, don't let it happen. In ancient times, no matter how much some great beings were beaten, they still accepted the blows. Even now some great beings accept blows. I don't. Even before someone hits me, I give him two blows, and he gets scared and leaves. He never touches me. Some people have the habit of oppressing others. They get addicted to beating up people if nobody resists them. But if you respond to them harshly, they give up their violent habit. It is fine to bear these things to a certain extent. A great being said that if somebody gives you a blow on one cheek, you should turn the other cheek to him. That's all right for him, but I say that if a person gives you one blow, you should give him three blows — one on each cheek and one on the head. Only then can he improve and get rid of his habit of abusing others.

However, self-restraint is also very necessary. Years ago I beat a *sādhu* with a stick after listening to a thousand abusive words from him for two days. I didn't beat him after listening to only a single word of abuse. I also knew that nobody had ever stood up to him in his entire life, so it was very necessary for me to do so. What I did was good for him, but it would not be good for you to do what I did.

He wins who bears everything. If somebody uses a harsh word, you should be able to bear it. Only then will you be a winner. If you react with a harsh word to someone, both of you will be defeated.

Don't worry. Whatever happens, let it happen. Whatever God wishes to happen, will happen. There are many people who speak in dry, abusive terms.

When confronted with potential violence, should one take the position of self-defense or nonviolence?

If you are completely stabilized in the state of nonviolence, that is best, but if you are not, it is better to take the position of self-defense. In these times you have to defend yourself; there is no other way.

Once there was a big serpent lying on the main street of a city and it was biting many, many people. One day a saint came to live there. The snake wanted to bite him too, but when it saw the saint, it couldn't do it.

The saint lived there for a while, and he instructed this snake to give up biting. Then the saint blessed him and left.

The next year the saint came again to the same place. He saw that the snake was completely beaten. Its bones were broken, its muscles were torn, its tail was twisted. All the children in the neighborhood would come and pull the snake's tail and throw stones at it, so that the snake was now half dead.

When the saint saw its condition, he asked, "O brother, why are you in such a predicament?"

"Should I speak the truth?" the snake asked. "This is the result of following your teaching. You taught me to be nonviolent, and because I am in that state, all these children come and drag me by my tail and throw stones at me. I promised you that I would follow nonviolence, so I didn't do anything."

The saint said, "Now I am going to give you more teaching."

"Please," said the snake, "not again. I've had such a hard time with your teaching."

"No, no, this will be good," the saint said. "If you see people walking by, just hiss at them as if you are furious. Then no one will come close to you."

Then the saint left. Afterward, the snake began to do that. Whenever someone passed by, the snake raised its head and made a hissing noise; and sure enough, no one came close to it. The children stopped tormenting it. And soon the snake recovered its good health.

So if a person always endures other people's violence, they will always be violent. If someone hits you once, you should hit him twice. If you do that, he won't harass you again. The times are such that this is what you have to do.

The other day you were talking about how we shouldn't be angry or mad or hateful, but can a person really deny how he feels?

With positive feeling you should erase those negative feelings.

Just as when your clothes get stained, you use soap and water, and you wash away the stains, in the same way, with good feelings you should erase bad feelings. God's Shakti exists within everyone. God is not a being who is a certain size and lives somewhere up in the sky. He pervades everywhere, so it does not matter who worships Him — whether he is a Jew or a Hindu or a Christian or a Muslim. If God were not everywhere, Moses wouldn't have found Him on the mountain. He would have had to go somewhere else where God was.

To have positive feelings, remember God all the time, have a good attitude, look at everyone as good. Don't try to look for others' faults; see the Self. There is Consciousness within; always remember that Consciousness so you can have positive feelings. Understand that negative feelings are your enemies and they chase you. They are like the Berlin wall. The countries on either side are part of Germany, but there is a wall that divides them. So give up negativity.

As long as you have these negativities, they don't allow you to really meet another person, to really see another person. Negativities don't allow you to see God, to experience the Shakti. *But sometimes I get so mad, and it seems so difficult to let it go. Should I just keep on saying the mantra?*
Repeat the mantra and just drop the matter. Even that feeling is momentary; it changes very fast. You should just leave wherever you are when you get angry. Go and look at the sky and pray to the Lord. Once some time passes, the feeling just goes away. Anger is not good. Regardless of how it affects other people, it is terrible for you. When you are angry, you won't be able to digest your food well; you won't be able to sleep well either. Anger won't allow good thoughts to arise. Therefore, our Bible, the *Bhagavad Gītā*, says anger is the enemy.

There are those who say it is important to feel your feelings in order to release them. They say you should get a counselor and pound a pillow if you're angry. What do you feel about that?

They must be psychologists! If you get angry, just go out in the open air; just pray to the Lord; pray to your own inner Self.

Become calm and still. Even anger has its own limits, it has its own reason. And after a while, it leaves you. Don't give too much importance to it. With anger, the friend of the morning can become the enemy of the evening, and the enemy of the morning can become the friend of the evening. With the freedom of the Self man should try to improve himself.

A human being is not so weak that he has to receive advice from others. People who follow Siddha Yoga don't really have to go to others for instructions. They receive it from their own Self. For example, you're angry and I give you some advice. Even if I don't give you any advice, after a few moments your anger will leave you. If you use discrimination, you don't even need advice. If you are angry and you look to somebody else for advice, it's a vicious circle.

But there are those who say that some people need to be yelled at, or that sometimes it is good for a parent to scold a child.

When parents get angry at their children, it is not really so bad, because their only desire is the good of the children. Sometimes a lot of work has to be done and the parent or teacher gets angry, but it is not real anger; it is just the way to get the work done. This kind of anger may remain in a person, but you should not give it so much importance.

I guess that's a good point because in my family there was a lot of love and a lot of yelling.

Anger always goes along with love. Just don't attach too much importance to it; that is all you have to remember. Anger is very mundane. The moment you stop giving much importance to it, it dies.

BECOMING FEARLESS AND CONTENT

How can we combat the everyday fears of life that prevent us from being happy?

If you were to find the place of total bliss inside you, those fears would leave you. When do you feel frightened? Don't you feel fear when you are confronted by someone who is different from you? If, instead of seeing people as different from you, you were to see them as the same as yourself, you would not experience any fear. If you were to insure yourself with God's insurance company, you would become totally fearless.

I have been in pain since my sister died ten years ago.
Please help.

Forget that. Don't keep it in your memory. She must have taken birth somewhere else by now, but still you are sad that she died.

Once there was a sage called Gadhi. He had two disciples —one had perfect knowledge and the other had ordinary knowledge. When Gadhi passed away, the younger one cried for a long time remembering his Guru. The other one called him close and asked, "Why are you crying?"

He said, "Because our Guru died. He was like a father."

The older one said, "In every moment, so many of your fathers die; why are you crying for this one father?"

Who knows how many times you have taken birth in how many families in this world? Everyone is your relative, everyone is your friend, and everyone belongs to your family. However, you remember only this one family. Among all these people, so many die and so many take birth. Why do you have to cry for this one? Look at the Self. Does it have any birth or death? If the old body goes away, a new body comes to you, so why do you have to cry for yourself? Don't worry about those people who have already gone. Think about the time that is left for you and how to make good use of it.

How can the lonesome hole inside my heart be healed?

This will be healed when you find the Being who dwells inside you. This Being has the form of light, and that is nothing but Consciousness or the Self. If a person doesn't have any trust in God, if a person doesn't accept God, the only mantra he can repeat is this: I am lonely. He considers himself an orphan all the time and is filled with fear. You are not alone, He is with you. However, you don't know Him. From now on, understand that you are not alone. Understand that God is with you. He is before you, behind you, on all sides. He is above, below, everywhere. If a person experiences that he is far away from God, he feels lonely. Man should have complete trust. He should have this awareness: as much as God belongs to others, He also belongs to me.

What does aloneness mean to you? How did you deal with it?

I like being alone. When I came to this earth, I came alone; I didn't come with anyone. When I leave, I will go alone; no one is going to accompany me. Why should I be sad being alone? I am happy being by myself. I don't live alone; I live with God. If God seems far away from me, I repeat the mantra on my *mālā*. So I am never alone.

When I see what is creating my suffering, how do I get the power to stop creating it?

You have to go through the pain that comes to you. No one can stop it. Suffering comes according to your fate, and you have to experience it. However, if you meditate more and more, you will attain the state of witness-consciousness. In that state you can watch pain and suffering without being affected by them. Meditate very well, and you can attain this state.

Pain and pleasure will always exist; they are included in this creation. There will always be opposites. The brother of happiness is pain, and the brother of virtue is vice. In every field there are pairs of opposites, and the world is created of these opposites. If opposites did not exist in this world, the sages would have written, "Eat a lot, and drink a lot; make merry a lot; indulge in your senses a lot; get married over and over again." They would have told you that. Instead, they tell us to restrain our senses. We feel that they have written advice contrary to our best interests, but it is not so. They have written the right thing. They experienced everything and found the Truth, and that is why they wrote what they did.

Once there was a man who became very aware before he died. On his deathbed he spoke a few intelligent words: "I thought that I enjoyed all the pleasures, but now I find that I did not enjoy anything—those pleasures have enjoyed me. I used to think my thirst and my cravings would become weak and leave me, but instead, they have made me weak. I used to think I was spending time, but now I know that time has been spending me."

When you are dying, what will you think of? Think about your final days. What is going to happen at the end? Make your life better now and be happy. Have all the good things for your children and enjoy all the pleasures in this material world, but understand that there is more to life. You have to do something more, and that is to attain the inner Self. Once you attain that state, then your death dies—not you. Becoming absorbed in this worldly life, do not lose yourself. You should not die; your death should die. Bring death to your death. Have fun in this life and be happy, but along with that have a lot of faith in your inner Self.

How does one overcome doubt and fear?

By having trust in God and by fearlessness. Fear makes you weak; you don't need it. Fear is a mental addiction. The main reason for it is ignorance of the Self. A great being said, "How can that person who has attained the bliss of the Self, the ocean of the bliss of the Self, have any fear?" The nonrecognition of the inner Self and of the inner Shakti is the cause of fear. Once you recognize the Self and the Shakti, that creates fearlessness.

At night I have terrible nightmares that bring fear and anxiety to my body and mind. I see animals rushing to kill me or a lot of angry people condemning me. When I try to get up after such dreams, it is very difficult because my body is very heavy and painful. Will you help me?

Of course I will help you. You have these dreams because of the weakness of your heart. You conquer fear in the waking state, but you are afraid of the fear in your dream. When a person dreams that he has become a pauper or a rich man, it is mere delusion — he doesn't become that in the waking state.

I am going to tell you something very effective. It is called *Rāmabāna*. The arrow of Rama was very sharp. If he released an arrow, it never went to waste — it always worked. Therefore, before you go to sleep, wash your feet and hands. Have a photo of my Baba near you, and wave an incense stick to it. Repeat, *"Guru Om, Guru Om, Guru Om,"* and fall asleep. Then see what happens and report to me.

I experience intense fear and tension these days. It feels as if my heart is frozen and the rest of me is paralyzed. I meditate, do japa, and chant, and I call for you to heal me. Yet once I am in one of these states, it is very hard to let go and be open. I am not sure who I am or how to remain open to you. It is like facing my own death. Would you advise me, please?

You have this kind of feeling, but you are not really facing death. Death will come to you when it is time. Repeat the mantra peacefully and warm yourself up. One who repeats the mantra constantly should eat butter and drink milk or cold drinks because heat is created in his system as he repeats the mantra. Don't be scared about this matter. Don't remember your death. Everyone has this fear — some people have intense fear and others have mild fear. To become fearless, take the support of the inner Self, of the supreme Principle. Insure yourself with God's insurance company. Your feeling of facing death is nothing but emotion. Death will come to you when it is time for you to leave, so don't worry about that now.

Once a camel began to chase Sheikh Nasruddin so he ran from it and fell into a pit. As he lay there, he became afraid the camel would come and kick him, so he lay still, pretending to be dead. Because he had been lying there for such a long time, he thought he really had died. He began to worry. "Oh," he thought, "I didn't let my wife know that I died!"

He looked up and saw a man passing by, so he called him over and said, "Please do a favor for me. Tell my wife that

Nasruddin died in this pit." Then he lay back down again.

When the news reached his wife, she came running, thinking her husband had died. She was screaming and shouting, "O God!"

Nasruddin told his wife, "Hey, don't scream and shout — if you do, the camel will come again. If you want to cry, cry softly."

"But they said you died," his wife said. "What kind of death is this?"

Nasruddin replied, "Well, I just *felt* that I had died."

So you have all these different kinds of emotions and feelings. But you should feel that you are immortal, that you will never die. You should contemplate in this way: the Self is immortal, the Self is eternal, the Self is supremely pure.

Don't have any more inferior feelings.

I have such a longing to experience release and to flow freely in Consciousness, yet I am filled with so many fears and blockages. I meditate regularly. I practice Kundalinī yoga. What else can I do to get away from self-consciousness, to let go and flow with God?

You should continue to meditate regularly despite your fears. Fear is a common condition. Only one who has seen the inner Self is totally free from fear. After that, he devours fear. This is true of everyone whether they admit it or not. Some people admit their fear and others hide it secretly in themselves. A saint has said that one who has experienced the Self is totally fearless. Let your fears remain; it is this intense longing to be free that is important. That is what will bring you freedom. There was a great saint in Maharashtra who said that intense longing for anything brings that thing to you. If you have intense longing for God, you will surely attain Him because that longing brings Him toward you. If you want to flow with God, keep chanting His name with love; that will release tremendous love in you and you will flow in that ocean of love.

You have asked a very good question. It is good for me, for you, and for everyone who is listening.

Why in the course of sādhanā does one go through prolonged periods of feeling absolutely terrified? Would you please talk about your own experience of this fear during your sādhanā?

In the course of sadhana you do come across the center of fear in the heart *chakra*. When you go on an external journey, you come across rough roads and you have to go through thick forests. In the same way, when you are on the inner journey, you come across different energy centers. When the time comes for you to merge into Him, all of a sudden there is fear. You are terrified of letting yourself go and becoming one with Him, and it is that very fear that stops you from becoming one with Him. Sometimes a meditator gives up meditating forever because he is so terrified. Watch out for this center of fear. If you can face it, you can go beyond it. Then you become completely fearless. With great courage, if you lose yourself, you attain That. If you hold yourself back because of that fear, you lose everything.

There was a great Sufi saint called Shams-i Tabriz. *Shams* means "the sun," and he was called Shams-i Tabriz because he was always shining like the sun. He said that if you want to attain God, you should merge your individuality into Him. It is your ego that is the worst enemy, so you should obliterate this ego. If you want to attain something great, eradicate your individuality. If you maintain your individuality and think that you are going to attain Him, you are mistaken. If you lose yourself, you will attain Him. Don't get stuck in a particular condition or in your wrong understanding. Give up your wrong understanding. Then you will merge into Him.

Shams-i Tabriz used to give a beautiful analogy. He said that a grain of wheat merges into the earth and it loses itself there completely. Then once again it sprouts. It becomes a beautiful plant and it produces so many more grains of wheat.

As long as your ego exists, as long as your individuality exists, you cannot attain God. When you lose the ego, you will have the awareness — I am God.

And you *are* God.

THESE FEELINGS WILL CHANGE

Sometimes the desire for material things seems to become stronger than the longing for the great and the true. Is it better to let the desire fulfill itself and be done with it, or to struggle and overcome it?

If you know the knack of it, turn the direction of the desire toward God. Make yourself aware that God is the source of all fame and that you can get all fame from Him. God is the source of all valor and you can get all courage from Him. He is the source of all love and you can get all love from Him. He is the storehouse of all beauty and you can get all beauty from Him. This is how you should change the direction of the desire.

Rabi'a was a great saint, and once some Moslem priests asked her, "Don't you feel any desire for anything in the world?" She said, "Yes, I feel desire but all my desires are fulfilled in God."

Often after a period of very intense contact with my inner Self, I get depressed and rebellious. Why does this happen?

When you become separate from the inner Self, you experience this state for a while because you really don't yet know how to stay in the Self for a long time.

I have been meditating for the past five years, and I have practiced kriyā yoga. Ever since I left the retreat, I have been unable to meditate and I feel all this negativity coming up.

This will pass. Just endure it.
Am I burning up karma by having this come up?
It is inner cleansing. However, do sit for meditation regularly.
I can't concentrate on meditation for long — just one minute or two.
Let the mind go.
So much negativity comes to the surface — awful things and feelings. Does this have anything to do with shaktipāt?

Yes, it has a lot to do with Shakti. That is why I am asking you to let it happen. Let it all come up. You should just meditate calmly, and whatever feelings emerge from within, let them emerge.

During the two retreats I spent with you, I am pretty sure I received your grace. Yet within the last two months I have been unable and very reluctant to meditate. I am just now coming out of that. I would like to know why these periods still keep coming up.

It happens because of past samskaras, past habits or tapes. However, once you have received the Guru's grace, you will not lose your interest in meditation forever. It may go away for a short while, but it will come back. There are twelve different phases that the mind can pass through after you have received grace. Sometimes you will find it filled with faith. Other times you may find it devoid of faith. Sometimes it may be filled with love; at other times it is devoid of love. Sometimes it may become insensitive. Or it may become very agitated, very disturbed, or very empty. You may lose enthusiasm, you may feel listless. All these are phases, and all these phases are workings of the same Shakti — that is what you should understand.

We are born into this world with all its conditioning and then we come into contact with Truth. Then we are expected to change and pursue a spiritual path. Why is it so hard?

It is not hard. It is only because you are resistant to unfolding that you find it hard. There is nothing limiting you. Because you limit yourself, you feel that everything is conditioning. For example, now you might see something as very negative, but once you reach perfection, everything appears as nothing but love. The world, which is full of so many different things, appears later on as nothing but love.

What can I do to overcome a sudden feeling of antagonism toward divinity and God?

If you have a feeling of antagonism toward God, increase it. Have that feeling twenty-four hours a day. Be very friendly with all your neighbors and all the people around you. However, get really mad at God. Ask Him, "Why did You give me this birth?" Fight with Him. Ask Him, "Why did You give me such a beautiful body?" You can also get mad at Him by saying, "Why did You sit so close to me? Why couldn't You sit far away from me?" Day and night, get mad at Him.

Jnaneshwar Maharaj wrote a beautiful commentary on this subject. He said that if you want to have enmity, make God your enemy. When you think of God as your enemy, these feelings will change; divine feelings will surge within you.

There was a demon called Hiranyakashipu and his son was Prahlada, who was a great devotee of God. But Hiranyakashipu hated God. Although he hated God, he thought of Him so much that finally he attained God. Whatever action a person performs, that is what he attains. Regardless of how you feel about fire, it will still give you warmth. If you touch it, you will feel the heat. If you put yourself in the fire, it will burn you. Therefore, antagonism toward God is very good. That very feeling will change into the feeling of a friend.

Why are there blocks along the spiritual path?

As you travel along the nonspiritual path, have you noticed any blocks? Aren't there blocks on your mundane path? Have you looked at your own life? How many psychologists have you had in your life? How many doctors? How many girlfriends? How many boyfriends? How many enemies? How many other people? Do you find blocks only on the spiritual path? If you have all these things in your bound path, why should the spiritual path be so different?

The spiritual path is not as difficult as the mundane path; it is much easier. On the spiritual path you do not have any fistfights, you do not have to give or take, you do not have to do anything with others. All you have to do is just turn inside and meditate on the Self very peacefully. Isn't that true?

When we have an obstacle in our sādhanā, how can we know whether to ask you about it in person or to rely on the inner Guru?

Of course you can come up and ask me your question in person. You can also ask it at the question-and-answer session during the evening program. This session is intended for people who have obstacles in their sadhana. However, if you have an obstacle, just wait for a while. Don't come running to me the moment you get an obstacle; just wait and it will go away. Nothing can hinder a person who has an ardent desire to pursue sadhana. If you are lazy about pursuing sadhana, you yourself are the obstacle, and you only imagine that other things are obstacles.

Is it all right to pray to the Guru for help in difficulties?

Yes, it is all right to pray to the Guru for help. When you pray to the Guru, you do get his help. Some people, however, no matter how many difficulties they have to face, bear them without asking anything of God or the Guru. They face difficulties with the understanding that they are undergoing them because of their karmas. They devour their difficulties; they do not become miserable or anxious or depressed.

In the Upanishads I read about a great saint called Vyita. He was free of lust and other desires. He was a great enlightened being, a learned man, and he had the knowledge of the Absolute. Vyita had no legs, and he walked with the support of his hands. He was a great yogi, a great *brahmajñāni*, a knower of the Absolute.

A king named Janasruti went to him to receive knowledge. He said, "Please impart the knowledge of the Absolute to me." He had taken some gifts and he gave them to the saint.

"What are these?" asked Vyita.

"These are gifts for you," said the king.

"What makes you think you are going to buy this *brahmajñāna*, the knowledge of the Absolute, with these things? You should leave."

Brahmajnanis, great beings and saints, are like this. If they

447

have everything, that is all right with them. If they do not have anything, that is all right too.

After Vyita told him to leave, the king said, "Well, I will give you two people to serve you because you are not able to walk by yourself. I will also give you two chariots."

The yogi cried, "Get out of here! What makes you think that you are going to buy this brahmajnana with two people and two chariots? What makes you think that you are going to buy it so cheap?"

The king said, "Well, I'll give you half my kingdom, and I will also give you a wife."

Vyita laughed and said, "You think it's so cheap? You think you're going to attain this brahmajnana by giving me half of the kingdom and a girl?"

Finally the king said, "Okay, I will give myself to you along with my kingdom. Please impart that knowledge to me."

"*Now* you can sit down," Vyita said, "I will impart knowledge to you." And Vyita gave the king what he was supposed to give.

After a while the king asked, "What are you going to do with the kingdom?"

Vyita replied, "A kingdom belongs to a king, so you should go back to your kingdom and rule it. Go back and rule the kingdom with the knowledge that I have given you."

So it is all right to pray to the Guru for help in difficulties, but it is better to turn your difficulties into nectar and then try to digest that nectar with great joy. It is very valuable, very important, to digest your own difficulties.

EVIL IS HURTING OTHER PEOPLE

What is the nature of the evil forces that seem to be working in the world?

There are no evil forces as such. But we can create them, and since we create them, we can erase them. Rain falls from the sky, but evil forces are not created in that way. God does not create them for us; we create them for ourselves.

Therefore, we should try to erase what we have created. If every person maintains respect for everyone else in his heart, all evil forces will disappear.

What is evil? What can people do about it?

Evil is hurting other people. There is no worse evil. People talk about heaven and hell but there is no hell worse than hurting others. Even to think of torturing or hurting people is hell. People should give up this tendency; they should think about helping other people. This is just a matter of mundane life, but if you just rise a little bit above this level, evil has a different meaning.

If one does not respect his own Self, that too is evil. The worst sinner is one who does not understand his own Self, one who insults his own Self, one who does not attain his own Self. It is because we do not understand our own Self that we do not understand another's inner Self. Because of this ignorance, evil is created. So when one perceives his own inner Self through meditation and knowledge, he finds the divinity that lies within. Then he will not see anything bad in others; he will not find anything evil.

This is a fact: only one Self resides within everyone. That Self is all-pervasive and we should become aware of this. There is only one Self, but many, many forms. All these clothes, all the makeup that you put on, all the decorations that you put on your body, and all these outer appearances have no significance. Only the inner Self has significance. There is only one Self for this whole world. That Self belongs neither to the East nor to the West, neither to white nor black, neither to man nor woman, neither to high nor low. That Self is supremely beautiful and full of light. It is within everyone in the form of light. When this is so, if you hurt other people, that is the greatest sin you can commit in your life.

If a person understands his own true nature, he finds that everyone is his own Self. We should always think of That. It is amazing that even though the supremely beautiful Self is within us, even though it is God's flame that has taken birth in different forms, still we are unhappy, still we are sad. Because of the ego, we consider ourselves great and high in other ways, but we should try to understand our true greatness. Even though the Self is so close to you, if you have not discovered that Self, if you have not attained that Self, what good is that ego?

To hurt other people is evil. You should also try to give up the things that intoxicate you, the things that disturb or upset your mind. They are also evil. Some people take drugs, which are nothing but poison. There is greater intoxication in your own Self. Once you get high on that, you will never come down. It never spoils you, it never gives you any trouble, it does not make you bad.

The great Siddha Tukaram said that to help other people is the greatest merit and to hurt other people is the worst evil.

I know that criticism and fault-finding are very foolish and I'm becoming more aware of this all the time, but sometimes it comes out against the people I love the most. Why does this happen?

You see faults in the beloved ones when your love is coupled with desire or selfishness. If you were loving for the sake of love, and if your love were totally selfless, you would not see faults. Seeing faults is not good for the one who sees them; it's not good food. If you remember the good that you did for those people, you will see even more faults in them. If you don't remember the good you did them, you will probably ignore their faults.

What should my attitude be toward bad actions that others inflict on me?

If you consider the evils done to you as a gift from God, and if you endure them, they become very good for you. In Sufism there was a great child saint named Rabi'a. She led a very pure life even from her childhood. Her name is famous in our literature and throughout the world. Rabi'a was sold into slavery. During the daytime, no matter how much she was bothered by her master, she would endure everything patiently. During the night, she would repeat the Lord's name constantly. One night her master visited her room and was astonished to see blue light everywhere. He was terrified, and the following day he told her that he would release her from slavery and he offered her good lodgings in which she could spend her whole life. She told him that she had no need for a house to stay in, but that if he wanted to, he could release her.

If you too develop this power of endurance, it will be very good for you. There is no meaning in enduring a painful experience if you cry and complain, but if you can endure hardship with composure, it will be very good for you.

UNTIL THEN, DO SOME TAPASYA

I experience a lot of pressure in the head. It is just incredible and sometimes lasts for a week at a time. I have heard of different remedies such as applying sandalwood oil. Would this help?

That is no way to treat it. As you keep practicing, that kind of pressure will be there all the time but you will be able to bear it. You will find peace through it, and you will be able to function. It is this pressure that brings the permanent state. Don't get frightened by it; you will develop the power to endure it.

Sometimes I experience a very great sense of frustration located in my chest. It feels as though I have a longing for something. What is it? Am I craving the experience of my Self?

It is a state of the mind. At these times concentrate on repeating your mantra. Just identify yourself with your inner Self, and that state will change immediately. The only remedy is repetition of the mantra and prayer. Because you allow your frustration to grow, it grows. It has no power of its own to grow.

Is it very difficult to get rid of lust, anger, and desire completely?

If you really want to get rid of them, it is not very difficult. If you really do not want to get rid of them, it is incredibly difficult.

451

I suffer from tremendous lust and anger, and I am unable to control my mind. Because of this, I am unable to surrender to you. But after I leave, your love influences me so much that I am again drawn to you. Do I come here because of my love for you or because of my weak mind? What should I do?

Your actions reveal your weakness. Still, you keep coming here. Even then, you don't understand your weakness. When you leave this place, you are controlled by your lust and anger. After a while, you lose interest in them and you think of coming here. Then you come here and you miss those things, so you leave this place. As this goes on continually, one day you will find that you are on the right path and everything will be all right. After you suffer many times in this way, you will obtain happiness. You are not the only one; it happens like this for many others too. However, try to cool down both tendencies, either through meditation or chanting.

How does one transmute the lust of sexual passion into light?

To transmute the lust of sexual passion into light, you have to meditate and chant a lot. The great *yogini* Rabi'a was asked by a priest, "O Rabi'a, doesn't this sexual tendency harrass you?"

She said, "Yes, it does, but only when I forget God. Only then does it give me any trouble; otherwise it doesn't."

Do you understand this? That is why you should transmute your sexual passion into God's love. Everything should be moderate. Sex is all right, but it should be moderate. If something is disciplined, you can derive joy from it. Otherwise, you cannot attain anything from anything.

I feel so much fire inside me, but instead of shining in it, I often burn in it. How does fire work? I haven't gotten past purifying and I just keep roasting.

If there is too much fire inside you, don't worry, it doesn't matter. I will throw the water of contemplation on it and it will be extinguished. A sage said it doesn't matter how much the fire is blazing, it doesn't matter that the fire is burning down the whole forest on the mountain. Sprinkling the nectar of the name of God can extinguish any kind of fire. If nothing bad exists inside you, don't try to fill yourself with bad things. Change yourself and understand yourself in that way. Understand that the Self is very clean and pure. Also understand that as a person contemplates God, he becomes free from sins. Don't burn yourself in the fire of thoughts. Soak yourself in the nectar of the name of God. The name of God is nectarean. It is extremely cooling.

Why do we have to have tests?

In ancient times realization was attained with great difficulty and one had to undergo a lot of tests. Who knows why it has become so easy in Kali Yuga? Still, it is necessary for a person to follow sadhana with firm faith. This is the Siddha path and you cannot measure this path, you cannot limit it.

Once a disciple called Yusof Ibn Al-Hosain from Egypt was living with a Siddha Guru called Dho'l-Nun. He went there to do seva. When he got there, the Guru said, "Hey! Sit over there."

So he sat there and after a year the Guru called him. "Where have you come from?"

He said, "I come from Rayy."

The Guru said, "All right."

Then another year passed. Again the Guru called him close and asked, "For what work have you come?"

Hosain said, "I have come for your *darshan*."

Then the Guru called him a third time after three years. "Hey, Hosain, what do you want?"

He said, "I want the touch of your divine inner Shakti and also the secret mantra that you have."

He gave him a box and said, "Take care of this; don't open it. Across that river lives a great saint called Hazrat Hussain. Give him this, and he will give you everything."

Yusof walked and walked, and when he was approaching the river, he heard a rattling noise inside the container. He became very curious about what the rattling was, so he opened the top.

A mouse jumped out of the box and ran away. He wondered what to do. He thought it was better to keep on going, so he went on to the saint. Even though the saint was old, he was strong. He kept a stick with him as he sat there.

Great Siddhas do not flatter others; they do not feed them chocolates, saying politely and formally, "Please take the mantra, please repeat the mantra. Your inner Shakti will be awakened." Other people talk like this; it is useful in mundane life.

Yusof said to the saint, "I came with a gift from Dho'l-Nun. But when I opened it, the mouse that was inside ran away. Please sir, I've come to receive a secret mantra from you."

The saint was very forceful. He said, "Get out of here, you rascal! You couldn't even take care of a mouse. What would you do with the mantra? The great mantra contains divine Shakti. Get out of here! Leave immediately!"

The man put both hands to his head and went back. He told the entire story to his Guru, Dho'l-Nun.

The Guru said, "It's all right. It's not your time yet. Go back to your house. After twenty years you will either meet someone or else you can come here and I will give you the mantra. Until then, do some *tapasya*. Go."

The Siddha path has its strange ways.

What is the nature of māyā and how can we deal with it?

Maya is very difficult to comprehend. Everyone seems to think he understands the secret of maya, but the fact is that it is maya that has the upper hand. It is difficult to know maya directly. Even the great ones become deluded by maya; they become caught in her trap and fall. It is difficult to describe the reasons why this should happen. Maya is hard, terrifying, difficult. Maya is always alert, always trying to pull you down. The moment you are off your guard, she will lay you flat, and it is only after you are down flat and your back is broken that you realize something has happened.

The subject of maya has been discussed in the *Yoga Vāsishtha*, which is a great work. Maya is the force that makes what is not real appear to be real. She presents what is temporary and short-lived as eternal and everlasting. Maya is only another name for delusion. It is just like seeing a city of clouds in the sky or perceiving a rope as a snake. Even though there is no city and no snake, your mind is affected.

All of us are oceans of divine Consciousness, and yet we do not experience ourselves as such. This concealment is maya's most important function. Maya conceals your divinity and makes you experience yourself as a petty, limited individual being, and so she keeps you trapped. You are a child of God, but maya prevents you from knowing this. She makes you feel yourself as a petty, ephemeral, pathetic being, even though you are divine. Maya is keeping you from the Truth.

You are supremely free. Your real nature is the Self and you are divine in your innermost nature. Everything in the outside world lies hidden in the Kundalini Shakti, yet you are looking for satisfaction in the outer world. This is all due to maya. That is why the Lord says in the *Bhagavad Gītā*, "My maya is mysterious. All those who join their hearts to Me, who are constantly thinking of Me and who see Me in others, all those who see not others but My manifestations, will be able to cross this ocean of maya." All the rest are bound to sink.

I'm undergoing so much tapasya. No one speaks about this when we hear talks on Siddha Yoga. It makes me sad. Please talk about tapasya.

Siddha Yoga is the greatest tapasya. The culmination of tapasya is Siddha Yoga. *Tapas* means "to burn." What you burn in Siddha Yoga is your outgoing senses and your wandering, outgoing mind. It does not mean that you have to stand in the hot sun or in water or that you have to give up eating food and become very skinny and dry. Try to imbibe the teaching of Siddha Yoga. What is this teaching? Siddha Yoga teaches you about the inner Self. It teaches you that your inner Shakti should be awakened, and that you should become established in it. The inner tendencies are always outgoing. They keep taking a person outside, and they make a person fall. Siddha Yoga makes a person hold his tendencies inside and become established in his own inner Self. This is the supreme tapasya.

There are many kinds of external tapasya that only make

you burn. However, Siddha Yoga reins in the outer tendencies and makes the senses burn. Tukaram Maharaj said by doing outer austerities, one cannot attain the inner Self. Only when one becomes completely anchored in firm inner determination, and in that determination makes an attempt to attain the inner Self, can one attain it. If a person lacks firm determination, a disciplined heart, and control of his tendencies, what is the use of his life? Such a person is called a wanderer; he has a wandering life because he is not firm anywhere.

Siddha Yoga itself is the supreme tapasya, the pinnacle of tapasya.

He Was Always Testing Me

You tell us that we should test a Guru well. In what ways did you test Bhagawan Nityananda?

I never got any time to test him because he was always testing me. By the time he finished testing me, he was already tested.

I kept going back and forth, back and forth to my Baba for many years. I pursued him all my life. Nowadays people write me letters saying, "I don't have any time to come to you. Will you send me shaktipat?" I spent many years with him. He tested me and he taught me, and it took many years. I don't test anybody as severely as he did. I spent so many years with him and he tested me so severely. It was not just that he tested a person, but when he did, you gained the strength to digest everything, you became so strong.

In the old days, I never wanted to hear lectures from my Guru. I didn't think it was necessary to listen to his talks. But I had one-pointed love for him, and I had the confidence that one day or another I was going to receive his grace, and from that I would attain everything. So thinking like this, I used to do different kinds of seva at his ashram.

Now Gurus test you in different ways. And at that time people used to laugh at me and say, "Well, he scolded Muktananda, he did this to Muktananda, he did that to Muktananda." They would laugh. My Baba used to receive a lot of sweets and fruit, and he would distribute them to people. They would get in line to receive a sweet, but when my turn came, he would keep the sweet aside and look the other way. People would laugh, saying, "Oh, Muktananda didn't receive a sweet, he didn't receive prasad; he is an unfortunate being."

Sometimes I used to say, "Well, when my karma opens up, when it brightens up, I am going to get everything. You eat the sweets and be happy. But I will wait for my time."

My Guru was very strict when it came to discipline. If anybody spoiled the discipline even a bit he would say, "Go! Go to your own house. Go and lead your family life." He would kick that person out of his ashram.

You never knew when he would teach something. Even if he gave just one lesson a month, it was enough for the entire year. You could learn everything from him just by watching him coming and going, sitting down and standing up. All his activities contained lessons. If you were to ask him a long question, he would answer it with a few words. (Here people ask short questions and I give them long answers.) If you were to nag him a little more, ask him a little more, he would turn over and go back to sleep for two hours. He contained divine lessons and everything was worth learning from him.

After dark he never liked too many lights. At night they had to turn the lights off and he just sat in the dark. Even then, people sat around him. Sometimes people started behaving like him. They wore fewer clothes and kept their fingers straight just as he did. He would never bend his fingers into a fist. That is very rare. He never accepted anything with his hands. People went up to him and put things at his feet. Money was left there too, and for a couple of days things would lie there in a big heap. Then someone would go and put everything away systematically.

He was a great being, without any worries. He was very powerful. He was omniscient, but he never let anybody know that he knew everything. He was a great scholar, but he did not let anybody know that he had studied anything. You can tell from his pictures that he led a very simple life. His food was simple, and his speech was very simple too.

He sat very quietly and still without doing anything, yet people were so afraid of him. They were afraid to cough before him; they were afraid to sneeze or make any sound before him.

He would wake up in the morning at three o'clock and take a bath. Before the sun rose, he would walk for two hours. While walking, he would keep his head down, he would not lift it up, and he kept his eyes closed too — that is how he walked. He either looked down or he looked up. He never looked straight out.

He was easy on the devotees, but when it came to disciples, he was terribly strict, really hard. That is how he was. He was so tough when it came to discipline, he was so strict, that no bad tendencies could live in any disciple.

COMPLETING THE JOURNEY

CHAPTER 19

A Place of Tremendous Joy

One has a birthright to liberation—to total freedom and total bliss.

Prior to liberation, did you feel or know somehow that you would attain liberation?

Why not? I had unshakable faith in the Lord, and one who has such faith will fully attain that state. Liberation is the birthright of a human being, so one need not even depend on the grace of the Lord. I had the faith that I would get it, that *mukti* would be attained.

Will you take my wife and me all the way across the ocean of samsāra? We would surely drown if it were not for your grace and blessings.

Are you ready to sit in my ship? Or do you want me to take you across from your home? If you are ready to sit in my ship, it is very likely that you will go across the ocean of samsara. The ship is already moving, so you just have to sit in it.

Is finding a Guru the whole key to finding God? Does it depend not on what meditation you do but what teacher you get it from?

Yes, that is completely correct. I practiced so many techniques and studied so many scriptures, yet none of those practices and none of those studies were of any help to me. It was only after receiving the touch of my Guru that I attained what I was looking for. Then I came to realize the truth of all the scriptures I had studied. Then I attained the goal of all the techniques I had practiced.

Is it possible that the practice of all those techniques was a way of overcoming obstacles in order to reach Bhagawan Nityananda?

Yes, it is true that no matter what techniques you do, they are bound to purify you to a certain degree. I can also say that all the scriptures I read and all the practices I performed led me to my Guru. But even if they had not done anything for me, I would have gone to him all the same.

Meditation and experiencing God within are not easy for me. When I read your autobiography, I do not think it was easy for you either. Why then do you say that realizing God is easy?

Although it wasn't easy for me, it could be easy for you. I read a story about the Singer sewing machine. It took the entire life of the man to invent that sewing machine. At the end of his life he still hadn't finished it and he realized that he was going to die without completing his work. Suddenly he had the idea that he should place the needle upside down. When he did that, the machine was ready. At the end of his life it was complete. So if I were to open a sewing machine factory now, I could make thousands and thousands of them in three months and sell them so easily.

In the same way, meditation won't be that difficult for you now. Pursue *Hamsa,* and then realizing God will happen very easily.

I am confused about samādhi. On a number of occasions the energy has risen to my head and I was bathed in total light and indescribable joy and bliss. Then I came back down from the experience. I thought that in real samādhi you remained in that state. But within three days I went into a deep depression. What is a true samādhi state?

What you experienced was a sample of true samadhi. It lasted just a brief while. The samadhi that you have in mind lasts for a longer time, but for that you have to practice for a longer time. To stay there you must meditate with regularity. But your experience is authentic. Now through your practice you should earn the same state for longer periods of time. Sometimes salesmen come and give you samples of their goods. And if you want more, they ask you to go to their stores and get some there.

Would you explain the difference between pleasure and bliss?

Pleasure is a mere appearance and it is momentary. Before you have contact with an object of pleasure, you don't experience it, and after your contact ceases, again you don't experience it. Even during the period of contact you may not experience it all the time. Pleasure flashes like lightning. The pleasure that you experienced earlier does not exist any longer and the pleasure you experience now will not exist in the future.

But bliss is absolute; it is unconditional. Once it begins to rush up from inside, it never ceases, it continually grows. It is self-determined and self-existent. Bliss is completely independent of the friction of the senses with their objects. Pleasure arises from this friction and since it depends on this friction, it is momentary. While you are still enjoying it, it disappears.

First I am awake, and then I am asleep. Where does the waking state go when I am asleep and the sleeping state go when I am awake? Do these states exist in other worlds?

These states exist everywhere. Wherever individuality exists, these states also exist. One state or another will always exist; it all depends on the individual person and the particular world. A man who tries to understand the three states really knows God. Because of these three states, the *jīva* exists. In some beings there are four states, in some there are three, in some there are only two, and in some other creatures only one state exists.

You have asked about two of these states; it seems you don't know about the other two. There is a third state called the deep-sleep state in which you are not aware of yourself at all.

Trees, mountains, and water are all in this state. There is a second state called the dream state. Through the inner organs, the inner senses, you come to know this state. All animals experience this state. Then there is the first state, the waking state, and this you know through the outer senses.

However, these three states depend on the fourth state. The scriptures call the fourth state *turīya*, which means the state of Shiva, the state of God. Because of this state the other three — the waking state, the dream state, and the deep-sleep state — arise and subside. They arise and subside in the fourth state.

Shaivism says that for a man who tries to understand the three states — for him the state of turiya unfolds and then he understands the state of Shiva. He attains the state of God. When man becomes established in this state, he is happy in happiness and he is happy even in unhappiness. He remains joyful. He considers pain and pleasure, happiness and unhappiness, as relative; neither of them exists. According to him, pain is not pain, pleasure is not pleasure. Sometimes pain can turn into pleasure and pleasure can turn into pain.

You have asked a very good question. All three states arise and subside in the Self, in the fourth state, the divine state that is beyond the other three. For this reason man should know his own Self. Man should meditate. Man should perform every action with good feeling; he should perform good actions and offer them to God. These three states are very ordinary. When one state exists, the other states do not exist. So man should try to contemplate and perceive this: how does the sleeping state arise and where does the waking state subside? Due to the inner supreme Shakti these states exist, this dance goes on. We become happy in these states. But you must understand that this happiness is nothing but unhappiness compared to the happiness of the fourth state. So there is no happiness and no unhappiness; everything depends on our understanding. We consider unhappiness happiness and we pat ourselves on the back and say how great we are. With this understanding we consider ourselves brave and clever.

I spent a lot of time with my Baba. I was close to him for at least twelve or fifteen years and I never saw him sleeping at night nor did I ever see him get tired. I never felt that he ever wanted to sleep.

In meditation try to go beyond the three states and then you will understand the true state. I am very happy with your question.

How can we attain the turīya state and become established in it?

You have already attained the turiya state. It is inside you. But in order to make it completely yours, you will have to meditate. What is turiya? It is a state without thoughts, an inner state where pain and pleasure don't reach. The scriptures say that when you become surprised, there is a moment of stillness. When one friend meets another friend and loses himself for a few moments, that state of losing oneself is the turiya state. You have experienced this many times in your life, but you are not aware that it is the turiya state. It is inside us. To attain it, you have to meditate.

The great beings in these pictures all lived in the turiya state. On the outside they looked like us, but on the inside they were different from us. What is the waking state for us is night for them. What is night for us is day for them. It is a great state.

The Upanishads say that the heat of the sun does not reach there; the air does not move there; pain does not enter there; death cannot reach there. Bliss exists there all the time. It is not momentary like our sense pleasures. We eat some sweets and experience a bit of joy. We meet some friends and experience a little joy. We have just a touch of joy. But that joy is not like this; it is ever blissful. Even though we think we are experiencing great joy, still it is only for a few moments. The scriptures say it is like lightning; it flashes, and even before we see it, it disappears. Turiya is not like that. That state is ever blissful, supremely blissful. It is in the hearts of *yogis*; it is the goal of yogis. It is indestructible.

Although it exists within everyone, some have attained it and some have not. Because of the joy of turiya, we enjoy eating, drinking, listening, and touching. There is so much ecstasy in that state. After attaining it, man becomes intoxicated and delights in his own Self. He does not expect joy from others. That bliss is mysterious and very significant. It contains no distinction of caste, creed, deity, worship, or devotee. During all the hours of the day and night, there exists only bliss, nothing but bliss.

As a person meditates, he becomes established in the turiya state. He does not have to make an effort. The awakened Kundalini takes him and establishes him there. Her work is accomplished there. For this reason Siddha Yoga is called *mahā yoga*, the great yoga.

What happens after a soul is liberated?

After you become liberated, you become aware that everything is only Consciousness. Then you see everything in the world as pure. All the hopes that you put in outer things are fulfilled inside. Then you revel in the Self, you delight in the Self, you are friends with the Self, you find fulfillment and contentment only in the Self. And you attain total freedom. Then you begin to see that everything is as you are.

Does Self-realization mean that you have no ego at all, or that you are not affected by whatever ego you do have?

Even when you realize the Self, the ego doesn't leave you, it stays. But the quality of ego changes. Before you realize the Self, you identify with whatever you have and whatever you are. You think, "I am a woman, I have children, I have a husband, I am a writer." Once you realize the Self, you experience, "I am the Truth, I am the Self, I am happiness, I have merged into God." So the quality of ego changes once you have realized the Self.

For seven years I had an intense desire for liberation. I meditated but nothing happened. Now I do not particularly desire anything and nothing seems to be happening. Can you deliver me from desire and emptiness? Will you be the grace for me that your Guru was for you?

Give up the desire for liberation. This desire is a hindrance. When you do not have any desire to attain anything, that is when you attain everything. When you give up the desire to find something, you find everything. So give up that desire totally; then you will attain everything.

Is one's Self-realization predestined?

Destiny is made by one's endeavor, by one's own actions. What we do now, the kind of effort that we put in now, will determine our future destiny. Therefore, effort is more important than destiny for Self-realization.

There was a great saint in our country called Dharanov. His life story is most amazing and miraculous. He was afflicted with leprosy; still he would chant in ecstasy.

Dharanov's Guru, Eknath Maharaj, was a very great saint. The Lord commanded Eknath Maharaj to ask his disciple to compose a commentary on the *Bhāgavatam*. So Eknath said to Dharanov, "Dharanov, what keeps you busy?"

"I chant, I keep chanting *Hare Rāma*."

"Why don't you write a commentary on the *Bhāgavatam*?"

"I will certainly do your bidding; I will write it."

In a vision, Dharanov came to know that the command was from the Lord Himself. The Lord appeared to him and said, "Write this great work and your leprosy will disappear."

Dharanov replied, "My leprosy doesn't bother me. After all, everybody is diseased, though maybe I'm a little more diseased than most. But I'm quite happy with this disease because nobody bothers me. So I wouldn't want to compose something in order to overcome it. However, for inner peace and for inner joy I will certainly compose this work."

By the time he finished the commentary, his body had become completely pure and healthy; the leprosy had disappeared. Dharanov says that wealth and pleasures are determined by your past merit, but as far as remembrance of God is concerned, you are completely free to do that every moment, and you must make a very strong and earnest effort to keep your mind engaged with God all the time. Self-realization comes through strong effort.

What is the significance of intense craving for the Guru? Is there any danger in this? Does it ever leave?

Intense craving for the Guru is very significant. If you have this desire, the Guru's Shakti will enter into you and begin to work within you and it will do great work. Any work is completed only through intense craving. On the spiritual path you should have intense craving for God, for the attainment of God. You should say, "I am going to attain God, I am going to attain the spiritual path, I am going to meditate to attain Him." So intense craving for the Guru is very good.

It is only your doubt that is very dangerous — nothing else. First of all, remove the doubt, and then everything will be fine.

What is Self-realization, and what kind of understanding does one have after attaining it?

After you are Self-realized, you have the understanding: I am not this body; I am not an ordinary being. I am God; I am supreme Consciousness. Whatever concepts you had before you became realized cease to exist. Many people wonder what will become of their individuality if they become Self-realized. Nothing will happen to your being. However, your old concepts will be destroyed; your understanding will change. Owing to your understanding, you experience pleasure; owing to your understanding, you also experience pain.

Different concepts and thoughts arise and subside in the mind. As various thoughts arise in the mind, you become them. You are filled with pain, pleasure, anger, greed, jealousy, and other feelings. All these feelings are created through your own understanding. In the same way, once you are Self-realized, you obtain divine understanding. You become aware of your original nature. For example, when a person is sleeping, he may have nightmares and become afraid. However, when he wakes up, he does not have any fear. His nightmare has disappeared and once again he is happy.

So if you have the vision of your inner Self, if you wake up from the nightmare of your wrong understanding, that is called

Self-realization. Right now, you are aware of your body. Later, you will become aware of That.

Once you are realized, can you still lead a normal life?

Certainly. Even after a person is realized, his normal life continues. Don't be afraid that your life will be ruined. All the great sages led their normal, daily lives. In Maharashtra there were great Siddhas, perfected beings, and many of them led very normal lives. Some of them were shopkeepers, some were gardeners, some were barbers, and some were tailors. Your normal life won't be spoiled or destroyed. On the contrary, it will become better.

Eknath Maharaj was a great saint who was a householder. He used to say, "I will lead my life in such a way that in all the three worlds I will enjoy only happiness. I will become blissful."

Because of ignorance, you consider yourself a jiva, an individual soul, and you consider this world a mere world. However, once you attain that knowledge, you become aware that this world is made of God, this world belongs to Ram. The moment you become aware of God within yourself, you see this entire world as heaven.

As long as God hasn't revealed Himself within you, this world is a mere world and it is painful. However, the moment He reveals Himself to you within, you will see the world as it is. For that reason, if you become realized, you will have no worries. You can lead a normal life with great joy.

What are the signs of a realized being? How can we recognize one when we meet one?

This is a great question. If you really want to know the signs of a realized being completely, become realized. Otherwise, I can just tell you the external signs. You can say that a realized being is a happy being. He knows the Truth and he has the ability to make others know the Truth. He is a being who experiences only bliss, nothing but bliss, everywhere in the world. He takes delight in God. His main goal is to be absorbed in God all the time. He doesn't belittle his daily actions; he considers his daily actions the worship of God. He makes his own home the temple of God. He considers his wife and children God also. He considers all his actions the articles of worship of God. Shaivism says that such a being has the understanding that God pervades the entire world, that it is God who dwells in all beings. Because of this awareness he experiences the bliss of samadhi and then he becomes established in that bliss.

In a very few words, he is a realized being who has seen the Truth in his heart as it is.

How long does the energy that is awakened from shaktipāt last? Can one undo its effects?

The Shakti awakened by a real Guru will last until it has made you complete. It cannot be broken in the middle. If you do not become complete in this lifetime, it will continue to be with you in the next lifetime. It will certainly make you complete. It will keep increasing. However, to make it increase more and more, you have to have faith in your own Self, in the Shakti, and also in the Guru. It is God's Shakti that makes you become aware of God. God has five powers and He performs five actions; one of them is the bestowal of grace.

I have heard that a Siddha student is expected to finish all his karma during the same lifetime in which his Kundalinī is awakened. What part can self-effort play after this awakening to ensure this culmination? Or is everything predestined?

What you have heard is completely true. Compared to the fire of Kundalini, a forest fire is like a blade of grass burning. The Upanishads say that when your inner Shakti awakens, the inner light begins to blaze, and when you perceive that light, all your karmas are burned up. The knot of your heart is released, and all your doubts are destroyed.

Siddha Yoga is a great yoga; it is called the emperor of all paths. It is not the kind of yoga that happens when you are walking on the road and some flash comes to your mind and you begin to cultivate your own ideas and preach them. It is not like that at all. This yoga has existed since ancient times. When the creation came into being, Siddha Yoga also existed. Since then, this Siddha Yoga has prevailed. It is true. Its lineage is millions and millions of years old. It is not a yoga that is formed by the mind. It is a complete yoga, a great yoga.

Your self-effort is very important. You should keep on meditating constantly until you reach the Blue Pearl. It doesn't have to be predetermined that you are going to attain the Blue Pearl. It is not like that. Through your self-effort you can attain that Blue Pearl. It is true that through the virtues of your count-less lives, eventually you reach a life in which you begin to know Siddha Yoga. You become liberated, you become the image of this liberation, and you become completely pure.

REBIRTH AND REALIZATION

After receiving shaktipāt, how many times does one take birth again before reaching the final goal?

It isn't like that. You can attain the final goal in one lifetime. Shaktipat takes you to that place. For that, meditate continu-ally. If meditation really enters you, it does not matter whether you sit for meditation or not. Whatever work you are doing, meditation just happens. Even if you cannot see that energy, it is alive in you.

If your loyal followers perform the sādhanā you set for them, will all of them attain nirvikalpa samādhi within twelve years?

If they pursue sadhana they will attain everything — years are not counted. If they do sadhana every day, they can attain this within twelve years.

Don't think that getting into this nirvikalpa state — the thought-free state — is very exhausting work, like flying to Venus on a rocket. *Nirvikalpa* means free from imagination, free from thoughts, aware only of unity; it is the peaceful state. It occurs when you are established in the Self, when the mind is very quiet. In your mundane life you experience many moments without any thoughts, even though you are unaware of it. Tomorrow you can try this out. During the day, notice as your mind becomes free from thought, free from imagination, even just for a second. When you meet a friend you haven't seen for a while, you say, "Hey!" and at that instant you are free of thoughts. When something amazing takes place, the same thing happens: at that moment you are free of thoughts. In your life you experience this state many, many times, but it lasts for only a very short moment.

Everything happens inside a person. You should think about that. You also have this nirvikalpa state within you.

If the disciple of a Sadguru doesn't attain liberation in this lifetime, how will he recognize his Guru in the next incarnation? Or will he have another Guru?

Generally speaking, if a person receives the Guru's grace in this lifetime, he will be liberated in this same lifetime. However, if he were destined for a shorter life this time and were to give up this body, he would go to a higher world and pursue sadhana there and become liberated. The Upanishads say that a person who does not finish his sadhana in this lifetime, who leaves his body halfway through, will attain *brahmaloka* — which is the same as *siddhaloka* — and there he will pursue sadhana and attain liberation.

There are seven levels of knowledge. Siddhaloka is for those people who have reached the fifth or sixth level of knowledge. If a person has obtained the fourth or fifth level of knowledge, he is reborn immediately.

In the *Bhagavad Gītā* Arjuna asked Lord Krishna what would be the state of a person who had given up his body before attaining That. The Lord said that he would take birth immediately and be born into a very rich family; he would begin his sadhana from wherever he had left off in his last life. Then he would reach his goal. His past destiny would make him meet one Guru or another.

So a Guru's compassion, a Guru's grace, will never go to

waste. I read some philosophy in the Kannada language by Nijaguna Shiva Yogi. He said, "Once you receive Guru's grace, it will never leave you, no matter how many lifetimes you go through. The Guru's grace will continue to chase you." Therefore, have no worries.

It seems from what I have read that most of those who have reached God-realization started having spiritual experiences when they were young. Does this mean that if someone were to reach God-realization in this lifetime, he would necessarily have to start on the spiritual path as a young person?

You can begin having spiritual experiences at any time — when you are a child, or when you are middle-aged, or even when you are quite old. When the time is right, you will begin. People who start their sadhana when they are very young usually practiced sadhana in their previous life, but died before reaching God-realization. Such people are *yogabhrashtas*. Their family circumstances are comfortable, and the moment they are born, they begin their sadhana. Sadhana vibrates in their bodies because of their practices in previous lifetimes. In the same way, if you have received shaktipat but die before reaching God-realization, your Shakti is reawakened in your next lifetime.

That is the specialty of this yoga, the great mark of this yoga — that you won't remain incomplete. There will be a day when you will be realized. If you become complete and perfect right in this world, it's great; you can enjoy life. But even if you don't become perfect in this world, still you will become perfect in Siddhaloka.

When people finish their sādhanā in siddhaloka, do they come back to this loka, to earth?

No. They are liberated.

Does that mean they are not separate any more?

They are not separate at all, even from the beginning, even when they start doing sadhana. After completing sadhana, they are definitely not separate. Even people who don't do sadhana —

they are not separate either. It is just that their understanding is separate.

It is not that you attain something new after sadhana: you attain what you already have. The thing is that after you do sadhana, you become aware that you already have it; you attain what you already have inside. The Self is already supremely pure, and still you put it in the washing machine. It is already clean, but you are not aware of it. Siddhas are like that — completely pure. Siddhas purify what is already pure. So through sadhana you attain what you already have.

Does it take years to become Self-realized to the point that you are never separated from the Self during the course of the day?

If your eyes are closed, how much time does it take to open them? To become Self-realized takes only that much time. But only one who has full faith, full understanding, and full worthiness can attain Self-realization quickly. Otherwise, it takes many ages to become Self-realized; it might take millions of years. It all depends upon your worthiness.

Once Swami Vivekananda went to Ramakrishna Paramahamsa. Swami Vivekananda was a smart young man, and Ramakrishna was a man who belonged to the old tradition. When Swami Vivekananda approached him, he asked, "Have you seen God?"

Ramakrishna said, "Yes." Then he said, "You are too far away from me; I see God closer than that."

"Will you show me God?" asked Vivekananda.

"If you can see Him, I will certainly show Him to you."

"Please show Him to me."

"Put your head down on my foot."

The moment Vivekananda put his head down on Ramakrishna's foot, he got a shock of Shakti. So it took only a moment for Vivekananda. Yet to attain the same Shakti it took Ramakrishna's Guru, Totapuri, thirty-five years.

Shankaracharya was a *jagadguru*, a world Guru. It took him twenty-four years to attain God. One of his disciples was Hastamalaka. Just by uttering one phrase, Shankaracharya made him attain God. The disciple asked, "Who is God?" Shankaracharya said, "The witness of your mind," and just by hearing that, Hastamalaka attained God.

It took Inayat Khan a long time to attain God, but it took his disciple Sheikh Shibli only an hour to attain Him.

You can attain That within a minute, or you can attain That after years and years, or you can attain That after countless lives. No matter how long it takes, still you should have great feeling for Him and you should always remember Him in your heart — that is the greatest sadhana. Don't use up a lot of your time in pursuing languages or scriptures or philosophies. Use your time to turn inward and ponder the Self.

Does your grace extend beyond death?

Once you receive God's grace or the Guru's grace, it will never leave you. Nonetheless, you should put forth self-effort.

Tukaram Maharaj said, "With these very eyes, in this very body, I will see divinity. I will perceive Him." He had such a great heart, he had such great determination. Why assume you will attain Self-realization after death? Why not now? You should have that much trust within yourself. However, even if you can't do this, still, grace won't go to waste.

In California, somebody asked me, "Why do we need to have a Guru? Ramana Maharshi did not have a Guru."

"How many Ramana Maharshis have there been?" I asked him. He just shook his head; he didn't know the answer. There was only one Ramana Maharshi — he was extremely rare. He was a yogabhrashta; in his last life he died before attaining That, so in this life he was a born yogi. When he was fifteen, he left his house and pursued sadhana intensely. In his body in subtle form there were impressions of his past sadhana.

Even Then There Was Only One Thing on My Mind

Will you please tell us about the first fifteen years of your life?

I came from a family that was full of wealth and happiness, and I had a very happy boyhood. Since I was the only child and my parents were very much attached to me, I didn't get much chance to go away from home and see the world. I would go to school and I would come back home and then go to school again.

I had great love for sadhus, for holy men. Even then there was only one thing on my mind, and that was the miracles performed by these holy men, how to receive their grace, what would happen if a holy man cursed someone, and so on.

My mother gave birth to me after wanting a child for a long time. She prayed intensely for a child and then she gave birth to me. So right from the start she gave me a deeply religious training. She would ask me to repeat the mantra Om Namah Shivaya, and if at meals I didn't do it, she would take my hand and tell me, "First say your mantra and then eat your food."

I was very fond of watching spiritual plays and I used to attend them often. I acted as Lord Krishna and Narada many, many times when I was at school. I had a simple and natural interest in God. At the age of fifteen or so I left my home in search of God.

In Indian mythology there is a story of a child devotee called Dhruva. His father had two wives, and Dhruva was the son of the older wife. The younger wife was his stepmother. One day Dhruva went out to play somewhere, and when he came back, his father was sitting on the throne. Dhruva rushed to his father and climbed on his lap and sat there comfortably. But his stepmother didn't like it and she pushed him away. Dhruva began to weep and he went to his mother and said, "I was sitting in my father's lap, but my stepmother couldn't stand it and she pushed me away."

His mother said, "Don't complain to me. Complain to the One who is the real Master of the throne. Complain to God."

"Shall I complain to Him?"

His mother said yes. So even though he was only nine years old, he left his home and went into a forest. There he did severe tapasya, he performed austerities. All the Siddhas and saints in that forest supported and helped him, and the wives of the seers helped too in various ways. God was pleased with him and granted him immortality. According to the legend, Dhruva became the Pole Star. I used to read this story quite often; I was very fond of it.

Even in my early life I didn't fear anything, and that's how it has been all my life. I haven't been afraid of any law. I haven't been afraid of any particular government. I haven't really been afraid of anything. So one day I left my home. That's all that I remember of my boyhood.

CHAPTER 20

The Music of Consciousness

*Nāda is the great mantra that emanates
from the inner sky.*

*Before I go to sleep, I hear sounds in my ear, but they seem to
be coming from inside the ear. Is this Shakti or should I question
if my ear is operating correctly?*

Your ear is operating correctly, because in the waking state
your hearing is quite normal. The *Vijñāna Bhairava* speaks of the
unstruck sound, which arises on its own without the contact of
two objects. In the scriptures this sound is called *nāda*, divine
sound. It is vibrating all the time inside man, in the earth, in
water, in fire, in air, and throughout the entire world. The entire
universe came into existence due to the vibration of this sound.
It is explained in the *Spanda Shāstra*.

Recently some scientists discovered evidence of a particular sound in the background of the universe, a sound that is
always reverberating, always pulsating. According to their the-
ory, the entire universe came into existence because of the pulsation of this sound. Chanting has its foundation in this divine
sound, not in any particular country or religion. Because of the
original sound, we chant, we repeat the mantra. We do this so
that we can hear the inner sound. Although the inner sound
reverberates constantly inside us, only very rare people can hear
it. This inner sound is fascinating music, it is very joyful. No
human being can sing like that. Musicians have tried to imitate

the inner sound; that is why they have created all these musical instruments. Still, they cannot duplicate the inner sound, which is joyful, nectarean, and absorbing. Because you have received God's grace, you can hear the inner sound.

I have started hearing nāda but I haven't progressed beyond that yet.

Who said you haven't progressed? It is only due to your progress that you have started listening to nada! Now you should progress in listening to it; you should become immersed in listening to it. Lose yourself in that sound at least for a while. Nada arises from the space of God. Jnaneshwar Maharaj said, "God's house exists a little beyond where the sound arises." It is true, and that house is called *turīya*. Keep listening to that sound. That is your progress.

For two years I have heard a buzzing sound in my head, something like the buzz of a transformer — sometimes stronger, sometimes less strong. Does that result from yoga? Will it develop further? Or will it eventually cease?

As a person pursues yoga more and more, ten divine musical sounds spring forth to remove the fatigue of yoga. It is a great music, it is the music of the inner Self. This morning we had music here and it was played very well, but that kind of music is completely dependent on outer things. One person has to tune the strings, another has to tune the drum with a hammer. But this inner music is completely independent; there are no instruments inside, no sitar, no *sarangi,* no *tabla.* This divine music arises in the inner space of a human being. The music you hear through outer instruments is nothing but an imitation of the inner music. Our classical music was composed by sages so that people could learn to hear that inner music.

Keep listening to this nada; it won't stop. Now your meditation should be to listen to that. That music will change; it will culminate when another music called *megha nāda* arises. If you keep listening to this music from the *sahasrāra*, nectar will flow to the end of the throat and you can taste it with your tongue; it is very delicious. Then this nectar will pervade all the nerves of your body, and joy will spring forth; you will experience joy in every pore of your body. At that time a *yogi* begins to dance for joy. That is the glory of this inner music. If you go to sleep while listening to it, you will keep hearing it even when you wake up. You will have your sleep, and you will also listen to music.

Kabir said, "In the upper space, the inner music has been playing on its own. As I was listening to that music, the pot of nectar turned upside down. I tasted that nectar, and after that all my miseries went away." There is nectar inside, and when the inner music is sounding, it releases its flow. This is the glory of nada. This is the greatest attainment of meditation. Through this, one merges in the supreme Truth, where one already exists.

During meditation I hear high-pitched sounds in my head and lower sounds in my heart. What are these?

You should focus on the sound that seems to come from the top of your head. That is the music of Consciousness. There is a great space there. Doctors may not have accepted it yet, but it is real. When Kundalini rises, you begin to hear this music, which is reverberating all the time in the inner spaces. If you were to hear more of it, you would find it very blissful. The elixir which is released as a result of your hearing the divine inner music has tremendous medicinal value; it has the power of ridding your system of many diseases.

The heart center and the crown center are connected with each other. It is mostly from the crown center that you hear divine music. Whatever you hear from the heart center, you will also be able to hear from the crown center and vice versa.

Don't try to force your attention on the heart; let it stay wherever it goes. Don't try to direct your meditation by your will. Let it direct itself, and you go along with it.

Would you please speak about nāda?

Nada is divine sound; nada is the great attainment. The yoga scriptures say there is no greater mantra than nada. As the inner Shakti is awakened through the grace of Kundalini, the nada of the divine sound arises. There are different types of nada. Ordinary sounds arise when two things come in contact, but the inner sound, *anāhata nāda,* is the unstruck sound, the sound that emanates without two objects clashing. Because the inner space is empty, there is nothing there to clash, nothing there to make an ordinary sound.

In the heart and also in the crown *chakra* at the top of the head, there are inner spaces. In these spaces, divine bliss springs forth, and the vibration of this supreme bliss is nothing but this sound. For a yogi or a meditator, nada is a special vehicle for travel. Through the help of nada you can reach the space of God instantly, because it is from the space of God that nada arises. Nada is the great mantra that emanates from the inner sky.

There are ten different types of nada: the sound of cymbals, the sound of the sarangi, the sound of the conch, the sound of the *mridang,* and other instruments. The final divine sound is heard as thunder. When you start hearing that, nectar begins to flow and you taste it. As you taste this nectar, you regain youth; you feel very young within yourself. This is the blessing of Kundalini, the *prasād* that you attain after meditating for a while.

What is the significance of hearing the sound Om *within one's inner being in meditation? This happened right after I ate some of your prasād.*

Om is the final divine sound. To hear *Om* is to talk to God. *Om* itself is God. It is the divine sound, and it resides within you. As you meditate and meditate, this divine sound will begin to arise within you. Kabir says, "My Guru imparted to me a word and he kindled my light. He opened my heart." That is why I say that there is no creature greater than a human being.

After one hears nāda, what is the next step on the spiritual path?

The only thing left to do is to keep listening to the nada. Combine your mantra with the sound of the nada. Then whatever mantra you repeat, you will hear that mantra coming from the nada. As you keep listening to it, your mind will follow it. The space of Consciousness lies where nada arises. Jnaneshwar Maharaj said, "Just beyond nada lies the house of God." From there nada arises. Nada arises from *anāda*, from no sound, and it arises from Consciousness. Nada is the music of Consciousness.

Whose voice is it that I hear singing so beautifully above all of us?

If you can hear the singing within yourself, you are hearing God's songs. That is the music of the Self and it is divine music; it is not ordinary music. Once you hear the divine music for quite a long time, nectar begins to flow from the sahasrara.

Where does the inner nāda originate? How does it affect me?

You must be hearing the inner nada every day, so starting tomorrow, try to determine where it originates. Within the physical body there are three other bodies: the subtle, the causal, and the supracausal, one inside the other. Corresponding to these four bodies there are four levels of speech: *vaikharī, madhyamā, pashyantī,* and *parāvāni.* There are also four states: the waking state, the dream state, the deep-sleep state, and the state of turiya, or the transcendent state.

Everyone knows the waking state and the dream state, and during meditation we can also experience the other two states, the deep-sleep state and the transcendent state. Nada emanates from the paravani, or transcendent level of speech. From there the vibrations — the *vāni* — move to pashyanti, from pashyanti to madhyama, and from madhyama to vaikhari.

The effects of nada on your being are many. Whatever a person needs takes place because of nada. If you listen to nada each day in meditation, it increases. Each of the ten main varieties of nada has the power to destroy certain diseases and to cleanse the body of its impurities. Keep listening to this music because it is from these sounds that you attain the divine nectar which makes the body beautiful and strong from within.

If it is quiet enough, I am able to hear nāda at any time without having to mentally articulate the sound. May I use the So'ham *mantra, which I hear spontaneously, instead of* Om Namah Shivaya, *which you gave me earlier?*

Yes, you can repeat the mantra *So'ham.* This is the outcome of your earlier mantra. It is true that you hear this mantra very naturally, because it is being repeated inside you. It is very significant when this mantra begins to repeat itself from within. It seems you are a good meditator. When the mind becomes still and free from mentation, you begin to hear this mantra going on inside you. The nada that you hear is the music of God, which is being played of its own accord inside your head. This nada is inspired from the place of the supreme Principle. Nada is very valuable.

Keep on listening to this nada and as you do, you will get into *samādhi.* You will be very close to the supreme Principle, very close — only half an inch away. I thank you for this question.

If I hear nāda during meditation, can I meditate on these sounds as my mantra?

Nada itself is a great mantra. It is divine sound. Once nada is unfolded, it is very beautiful to keep listening to it. When you join your mantra with nada and keep listening to it, that itself is meditation. There is no mantra greater than nada. One of the final forms of nada is megha nada, the sound of thunder. When you hear it, you become so scared that you begin to run here and there; it feels like your head is going to burst. After this you hear the last nada, which springs forth with the sound *Om.* Then you become perfect. To listen to nada is very great; keep listening to it.

What is the benefit of listening to the various nāda?

They purify your body. They make your senses stronger. They make your muscles stronger. At the end you reach God through nada. Nada is the rocket on which you fly to God.

Lately I have had strong rushes of energy between my eyes, followed by a vast roaring of thunder. Then I experience leaving the body. What is happening? During this period I am always doing japa rapidly.

What you hear as the roaring of thunder is called *megha nāda*. In the scriptures that is the music of inner thunder. One who is devoted to God, one who meditates, one whose inner Shakti has been awakened is blessed by God with the gift of inner music. Megha nada, or the music of thunderclouds, is a very high form of nada. You know what happens when there is thunder — it is followed by a heavy shower of rain. Likewise, this roar of inner thunder will be followed by a shower of elixir that falls on your tongue. You must be experiencing this roaring in the crown center. When you hear it, don't do japa; try to hear your mantra in the sound of this thunder. Your *sādhanā* is going very well.

One Day a Great Musician Came to Meet My Guru

One day a great musician came to meet my Guru. The people who had brought the musician asked him to sing for Babaji. Now my Baba lived in a very simple manner, and this musician was quite eminent; he used to sing for other distinguished people — cabinet ministers and other important officials and wealthy people. When he was asked to sing for a simple saint, he turned up his nose.

So Babaji asked the others to take him to a nearby hotel and give him some food and put him up there. He stayed there for two days, and during that time an unusual change took place inside him. On the third day he himself offered to sing for Babaji.

At that time I used to sit at quite some distance from my Guru, off to one side. I never sat close to him. On that day everybody said, "Look, Babaji! That great singer is now ready to sing. Kindly allow him to sing."

But Babaji said, "His music is not classical enough; it is not first-rate."

After making that remark, Baba turned his back on him. The musician stood there and wondered why the saint had said such a thing about his music. Two or three people told him he should speak to one Muktananda Swami who was sitting in a corner and ask him about it. Babaji fell asleep, and the musician, along with the others, came to me.

One of them said, "How is it that Babaji said his music is not classical enough, not first-rate?"

I told them that when a yogi's mind becomes stabilized in the upper akasha, the space in the crown chakra, there emanates a divine melody. This divine music is produced without the help of any instruments. It is this music alone that is truly first-rate. All outer music is only an imitation of this inner divine music; it can never be as great. So this is why Babaji had said that he didn't care about his music: it lacked depth.

As a yogi perceives the pure radiance of this divine music, as he enjoys the divine melodies, nectar is released from the cranial region, and this nectar spreads throughout all the nerves and gives him new life and youth.

CHAPTER 21

The Blue Light of Love

*The Blue Pearl exists within you in order to be seen
and perceived by you, in order to be realized by you.
This Blue Pearl may appear to be tiny,
but it contains the entire cosmos.*

*Would you please tell me what the beautiful light was that I saw
pulsating in the area of your heart chakra?*

This blue light is in everyone's heart. The supreme Principle is
the color of blue light. There is no color in the sky, in the ether;
still the sky appears to be blue. The *Bhāgavatam* says,
"Consciousness is of the color blue." In meditation it appears as
blue. You may have seen your own blue light superimposed on
me. Sometimes that happens.

*Why does the Self necessarily manifest as a blue light? What is
the difference between experiencing a blue light or a white light
or whatever color? Isn't the Self essentially without attributes?
Why blue?*

The light of the Self is blue. Just as the sky is blue — and because
of the sky even the ocean is blue — the Self lives in that blue.
This is the attribute of the light of the Self. The attributeless Self
doesn't have any color, any shape, or any form. It is free from
attributes, free from thoughts, and beyond all feelings. The One
which has no form, the One which is nothing, manifests as this
universe. The sky has nothing, but it is blue.

Why is Chiti perceived as blue?

It is not that it is *perceived* as blue; it *reveals* itself as blue. When something is empty, when it has no form, it appears as blue. For example, look at the sky. The sky has no solid objects in it, but it appears as blue. A meditator sees scintillating blue light within him. All colors belong to that light. So it is not perceived as blue. If it were a matter of perception, we could also perceive it as yellow, but it does not happen that way.

In meditation quite some time ago, I experienced many pulsating visions of light intensifying with overwhelming energy and joy. All of a sudden the visions ceased and, as if piercing a veil, I merged into waves of white, indescribable energy and joy. Can you please explain this?

You have had a wonderful experience, and you should congratulate yourself that you have been blessed by God and the Guru. You had a momentary vision of Truth. It is love which is the true form of the Lord — love and nothing else. Supreme love, the highest love, is the beautiful form of the Lord. The light you saw is the light of love. Your experience is very good and you should continue to meditate. It is not without reason that I ask people to meditate; I'm not interested in wasting their time.

I walk around feeling open and physically drained by people around me because I don't know how to protect myself effectively.

This state will last only until the Kundalini merges into the *sahasrāra*. After that merging you will be like the ocean, which can give out any amount of water and yet never be drained. When Shakti is united with Shiva, the river becomes one with the ocean. This feeling of being drained will occur until that final union takes place in the sahasrara. After that, you will not be affected. You are close to perfection but you are not quite there. It is the difference between watching the ocean and being in it.

Later, you will see a complete sphere that will explode and you will see a million tiny suns. Then you can say that you have achieved the final goal, but until you have reached that, you will be without the grace of the Being dwelling there. Within the middle of the sphere there is the blue light that we call the Blue Pearl. When that sphere explodes, the Blue Pearl will emerge. That will be the consummation of your *sādhanā*. Until then, you must meditate intensely. You will see lots of visions, but the most important is the Blue Pearl.

Thank you so much for the grace I experienced last time we met. During meditation I experienced the whole room filled with a blue color. Would you say something about this?

The truth is that this light fills not just one particular room, but the whole cosmos. You can see it spreading everywhere, and later you will see heaven and hell and other worlds in meditation. Then you will realize that these worlds are real. The blue light precedes the final realization of God's form, the beatific vision. The natural color of the sky and of water is blue. Likewise, the innermost light of God is blue.

It is not only I who deserve to be thanked, but you also deserve to be thanked because you have had such a marvelous experience in meditation. The blue light is an indication of a very high state. In the center of this light there is a spot that we call the Blue Pearl. You will see it in meditation. The light of this Pearl is so brilliant that it is sufficient for an entire cosmos. In the Bible it is said that the effulgent kingdom of heaven is within you, and that is completely true. One seer says, "O Lord, we see You as pure light that blazes in the form of a flame." The saints in our country have said that one who sees divine lights is supremely blessed. It is that very light that is reflected in the light of the sun, the moon, and the stars.

The other night after chanting the Guru Gita, *I bowed to your picture and felt overwhelmed with yearning for you. As I sat up to meditate, the Blue Pearl appeared. I opened my eyes and it remained. The next night I had a similar experience. Could you speak about this?*

Your vision is very beautiful. The Blue Pearl is in the fourth body and it is in the Self. In the Bible, the Blue Pearl is referred to as a mustard seed. All the great beings experienced the same thing. Keep doing sadhana; there is more to go. However, what you have experienced is very good. To see the Blue Pearl once and to see God once are the same.

I haven't seen the Blue Pearl yet and sometimes I feel that I never will.

It is not difficult to experience the Blue Pearl. Don't feel that you can't. If you couldn't, why would it be dwelling within you? It is only waiting for you to experience it, waiting to reveal its glory and its splendor. Your search will be fulfilled once you have reached it. This divine Pearl is the supreme goal of human life. It represents the ultimate destination of the spiritual path.

Tukaram says that the Blue Pearl is most marvelous. Though it appears to be tiny, it contains the three worlds within it — heaven, hell, and this world. Because of the presence of this Blue Pearl, you are able to feel love for each other and you are worthy of each other's love. The moment this blue radiance leaves you, nobody wants to see you; your body has to be taken away. After the Kundalini has been awakened and has performed its various inner functions, when it has purified the body and reached the sahasrara, and after your mind becomes stabilized there, you will be able to see this Blue Pearl. It is most miraculous.

Just as a piece of iron becomes transmuted into gold when it is touched by the philosopher's stone, similarly when a person experiences the Blue Pearl, his entire being becomes transmuted. He does not experience himself as a perishable being but as divine. The Blue Pearl has such potency that it transforms you completely. It remolds your tendencies, your habits, and it gives you an entirely different state. The scriptures describe this blue light as the light of Consciousness, which is divinely effulgent and dwells within each of us. This blue radiance will put an end to your bondage and make you realize your own perfection, your own Shivahood.

I saw the Blue Pearl a few days ago — just for a moment and then it left.

The Blue Pearl has the highest value. Make your experience of it steady. There are many *yogis* who long for a vision of the Blue Pearl and don't get it.

Should I try to sustain the Blue Pearl?

That is the object of meditation.

Can you use it in dying also? You spoke about that yesterday.

That depends on the worth of a person. In a very evolved person the Blue Pearl will leave through the right eye; in a less evolved person it will leave through the left eye. You don't have to work on the right eye — you have only to meditate, the eye will take care of itself. You need three things: devotion to the Guru, faith in your own Self, and attachment to the Blue Pearl.

Is the Blue Pearl the same as the soul?

Yes, it is the *ātman*. Even though it looks so tiny, it is infinite. When you look at me, you see just a physical form, but my soul is different from what you see. The Blue Pearl is the innermost body of the inner Self, and it is a matter of great fortune to be able to see it. After seeing it, one should be able to penetrate it. For that you should read *Play of Consciousness*.

I've done only one Intensive two years ago, and I'm not truly a meditator — yet I believe I have seen the Blue Pearl. Is this possible?

Absolutely! It is possible. When the Blue Pearl exists inside, what's so surprising? It is right in the center of the head, and it goes out of the eyes and comes in again very quickly. It is exquisite. It is the last of the four bodies. It is the Blue Pearl that lets you travel to different worlds. The Blue Pearl contains the entire universe within it. It seems so tiny; nonetheless, inside it the entire universe is as tiny as that.

Sometimes I see several blue splotches of light about the size of a chickpea, sometimes smaller. I see these both in and out of meditation. What are they?

What you see is very good. It is the Blue Pearl and its real size is that of a sesame seed. Around the Blue Pearl there is a glow. This Pearl is inside you, and sometimes you may see it outside. The saints say that to see it is very fortunate. The *Bhāgavatam* says it is Consciousness, it is the light of God. When a person's impurities have decayed, he sees that Blue Pearl with his very eyes. The goal of every sage is the Blue Pearl. Mostly it dwells in the sahasrara. It goes out through the eye and comes back inside through the eye. Because it is so subtle, the eyes never feel it when it goes in or out. But still the eyes can perceive it.

The sages mentioned this Blue Pearl in their poems but always briefly. Jnaneshwar wrote four *abhangas* about it; Amrit Rai wrote two. They describe the Blue Pearl very briefly, and then they drop the subject. The main purpose of Siddha Yoga Meditation is to see that Pearl. Even though it appears to be a small dot, still, compared with that Pearl this whole world is a mere dot. In meditation, we travel to different worlds through that Blue Pearl; it becomes a vehicle. Tukaram Maharaj said that this small Blue Pearl pervades all the three worlds.

So your experience is very good, and you asked a very good question; it's a happy thing. Now as you meditate and meditate, you should be able to make that Pearl stand in front of you. Then it will grow larger and larger and eventually explode. Whatever you see inside that, whatever understanding you derive there — that is the Truth. The journey of Siddha Yoga culminates there.

During the past year and a half, I have seen only one vision.
It is a tiny, radiant blue light resembling the Blue Pearl you
describe in your writings. I have seen it many times in relaxed
moments in the waking state, while doing japa, chanting, or
thinking of you — but not in meditation. Was it the Blue Pearl
I saw? If so, how could I have seen it before seeing the red, white,
and black lights and experiencing the visions you describe in
Play of Consciousness? *What does this blue light mean?*
Since your arrival, I have begun to see human beings, animals,
the ocean, an auto accident, and other scenes during meditation.

The Blue Pearl is supremely free. Don't think that it can be seen only in meditation; it can be seen out of meditation too. However, it is true that the Blue Pearl is the goal of our meditation. It is good that you are able to see it outside of meditation. It seems that the Blue Pearl is quite fond of you. If you do japa in order to see God sometime in the future, and you happen to see God that very day, what possible objection could you have?

All these visions are quite authentic and you will have many more like these. The deeper you go into yourself, the more of the outer world you will be able to see in meditation. Meditation has such great power. It is nothing extraordinary to be able to see humans, animals, horses, and elephants in meditation. While I was meditating this morning, I saw which person brought which cap. I also saw what brands of chocolate were brought by which people. But I don't attach any importance to this because you can see all those things without even meditating. You can see chocolates by going to a store, so what is the point of meditating to see these things? I like to go to the place beyond all these visions where you see nothing, where there is absolutely nothing to be seen.

The Blue Pearl is free. If it likes, it can reveal itself to you before you see the red, black, and white lights. You cannot control its movements. Suppose somebody is working in a big company and his boss has told him he will be paid a thousand dollars a month. But the boss becomes very pleased with him and gives him a thousand dollars the first day and says, "You don't have to come to work for the rest of the month." You can't prevent the boss from doing him that favor.

This experience is very good; your meditation is going very well. It seems that the Blue Pearl is very pleased with you.

In your autobiography you describe experiences such as seeing the Blue Pearl. If I do not have any of the experiences you describe, does this mean that I am a long way from being realized or does it mean that I am just at the beginning of my sādhanā?

Even if you have not had these experiences yet, one day you will. Your entire body functions due to that Blue Pearl. Without it you cannot function.

In meditation you can literally see it. As you continue to see it, you will start changing, you will be transformed, you will have the knowledge of the future. It is right in the center of the head. It goes out and comes in through the eyes, but the eyes cannot feel it. It is so subtle but so exquisite. It is called *jīvātma*, the individual soul or Consciousness; it is also God. Although it looks so tiny, it is bigger than this universe.

Modern scientists have discovered the laser beam, which is somewhat similar. I met the man who discovered it. He said that the laser beam is so strong, so subtle, and so powerful that it can tear down the biggest wall. However, the Blue Pearl is greater than that. It manifests in meditation. Even if it has not manifested yet, know that it is inside. Have some trust.

Would you give me a technique for expanding my awareness?

Meditate on the inner Self. Along with that you could also study spiritual philosophy. The only knowledge you need is the awareness that the same Consciousness pervades every object. Combine that with meditation. Meditation is essential. Once the inner Shakti awakens, everything else will follow. There is a light which is the size and color of this tiny blue flower, and it dwells right here in the top of the head. You can see this light through meditation.

There are thousands of scriptures in our country, but *Play of Consciousness* is the first book containing a systematic account of spiritual experiences. In the last part of that book I made it very clear that the Shakti comes from a great lineage of Siddhas. Other sages and saints had these experiences but they usually didn't describe them, although Yogananda Paramahamsa describes the blue light and the Blue Pearl in his *Autobiography of a Yogi*. There is quite a bit more that has yet to be revealed.

What usually happens is that after getting a few experiences on the path, people begin to think they have everything. Then they leave sadhana. There are very few who reach the journey's end. Even after I had a vision of the final Truth, I meditated for a long time. If I were to narrate the miracles that followed all those inner experiences, it would fill a thousand volumes. All miracles reside in the experience of the Blue Pearl.

When you were doing your sādhanā, how long did you see the Blue Pearl before it shattered?

I saw the Blue Pearl for three years before it exploded. Once you see the Blue Pearl, it takes at least several years to make friends with it so that it will stand steady in front of you all the time. After it becomes steady, then it explodes. That is called divine realization.

As your sādhanā approached its consummation, you were exhorted to press beyond the Blue Pearl to the Self. What is the relationship of the clear light of the void to the other three bodies of the individual soul?

You don't have to be exhorted to press on. Even if you are exhorted, that's not so very important. What is important is that when you have the final vision of the Blue Pearl, contentment arises in your heart, and that contentment itself urges you forward.

How can the void have any light? Light is beyond the void. The state of the void marks only the third stage of sadhana — the state of sound sleep. But the experience of Consciousness transcends the void, and that is supreme light. When you see that supreme light, it is possible that for a while your eyes may stop seeing, your mind may stop thinking, and your intellect may stop functioning; but when you return to the normal state, they will function normally once again.

The three bodies are related to one another as cause and effect. All three bodies spring forth from the Being which is pure Consciousness, which is beyond all thought. The gross body is supported by the subtle body, the subtle body by the causal body, the causal body by the supracausal body. The supracausal body is supported by the highest Truth, which is without a body.

For a simple analogy, think of an onion: when you begin to peel off its skin, you remove one layer after another and finally, you are left with nothing. Your question was very good.

You spoke of a time when the Shakti penetrated your physical eye. Could you speak about the change in the eye itself as a result of this awakening?

The normal eyes of a human being generally see diversity in objects and people. In the course of our sadhana, a process known as *bindu-bheda* takes place in which the eyes begin to revolve very fast; it is a painful process. Then the eyes obtain the power of seeing within. Your entire perception changes completely and you look at people with a positive attitude all the time.

Then the Blue Pearl comes out of the eye and stands before you. But even that is not the culmination of sadhana. There is something beyond that experience which cannot be described. Only after the vision of the Blue Pearl does one experience that indescribable state. Only then does one develop true witness-consciousness. It is not difficult to become a *jñāni* or a *yogi*, but it is very difficult to have this witness-consciousness all the time. Witness-consciousness means that you see yourself in the same way as you see other things or people. Even while performing all your activities, you continuously remain in witness-consciousness.

A state that is beyond description is not so unusual — even a drug addict or a drunkard gets into that transcendental state for a while. But to have such an experience with complete awareness — there lies the difference. Without awareness anybody can pass through such a state. But when a person gets established in that state with awareness, he never again becomes a slave to the senses. All the senses become his slaves. One who is established in the Self is completely independent because the Self is completely free.

If the mind constantly runs after this or that, wanting this or desiring that, and at the same time you say that the mind is in a transcendental state, you are just talking childish nonsense; you are playing make-believe. A person should acquire complete independence — so much so that in his company other people also have a similar experience of independence.

I do not see the Blue Pearl, but I feel it. What can I do? Please grant me love and devotion to you and bless me that I may become realized in this life.

We are already on the path to realization. Why should you even raise that question? Our journey is directed toward that place.

Within the head is a most brilliant light. Even the light of a million suns cannot compare with it. To see that light is a most important experience. That light is very close to us, and that is why you feel you are about to see it — you *are* about to see it!

You should be able to see me once within that light. See how I look there. I'm also right in the middle of that light.

THE FORM WITHIN THE LIGHT

When I met you in Switzerland, you said that I was halfway to realization. Since then I have meditated regularly, and for the last few weeks my focus of concentration goes spontaneously to the sahasrāra. Sometimes I see a blue light with a yogi seated in it. Sometimes the yogi expands and merges into me. Does this indicate that the Kundalinī has risen to the sahasrāra? If so, how can I stabilize it there?

Keep meditating. You don't have to try to stabilize it; it will become stabilized on its own. The sahasrara is the abode of the Guru, the seat of the Guru, so it is very natural to see a yogi there. The true Guru dwells there; everyone's own Guru dwells there. Even if you receive the grace of the outer Guru, understand that you are receiving the grace of the inner Guru.

This experience does indicate that the Kundalini has risen to the sahasrara. Keep meditating and it will become stabilized there. The Kundalini has risen there to become one, to merge in Shiva, to become Shiva. That is the supreme attainment at the end of sadhana.

I had an experience in which energy came up around my body like fire. It came up to my head, and above my head I saw a figure sitting in the lotus position. Instead of a head this being had light, a very subtle bluish-gold light. What does this mean?

That's a very good experience. Though you didn't see the head now, you may be able to sometime. What you saw was the Guru's form; that is the embodiment of the light within.

About a year ago I awoke in the middle of the night and saw a small, shimmering Blue Being sitting on my pūjā. I got up to close the window and when I returned, it was still there. I became frightened, but soon after I fell asleep. Please tell me why this occurred and what it means.

God is like the Blue Being. If the Blue Pearl becomes pleased with you and stands in front of you, you see the Blue Person within that Pearl. Then he speaks to you. Saints call that the realization of the form. To see even this much is enough for your whole life. It's a fortunate thing; it's very good.

On several occasions I have had an experience where I saw everything around me turn into layers and patterns of light. When I looked around, there was a man standing there, also made of light. He was looking at me and at everything with a beautiful, compassionate look. Who is he and what is the significance of this experience?

This is an experience of true knowledge. The truth is that this whole world is made of light, but we aren't able to see it because of our inner impurities. Otherwise, everything is full of light; everything is nothing but light. It is within light that this house exists; it is within light that factories exist; it is within light that cars and trees exist.

The saints say, "O Lord, You are pure light, You are the divine flame, You are pure knowledge." This has been the experience of all the saints: they see a conscious light all around them. There is soft blue light that keeps shimmering and glowing all the time. It is within this blue light that you and I exist, that everything exists. It is this reality that all the saints realize.

Your experience is part of the experience of the Self. Keep praying to the Lord and you will have more experiences. The person that you see is a sublime Being; He is the supreme Person. Meditate more and you will be able to see many other things.

About three years ago while I was reading one of your books, I started to feel very happy and free. Later I couldn't hear anything. Then I could hear music which came from nowhere. During the night I saw a light in my forehead and then at the back of my head. I felt I was meditating with something supreme. What was happening, and should I try to attain this state again?

Of course you should continue to meditate! What happened to you was very good. Inside everyone lies supreme light. The scriptures say that this light is the effulgence of God. You had His vision, and you are very fortunate. However, you shouldn't give up your own good fortune. Start meditating, and once again you will see the same vision.

Once you start perceiving that light, you will see it everywhere since everything is filled with it. It is only because our eyes are not pure that we don't see that light everywhere. The light we see in a room and think of as light is not really light; compared to the inner light it is nothing but darkness. The true light is the light you perceived. The entire world exists in it. This light scintillates and shimmers everywhere — before you and behind you, above you and below you. Some people are able to see it, and others are not.

The great sage Shivaji said that in this very body exists a self-born, brilliant light, which is nothing but God. Only he is able to see it whose sins are destroyed, whose eyes have become pure.

Sometimes God manifests as that light or in a form made of that light.

Would you please describe your own experience of enlightenment?

After you receive *shaktipāt*, yoga begins to happen within you spontaneously. Through that yoga all the nerves of the body are cleansed and after this purification, you enter that place in the heart where you experience divinity, where you experience the divine light. There you can see things out of the range of normal sight and hear things out of the range of normal hearing. Once you get to that place in the heart, you will want to stay there. Once you live there, you will be able to understand and see through people. You will be able to move through different worlds.

Then the Shakti rises to the chakra in the crown of the head. When your attention travels there, you begin to hear celestial sounds and smell celestial fragrances. Then in the upper spaces you see a most glorious light whose brilliance surpasses even the light of a thousand suns. Such is the greatness of man.

The inner skies are most beautiful. The lights that you see there are colorful and fascinating; and in the middle of those lights is a blue light which we call the Blue Pearl. That is the very life of man, the very center of the universe. Using that Blue Pearl as a vehicle, one is able to travel through this cosmos from one world to another. I have seen heaven and also hell by traveling in the Blue Pearl. After one dies, the soul leaves the body using the Blue Pearl as a vehicle, and it departs to some other world. One day or another, once you have received Guru's grace, that Blue Pearl emerges and stands in front of you. Within the Blue Pearl you have the final vision, the beatific vision, and you receive a message from That.

What is the message?

This is not a question to be answered.

Does knowledge come with that vision?

Yes, knowledge springs from within, and your understanding becomes fully evolved. Supreme divinity dwells within the Blue Pearl.

Does it give you immortality?

Yes. You get everything — immortality, supreme knowledge, supreme bliss, and supreme liberation. That light is the supreme Truth of life. Even though that spot of light is very tiny, it is vaster than the entire cosmos. It is because of that light that the body, the mind, and the intellect function. It is only after seeing that light that your being a yogi is justified — not until then.

Is it the job of a yogi to spread knowledge and Truth?

Yes, it is. That light gives knowledge. Once you reach there, you get to know everything. It is that light that enters the disciple, and then the transmission of Shakti happens. Though you may see me in this body, I live in that place continuously. If I had not seen that place, I would not be here teaching.

I Began to Revel in
that Blue Dot

The more I watched it, the more I loved it. The more I loved
it, the happier I became. I thought I had attained everything.
I began to revel in that Blue Dot. At this point I was very
proud and I went to meet my Guru. He said, "You have a
long way left. Go! Just go! Right now, leave this place."

So I turned away and went back. Once again, I became
absorbed in meditation. I received a lot of understanding
from that Blue Pearl. One day the Blue Pearl came out of
my eyes and it was so active, so fast; within a fraction of a
moment it would go outside, then it would go inside. It was
fascinating! The Yoga Shastra *calls it the embodiment of*
Consciousness, chinmaya.

Finally, there was a day when it came out of my eyes and
it just stood before me. It did not go inside. I kept watching it
and watching it, and I became happier and happier.

As I kept watching it, it began to grow. I saw a Blue
Being appear right in the center of it. Even now, I can't say
whether it was male or female. Just as I am watching you
right now, I watched that Being in meditation very clearly.

It was beautiful. It was right before me — about two
feet away. It began to speak to me. It showed me one of its
legs and said, "I can speak to you through this leg and I can
see you through this leg. I can see you through this hand and
I can also speak to you through this hand." It said a lot more
and I listened to everything. Many of those things I cannot

tell you now. Then it gave up the human form and dissolved into scintillating blue light, and the particles began to pervade the universe. I saw the entire universe in it. I'm still watching it with great joy.

Then it began to contract; it became smaller and smaller and smaller. It became a dot and it entered inside, and once again I was normal. However, I was in bliss. I realized that I was God, that I was the Self — not because it was written in the scriptures, but because I experienced it from within. I became extremely blissful. Then in meditation joy began to spring from every pore of my body.

CHAPTER 22

Merging into the Absolute

*If we look from the highest point of view,
every individual is a fully realized, perfect being.
There is no doubt about that. So it is a question
of awareness, of having a personal experience of this
reality in one's own being.*

*I feel very quiet during meditation, and it seems that repeating
the mantra is a disturbance. Should I do so anyway or should
I remain silent and deepen the silence?*

Deepen your silence. Silence is the goal of mantra. When you
get into that state of silence, that is the truest meditation. In real
meditation, the mind becomes totally still, so when your mind
becomes still and silent, let go of the mantra and just stay there.
That is the highest Consciousness, the state of Truth. The highest meditation is that which does not change, where there is no
agitation, no passion, and no thought. Merge into that. What
remains after you have merged completely into that state is the
Truth. That is the pure Being from whom this entire world has
emerged.

One of the *gopīs*, a lover of Krishna, sang beautifully to her
Lord: "I meditate on You and all my thoughts and feelings dissolve; I am no longer conscious of myself, I am no longer conscious of the outer world. I have only one tiny request to make
of You — that You play Your flute. I would like to hear that

within the total inner stillness." The music of the flute is one form of inner music or *nāda*.

You are in a very good state, and I thank you for being in it.

I want to thank you for your love and your grace, but how can I?

If you truly want to thank me, then keep silence. Love has no speech. Speech lies on the surface, but love lies deep inside. There is a difference of at least eight finger-widths.

I've been asking you my questions during darshan and you have answered them all. What will I do after you leave? Who will answer my questions?

Stop asking questions—you won't need answers! If you don't allow questions to arise from within, you won't need any answers. Then your addiction to asking questions all the time will leave you.

What is solitude?

Solitude is that state in which even the concept of other does not exist. If people go to the mountains but keep thinking about cities, what kind of solitude is that? Solitude is that state in which you are not at all conscious of the existence of another.

Yet there is a still greater solitude, and that is the solitude in which saints dwell. A saint is aware that the supreme Spirit has become everything; it is all-pervasive, it has become man and woman and every other creature. A saint lives in this awareness all the time, no matter whether he is in a market-place or in a club or anywhere else. That is the most solitary of solitudes. It is not a solitude that seekers would be able to dwell in. It is the solitude of the realized ones. A realized being is aware that there is nothing separate from him, nothing apart from him. Whatever there is, is his own Self.

It is only when you are conscious of others as others that you are not in solitude. If you are aware of others as yourself, you are in solitude all the time.

I used to have so many questions, but now it is as if I have become dumb.

It is not that you have become dumb — it is just that the questions have disappeared.

Please speak about the law of divine love that is so much in force here.

If divine love exists here with so much force, why should I talk about it? Love is dumb; it has no tongue to speak with. Love has no speech. As long as there is no love, there is speech. The moment there is divine love, there is no speech. The great sage Narada said, "To talk about love is like a dumb person who has eaten a sweet and tries to describe it." What can he say?

What is the best and most important question to ask one's Guru? And what is the answer?

(*Baba puts a finger over his lips and remains silent for a moment before answering.*) The best question is asked in silence — and the answer is given in silence.

There is a great scriptural and philosophical work called the *Yoga Vāsishtha*. There is no greater book; it is divine. It is huge; it contains thousands of stories and lectures and commentaries. Much of modern science is already written in this book — for instance, the idea that there is energy in every particle of the universe.

In the *Yoga Vāsishtha* the great sage Vasishtha teaches Lord Rama about the ultimate Truth. He answers all of Rama's questions by telling him stories. At the end Rama asks, "Lord, please show me Parabrahman, just as He is."

When the great sage hears the question, he falls silent for a long time. His breath doesn't move; his body doesn't move; his eyes stay closed.

Rama is taken aback. "What happened?" he wonders. "I just asked him a simple question and he has done this. Perhaps my question wasn't right."

As Rama is thinking this, Vasishtha slowly opens his eyes, but still he doesn't say anything.

Rama says, "Lord, can I ask you something again?"

"Yes, yes."

"Did I make a mistake when I asked you that question? Was it unsuitable or unscriptural or improper?"

"No, no. It was a very good question, a true question, the kind of question that should be asked."

"But you didn't say anything. You were completely silent."

"No, no, Rama! I was showing you the answer as it really is. You asked me to show you the nature of the ultimate Truth as it really is. And that's how it is — detached, without speech, beyond the mind, without vibration, without sound, beyond the senses. That is why I became like that. Giving lectures is commonplace, but the reality of the Lord is not commonplace."

Absolute silence is the most perfect lecture, the greatest lecture, and therefore the Guru removes the disciple's doubts through his silent teaching. You read every day in the *Guru Gītā* that God is silence. He is without memory, without thought, without reflection, without outside, without inside, without height, and without depth. When everything has been denied, the Self is all that remains.

To speak about Him and to know Him as He is, is nothing but silence. The Guru's long and silent lecture destroys a disciple's doubts. The best question is silence, and the best answer is silence.

Is it in the power of silence that you begin to know yourself?

The final knowing is silence. When the mind and the intellect merge, when they dissolve — in total stillness free from thought — then you know That.

And when you reach that state, are there no doctrines, no rights, no wrongs?

That is the end. The supreme silence is the final state, the end, nothing more. When you are in that state and you look outside, you know that it is all the same. Then there is love for each other, there is friendliness. Before you reach that state, the color of the world and your own understanding are different. After you perceive that supreme silence, this world looks new to you.

THE RIVER IS NO MORE

Is the goal of life to dissolve in bliss and lose one's identity? Or is it to move toward a more and more subtle identity?

The goal of life is the attainment of Truth. According to the *Katha Upanishad*, it is the cessation of all thoughts and the attainment of bliss. According to the *Bhagavad Gītā*, it is *brahma-nirvāna*, the all-pervasive Brahman attaining Brahman. That is inner unfolding, or you could call it dissolution in highest bliss. That is the goal, and, paradoxically, individuality is dissolved, yet one does not cease to exist.

What do you mean by "inner unfolding"?

In *Play of Consciousness* you must have read a description of the Blue Pearl. The highest goal of life is beyond the Blue Pearl. When we speak of the disembodied state, don't interpret it literally. It means the state in which you transcend body-consciousness. As you grow, your individual identity is dissolved, and it expands to embrace the entire cosmos. Either through meditation or knowledge, you cease to look upon yourself as a limited person and you expand into infinity.

Then what?

That is the supreme Truth. There is nothing beyond supreme Truth.

Does the supreme Truth unfold?

Yes, the supreme Truth unfolds itself in the heart.

In the highest Consciousness, when man is one with God, does he have the powers of God — for instance, to create a universe — or is it just a friendship with God?

It is like a river that is moving toward the sea. When it flows into the sea and becomes one with it, it becomes the same old sea; it does not become a new sea. Just as the river does not stay separate from the sea, when you merge into Consciousness, your individuality disappears, and then whatever you do is the work of Consciousness.

Driving back from the retreat I had the physical sensation that I was the same as the mountains. It was a physical reality, not a mental thing. Will this kind of awareness continue?

Yes, this is how it will grow. You will also grow into the awareness of God everywhere. When your awareness expands like that and you become established in it, that is known as *brahma-bhāva*, or the state of awareness of God.

When one obtains realization, is it for the first time or is it a return to a state once known but temporarily lost?

The latter part of your question is absolutely right. You already had this state, but for a while you forgot it, so once again you return to it. For a very long time you lost this state — more than years — a very long time. As you return to it once again, you realize that you have attained it, and you experience supreme satisfaction. You feel like a person who had been lost in a jungle, but after a long, long time, you found your way again.

Once a person has attained God-realization and no longer has to exist within a physical body, does he continue to have some individual aspect in order to serve God? Does he continue to be God's servant eternally, or does he actually merge with the Absolute and become God?

Once a person's individuality is merged with God, that whole thing is finished. What is left is the feeling of God or Godhood. What happens is that one's individuality is merged into God and he attains cosmic awareness. After that, he can serve other people. Many people have the feeling that once man attains God-realization, he becomes useless. But has God retired? No! He has not retired; He is still functioning. In the same way, a person who has attained God will continue to serve other people. However, the goal will be that he will help other people attain God.

At the end of this search for the Self, do we realize that God is in everything and that everything is perfect?

Yes, that is exactly how it is. Your understanding is very good.

I can see that everything is in its perfect place, so I don't know what is bad or good. Are they both the same thing?

Bad and good become the same when you realize the Truth. At that point everything is the same for you. However, until then a person should follow morality. Your question is a great question. If you ask this question from a small heart and try to understand it, you can't. You have to have a big heart to understand it. In reality, it is we who have chosen good or bad. However, don't misuse these words. With great care, understand them.

A great being said, "What is different from me that I can reject? What is other than me that I can accept?" For a sensible person everything appears the same. Truly, everything is the same. It is like the dollar bills which come from the same printing press.

In some big shops there is a sign that says, "Fixed Rate," meaning you cannot bargain; the price is not less, not more. It is fixed. In reality, that is how everything is in the world. Only Consciousness pervades everywhere. You will know this when you know your own Self.

It appears to me that the final barrier to Truth is the fear that manifests as utter loneliness or the absence of others. When I am ready to receive Truth, it never comes, and when it comes, I scream that I am not ready and it disappears. Can you help me?

This is the delusion of your understanding. If this delusion leaves you, everything will be good. Man has already attained the Truth, he lives with the Truth, the Truth will never leave him. The Truth pervades everywhere and it will never disappear. Change your way of understanding. It seems that you are

515

creating your own world. You say that when you are ready, the Truth does not come. But when the Truth is with you, when the Truth is right there, how can it be that you aren't ready? A person's own thinking, his own cleverness, sometimes becomes his enemy. So don't think about it. The Truth is with you.

What is the bhramara's state of realization, and how can we attain it?

The *bhramara* is a bee that is always absorbed in sucking honey. It is used as an illustration. A bee is always tasting honey; it doesn't like anything but honey. After one is stabilized in realization, he is like that bhramara.

Anyone can have a momentary realization because the Self is already attained; it is always revealed. We are the Self; it is not different from us. So one can have a glimpse of Self-realization; it can last for a moment and one can be Self-realized for that moment. But one should be stabilized in that realization — this is what the bee illustrates. It is always engaged in collecting more and more and more honey, always engaged in tasting the honey. So when one is realized, he should be in that state constantly; there should be no moment when he is not in that state of realization.

When you leave here, I'm so afraid I'll lose my connection with your love.

These programs will come to an end, but the love between you and me will never come to an end. It will always remain alive. It is true that I am inside you and you are inside me. It is also true that I love you a lot and you love me a lot too. Nonetheless, both the loves should merge into each other and only one should exist. This is the attainment. Remember, you belong to me and I belong to you, and we all belong to God. This is the true understanding.

Baba, would you explain how you see the world? Do you see Blue Pearls everywhere? Or one continuous blue field? Or do you see colors and shapes as we see them? Do you see our chakras when you look at us? Please describe this so I can understand what your yogic vision is like since you have merged with the Absolute.

Your question is very beautiful, and your vision is very beautiful too. I see the world as my own Self. You should learn to see the same way. If a person sees everything as his own Self, he truly sees. The *Bhagavad Gītā* says that one who sees the world as his own Self has learned how to see everything. People see everything according to their own worthiness. What is the world? The scriptures say that the world is as you see it. Man sees himself in others. Therefore, have good vision and see only good things.

There is a story from Swami Ram Tirth about somebody famous who built a house of mirrors. A sensible person went inside to look at it. There were thousands of mirrors on the walls. When he entered, he saw his own reflections everywhere; he saw himself as thousands. He said, "How wonderful! Only I exist everywhere." He became very happy to know that only he existed in everything and that he was so many.

Soon afterward, a dog came into the house of mirrors. Right away he saw another dog approaching. He got scared and went to the opposite wall. But there was another dog there. He looked up—and there was another dog. He looked down—there was yet another dog, and he was terrified. Then he began to bark loudly and the dog in the mirror began to bark loudly too. The louder he barked, the louder the dog in the mirror barked. He kept on barking and jumping up and down in a frenzy. Finally he collapsed and died.

In the same way, man has two kinds of vision. Therefore, have good vision so that you can see everybody as your own Self. Shaivism says to fill your eyes with the knowledge of Shiva. Then you will see only Shiva everywhere.

I don't have to look at your chakras. When you come before me, your chakras are very apparent. They reveal themselves in your eyes, in your speech, and through your actions. I can tell who you are. So naturally, they appear before me.

To yogic vision the world appears as a blue radiance. Say that forty people are swimming in the ocean; you see all these people as part of the blue ocean. In the same way, for a *yogi* the world appears as the blue radiance.

Meditate more, unfold the inner Shakti, and then you will see the same thing.

I Attained My Own Divinity

What accomplishment would most satisfy you?

I have already attained what I wanted. I don't want to attain anything more. What I wanted to attain, I did — from my Guru. I will live for the rest of my allotted time. And as long as I live, I will continue to help people. I don't want anything else.

What did you achieve from your Guru?

I obtained the inner power and the knowledge of my own Self. I understood the ways of the world. I assimilated the true disciplines of the world. I also learned from him how to help other people. The main thing I attained from my Guru was my own inner Self; I attained my own divinity.

And you didn't have that before?

I wasn't like that before; I was just like every layman in this world.

Really?

Yes, before meeting the Guru.

So it happened to you, and you do the same thing for other people?

Yes, I reveal to people what I attained from my Guru.

Do you still feel that the Guru is with you?

Yes. In the form of the Shakti the Guru enters the disciple and remains with him as long as his life continues.

Is this your greatest accomplishment — this achieving of Oneness?

That is the highest goal — to become one with the Self.

CHAPTER 23

Being a Siddha

*To become an enlightened being is this—to live
with people, to be with people, and at the same time to
be in your own ecstasy, knowing that everything
is Consciousness.*

*Are there times when you are happier than other times? When
are you the happiest? When you are doing your work?*

I am happy doing my work and I am happy not doing my work,
because for me there is no relationship between work and happiness. Happiness is different from these things. A person who
is happy naturally is happy when he is doing work and when
he is not doing work. He is happy when he is living; he will be
happy when he dies. He is just happy.

*Are all fully realized beings Gurus? Does one have to become a
Guru in order not to be born again?*

Not all fully realized beings are Gurus. Some become Gurus,
and some remain in themselves. However, even they carry out
their mission through one person or another. Even though the
inner state is the same for all realized beings, their outer actions
differ. According to their destiny and austerities, their outer
conditions are different. Still, people respect them as Gurus.

There on the wall are pictures of four great beings—Sai
Baba of Shirdi, Zipruanna, Hari Giri Baba, and Akkalkot
Swami. Hari Giri Baba and Akkalkot Swami did not instruct

anybody — still they had divine Guruhood. Every great being's destiny is different. Some may appear inert, some may appear intoxicated, yet they are all absorbed in supreme Consciousness. They act according to their destiny, but their inner state, their perfection, is complete.

Bhartrihari was a great poet-saint who said, "You find some beings for whom the earth is their bed." Zipruanna was such a being. "Some beings become maharajas, even greater than kings, and some beings become very tender." Sai Baba was very tender. "Some beings become very serene and tranquil." All these beings were serene. "Some beings remain lying down like pythons." They couldn't have cared less about the world; they were totally immersed in inner Consciousness.

Now don't feel that you have to stop your *sādhanā* because you don't want to reach this state. I'm telling you, not all of you will attain these states, so don't get scared.

So you do not have to become a Guru in order not to be born again. However, you do have to realize the inner Self. The true cause of birth and death is nothing but ignorance, nothing but lack of understanding of your own Self. The knowledge of the Self frees you from birth and death.

Is there a chance of becoming a perfect being like you?

There is a perfect chance of your becoming a perfect being. Why should there be a partial chance? There is a total chance.

And then what happens?

Well, that is the place beyond questions and answers; that is the very end of the journey, the culminating point. There everything merges into perfection and completeness, and that is what is called supreme peace. Anyone who reaches this place becomes aware that he can't go any further, and so he rests calmly there.

What did you feel when you found that place of perfection?

I felt supreme peace. There are so many things along the road, but the final goal is supreme peace, centering in the inner peace. In that place all desires cease, and one acquires the ability to function in the world without being subject to agitation.

Of all the things I've read about yogis, it seems they all have been pure beings right from the beginning. I was wondering if you knew of anybody who started out on the wrong foot.

Many, many of them. Some were great thieves or bandits. In the course of their lives they would come across some great saint and give up banditry and become a great yogi. There have been prostitutes of absolutely irresistible charm. One such prostitute tried to initiate a Siddha, but so great was the power of the Siddha that instead of her initiating him, he initiated her. There was one fellow who was a murderer, who did not kill bad and fallen people, but would pick out good people to kill. He once set out to murder a Siddha, but he was so powerfully affected by him that he became godly.

There have been many saints of this category. When you become bored, when you begin to feel sick of sense pleasures, when you become disgusted with your ways, then you repent. In that single moment of repentance, you become pure. Devotion to God burns up all your *karmas*. Even if the conduct of a person has been very, very bad, very, very wicked, if he becomes a devotee of God, his devotion burns up all that evil.

You should not nurse the memory of earlier bad deeds while meditating — or you drain a meditation temple, you drain your life.

I understand that you have reached the state of nirvāna and I would like to know if this is something you spent your whole life working at, or is it something that just happened one day without any effort on your part?

The state of nirvana I have attained is within everyone. Many years of my life were spent in quest of it. People spend many, many years — even lifetimes — in their quest, practicing different techniques, yet nothing comes into their hands. However, if you could find a being like Bhagawan Nityananda, whose picture you see here, and if you could obtain his grace, through his mere touch you could have a direct personal experience of that state in an instant.

When everyone becomes realized, will the earth continue?

The earth will acquire new youth; it will become young again. Its burden will be lighter, and it will dance and shed light. In any case, don't worry about it. If you can, you should work in a way that helps everybody become realized. There is great innocence in this question.

What is the experience of a realized being? Does he experience the Self without attributes and qualities? Or does he continue to experience dazzling colors and blue lights even after attaining realization?

The experience of a realized being is the true vision, the real vision of God. The final realization of God has no attributes, no forms, and no colors. Once you reach that state, the mind is finished; the mind no longer exists to see differences. The mind makes no distinctions about red, white, black, or yellow. Experiences and visions occur on the road to realization. Realization itself has no speech. The *Bhagavad Gītā* says that the experience of realization is beyond all senses. It is beyond speech; words cannot catch it. It has no shadow, no shape, and no gender.

When salt falls into the ocean and merges there, it loses its individuality, its solidity, its existence. It becomes one with the ocean, it becomes absorbed in the ocean. In the same way, the final experience is like that. A saint said, "When I perceived the holy and divine manifestation of God, I lost myself completely in Him; I do not know myself any longer."

The *Gītā* says that only the intellect that has been purified can perceive That, can experience That. The final experience is the surge of inner bliss, the surge of inner love. There are many different experiences, but this is the final one — the experience that the *ātman*, the Self, is without attributes and without qualities. It is supremely pure. The *Gītā* says that even though it lives in this body, still it doesn't get involved in the *dharma* of this body. The Self is filled with knowledge; it is filled with perfection. If anybody imposes attributes on the Self, he lacks understanding.

A knower of the Truth has explained knowledge in two ways— *savikalpa* and *nirvikalpa*. Nirvikalpa is a state beyond imagination, beyond all thought. In savikalpa, a yogi experiences the Self as dazzling lights, as dazzling colors. In the nirvikalpa state, there is no longer a seer and therefore there is nothing to be seen.

Even after becoming realized, a Siddha will continue to experience moments when he is not in that state completely. When he is slightly out of that state, when certain tendencies still exist, he will experience these colors and lights. When he goes beyond all these inner tendencies, he will no longer experience such things.

In the state of full realization are you omnipresent, aware of everything in the universe all the time? Or are you in the state of awareness that is only conscious of the body you are occupying and your immediate surroundings? If you have the experience of omnipresence, is it possible to maintain it while walking and talking as well as while formally meditating?

When you dream, after you wake up, you know what dreams you had. They are not true knowledge; you still lack true knowledge. When you attain the state of God, then you become aware of everything. You lose yourself completely, you don't hold yourself back. A great saint said, "If a person holds himself back, if he is still aware of his individuality, he is not completely absorbed in the state of God. The river water that merges into the ocean is no longer aware that it is river water."

If I want to know what is happening in the universe, I can know. But why should I bother? The state of God is such that you are always aware that you are everything. The state of God does not want just to keep looking outside at mundane life; it transcends mundane life. Mundane activities exist only right here, but the state of God is completely beyond these things. What makes you think that I should see the same things in meditation that I see at other times?

Now we are watching Melbourne people, Melbourne buildings, flowers, and airplanes. Should I see the same thing in my meditation as in my waking state? The state of God is nothing but the state of God; no mundane activities exist there. When you lose yourself completely in Consciousness, when you know where and who you are, only then do you attain the perfect state of God.

The other day in Sydney there was a big robbery. If I had wanted to and if I had tried, maybe I could have seen that event in my meditation, but I can see it just as easily on television.

How is it that an enlightened being has an individual personality while also being beyond the mind and one with God?

Even after attaining That, an enlightened being still has an individual personality. However, his understanding changes. Before he becomes enlightened, he has the awareness that he is his body, that he belongs to a certain country, a certain caste, and is of a certain color. Because of the awareness of this body, he feels that he is a father, a son, or something else. With this awareness, he leads his life.

Once he attains the realization of the Self, his understanding changes. He experiences himself as something different from this body: he experiences himself as Consciousness. A person who is sleeping feels that he is different from this gross physical body. In the same way, through knowledge, meditation, and the realization of the Self, an enlightened being's understanding changes; his pain and pleasure also change. This very world becomes new for him.

Even though we are inside this ashram, still we experience that we are different from this ashram. In the same way, even though an enlightened being lives in a body, even though he still has a personality, still he is different from the body and the personality.

Since your mind is still, even amidst action, what is your relationship to the play that goes on? Do you feel like a spectator, an actor, or what?

This entire world is nothing but a play. Shaivism says that the Self is a great actor. Everybody has taken a different part, a different role, so I also play a part. Even though I live amidst people, even though I am right in the center of all the activities that go on, I don't get involved or trapped in the awareness of doing any actions. Because they happen, they are supposed to happen.

If a person conquers his senses and becomes established in his own inner Self with great serenity, he becomes the witness. He becomes the spectator. No matter what happens, he just watches everything. He is not bothered by the pairs of opposites such as heat and cold, pain and pleasure, honor and insult. Man should learn how to live with the awareness of being a witness. Even though I did so much work this morning, I am still in a serene state. This morning there was the finale of the *saptah* and the weddings, and now I am meeting you all. But I don't absorb in my mind the feeling of any action.

Once Lord Buddha gave initiation to a certain man. His family didn't like it so they went to Lord Buddha and abused him. They used many, many abusive terms. Even though they used so many swear words, still Lord Buddha listened to them very quietly because he was a great being. After they finished abusing him, they were tired, so he asked them to sit down for a while.

He said, "If you invite guests to your house, wouldn't you cook delicious dishes?"

"Of course, if we invite guests, we would cook delicious food," they said.

"And if the guests don't eat it?" asked Buddha.

They said, "If the guests don't eat the dishes we have cooked for them, then after they leave, we eat them."

"Very good," he said. "Now, you have used so many abusive terms and I haven't eaten a single one of them. What will you do with them?"

So when you perform a particular action, do not absorb the feeling of that action. I have no relationship with what goes on. It is supposed to happen, so it happens. I am just the witness. An actor plays a part and he cries and cries. But does he really cry? No, he is just playing his role. Man should live his life in the same way.

*Can we live permanently in the state of samādhi, even in our
daily lives, or is it just a temporary state?*

If your practice has been good, you can stay in the state of
samadhi even while functioning in the world. Samadhi does
not mean to close your eyes and become like a lump of wood,
like a dead log. Samadhi means that your mind becomes centered in unity-awareness, and it treats pleasure and pain alike.
A being who is in the state of samadhi does not get tormented
when surrounded by sorrow; he does not get elated when surrounded by joy. If anybody speaks ill of him, he does not get
hurt, and if anybody praises him, he does not start jumping up
and down with excitement.

*Yesterday you said that only a few can maintain the state of
sahaja samādhi. What is the criterion for a person who can
maintain that state? Is it a genetic trait or could it be a matter
of lifestyle?*

In a certain sense it is genetic, because for sahaja samadhi you
have to prepare yourself through a number of lifetimes. It is
extraordinary to become anchored in that state in which there
is no sense of differences, in which you are not subject to any
agitation or change. Even if such a being were to open his eyes
and see things, his samadhi would not be interrupted. And if
he were to close his eyes, his samadhi would not be enhanced.
If he were to speak, the silence of his mind would not be broken. If he were to become silent, he would not be observing a
vow of silence any more strictly. Such a being, though living in
the body, lives apart from it.

The scriptures describe this state as witness-consciousness.
Such a being may appear to be in a body but there is no sense
of body in him. This is the very final attainment of meditation.
In the states of waking, dream, and deep sleep, there is still some
awareness of phenomena, but in that state there is no such
awareness. It is a very, very high state of sadhana. It is also called
the state of steady wisdom — the state in which your intelligence becomes so firmly anchored in unity that all the apparent

diversity of the world cannot disrupt that sense of unity.

Would you kindly explain the meaning of lokanandah
samadhi sukham?

This is one of the sutras from Shaivism. Lord Shankara Himself
with His trident inscribed this sutra on a rock. As a person turns
inward, as he continues his sadhana, he attains his own joy. It
is absolutely certain that the Self is filled with bliss. It is only
because a person turns outside that he is far from joy. Once he
turns inward and attains that bliss, then when he turns outward again, he feels the same bliss in everybody. As he perceives people with the awareness that they are also filled with
bliss, he attains the bliss of samadhi. With whatever feeling
man perceives others, the same feeling arises within him too.
Therefore, man's vision is his own creation.

It is said that the world is as you see it. There is no other
world; it all depends on attitude. An enlightened being perceives the same bliss within everybody that he has attained
within himself. In that way, he enjoys the bliss of samadhi and
he doesn't have to meditate in a new way. A saint of Maharashtra said, "The root of supreme bliss is shining within
everybody," and this is absolutely true. My Babaji always used
to say, "Everything is Brahman. All this is the Absolute." He
had this experience and this understanding.

In the *Shiva Sūtras,* Lord Sadashiva has explained the characteristics of a yogi and also the kind of bliss that he experiences in his samadhi. Such a yogi does not have to run away
from people; he does not have to lock himself inside a room
and close his eyes and turn off all the lights. He enjoys the bliss
of samadhi just by perceiving others. We should feel happy seeing people. Our hearts should not hate others when we see
them. If a person becomes dejected or disturbed by seeing others, understand that he has some kind of mental problem and
he hasn't attained the Truth. So when a being attains That, he
perceives that everyone has this joy and he enjoys the bliss of
samadhi when he sees people.

Do enlightened beings need to go into solitude?

If an enlightened being needed to go into solitude, what kind of realization would that be? In order to attain enlightenment you might go into solitude to meditate for a while. But you can become enlightened wherever you are, and once you reach that state, you are an enlightened being. For enlightened beings every place is a solitary place.

If one has attained divine realization, why would he have to go away from people? Why would he have to get angry with people? Enlightened beings give up their caves and their mountains and they come and live with people. My Baba did his sadhana in secret places, very privately, but after he had become perfect, he came out and began to live among people.

There are many saints, and once their delusions leave them, they don't have to search for solitude. All they see is solitude everywhere; they don't see mere people. A realized being once said, "My feelings of rejection and possession have left me, and I have attained unity-awareness. I see equality everywhere. I see only Consciousness everywhere." This is the understanding you attain once you become realized.

What makes you think that realization is for getting angry with people? What makes you think that to become realized is to hate people and run away and lock yourself in a room? No! To become an enlightened being is this — to live with people, to be with people, and at the same time to be in your own ecstasy, knowing that everything is Consciousness.

As long as you have this sense of duality, you are a great fool, and if you consider yourself an enlightened being, you are nothing but a greater fool. The Vedas say that when you have this sense of duality, when you see diversities, when you think you are different from people, then you have this fear. That is why you might want to chase after solitude. But sainthood isn't like this.

In Indian mythology there is a story about a mythological eggplant. During a certain season called *shrāvana māsa,* the priests tell the people stories of God from the Puranas.

Every day a father and his son would go there to listen to

these stories. One day the priest said, "It is very bad for a Vaishnavite — a worshiper of Vishnu — to eat an eggplant in this season. It makes you completely impure and you go to hell."

After the story was over, the father and the son went home. Now the wife had cooked eggplant that day. She had fried it in oil, and it was very tasty. They were eating the eggplant when the boy suddenly remembered what the storyteller had said, and he cried, "O Father, don't you remember what we heard today? If you eat an eggplant in this season, you go to hell!"

The father said, "What are you talking about? That was a mythological eggplant — not a real eggplant! The priest wasn't talking about what we're eating right now!"

So if you are mythologically enlightened, if you have mythological solitude, if you have mythological unity-awareness, and if you have mythological equality-awareness, they don't make any sense. All these things should be practiced; they should be active. Mythological enlightenment is of no use. It must be real.

I called my home in Kansas City last night and my five-year-old daughter told me that she had a dream in which she was Muktananda, and Muktananda was her. Could you tell me what that means?

That's very good — that's how it really is.

The Greatest Sadhana

*There are many sadhanas, but there is also a final sadhana.
The best and greatest sadhana is to worship the lord of prana.
Prana is the highest deity, the vital force of the universe.
Everything is under its control. If the lord of prana is even
a bit angry, everything is finished. In that recent typhoon
in Andhra Pradesh, the prana was so angry that everything
was demolished there.*

*Shaivism says that the universal Consciousness, which
is nothing but God, is inside you in the form of prana, which
constantly comes in and goes out. When the incoming breath
and the outgoing breath become balanced and equal, that is
when you have God's darshan.*

*As long as you don't attain equality, you don't attain
anything except dissatisfaction. So one should worship the
lord of prana. How can you worship the prana so that it will
become pleased with you? The greatest worship is to have
the perpetual awareness that when the prana comes in and
goes out, it is uttering the mantra* Hamsa. *To understand
the repetition of the mantra is to worship the lord of prana.
When the prana becomes quiet, you begin to experience joy.
So combine your mind with the lord of prana to worship him.*

*The coming and going of the mantra has existed since
the beginning of the universe. It is beginningless; it doesn't
depend on any language or any country.* Ham *merges into
the Self, which is formless, pure, and conscious. Afterward,
it once again arises and goes out with the sound* sa. *You can*

watch it. When sa *goes out, it also merges. It doesn't retain its form.* Ham *merges into the inner Consciousness and* sa *merges into the outer Consciousness. The same Consciousness pervades both inside and outside. This is the wisdom of the Guru. Understand this. When* ham *merges inside and when* sa *merges outside, there is a thought-free state before any positive or negative thought arises.*

That is the true state — that is God. It is inside you and you have already attained it. It is not that I make you attain something.

Put forth self-effort to enhance this continual awareness. Without self-effort, you cannot attain anything. Don't worry about not attaining That because you can. Don't be afraid of your downfall because you can also rise up again. Don't worry if you are not happy because you can become happy. Do sadhana very privately because if it remains private, it will flourish abundantly. True sadhana is the awareness of Hamsa. *Gradually* ham *merges and the state of formlessness manifests. That is the state of samadhi. When* sa *merges outside, that is the outward state of samadhi. It will keep growing. As it grows more and more, you will obtain the knack of being able to stay established in that state for a long time. That is attainment.*

Get rid of your ignorant understanding, which is bondage, which is infatuation. Shaivism says that knowledge is bondage. What knowledge? The knowledge we have that is opposed to the Self. The moment you discard your wrong understanding, you start worshiping the inner Self with the awareness "I am That." This is exalted worship and this is sadhana. This is the goal of meditation. Everything is this unbroken awareness.

So become established in this awareness. When you are coming or going, walking or sitting quietly, focus your attention on the lord of prana. See how the prana comes in and goes out. Through repetition of the mantra, the lord of prana becomes pleased. Don't consider it mere prana because it is a deity; it is the Lord. Prana is the universal Consciousness. It is your understanding which is like the devil. Get rid of it. No matter where you go, the devil of wrong understanding is standing before you. He will see to it that you have his darshan rather than that of your own Self.

Have this understanding: prana dances and plays by itself, going out and coming in with the maha mantra, the great mantra. Lose yourself in the play of prana and dance in that. Don't dance pursuing the senses but dance pursuing God. In that way this whole world is the play of God. You too should dance in His play. Become the bubbles and waves in the ocean of love. Then see if joy and peace are far away from you or if God is different from you.

EPILOGUE

Now my time for answering your questions is over. Maybe some of the questions were not answered. Even if they were not, it does not matter, because questions are questions. The supreme Truth, which dwells within you, is completely detached from all your questions.

Let me tell you this: when any question arises in your mind, know that it is just a question. And when another question arises, know that you are the Self and it is just a question — and it will be answered.

Then yet another question will come up, and you should say to it: "You are a question and I am the Self!"

GLOSSARY

Abhanga
A devotional song in the Marathi language, expressing longing for God.

Abhinivesha
False identification of the Self with the body or the mind; the instinct to cling to worldly life and the fear of non-existence after death.

Abhisheka
A ritual bath given as part of a *pūjā* to a deity or an idol.

Absolute
The highest Reality; supreme Consciousness; the pure, untainted, changeless Truth.

Advaita Vedanta
The philosophy of absolute nondualism. *See also* Shankaracharya.

Aham
(*lit.* I) The pure inner Self; absolute I; the experiencing subject; I-consciousness.

Aham Brahmāsmi
One of the four great statements of Vedanta; it means "I am Brahman," the supreme Absolute. *See also* Mahāvākya.

Ajapā-japa
The natural, involuntary, and effortless repetition of the *mantra* that goes on within every living creature in the form of the incoming and outgoing breath; repetitive prayer. *See also* Hamsa.

Ājñā Chakra
A center of consciousness located between the eyebrows, sometimes called the third eye; the seat of the Guru. *See also* Chakra.

Ākāsha
(*lit.* space) The inner ether; the first of the five elements (ether, air, fire, water, and earth) which constitute the universe; a substance subtler than air.

Anāhata Nāda
The "unstruck" sound heard in meditation; the inner divine melody. *See also* Nāda.

Anandamayi Ma
(1896-1982) A great woman saint

who lived in Hardwar, a town on the bank of the Ganges. Thousands of Indians venerate her as an embodiment of the Divine Mother.

Anāsakti Yoga
The *yoga* of non-attachment, of desirelessness.

Apāna
Inhalation; one of the five types of *prāna;* downward moving energy which controls the abdomen and excretion of wastes from the body. *See also* Prāna.

Āratī
A ritual act of worship during which a flame, symbolic of the individual soul, is waved before the form of a deity, sacred being, or image that embodies the divine light of Consciousness. Arati is preceded by the sound of bells, conches, and drums, and accompanied by the singing of a prayer.

Arjuna
Third of the five Pandava brothers and one of the heros of the *Mahābhārata,* considered to be the greatest warrior of all. He was the friend and devotee of Lord Krishna. It was to Arjuna that the Lord revealed the knowledge of the *Bhagavad Gītā.*

Āsana
1) A *hatha yoga* posture practiced to strengthen the body, purify the nervous system, and develop one-pointedness of mind; the *yoga* texts refer to eighty-four major *āsanas.* 2) A seat or mat on which one sits for meditation.

Āshram
(*lit.* a place that removes the fatigue of worldliness) The abode of a Guru or saint; a monastic place of retreat where seekers engage in spiritual practices and study the teachings of yoga.

Ashtānga Yoga or Rāja Yoga
(*lit.* eight limbs of *yoga*) Eight stages of *yoga* described by Patanjali in his *Yoga Sūtras,* the authoritative text on *rāja yoga.* The eight stages are self-restraint, daily practices, steady posture, breath control, sense withdrawal, concentration, meditation, union with the Absolute. *See also* Patanjali; Yoga Sūtras.

Ātman
Divine consciousness residing in the individual; the supreme Self; the soul. *See also* Aham Brahmāsmi; Sat chit ānanda.

Avadhūt
An enlightened being who lives in a state beyond body-consciousness and whose behavior is not bound by ordinary social conventions.

Avidyā
(*lit.* ignorance) Wrong knowledge; failure to apprehend the unity behind all manifestations of nature.

Baba, Babaji
(*lit.* father) A term of affection and respect for a saint, a holy man, or a father.

Bhagavad Gītā
(*lit.* Song of the Lord) One of the world's greatest works of spiritual literature, part of the epic *Mahābhārata*. In the *Gītā*, Lord Krishna explains the path of liberation to Arjuna on the battlefield, as they wait for the fighting to begin. *See also* Mahābhārata.

Bhagawān
(*lit.* the Lord) One who is glorious, illustrious, and venerable. A term of great honor. Baba Muktananda's Guru is known as Bhagawan Nityananda. *See also* Nityananda, Bhagawan.

Bhajan
A devotional song in praise of God.

Bhajia
An Indian snack; a spicy, fried vegetable dish.

Bhakti
Devotion.

Bhakti Yoga
The *yoga* of devotion; a path to union with the Divine based on the continual offering of love to God and the constant remembrance of the Lord. *See also* Narada.

Bhartrihari
(5th. century A.D.) A philoso-

pher and royal poet who renounced his kingdom to become a *yogi*; the author of many spiritual poems.

Bhāva
(*lit.* becoming, being) Attitude; emotional state; a feeling of absorption or identification, which becomes action.

Bhīmeshwar Lingam
A *shivalinga* that is worshiped in the Shiva, or Bhimeshwar, Temple in Ganeshpuri. *See also* Lingam

Bindu
(*lit.* a dot, a point) *See* Blue Pearl.

Bindu-Bheda
A *kriyā* of the eyes; a subtle piercing of the eyeballs after which one begins to perceive the Blue Light vibrating everywhere; the purification of the eyes.

Bistami, Hazrit Bayazid or Abu Yazid Al-Bistami
(d. 875) An ecstatic Sufi saint of the Naqshbandi Order who lived in seclusion at Bistam in northeastern Persia. His many poems boldly portray the mystic's total absorption in God.

Black Light
See Four Lights.

Blue Light
See Four Lights.

Blue Pearl
A brilliant blue light, the size of

a tiny seed, which appears to the meditator whose energy has been awakened. The *bindu* is the subtle abode of the inner Self. *See also* Four Lights.

Blue Person
The form that exists within the Blue Pearl; the Lord who grants the final vision.

Brahma
The supreme Lord in Vedic terminology; in the Hindu trinity of Brahma, Vishnu, and Shiva, the aspect of God as creator of the universe. *See also* Shiva; Vishnu.

Brahmabhāva
Identification with the all-pervasive Reality.

Brahmajñānī
One who has realized the ultimate Truth by following the path of reason and discrimination.

Brahmāloka
(*lit.* the world of Brahma) The highest heaven; the world of supreme joy. Those who reach this *loka* after death are beyond rebirth.

Brahman
(*lit.* expansion; swelling of spirit) Vedantic term for the absolute Reality. *See also* Sat chit ānanda.

Brahmānanda
The root of all happiness; the bliss of Brahman, the bliss of the Absolute.

Brahmanirvāna
Resting in a state of pure spiritual wisdom, devoid of activity and free from *karma*; the attainment of the all-pervasive Brahman; dissolution in the highest bliss.

Brahmanishtha
One who is firmly established in the Supreme Being, in Brahman, the absolute Reality.

Brihadarānyaka Upanishad
An important Upanishad, which teaches the identity of the individual and universal Self, gives instructions on worship and meditation, and describes the steps of *sādhanā* according to the philosophy of Vedanta. *See also* Upanishads; Vedanta.

Buddhi
The intellect. *See also* Chitta.

Causal Body
One of the supraphysical bodies; the state of deep sleep occurs here. This body is black in color and the size of a fingertip. *See also* Four Bodies.

Chakra
(*lit.* wheel) A subtle energy center, or nerve plexus, located in the subtle body. There are seven major *chakras*: *mūlādhāra, svādhishthāna, manipūra, anāhata, vishuddha, ājñā,* and *sahasrāra.* When it is awakened, the *kundalinī* flows upward from the *mūlādhāra* at the base of the spine to the *sahasrāra* at the crown of the head. *See also* Kundalinī.

Chapāti
Unleavened Indian bread which resembles a thin pancake.

Chidākāsha
The subtle space of Consciousness in the *sahasrāra* and in the heart.

Chinmaya
The embodiment of Consciousness; full of Consciousness.

Chiti
Divine conscious energy; the creative aspect of God.

Chitta
The mind.

Consciousness
The intelligent, supremely independent divine Energy that creates, pervades, and supports everything in the cosmos. *See also* Sat chit ānanda.

Dāl
Split legumes of many varieties used as a staple in Indian cooking.

Darshan
(*lit.* viewing) Being in the presence of a holy being; seeing God or an image of God.

Devi
(*lit.* resplendent) The great Mother Goddess; Shiva's consort who represents Shakti or cosmic energy. In Her benign form, the Devi is known as Parvati; in Her fierce aspect She is known as Durga and Kali. *See also* Durga; Kali; Parvati; Shakti; Vajreshwari.

Dharma
Essential duty; the law of righteousness; living in accordance with the divine Will. The highest dharma is to recognize the truth in one's own heart.

Dho'l-Nun
A 9th-century Sufi saint and poet.

Dhoop
Incense made from herbs, plants, and flowers which is burned as an offering in worship.

Dhyāna Yoga
Meditation; the seventh stage of *yoga* described by Patanjali in the *Yoga Sūtras. See also* Yoga Sūtras.

Durga
(*lit.* hard to conquer) The fierce aspect of the universal Shakti. She is often depicted as an eight-armed goddess who rides a tiger and carries weapons. The destroyer of evil tendencies. *See also* Devi.

Dwaraka
One of the principal holy places in India; an ancient town which was the capital of Krishna's kingdom. Located on the west coast of India, Dwaraka is today the site of a famous Krishna shrine and a place of pilgrimage.

Ego
In yoga, the limited sense of "I" that is identified with the body, mind, and senses; sometimes

described as "the veil of suffering."

Eknath Maharaj
(1528-1609) A householder poet-saint of Maharashtra, the author of several hundred *abhangas*, who was expelled from the *brāhmin* caste because of his attempts to banish untouchability. By writing on religious subjects in the popular vernacular, Eknath ushered in a spiritual revival among the people. *See also* Abhanga.

Enlightenment
The final attainment on the spiritual path, when the limited sense of "I" merges into supreme Consciousness. *See also* Liberation.

Four Bodies
The physical, subtle, causal, and supracausal bodies which are experienced respectively in the states of waking, dream, deep sleep, and *samādhi*. *See also* Blue Pearl; Turīya.

Four Lights
The red, white, black, and blue lights associated with each of the four bodies and experienced respectively in the physical, subtle, causal, and supracausal bodies.

Ganeshpuri
A village at the foot of Mandagni Mountain in Maharashtra, India. Bhagawan Nityananda settled in this region where *yogis* have performed spiritual practices for thousands of years. Gurudev Siddha Peeth, the *āshram* founded by Baba Muktananda at

his Guru's command, is built on this sacred land. The samadhi shrines of Bhagawan Nityananda in Ganeshpuri and of Swami Muktananda at Gurudev Siddha Peeth attract many thousands of pilgrims.

Ganges
The most sacred river in India, the Ganges is said to originate in heaven. On earth, it flows down from the Himalayas across all of North India to the Bay of Bengal. It is believed that whoever bathes in the Ganges is purified of all sins.

Gāyatrī Mantra
A sacred verse from the Vedas; a hymn to the sun which is recited by *brāhmins* at dawn and at twilight.

Ghee
Clarified butter used in Indian cooking and in worship.

Gopala or Govinda
(*lit.* master of the cows) Lord of the senses and the mind. In the *Bhagavad Gītā*, an epithet of young Krishna.

Gopīs
The milkmaids of Vrindavan, who were the companions and devotees of Lord Krishna. The *gopīs'* devotion to Krishna was so complete that they saw Him in everyone and everything.

Gunas
The three basic qualities of nature which determine the inherent

characteristics of all created things. They are *sattva* (purity, light, harmony, intelligence); *rajas* (activity, passion); *tamas* (dullness, inertia, ignorance).

Guru
(*lit. gu*, darkness; *ru*, light) A spiritual Master who has attained oneness with God and who is therefore able both to initiate seekers and to guide them on the spiritual path to liberation. A Guru is also required to be learned in the scriptures and must belong to a lineage of Masters. *See also* Shaktipāt; Siddha.

Guru Gītā
(*lit.* Song of the Guru) An ancient Sanskrit text; a garland of *mantras* that describe the nature of the Guru, the Guru-disciple relationship, and meditation on the Guru. In Siddha Yoga ashrams the *Guru Gītā* is chanted every morning. *See also* Guru; Swādhyāya.

Guru Om
The *mantra* by which the inner Self is remembered in the form of the Guru.

Gurubhakti
Devotion and love for the Guru.

Gurubhāva
Identification with the Guru. *See also* Bhāva.

Gurudev
(*lit.* divine Guru) A traditional term of address and reverence, which signifies the Guru as an embodiment of God.

Guruji
A respectful and affectionate term of address for the Guru.

Gurumayi
(*lit.* one who is absorbed in the Guru) A Marathi term of respect and endearment used in addressing Swami Chidvilasananda.

Gurusevā
Service to the Guru. *See also* Sevā.

Hamsa
(*lit.* I am That) The natural vibration of the Self, which occurs spontaneously with each incoming and outgoing breath. By becoming aware of *Hamsa*, a seeker experiences the identity between his individual self and the supreme Self. Also repeated as *So'ham. See also* Ajapa-japa.

Hanuman
(*lit.* heavy-jawed) A deity in the form of a huge, white monkey who is one of the heros of the *Rāmāyana.* Hanuman's unparalleled strength was exceeded only by his perfect devotion to Lord Rama, for whom he performed many acts of bravery and daring.

Hari
The one who stills the fluctuations of the mind; the aspect of the Lord which takes away shortcomings and attachment to worldliness; a name for Lord Vishnu.

Hari Giri Baba
A Siddha from Vaijapur, Maharashtra, who bestowed great love and affection on Swami Muktananda during his *sādhanā*.

Hatha Yoga
Yogic practices, both physical and mental, done for the purpose of purifying the physical and subtle bodies. The goal of *hatha yoga* is to awaken the inner energy, or *kundalinī*.

Hridaya
The space where the inbreath and outbreath merge; "the true heart"; the place where the breath is still in the state of merging.

I am That
The pure, unconditioned self-awareness of absolute Consciousness, beyond all limiting attributes, that dwells within all human beings. *See also* Aham; Hamsa.

Indra
In the Vedas and Puranas, the lord of the heavens; the god of thunder and lightning.

Intensive
A program designed by Swami Muktananda to give direct initiation into the experience of meditation through the awakening of the *kundalinī* energy. *See also* Shaktipat.

Jagadguru
A world teacher; a great Guru.

Jainism
An Indian religious sect, founded in the 6th-century B.C., which stresses strict asceticism and concern for the well-being of all manifestations of life as a means of ending the cycle of death and rebirth.

Janaka, King
A Siddha who ruled a kingdom in ancient India. He was a disciple of Yajnavalkya, and is mentioned in the *Mahābhārata* and the *Rāmāyana*. The father of Sita, Rama's consort.

Japa
(*lit.* prayer uttered in a low voice) Repetition of the mantra, either silently or aloud.

Jīva
(*lit.* living being) The individual soul, which is conditioned by the experiences and the limitations of the body and the mind.

Jīvabhāva
A feeling of identification or absorption with the limitations of the body and the mind.

Jīvanmukti
(*lit.* liberation in life) Attainment of liberation while still alive.

Jīvātma
The individual or personal soul. *See also* Jīva.

Jñāna Yoga
The *yoga* of knowledge; a spiritual path based on continuous contemplation and self-inquiry.

Jnaneshwar Maharaj

(ca. 1275-1296; *lit.* lord of knowledge) Foremost among the poet-saints of Maharashtra, he was born into a family of saints, and his elder brother Nivrittinath was his Guru. His verse commentary on the *Bhagavad Gītā*, the *Jñāneshwarī*, which he wrote at the age of 16, is acknowledged as one of the world's most important spiritual works. At age 21, he took live *samādhi* (a *yogi's* voluntary departure from the body) in Alandi, where his samadhi shrine continues to attract thousands of seekers each year.

Jñāneshwarī

Also known as *Bhavārthadīpikā*. A sublime commentary on the *Bhagavad Gītā*, written by Jnaneshwar. It was the first original scriptural work written in Marathi, the language of the people of Maharashtra. *See also* Jnaneshwar Maharaj.

Jñāni

An enlightened being; a seeker of spiritual knowledge.

Jyota se Jyota

A chant; an invocation to the Guru entreating him to kindle the flame of divine love in the disciple's heart.

Jyoti

Spiritual light; *kundalinī*.

Jyotirlingam

One of the twelve great *Shiva-lingas* of India. *See also* Lingam.

Kabir

(1440-1518) A great poet-saint who worked as a weaver in Benares. His followers included both Hindus and Muslims, and his influence was a strong force in overcoming the fierce religious factionalism of the day.

Kailas

A mountain peak in the Himalayas, considered to be the abode of Shiva.

Kakabushundi

A sage in Tulsidas's *Rāmāyana* who, by the curse of Shiva, was turned into a crow, but through constant devotion to Rama, attained liberation.

Kālī

(*lit.* the black one) The fearsome aspect of the universal Mother, or Shakti, Kali embodies the power of time. She is often depicted as "the black goddess." *See also* Devi.

Kālī Yuga

(*lit.* the dark age) The present age in which righteousness and truth have degenerated; the age of moral and spiritual decadence, at the end of which the world will be purified.

Kannada

The main language of Karnataka state in South India; Baba's native tongue.

Karma

(*lit.* action) 1) Any action — physical, verbal, or mental; 2) destiny, which is caused by past actions, mainly those of previous lives. There are three categories of *karma*: that destined to be played out in the current lifetime; that for future lives, currently stored in seed form; and that created in the present lifetime. The first occurs even if the individual attains liberation in this lifetime; the other two are burned up when liberation is attained. *See also* Samskāras.

Karma Yoga
The *yoga* of action. A spiritual path in which one performs actions as an offering, while remaining detached from the fruits of those actions. *See also* Sevā.

Kashmir Shaivism
A nondual philosophy that recognizes the entire universe as a manifestation of one divine conscious Energy; a branch of the Shaivite philosophical tradition which explains how the formless supreme Principle, Shiva, manifests as the universe. Kashmir Shaivism, together with Vedanta, provides the basic scriptural context for Siddha Yoga. *See also* Shiva Sūtras.

Katha Upanishad
A principal Upanishad which contains the story of the sage Nachiketa. *See also* Nachiketa.

Khecharī Avasthā
The state in which one roams in the inner spiritual skies; the bliss of movement in the vast expanse of Consciousness.

Khecharī Mudrā
An advanced yogic pose in which the tongue is thrust up. This *mudrā* pierces the *rudra granthi* (knot of Rudra) in the *sushumnā nādī*, causing the meditator to experience *samādhi* and taste divine nectar.

Krishna
(*lit.* the dark one; the one who attracts irresistibly) The eighth incarnation of Lord Vishnu, whose life story is described in the *Shrīmad Bhāgavatam* and the *Mahābhārata* and whose spiritual teachings are contained in the *Bhagavad Gītā*.

Kriyā
(*lit.* movement) Physical, mental, or emotional movements initiated by the awakened *kundalinī*; purificatory movements.

Kriyā Yoga
The *yoga* whereby the individual utilizes his senses, breath, and mind for Self-realization.

Kumbhaka
Retention of the breath; a process of *prānāyāma*, or breath control, described in *rāja yoga* and *hatha yoga*. *Kumbhaka* occurs when the inward and outward flow of *prāna* becomes stabilized.

Kumkum
A red powder used in Hindu worship; also worn as an auspicious mark between the eyebrows, in remembrance of the Guru.

Kundalini

(*lit*. coiled one) The supreme power, primordial *shakti* or Energy that lies coiled at the base of the spine in the *mūlādhāra chakra* of every human being. Through initiation, this extremely subtle force is awakened and begins to purify the whole system. As it travels upward through the *sushumnā nādī*, it pierces the various *chakras* until it finally reaches the *sahasrāra* at the crown of the head. Then the individual self merges into the supreme Self, and the cycle of birth and death comes to an end. *See also* Chakra; Intensive; Shaktipat.

Kurukshetra

A small plain north of Delhi; the battlefield on which the battle between the Kauravas and the Pandavas took place in the epic *Mahābhārata*.

Laya Yoga

Absorption of the mind into the Self; dissolution; the interiorization of consciousness.

Liberation

Freedom from the cycle of birth and death; the state of realization of oneness with the Absolute. *See also* Enlightenment; Jīvanmukti; Mukti.

Lingam

(*lit*. mark or characteristic) Shiva's sacred symbol representing his creative power; a phallic or oval-shaped emblem of Shiva, made of stone, metal, or clay.

Loka

(*lit*. world) Plane of existence, both physical and subtle.

Lungi, or Lunghi

An article of clothing traditionally worn by men in India; a length of cloth tied around the waist.

Madhya

(*lit*. central) 1) The pure I-consciousness. 2) The *sushumnā nādī*, also called *madhyadhāma*, the central abode of the awakened *kundalinī*.

Madhya Nādī

See Madhya.

Madhyādasha

(*lit*. middle space) The natural retention of breath; the state of God; the space between the inbreath and the outbreath. *See also* Kumbhaka.

Madhyamā

Sound in its subtle form as it exists in the mind before its gross manifestation. *See also* Speech, Levels of.

Mahā

Great, mighty, powerful, lofty, noble.

Mahā Yoga

(*lit*. the great *yoga*) *Kundalinī yoga*. *See also* Siddha Yoga.

Mahābhārata

An epic poem in Sanskrit, composed by the sage Vyasa, which recounts the struggle between the Kaurava and Pandava brothers over a disputed kingdom. Within this vast narrative is contained a wealth of Indian secular and religious lore. The *Bhagavad Gītā* occurs in the latter portion of the *Mahābhārata*.

Mahadev
(*lit.* great god) An epithet of Shiva; sometimes applied also to Vishnu.

Mahāpralaya
The great flood.

Maharashtra
(*lit.* the great country) A state on the west coast of central India. Many of the great poet-saints of India lived in Maharashtra and the samadhi shrines of Bhagawan Nityananda and Swami Muktananda are there. *See also* Ganeshpuri.

Mahāsamādhi
(*lit.* the great *samādhi*) A realized *yogi's* conscious departure from the body at death.

Mahāvākya
(*lit.* great statements) Four statements containing the wisdom of the Upanishads, asserting the oneness of the individual Self and God: *aham brahmāsmi (Yajur Veda); ayam ātmā brahma (Atharva Veda); prajñānam brahma (Rig Veda); tat tvam asi (Sāma Veda).*

Maitreyi
The wife of the sage Yajnavalkya, from the *Brihadāranyaka Upanishad*. She was a seeker who renounced her husband's worldly wealth and sought instead his spiritual wisdom.

Mālā
A string of beads, used like a rosary, to facilitate a state of concentration on the *mantra. See also* Japa.

Manas
The mind.

Mānasa Pūjā
(*lit.* mental worship) A chant in which a devotee worships Shiva through an exercise which includes mental offerings of flowers, jewels, fruit, and vegetables.

Mansur Mastana, or **Mansur al-Hallaj**
(858-922) An ecstatic Sufi poet-saint who lived most of his life in Baghdad. He also journeyed through Iraq, Persia, Gujarat, and Kashmir to the periphery of China. He was hanged as a heretic for his pronouncement *ana'l-Haqq,* "I am God," which orthodox Islam of those days would not tolerate.

Mantra
(*lit.* sacred invocation; that which protects) Mantras are the names of God; divine sounds invested with the power to protect, purify, and transform the one who repeats them.

Mātrikā Shakti
(*lit.* power of the Mother) The Mother Goddess or Shakti, in

the form of sound, as the creative force of the universe; the power of letters and words.

Māyā

The term used in Vedanta for the power which veils the true nature of the Self and projects the experiences of multiplicity and separation from God. The force of *māyā* conceals the ultimate Truth and creates the illusion that the real is unreal, the unreal is real, and the temporary is everlasting.

Megha Nāda

The roar of the clouds; the highest form of divine inner music; the sound of inner thunder followed by a shower of divine nectar flowing from the *sahasrāra*. *See also* Nāda.

Mirabai or Mira

(1433-1468) A queen and poet-saint of Rajasthan, famous for her poems of devotion to Lord Krishna. She was so absorbed in love for Him that when she was given poison by vindictive relatives, she drank it as nectar from Krishna and was unharmed.

Mudrās

(*lit.* seals) 1) Various advanced *hatha yoga* techniques practiced as aids to concentration in order to hold the *prāna* in the body, thus forcing the *kundalinī* to flow into the *sushumnā nādī*. *Mudrās* can occur spontaneously after receiving *shaktipāt*. 2) Symbolic gestures and movements of the hand expressing inner states.

Mukti

Liberation from the cycle of birth and death; freedom from the sense of duality and limitation.

Mūlādhāra Chakra

The first psychic center located at the base of the spine; the resting place of the *kundalinī* before the transmission of *shaktipāt*. *See also* Chakra.

Mumukshutva

Intense longing for union with God; yearning for liberation.

Nachiketa

One of the principal characters of the *Katha Upanishad*. When he was offered a boon by Yama, the lord of death, he asked for the supreme teaching of the knowledge of the Absolute.

Nāda

(*lit.* sound) Divine music heard during advanced stages of meditation; the spontaneous, unstruck sound experienced in the *sushumnā nādī*.

Nādī

(*lit.* duct, nerve) A channel in the subtle body through which the vital force flows. The three main *nādīs* are the *sushumnā*, the central channel through which the *kundalinī* travels upwards after awakening; the *idā* which is on the left side of the *sushumnā*; and the *pingalā* which is on the right side.

Namdev

(1270-1350) A poet-saint of

Maharashtra. Namdev, once a member of a murderous gang of robbers, was overcome with remorse when he heard the lamentations of a woman whose husband he had murdered. He turned to a life of devotion, becoming a devotee of Vitthal, (a form of Vishnu). He realized the all-pervasive nature of God after he met his Guru, Vishoba Khechar.

Nanakdev
(1469-1538; also known as Guru Nanak) The founder and first Guru of the Sikh religion. He lectured widely, spreading liberal religious and social doctrines — including opposition to both the caste system and the division between Hindus and Muslims.

Narada
A divine *rishi*, or seer, who was a great devotee and servant of Lord Vishnu. He appears in many of the Puranas, and is the author of the *Bhakti Sūtras*, the authoritative text on *bhakti yoga*. *See also* Bhakti Yoga.

Nasruddin, Sheikh
A figure originating in Turkish folklore during the Middle Ages, used by spiritual teachers to illustrate the antics of the human mind.

Neti neti
(*lit.* not this; not this) The steady negation of all unreal aspects of oneself and the world.

Nirguna
(*lit.* without a quality) The aspect of God without forms or attributes. *See also* Saguna.

Nirvikalpa, Nirvikalpa Samādhi
The highest state of meditative union with the Absolute, which is beyond attribute, thought, or image. *See also* Savikalpa Samādhi.

Nityananda, Bhagawan
(d. 1961; Bhagawan, *lit.* the Lord; Nityananda, *lit.* eternal bliss) Swami Muktananda's Guru and predecessor in the Siddha lineage. He was a born Siddha, living his entire life in the highest state of Consciousness. Little is known of his early life. He came from South India and spent many years traveling in the South, for a time living in a cave not far from Kanhangad. Later he lived in the sacred region around the Mandagni Mountain in Maharashtra, where many sages had performed fire rituals and done austerities. The village of Ganeshpuri grew up around him. Although he rarely spoke, spending many hours in silent ecstasy, thousands of people came to receive his grace. Often their questions were answered without words in the stillness of his presence. His samadhi shrine is in Ganeshpuri, a mile from Gurudev Siddha Peeth, the principal ashram of Siddha Yoga.

Nizamuddin Auliya
(d. 1325) A Sufi saint who lived in Delhi; the Guru of Amir Khusrau.

Om
The primal sound from which the entire universe emanates. Also written *Aum*, it is the inner essence of all *mantras.*

Om Namah Shivāya
(*lit.* I bow to Shiva) The "five-syllable" Sanskrit *mantra* of the Siddha lineage, known as the great redeeming *mantra* because of its power to grant both worldly fulfillment and spiritual realization. Shiva denotes divine Consciousness, the inner Self. *See also* Panchākshari Mantra.

Pādukās
Sandals worn or once worn by the Guru; *pūjā* is performed to them, and they are objects of the highest veneration.

Panchākshari Mantra
(*lit.* five-syllable *mantra*) The *mantra Om Namah Shivāya* is called "*panchākshari*" because it has five syllables, not counting *Om.*

Pandavas
The five virtuous sons of Pandu and heroes of the *Mahābhārata* epic. They are Yudhishthira, Bhima, Arjuna, Sahadev, and Nakula.

Pandharpur
A place of pilgrimage, and the center of worship for devotees of Vitthal in Maharashtra state.

Parabhakti
Supreme love of the Lord, characterized by complete selflessness.

Parabrahman
The supreme Absolute.

Parashiva
(*lit.* supreme Shiva) The primal Lord; the supreme Guru.

Parāvāni
The deepest level of sound; the level of supreme Consciousness from which all sound emanates. *See also* Speech, Levels of.

Parvati
(*lit.* daughter of the mountains) The wife of Shiva and daughter of the King of the Himalayas; a name of the Universal Mother or Shakti.

Pashyantī
Sound in a subtle form as it starts to manifest before reaching the mind. *See also* Speech, Levels of.

Patanjali
(4th century) A great sage and author of the famous *Yoga Sūtras*, the exposition of one of the six orthodox philosophies of India and the authoritative text of the path of *rāja yoga*. *See also* Yoga Sūtras.

Patanjali Yoga Sūtras
See Yoga Sūtras.

Play of Consciousness
The spiritual autobiography

of Swami Muktananda Paramahamsa (1908-1982). Written in 22 days at Mahableshwar in May 1969, it is a work of illumination, charged with the spiritual power of its author. It is unique in its description of the experiences of *kundalinī* awakening and the unfolding of the Guru-disciple relationship.

Prāna
The vital life-sustaining force of both the individual body and the entire universe.

Prānāyāma
(*lit.* restraining the breath) A yogic technique, consisting of systematic regulation and restraint of the breath, which leads to steadiness of mind.

Prasād
A blessed or divine gift; often refers to food that has first been offered to God and is thus blessed.

Pratyabhijñāhridayam
(*lit.* the heart of the doctrine of Self-recognition) An 11th-century treatise by Kshemaraja, which summarizes the *Pratyabhijñā* philosophy of Kashmir Shaivism. It states, in essence, that man has forgotten his true nature by identifying with the body and that realization is a process of recognizing or remembering (*pratyabhijñā*) one's true nature.

Pūjā
Worship. 1) Actions performed in worship. 2) An altar with images of the Guru or deity and objects used in worship.

Puranas
(*lit.* ancient legends) Eighteen sacred books by the sage Vyasa containing stories, legends, and hymns about the creation of the universe, the incarnations of God, the teachings of various deities, and the spiritual legacies of ancient sages and kings.

Puri
Deep-fried Indian bread.

Rabi'a
(714-801) A great Sufi poet-saint and mystic. She was sold into slavery as a child, but the man who bought her was so impressed by her sanctity that he set her free. She withdrew into a life of seclusion, and many disciples gathered around her.

Radha
The childhood companion and consort of Krishna who is celebrated in Indian tradition as the embodiment of devotion to God.

Rāja Yoga
Discipline of quieting the mind, according to Patanjali's *Yoga Sūtras*; it includes concentration, meditation, and contemplation. *See also* Ashtānga Yoga.

Rajas
See Gunas.

Ram Tirth
(1873-1906) Born in the Punjab of a poor family, he became a distinguished professor of mathematics, but out of his longing for God withdrew to the Himalayas, where he attained enlightenment. He lectured on Vedanta in India, Japan, and the United States (1902-1904). He wrote many beautiful poems in the Urdu language.

Rama
Seventh incarnation of Vishnu whose story is told in the *Rāmāyana*. *See also* Rāmāyana.

Ramakrishna Paramahamsa
(1836-1886) A great saint of Bengal; the Guru of Swami Vivekananda and the founder of the Ramakrishna Order of monks.

Ramananda
(15th century) A north Indian saint who revitalized the path of *bhakti* in the north. The most well-known among his disciples are Kabir the weaver, Ravidas the cobbler, and Sena the barber.

Rāmāyana
Attributed to the sage Valmiki, and one of the great epic poems of India. The *Rāmāyana* recounts the life and exploits of Lord Rama, the seventh incarnation of Vishnu. This story, so rich with spiritual meaning, has been told and retold down through the ages by saints, poets, scholars, and common folk.

Rasa
Nectar, flavor; a subtle energy of richness, sweetness, and delight.

Ravana
The ten-headed demon who captured Sita from Lord Rama in the *Rāmāyana* epic, and was finally defeated by Lord Rama.

Realization
The state in which the individual ego merges with pure Consciousness.

Red Light
See Four Lights.

Riddhis
Supernatural powers.

Rudra
The fierce aspect of Lord Shiva.

Rudram
A chant to Rudra from the *Krishna Yajur Veda* in which the Lord in His many manifestations is offered repeated salutations. *See also* Vedas.

Sadashiva
A name of Shiva meaning the all-pervading Shiva.

Sadguru
A true Guru, divine Master. *See also* Guru.

Sadgurunāth Mahārāj kī Jay
(*lit.* I hail the Master who has revealed the Truth to me) An exalted, joyful expression of gratitude to the Guru for all that has been received.

Sādhanā
Practices, both physical and mental, on the spiritual path; spiritual discipline.

Sādhu
A holy being, monk, or ascetic.

Saguna
Having attributes; the personal aspect of God. *See also* Nirguna.

Sahaja Kumbhaka
The natural retention of breath.

Sahaja Samādhi
The natural state of meditative union with the Absolute, which remains continuous throughout the waking, dream and deep sleep states. *See also* Samādhi.

Sahasrāra
The thousand-petaled spiritual center at the crown of the head where one experiences the highest states of Consciousness. *See also* Chakra.

Sai Baba of Shirdi
(1838-1918) One of the great Siddhas of modern times. His samadhi shrine at Shirdi is a popular place of pilgrimage.

Samādhi
State of meditative union with the Absolute. *See also* Mahāsamādhi.

Samādhi Shrine
The final resting place of a great *yogi's* body. Such shrines are places of worship, permeated with the saint's spiritual power, and alive with blessings.

Samsāra
The world of change, mutability, and death; the world of becoming.

Samskāras
Impressions of past actions or thoughts which remain in the unconscious and are stored in the *sushumnā nādī*, the central nerve channel in the subtle body. They are brought to the surface and eliminated by the action of the awakened *kundalinī* energy. *See also* Karma.

Sannyāsa
Monkhood; the ceremony and vows in which one renounces the responsibilities and privileges of worldly life and dedicates oneself exclusively to the goal of Self-realization and service to God; in India, traditionally, the final stage of life, which occurs after all worldly obligations have been fulfilled.

Sanskrit
(*lit.* complete) The language of the ancient Indian texts.

Saptah
(*lit.* seven days, from ancient tradition of seven-day chants) The continuous chanting of the name of God, which may be accompanied by dancing in a circle in a series of measured steps as an act of devotion and a kinetic form of meditation.

Sat chit ānanda
(*lit.* absolute existence, con-

sciousness, and bliss) The three indivisible categories used to describe the experience of the Absolute.

Sattva
See Gunas.

Satyaloka
The realm of Truth; the state of God-realization.

Savikalpa Samādhi
The state of absorption in an object of contemplation where the knowledge of the object is retained. *See also* Nirvikalpa Samādhi.

Seera
An Indian pudding made of wheat, ghee, and sugar, like a thick, sweet breakfast cereal.

Self
See Ātman.

Self-realization
See Realization.

Sevā
(*lit.* service) Selfless service; work performed with an attitude of nondoership, without attachment to the fruits.

Shabda-brahman
Ultimate Reality in the form of thought-sound vibration. State in which thought and word are identical.

Shaivism
See Kashmir Shaivism.

Shaivite
One who worships Shiva as the supreme Self.

Shakti or **Kundalinī Shakti**
Spiritual power; the divine cosmic power which, according to Shaivite philosophy, creates and maintains the universe. The dynamic aspect of divine Consciousness. *See also* Chiti; Devi; Kundalinī.

Shaktipat
(*lit.* the descent of grace) The transmission of spiritual power (*shakti*) from the Guru to the disciple; spiritual awakening by grace. *See also* Guru.

Shankaracharya
(788-820) One of the greatest philosophers and sages of India. He traveled throughout India expounding the philosophy of absolute nondualism (Advaita Vedanta). In addition to teaching and writing, he established *āshrams* in the four corners of India. The tradition of monks to which Swami Muktananda and Swami Chidvilasananda belong was created by Shankaracharya. One of his famous works is the *Viveka Chūdāmani*, "The Crest Jewel of Discrimination."

Shiva
1) In Shaivism, supreme Shiva (Paramashiva) is the all-pervasive supreme Reality, the unmoving, transcendent divine Consciousness. 2) In the Hindu trinity, Shiva is the third aspect

of God, the destroyer of ignorance. *See also* Brahma; Vishnu.

Shiva Āratī

A short *āshram* chant about
being in the joyful presence of
the Lord.

Shiva Purāna

An ancient treatise of legends of
Shiva; it describes the origin and
dissolution of the universe, its
different ages, and the genealo-
gies and deeds of famous kings.
It also expounds Shaivite rituals,
including the spiritual practices
that are means for attaining
liberation or union with Shiva,
or God.

Shiva Sūtras

A Sanskrit text revealed by Lord
Shiva to the 9th-century sage
Vasuguptacharya. It consists of
77 *sūtras* or aphorisms, which,
according to tradition, were
found inscribed on a rock in
Kashmir. The *Shiva Sūtras* are
the scriptural authority for the
philosophical school known as
Kashmir Shaivism. *See also*
Kashmir Shaivism.

Shivalingam

Phallic-shaped symbol of Lord
Shiva representing the imper-
sonal aspect of God; the symbol
by which divine Consciousness
is worshiped.

Shree or Shrī

A term of respect.

Shrīmad Bhāgavata Purāna

The scripture containing stories
of various incarnations of God,
Saints, Sages, Gurus, and their
disciples. Also called *Shrīmad
Bhāgavatam*.

Shuddha Vidyā

Pure knowledge.

Shuka or Shukadev

(dates unknown) A great sage of
ancient times, the son of Vyasa
and a disciple of King Janaka.
He is mentioned in many scriptures, but is most famous as the
narrator of the *Shrīmad
Bhāgavatam*.

Siddha

A perfected *yogi*; one who lives
in the state of unity-consiousness
and who has achieved mastery
over the senses and their objects;
one whose experience of the
supreme Self is uninterrupted
and whose identification with
the ego has been broken. *See
also* Enlightenment.

Siddha Yoga

The path to union of the individual and the Divine, which begins
with *shaktipāt*, the inner awakening by the grace of a Siddha
Guru. Swami Muktananda's successor, Swami Chidvilasananda,
is the living Master of this path.
Siddha Yoga is also known as
mahā yoga, or the great *yoga*,
because *shaktipāt* initiation sets in
motion a spontaneous and intelligent process in which all or any
form of yoga will occur within
the seeker according to need and
temperament. *See also* Guru;
Kundalinī; Shaktipāt.

Siddhaloka

Another plane of existence in which Siddhas live. Swami Muktananda describes this world in detail in his spiritual autobiography *Play of Consciousness*.

Siddharudha Swami

A great Siddha with whom Swami Muktananda studied Vedanta and took the vows of *sannyāsa*. All who came to him were given food, and in his *āshram* at Hubli in South India, the chanting of *Om Namah Shivāya* goes on continuously.

Siddhis

Supernatural powers.

Sitar

A stringed instrument used in classical Indian music.

Six Enemies

The inner enemies spoken about in Vedanta: desire, anger, lust, pride, greed, and envy.

So'ham

(*lit.* I am That) *See* Hamsa.

Spanda Kārikās

A 9th-century collection of 53 verses composed by Vasugupt-acharya. An important work of Kashmir Shaivism, it elucidates the *Shiva Sūtras* and describes how the *yogi* who remains alert can perceive the divine vibration, or *spanda*, in all of life. *See also* Shiva Sūtras.

Spanda Shāstra

Body of philosophical works in Kashmir Shaivism, which elaborate the principles of the *Shiva Sūtras*.

Speech, Levels of

Sound originates in the deepest level of unmanifest Consciousness, the *parā* level. From here, it arises successively through the *pashyantī* level to the *madhyamā* (subtle) level of speech until it manifests on the gross level as *vaikharī*, or articulated speech.

Subtle Body

See Four Bodies.

Sūfī

One who practices Sufism, the mystical path of love in the Islamic tradition.

Sufism

The Muslim mystical doctrine, which teaches that the goal of life is realization of the divine Principle in the heart.

Sundardas

(1596-1689) A renowned poet-saint born in Rajasthan. The main collection of his *bhajans* in Hindi is the *Sundar Granthavāti*.

Supracausal Body

The fourth of the supraphysical bodies. The state of *samādhi* is experienced here. This body is blue and the size of a tiny seed. *See also* Four Bodies.

Surdas

(1479-1584) A poet-saint who was blind. He was devoted to Krishna and spent his life at

Vraj, the place where Krishna
lived in his childhood.

Sushumnā
The central and most important
of all the *nādīs,* located in the
center of the spinal column,
extending from the base of the
spine to the top of the head. The
seven *chakras* are situated in the
sushumnā and it is through the
sushumnā channel that the *kundalinī* rises. *See also* Chakra;
Kundalinī; Nādī.

Swādhyāya
The regular, disciplined practice
of chanting and recitation of
spiritual texts.

Swāhā
(*lit.* it is offered) A *mantra* used
when offering oblations to the
sacrificial fire. *See also* Yajña.

Swāmī or Swāmiji
A respectful term of address for
a *sannyāsin,* a monk.

Tabla
An Indian drum.

Tamas
See Gunas.

Tamboura
A four- or six-stringed musical
instrument which plays the
drone accompaniment in Indian
music.

Tandra
A state of higher consciousness
between sleeping and waking,
experienced in meditation.

Tantra
An esoteric spiritual discipline in
which Shakti, the creative power
of the Absolute, is worshiped as
the Divine Mother through the
practice of rituals, *mantras,* and
yantras, or visual symbols. The
goal of *tantra* is to attain Self-realization through *kundalinī* awakening and through uniting the two
principles—Shiva and Shakti.

Tapasyā or Tapas
(*lit.* heat) Austerities; also the
experience of heat which occurs
during the process of practicing
yoga. The heat is generated by
friction between the mind and
heart, between the senses and
renunciation. It is said that this
heat, called "the fire of *yoga,*"
burns up all the impurities that
lie between the seeker and the
experience of the Truth.

Tat tvam asi
(*lit.* Thou art That) One of the
four *mahāvākyas,* "great statements" from the Upanishads; it
expresses the identity of the
individual self and the supreme
Self. *See also* Mahāvākya.

Third Body
See Four Bodies.

Third Eye
See Ājñā Chakra.

Thou art That
See Tat tvam asi.

Three Worlds
The waking, dream, and deep
sleep states.

Transcendental State
See Turīya.

Tukaram Maharaj
(1608-1650) A great householder poet-saint of Maharashtra. He received initiation in a dream and wrote thousands of *abhangas*, devotional songs, describing his spiritual experiences, his realization, and the glory of the divine Name.

Tulsi
A plant sacred to Vishnu; a type of basil, the leaves of which are used for worship.

Tulsidas
(1532-1623) A poet-saint from North India, author of *Rāma Charitāmānasa*, which is the life story of Lord Rama written in Hindi, still one of the most popular scriptures in India.

Turīya
The fourth state of Consciousness, beyond the waking, dream, and deep sleep states. The *turīya* state is the state of *samādhi*, the state of deep meditation. *See also* Four Bodies.

Uddhava
A friend and devotee of Lord Krishna.

Upamanyu
An ancient sage who did penance and was granted a vision of Lord Shiva; he narrated his experience and gave spiritual initiation to Lord Krishna; his story occurs in the *Mahābhārata*.

Upanishads
(*lit.* sitting close to; secret teachings) The inspired teachings, visions, and mystical experiences of the ancient sages, *rishis*, of India. These scriptures, exceeding 100 texts, constitute "the end" or "final understanding" *anta* of the Vedas; hence the term *Vedanta*. With immense variety of form and style, all of these texts give the same essential teaching, that the individual soul and God are one. *See also* Vedanta.

Ūrdhvareta
A perfect celibate whose seminal fluid flows upward.

Vaikharī
Shakti as gross word or speech. *See also* Speech, Levels of.

Vaikuntha
The celestial abode of Lord Vishnu.

Vaishnava or **Vaishnavite**
A worshiper of Lord Vishnu.

Vajreshwari
A village near Ganeshpuri, where Swami Muktananda did his *sādhanā* in a hut in the courtyard of an ancient temple of the Goddess.

Vasishtha
An ancient sage and Guru of Lord Rama. *See also* Yoga Vāsishtha.

Vasuguptacharya
(9th century) The sage to whom

Lord Shiva revealed the *Shiva Sūtras*, the scriptural authority of Kashmir Shaivism. *See also* Shiva Sūtras.

Vedanta
(*lit.* end of the Vedas) One of the six orthodox schools of Indian philosophy. It arose from discussions in the Upanishads about the nature of the Absolute, and was systematized by Shankaracharya. *See also* Upanishads.

Vedas
(*lit.* knowledge) Among the most ancient, revered, and sacred of the world's scriptures, the four Vedas are regarded as divinely revealed eternal wisdom. They are the *Rig Veda, Yajur Veda, Sāma Veda,* and *Atharva Veda.*

Vibhūti Yoga
(*lit.* the *yoga* of the divine manifestation) As described in the *Bhagavad Gītā,* in *vibhūti yoga,* the seeker experiences all qualities as divine and recognizes the oneness of God and His creation.

Vijñāna Bhairava
An exposition of the path of *yoga* based on the principles of Kashmir Shaivism. Originally composed in Sanskrit, probably in the 7th century, it describes 112 *dhāraṇās* or centering exercises which give the immediate experience of union with God.

Vikalpa
Imagination; mental oscillations.

Vikalpa Shakti
Power of imagination.

Vimarsha
Awareness; the aspect of consciousness by which things are known.

Vishnu
The supreme Lord. In the Hindu trinity, the aspect of God as the sustainer. It is said that during times of wickedness, Lord Vishnu incarnates to protect human beings and reestablish righteousness. Lord Rama and Lord Krishna are among the most important of these incarnations. *See also* Brahma; Shiva.

Vitthal
(*lit.* place of a brick) Lord Krishna went to the house of Pundalik, who, while tending to his aged parents, asked Him to wait and threw a brick for Him to stand on. This form of Krishna standing on a brick is known as Vitthal.

Vivekananda, Swami
(1863-1902) A disciple of Ramakrishna Paramahamsa and one of the most influential spiritual figures in modern India. During numerous visits, he introduced the teachings of Vedanta to the West.

Vrindavan
A district on the banks of the

Yamuna River where Krishna lived and sported with the *gopīs*.

Vyasa
A great sage, author of the *Mahābhārata* and the 18 Puranas.

White Light
See Four Lights.

Witness-consciousness
Remaining an uninvolved witness of events; supreme Shiva, who witnesses the play of the universe but is unmoved.

Yajña
1) A sacrificial fire ritual in which different materials such as wood, ghee, etc. are offered in gratitude to the Lord for all that has been received. 2) Any work done in the spirit of surrender to the Lord.

Yajñavalkya
A sage whose teachings are recorded in the *Brihadarānyaka Upanishad*; the Guru of King Janaka.

Yama
The god of death.

Yoga
(*lit.* union) The state of oneness with the Self, with God; practices leading to that state. *See also* Bhakti Yoga; Hatha Yoga; Jnāna Yoga; Karma Yoga; Kriyā Yoga; Kundalinī; Mahā Yoga; Rāja Yoga; Siddha Yoga.

Yoga Nidrā
The sleep of *yoga*, where the body is at rest as if in sleep, while the mind remains fully conscious, though all its movements are stilled.

Yoga Sūtras
The basic scripture of the path of *rāja yoga*; a collection of aphorisms written in Sanskrit by Patanjali in the 4th century. He expounds different methods for the attainment of the state of *yoga* or *samādhi*, in which the movements of the mind are stopped and the Witness rests in its own bliss. *See also* Patanjali; Witness-consciousness.

Yoga Vāsishtha
(also known as *Vāsishtha Rāmāyana*) A very popular Sanskrit text on Advaita Vedanta, probably written in the 12th century, and ascribed to the sage Valmiki. Vasishtha answers Lord Rama's philosophical questions on life, death, and human suffering by teaching that the world is as you see it and that illusion ceases when the mind is stilled.

Yogabhrashta
One who dies before completing his *sādhanā* and is reborn to complete it.

Yogananda Paramahamsa
(1893-1952) An Indian saint who travelled to the West, founded the Self-Realization Fellowship, and wrote *Autobiography of a Yogi*.

Yogi
One who practices *yoga*; also,

one who has attained perfection
through yogic practices. *See also*
Yoga.

Yoginī
A female *yogi*.

Yuga
Cycle or world period. *See also*
Kālī Yuga.

Zipruanna
A Siddha from Maharashtra,
dearly loved by Swami
Muktananda. It was Zipruanna
who sent Baba to Bhagawan
Nityananda.

INDEX

577

experience(s) of, 156-157, 193-194

instruction, 180-181

origin of, 164, 179

Omniscience, of Bhagawan Nityananda, 276-277

Oneness, experience of, 39, 75, 295, 339, 514, 519

gurubhakti and, 294-298

mantra and, 168

in meditation, 107

in name of God, 161

as a Siddha's state, 56-57, 93-94, 274-275

One-pointedness, 55

chanting and, 152-153

of love, 458

meditation and, 108

of thought, 307

Pādukās, Bhagawan Nityananda's, 48

Pain, 27, 427

chanting and, 144

creative, 83, 84, 90, 326-327

gurubhāva and, 300-301

as meditation experience, 126, 137-138

mind and, 378-380

Sundardas on, 342

transcendence of, 39, 256-257, 438, 439-440

of wrong understanding, 244-245, 305-311, 397

Panchadashī, 245

Panchākshari, 193

See also Om Namah Shivāya

Pandardas, 369

Pandarinath, 119

Pandavas, 154

Pandharpur, 158

Pantharāja, 37

Parabhakti, 288, 300

Parashiva, 152, 182

Parāvāni, 403, 485

Parikshit, 154-156

Pashyantī, 403, 485

Patanjali, 107, 118, 121

Patience, 25, 339

See also Discipline

Peace, inner, 21, 26, 75, 414

maintaining, 132

mantra and, 169

ritual and, 233

shaktipāt and, 38, 46, 47, 79

spontaneous, 88, 114

Perfect I-consciousness. See *Pūrno'ham*

Perfection, 19, 66-67, 78, 281, 492, 522

chakras and, 74

jīvabhāva and, 128-129

sādhanā and, 55

sevā and, 202-203

See also Blue Pearl

Perfume, divine, 96, 135

Personality, of enlightened being, 526

Pettiness, 254

Photographs, of Guru

meditating on, 121-122

reality of, 121, 234

Physical plane, 24

Plants, Shakti in, 76-77, 122, 377

Play of Consciousness, 43, 119, 122, 288, 334, 419, 495, 496, 498, 513

Pleasure

senses and, 58-59, 64, 398, 465

Shakti as source of, 45, 113

Postures. *See Āsanas*

Practices, spiritual, 67, 152, 294-295

culmination of, 167

devotion and, 258

discipline and, 223, 224, 241

faith in, 36

fear and, 441

secrecy of, 15, 46, 56
state required to transmit, 54-55, 123, 201-203
See also Awakening, inner; Grace; Purification
Shame, 427
Shams-i Tabriz, 443
Shankara, Lord, 171
Shankaracharya, 64, 93, 253, 476-477
    on retention of breath, 132-133
    on *sevā*, 208
Shibli, Sheikh, 477
Shiva, 31, 59, 81, 93, 110, 121, 167, 187, 270, 288, 315-316, 335, 492
    and ego, 348
    mantra, 182-186
    Rudram and, 152
    sevā and, 205
    understanding of, 245
    vision of, 137
Shiva Āratī, 152
Shivadrishti, 137
Shiva Purāna, 184
Shiva Sūtras, 381, 403, 529
Shivaji, 210, 503
Shivalinga, 243-244
Shrāvana māsa, 530-531
Shri Ram Baba, 358
Shrī Rām Jay Rām, 151, 168, 196
Shuddha vidyā, 404
Shuka (Shukadev), 57, 155-156
Shyam Chor, 281-283
Siddha(s), 57, 67, 122-123, 193-194, 210, 240, 314-315, 326, 421-422, 453-454, 505, 506, 507, 519
    being a, 521-534
    and God's name, 145
    meditation experiences of, 89, 93-94, 504, 506-507
    meeting a, 225-226

plane of, 29, 62, 66, 67
samādhi of, 56-57
from time of birth, 45
See also Guru; Saint(s)
Siddha Yoga, 15, 56, 225-226, 293
    attainment of, 267, 472-473, 496
    divine light and, 16-17, 38-39, 491-501
    idols and, 236
    and laughter, 80, 106, 109-110
    as *pantharāja* (king of paths), 37
    philosophy of, 23, 76, 113-114, 116
    and physical presence of Guru, 30
    tapasyā of, 456
Siddhaloka, 29, 62, 66, 67, 474
    sādhanā in, 475-476
Siddharudha, Swami, 33, 386
Siddhis, 45-46, 182, 317-318
Silence, 84, 511-513
    in meditation, 101, 509
Sin, 83, 184
    chanting and, 154
    mantra and, 184, 189
    meditation and, 106
    ritual and, 231
    and sinner, 267
    trust and, 329
Singer sewing machine, 464
Sitar, 149
Skepticism, 18, 427
Sleep, 74, 378, 386, 465-467, 485, 526
    center of awareness during, 39, 109
    Guru's presence in one's, 121
    mantra and, 5, 172
    meditation and, 5, 103, 108, 130-131
    Shakti and loss of, 81, 158
    witness state and, 117
So'ham, 39, 81, 179, 464, 532-534

SWAMI MUKTANANDA

SWAMI MUKTANANDA
AND THE LINEAGE OF SIDDHA YOGA MASTERS

SWAMI MUKTANANDA was born in 1908 to a prosperous family of landowners near the South Indian city of Mangalore. At around the age of fifteen he had several encounters with the great saint Bhagawan Nityananda, whom he would later recognize as his spiritual Master. These encounters were a turning point for the boy. Shortly thereafter, he decided to set out from home in search of direct experience of God, a journey that would ultimately take him three times across the length and breadth of India and last almost a quarter of a century. He met his first teacher, Siddharudha Swami, who was one of the renowned scholars and saints of that time, in an ashram in Hubli, two hundred miles to the north of his parents' home. It was there that he studied Vedanta, took the vows of *sannyāsa*, or monkhood, and received the name Swami Muktananda, "the bliss of liberation."

When Siddharudha died in 1929, Swami Muktananda began to visit one ashram after another, meeting and learning from more than sixty spiritual teachers, always looking for the one who would give him the experience of God. He searched for eighteen years. In that time he mastered the major scriptures of India, received training in an array of disciplines and skills — from hatha yoga to cooking and Ayurvedic medicine — and still he did not find what he sought.

At last one of the saints he met sent him to Bhagawan Nityananda, the Siddha Master, or perfected spiritual teacher, he had encountered so many years before. Bhagawan Nityananda

BHAGAWAN NITYANANDA

was then living in the tiny village of Ganeshpuri, fifty miles northeast of Bombay. Swami Muktananda recognized Bhagawan Nityananda as the Guru he had been seeking; he later said that this meeting "ended my wandering forever." From Bhagawan Nityananda he received shaktipat, the sacred initiation by which one's inner spiritual energy is awakened. This energy, known as *kundalinī*, is a divine potential that exists within each human being; once awakened, it enables a seeker to reach the most subtle levels of inner experience.

With his initiation Swami Muktananda became a disciple, dedicating himself to the spiritual path set forth by his Guru. This was the beginning of nine years of intense transformation, during which Muktananda underwent total purification, explored the inner realms of consciousness, and finally became steady in his experience of the fullness and ecstasy of his own innermost nature. In 1956, Bhagawan Nityananda declared that his disciple's inner journey was complete: Swami Muktananda had attained Self-realization, the experience of union with God.

Even after he had attained the goal of his discipleship, Swami Muktananda remained a devoted disciple, continuing to live quietly near Ganeshpuri. Bhagawan Nityananda established him in a small ashram near his own, and for five years Guru and disciple lived less than a mile from each other. Then in 1961, just before his death, Bhagawan Nityananda passed on to Swami Muktananda the grace-bestowing power of the Siddha Yoga lineage, investing him with the capacity to give spiritual awakening to others. On that day Bhagawan Nityananda told him, "The entire world will see you."

In the decades that followed, Baba, as Swami Muktananda came to be known, traveled throughout the world, imparting to others the same shaktipat initiation he himself had received and introducing seekers to the spontaneous yoga of the Siddha Yoga Masters. He freely bestowed the grace his Guru had given to him, opening to unprecedented numbers of people what he called "the royal road" of Siddha Yoga—a wide and accessible path to God. People who had never before heard of meditation found that in Baba's presence they were drawn into an inner stillness that gave their lives new focus and meaning. He introduced programs to give shaktipat initiation to vast groups and tirelessly explained to people the ongoing process of transformation that was unfolding within them. As Baba became world-renowned, his ashram (now known as Gurudev Siddha Peeth) expanded to accommodate the visiting seekers, and in time other ashrams and hundreds of Siddha Yoga meditation centers were established throughout the world.

In 1982, shortly before his death, Swami Muktananda designated Swami Chidvilasananda his successor. She had been his disciple since early childhood and had traveled with him since 1973, translating into English his writings, his lectures, and the many informal exchanges he had with his devotees. An advanced spiritual seeker from an early age, with a great longing for God, she became an exemplary disciple. She was guided meticulously in her sadhana by her Guru, who carefully prepared her to succeed him as Guru. In early May of 1982, Swami Chidvilasananda took formal vows of monkhood, and later that month Swami Muktananda bequeathed to her the power and authority of the Siddha Yoga lineage, the same spiritual legacy that his Guru had passed on to him. Since that time, Gurumayi, as she is widely known, has given shaktipat and taught the practices of Siddha Yoga to ever-increasing numbers of seekers, introducing them to Swami Muktananda's message:

Meditate on your Self.
Honor your Self.
Worship your Self.
Understand your own Self.
God dwells within you as you.

GURUMAYI CHIDVILASANANDA

FURTHER READING

BY SWAMI MUKTANANDA

Bhagawan Nityananda of Ganeshpuri

Does Death Really Exist?

I Am That

I Have Become Alive

Kundalini: The Secret of Life

Light on the Path

Meditate: Happiness Lies Within You

Mukteshwari

Mystery of the Mind

Nothing Exists That Is Not Shiva

The Perfect Relationship

Play of Consciousness

Secret of the Siddhas

Selected Essays

Where Are You Going?

BY GURUMAYI CHIDVILASANANDA

Courage and Contentment

Enthusiasm

Inner Treasures

The Magic of the Heart

My Lord Loves a Pure Heart

Pulsation of Love

Remembrance

Sādhanā of the Heart

Smile, Smile, Smile!

The Yoga of Discipline

To learn more about
the Siddha Yoga teachings and practices,
visit the Siddha Yoga website at:

www.siddhayoga.org

For further information about
SYDA Foundation books
and audio, video, and DVD recordings,
visit the Siddha Yoga Bookstore website at:

www.siddhayogabookstore.org

or call 845-434-2000, extension 1700.

From the United States and Canada,
call toll free 888-422-3334.